PROPAGANDA

Towards Disarmament in

the War of Words

PROPAGANDA

Towards Disarmament in the War of Words

John B. Whitton and Arthur Larson

Published

for

**THE WORLD RULE OF LAW CENTER
DUKE UNIVERSITY**

by

OCEANA PUBLICATIONS, INC.

Dobbs Ferry, New York

1964

PREFACE

This study of law and remedies bearing upon international propaganda was the first major research project undertaken by the World Rule of Law Center at the time of its creation in 1958. The study was made possible by grants from the Institute of International Order, Earl D. Osborn, president. The Center's gratitude for these grants is all the greater because they were made at a time when the Center was just getting its start.

The authors also wish to express their thanks to the following scholars who contributed analyses in the various legal systems indicated: Mr. Saad Samuel El-Fishawy (Islamic Law); Professor Robinson O. Everett (Common Law); Professor Hans W. Baade (Civil Law); and Mr. Robert D. Crane (Soviet Law).

The main substance of this book is a legal analysis of the rules, principles and remedies available to control propaganda of a kind that threatens the peace. However, in view of the central importance of propaganda in international affairs, an attempt has been made to present this legally-based material in a form suitable for use, not only by lawyers, but also by government officials, communications experts, members of international organizations, and opinion leaders generally.

JOHN B. WHITTON
ARTHUR LARSON

CONTENTS

Part I

THE PROBLEM

Part II

THE LAW

Part III

REMEDIES AND IMPROVEMENTS

Part I.

THE PROBLEM

Chapter I

Propaganda as a Threat to Peace

Propaganda helps to cause war.

In this role as a contributing cause of war, propaganda has much in common with armaments. Neither propaganda nor armaments is an "underlying cause of war." These "underlying causes," we are often told, must be found in deep-lying conflicts of national interest, stemming from ideological, religious, racial, economic, strategic, territorial and historical struggles and fears.

The essence of the practical problem of peace today is not to make these fundamental conflicts evaporate. This would be a good way to achieve peace, if it could be done. But we know that, even when all our best efforts in this direction have been made, intense clashes of interest will remain and new ones will continue to arise.

The everyday peace-keeping, job, then, it is keep these ever-present "underlying causes of war" from actually breaking out into war. It is at this point that the similarity between propaganda and armaments appears. Take a given clash of interests. Suppose that the nations on both sides of the dispute are relatively disarmed, and that they use all of the means of communications at their disposal to soften and conciliate the controversy. War will probably be avoided. Take the same clash of interests, and suppose instead that both nations are armed to the teeth, and use every technique of modern mass communciation to exaggerate the dispute, arouse hatreds and fears by false news and invented threats, and whip the people on both sides into a lather of war frenzy. The result will quite possibly be war.

For some years the greatest part of official effort in the direction of peace has been concerned with control and reduction of arms. This is good. But it is time we accompanied this effort with emphasis on a parallel theme: *propaganda is an armament*. While we are struggling to work out ways of dismantling the most dangerous weapons of physical destruction, we should also be struggling to work out ways of dismantling and controlling the psychological weapons used to exacerbate the causes of war. In short, while in past years we have often heard

1

the phrase "the propaganda of disarmament," we should now hold forth as an urgent need "the disarmament of propaganda."

The opening statement that propaganda in itself increases the danger of war is no mere theory or rhetorical flourish. There is convincing historical evidence of the actual hastening of war by deliberate propaganda techniques. Dozens of actual examples of propaganda will be cited in the appropriate places later, but at this point a single example may show how propaganda helped to usher in not only World War I but an entire era of global conflict. The relation between propaganda and armed conflict is relatively well known in more recent cases involving Hitler, international Communism and Middle Eastern outbreaks, to name only the most obvious examples. But, in view of the incalculable disasters which its Pandora's box released upon the modern world, the propaganda leading up to World War I deserves to be recalled in some detail as prime evidence of the relation between propaganda and war.

The story goes back long before 1914. The explosive situation which culminated in the assassination of the Archduke at Serajevo and the outbreak of war may be traced to the irredentist propaganda that had been carried on from the beginning of this century by Serbia in Bosnia and Herzegovina. Indeed, it is interesting to observe in retrospect that, while we may think of propaganda as a comparatively recent danger, the participants in these pre-World War I struggles were already acutely conscious of both the power and the danger of propaganda. As early as 1909 Serbia had agreed to renounce its opposition to the annexation of Bosnia and Herzegovina and had promised to live on good neighbor terms with Austria-Hungary. The latter interpreted this declaration as a promise to renounce subversive propaganda. But the Serbs, secretly encouraged by Russia, continued their agitation, which became all the more dangerous because carried on through underground channels. Some of this propaganda was definitely of a terrorist character. The clandestine activities of the Narodna Odbrana and the Black Hand were continued in Bosnia with the knowledge and even with the connivance of the Serbian Government. Not all the objectionable propaganda was clandestine. The daily press was also anathema to the Monarchy. No less than 81 Serbian publications were excluded from Austria-Hungary because, it was alleged, their contents were in flagrant violation of the domestic criminal code. For instance, after the attempt on the life of the Governor of Bosnia in 1910, Serbian newspapers extolled the assassin, who had killed himself, as a "heroic Serb whose name every Serbian will cherish with sorrow." It is not surprising, then, that after Serajevo, Austria-Hungary considered itself to be in a position of legitimate self-defense, not only against a military attack, but also against the corrosive maneuvers of greater Serbian" agitation. Consequently, the famous Austrian ultimatum of 1914 demanded of the Serbian Government an official condemnation of all propaganda directed against the Monarchy and an agreement to suppress by every possible means all criminal and terroristic propaganda. The Serbian Government, while denying all responsibility for agitation of a private nature, agreed to condemn the objectionable propaganda, to express regrets, and to adopt a number of other measures to prevent further political agitation. In actual practice, it made no effort to curb the violent attacks on the Monarchy appearing in the Serbian Press. Following upon the assassination of Archduke Ferdinand, the Serbian Government not ony failed to halt the continuing press attacks on Austria-Hungary but in fact almost seemed to condone the assassination. However, these attacks were in turn provoked by unbridled insults appearing in the Austro-Hungarian papers, which in addition republished the most insulting Serbian articles. Thus came the psychological preparation for the great war. In the opinion of competent scholars, this use of propaganda was one of the principal causes of the outbreak of the war. We realize today, as we look back on the explosive situation existing in the summer of 1914, that as a result of nationalistic propaganda the chance for a dispassionate consideration of the issues had already become virtually impossible.

REASONS FOR THE INCREASE IN THE DANGER OF PROPAGANDA

In the ensuing half century, several things have happened that have increased rather than diminished the relative part played by propaganda in international conflict.

One such development is the continued and accelerated shift of political power from a small minority of the people to the majority of the people. The more "the people" begin to rule, the more their governments see the necessity of controlling public opinion by various methods of mass persuasion. As the bases of political power broaden, every regime knows that its very life depends on its ability to hold the support of the majority of those it has to govern, and that in the long run this support has to be granted willingly. Even those dictators whose power is sometimes supposed to be absolute have realized that popular support was ultimately indispensable. Indeed, no popularly elected politician was more deeply conscious of the need to give attention to the press than Napoleon, Stalin, or Hitler.

The importance of propaganda was accentuated by a coincidence: this increase of the public's share in government went hand in hand with the remarkable development of the techniques of mass communication. This technical advance really dates back to the invention of printing. But it was not until the 19th and 20th centuries that the inexpensive daily press became general. Then came such inventions as telegraph, telephone, teletype, rotogravure, and radiophone, facili-

3

tating wide coverage, rapid reporting, and cheapness of publication. Simultaneously came rapid growth in literacy and education. Finally came radio, with which nearly everyone, whether literate or not, and however remote from the centers of civilization, could be reached by the purveyors of fact and opinion. Now, to the miracle of radio has been added the miracle of television, and, just recently, the amazing invention of Telstar. It is too soon to tell whether these new media will give us greater understanding among the nations, or merely greater opportunities for hostile, divisive propaganda.

The special characteristics of radio are such that when propaganda is harnessed to radio techniques, the menace of propaganda is multiplied many times over. This invention placed at the disposal of modern governments the most effective device yet contrived for the wholesale influencing of the minds of men.[1] Nor were governments slow to take advantage of its possibilities. It was in 1920, when KDKA broadcast the returns of the Harding election, that radio broadcasting first came into its own. But in May, 1922, the first warning of its possible perversion for purposes of propaganda was given by Owen D. Young, Chairman of the Board of the Radio Corporation of America. Upon his return from a visit abroad, he reported that European states were very fearful that their neighbors might make use of radio as a medium of propaganda.

No modern newspaper reader or radio listener needs to be convinced that Owen D. Young's apprehensions were well founded. But, while Soviet and Middle Eastern and Cuban propaganda are well known, it is sometimes not realized that in many other places around the globe the airways are constantly sizzling with savage electronic exchanges. Communist and Nationalist China tirelessly hurl insults at each other. Venezuela's radio tells the people of Santa Domingo:

> "Dominican people! However powerful a tyranny may appear, it cannot withstand the action of a people united and determined to recapture their freedom." (*Continental Radio*, March 2, 1959).

In counterattack, the *Dominican Voice* on August 25 broadcasts:

> "Arise, Venezuelans! Take the arms which your strength gives you, and use them against him who oppresses, enslaves and confuses you in order to sustain himself in power . . .

Meanwhile, the states of the Middle East lash out at each other in language of almost untranslatable fury. Egyptian radios call on the Jordanians to murder their own King, and spread false news reports leading to violent riots in Baghdad. At the same time, most of the Arab countries are not only uniting but trying to outdo each other in belligerent propaganda against Israel. President Nasser, in spite of

---

[1] Asa Briggs, *The Birth of Broadcasting*, New York, 1961.

4

an armistice with Israel, said on December 18, 1955 over the Near East Arab broadcasting station:

> "Egypt will be glad when both her and the Syrian Armies meet on the ruins of this treacherous people, these Zionist gangs, so that our dead may rest in peace with the knowledge that our countries have been liberated of all foreign encroachment."

King Hussein of Jordan declared over radio Ramallah on March 9, 1956:

> "We swear before Allah and history to sacrifice our property and everything dear to us for the sake of Palestine, to guard all her holiness and Arabism. We will not lay down our arms until we regain our rights completely."

And King Saud was reported in the *New York Times* for January 4, 1954 to have said:

> "The Arab nations should sacrifice up to 10,000,000 of their 50,000,000 people, if necessary, to wipe out Israel . . . Israel to the Arab world is like a cancer to the human body and the only remedy is to uproot it just like a cancer."

There are several reasons for the peculiarly lethal character of radio when turned to the uses of propaganda.

In the first place, radio, in contrast with the press, is subjected to a large degree of governmental direction and control in all states, not merely in the authoritarian countries. Real freedom of radio is a rarity. Thus, in democratic Sweden, radio is a governmental monopoly. In Britain, the British Broadcastng Corporation, although a "public corporation" must submit to a large degree of state control. Even in the United States, the government possesses at least the latent power to withdraw licenses from broadcasting stations through the intermediary of the Federal Communications Commission, and thus has a residual power in respect to the radio that is entirely absent in the case of the press. Moreover, as to overseas broadcasting, even in the United States this is almost entirely in the hands of the government.[2] While governments rarely publish a newspaper, they often own the radio, and typically own the overseas radio system. It is very unusual to find private broadcasting companies using radio to send harmful propaganda to other peoples. The reason is evident. Effective propaganda to other lands requires constant repetition and is not a paying venture. Particularly in those countries in which radio depends on the proceeds of advertising, it would be difficult if not impossible to find a sponsor for foreign broadcasts used mainly for the purpose of propaganda. But

---

[2] There are, however, several American-supported non-governmental radio chains broadcasting from overseas sites to the Communist bloc, especially Radio Free Europe and Radio Liberation.

when the government furnishes financial support, appoints a board of governors or otherwise maintains a certain degree of control, or operates the radio as a state monopoly, the temptation for governments to make use of such a powerful instrument as a weapon of policy is almost too great to be resisted.

Another reason why the radio is more potent than any other medium of communication is its tremendous range. While the press campaign from abroad stops at the frontier, the newscaster and radio commentator can speak to us from distant capitals. The entire world is their province. In 1959, it was reliably estimated that there were 315,-000,000 radio receiving sets throughout the world.[3]

The speed of radio communication is another signficant advantage. The radio wave takes only 1/7th of a second to encircle the globe. An American in Kansas City, listening to his radio, could hear Mr. Churchill addressing the British Parliament before the sound of the speaker's unaided voice reached the back benchers.

Not only is the range of radio almost unlimited; there is no adequate defense to its disturbances and dangers. Here it is in sharp contrast with the propaganda of the printed page, for usually the incendiary newspaper or pamphlet can be stopped at the border by postal and customs inspectors. During the 'thirties, even democracies were driven to prohibit the importation and circulation of foreign publications of an extremist character. Czechoslovakia passed a law covering all kinds of publications considered dangerous,[4] while Switzerland prohibited the circulation of material of Communist, anarchist, anti-militaristic or anti-religious character, and placed restrictions on public addresses delivered by foreign speakers.[5] But such measures have had little effect on checking radio propaganda from abroad. During World War II, even the death penalty for clandestine listening could not keep the determined Frenchmen—and even the occupying Germans—from tuning in on the BBC. Herculean efforts are made by the Soviet Union from time to time to jam the Voice of America and, in spite of considerable effectiveness of the jamming in the urban centers, available evi-

---

[3] George A. Codding, Jr., *Broadcasting Without Barriers*, The Hague (UNESCO), 1959, p. 27.

[4] Law of March 19, 1923, Karl Loewenstein, "Legislative Control of Political Extremism in European Democracies," *Columbia Law Review*, Vol. 38 (1938), Part I (April 1938), pp. 591-622, Part II (May 1938), pp. 725-774. See p. 755 for specific reference to Czech law of March 19, 1923.

[5] For a review of the development of Swiss law, see Lawrence Preuss, "La Répression des Crimes et Délits contre la Sûreté des États Étrangers," *Rev. Gén. de Droit International Public*, Vol. 40 (1933), pp. 622-631. See also the new American Statute, HR 7927, quoted at p. 205 *infra*.

dence indicates that the broadcasts reach a large number of listeners in the Soviet Union and satellite countries.[6]

It hardly needs to be added that new developments and refinements are constantly increasing the effectiveness of broadcasting. The potential of television is obvious. There are also interesting possibilities in an invention like Ultrafax which can transmit a 500 page book to great distances in half a minute,[7] and in the use of satellites to relay signals. The recent invention of Telstar, and the advent of other types of relay satellites, open up new possibilities for both good and evil.[8]

Another special reason for the effectiveness of radio is the peculiar appeal of the human voice. Many people will listen to a political speech who would not bother to read it. Nor should we forget that many millions of illiterates throughout the world listen avidly to the radio signal. Also, the voice, with its potentialities for emphasis and modulation, gives full scope to the eloquence and personal magnetism of gifted speakers. Or, as in the case of Hitler and Goebbels, a high pitch of vocal frenzy can be used to produce mass hysteria in a way that cold print could not.

Radio, moreover, seems made to order for the task of creating the "mass mind." Because of its range, universality and personal appeal, it seems to have the ability to create a mob, responding to crowd mentality, without the physical necessity of bringing people together in one place. When millions of people daily hear the same appeals and the same arguments, it is not surprising that they eventually begin to feel the same prejudices and harbor the same convictions, just as the propagandists intend that they should. Thus it is that the mob men-

---

[6] *New York Times,* September 16, 1959, pp. 1, 18; Foy D. Kohler, "Effectiveness of the Voice of America," *Department of State Bulletin,* May 14, 1951, pp. 780-783. On February 21, 1962, Henry Loomis, Director of the Voice of America, in a talk to the National Press Club estimated that, despite Communist jamming of 50 per cent of Voice of America programs, one-fourth of the broadcasts could be heard in most major cities behind the Iron Curtain and more than three-fourths could be heard in rural areas. *New York Times,* Feb. 22, 1962, p. 4, col. 3.

[7] David Sarnoff, *New York Herald-Tribune,* September 13, 1947. On that occasion General Sarnoff urged the establishment of United Nations short-wave stations with powerful transmitters at strategic points around the globe, to help win "the battle for the minds of men." He also advocated "freedom to look" and "freedom to listen." *Ibid.,* p. 6.

[8] Robert K. Doan, "A Town Meeting of the World," *New York Herald-Tribune,* October 26, 1962. Speaking of the prospects for better international communications opened up by Telstar, President Frank Stanton of CBS stated: "The strongest prop of a cynical and ruthless government or combine of governments is public ignorance. . . . But today we have at hand the tools to make an unprecedented beginning in wiping out ignorance and indifference forever, if we use them intelligently and venturesomely." *Ibid.* See also: Crowley and others, *Modern Communications,* New York, 1962.

7

tality, which formerly was a phenomenon only of the mass meeting, may now be extended to a nation as a whole. The mass hysteria created by the Invasion from Mars broadcast demonstrated such dire possibilities of radio.

For the future, an even greater danger may lie in television. The limiting factor today is its relatively short range and the relatively great expense of receivers. The range problem can now be overcome by means of relay stations on satellites and by other technical developments. As to expense, individual and communal receivers will undoubtedly become increasingly cheaper and more accessible. When to the appeal of the human voice is added human facial expressions, plus graphic film clips with pictures of atrocities and what not, the possibilities of television as an inflammatory medium become appalling. We begin already to approach 1984, with its omnipresent screens controlled by Big Brother.

In addition to all the developments of recent years heightening the dangers of propaganda, there must be mentioned the paradoxical fact that the stalemate in physical weapons may actually increase the use of verbal weapons. The course of national self interest is like a rapid river. If a dam is thrown across the main stream as by barring the use of those physical weapons which were always the last resort of national interest, the stream will try to break out into various side channels, such as economic and propaganda warfare. As nations are inhibited from forwarding their national ambitions through force, because of the nuclear stalemate, the outlawing of war, or the adoption of arms agreements, the pressure to pursue these aims through propaganda will be redoubled.

By now everyone is quite familiar with the theme that the unimaginable destructiveness and range of the H bomb and the missile have made the disarmament of physical weapons imperative. What is less well known is that technical developments in propaganda, including both the scientific advances in such media as television and the more subtle and sinister happenings in the realms of mass psychology, subliminal perception, and other measures to achieve "group-think" are rushing us toward the point where disarmament in the war of words may well be as important to the cause of peace as disarmament in the contest of hardware.

MEANING AND TYPES OF PROPAGANDA

This book is concerned only with propaganda that directly or indirectly endangers peace.

The term "propaganda" in itself can quite properly be given a

8

much broader meaning than this. There can be good propaganda as well as bad propaganda.[9] In general, propaganda means the use of facts, fiction, argument and suggestion, sometimes supported by an effort to suppress inconsistent material, with the calculated purpose of instilling in the recipient certain beliefs, prejudices, or convictions which will serve the interest of the author, usually by producing or tending to produce a certain line of action.[10]

Thus, it may be said that Moses led his people to the Promised Land by employing propaganda. Propaganda played a key role in the launching and carrying through of the French Revolution, the War of Independence, and the New Deal. Propaganda and politics are inseparable, both in the domestic and international fields. A political party up for re-election will flood the land with facts, figures, arguments and slogans. Similarly, a member of the United Nations whose policies are under attack will employ every medium of publicity to plead its cause. True democracy is founded on freedom to propagandize, and the United Nations is the greatest forum for rival international propaganda the world has ever seen. Such procedures are necessary and benefical, provided that all parties respect the rules of the game.

The word "propaganda" itself has gradually come to acquire a tainted and unpleasant connotation. It suggests that someone is trying to put something over on us. However, the concern of this book is not even with anything as broad as unpleasant, strident, or distasteful propaganda.

There is a line which our analysis will try to draw, beyond which the merely unpleasant becomes menacing, the obnoxious becomes inflammatory, and the argumentative or didactic becomes subversive and war-mongering. It is propaganda which goes beyond this line that is the concern of our discussion. It will be referred to by various names from time to time, such as dangerous propaganda or hostile propaganda or illegal propaganda. The essential feature of this "over the line" propaganda is that it tends to produce a breach of peace. Propaganda may threaten peace in three principal ways, and this division is followed in analyzing the pattern of legal rules and prin-

---

[9] E. H. Carr, *Propaganda in International Politics* (Pamphlets on World Affairs), New York, 1939. "Propaganda has no value in itself; it is neither good nor bad in its essence. There can be, there are, good propagandas, that is to say satisfactory in terms of the limits fixed in morals and in law, it being understood that we are speaking in relative terms." Quoted from Jacques Driencourt, *La Propagande, Nouvelle Force Politique*, Paris, 1950, p. 280. (Translation by the authors.) Also, Quincy Wright, *The Study of International Relations*, New York, 1955, p. 287.

[10] Leonard W. Doob, *Propaganda, Its Psychology and Technique*, New York, 1935, pp. 89-98; Quincy Wright, *op. cit.*, pp. 286-288.

ciples under these three headings: war-mongering propaganda; subversive propaganda; and defamatory propaganda.[11]

War-mongering propaganda directly undermines peace by actually fomenting war, preparing people for war, and building up incidents or ideas that will bring on war. Examples from the Middle East are innumerable. Thus, Yunis Bahri issued the following call over Radio Baghdad on December 12, 1956: "Come, let us close ranks in order, for once, to deal Israel a mortal blow and eradicate her from our land."

Subversive propaganda, although it may not be as blatant and obvious in its menace to peace, has perhaps done more to disrupt peace than any other form of propaganda. The objective of such propaganda is ordinarily to produce violence within a country—the violence necessary to overthrow the existing political order, to stir up domestic strife, to set class against class, and to turn people against their government. It is not surprising that the intended victim, acting in elementary self-defense, will react violently if it can and use all possible means to protect itself, with ominous consequences for international society. The Serbian subversive propaganda leading to World War I is an example of this kind of propaganda. That part of the world is still being constantly barraged by subversive propaganda. For example, the United Nations Commission of Investigation (UNSCOB) appointed to cope with the problem of disorders originating on the borders of Greece reported as follows:

> It appears to the Special Committee that the Greek guerrillas have received aid and assistance from Albania, Bulgaria and Yugoslavia; that they have been furnished with war material and other supplies from these countries; that they have been allowed to use the territories of Albania, Bulgaria and Yugoslavia for tactical operations. . . . The Special Committee further finds that moral support has been given to the guerrillas through Government-controlled radio stations, the existence of the broadcasting station of the Greek guerrillas on Yugoslavia soil and the systematic organization of aid committees. This assistance has been on such a scale that the Special Committee has concluded that it has been given with the knowledge of the Governments of Albania, Bulgaria and Yugoslavia.[12]

The third category, defamatory propaganda, also imperils peace,

---

[11] John B. Whitton, "Propaganda and International Law," *Hague Recueil*, Vol. 72 (1948), pp. 568 ff.; Von Johann Joeden, "Die Funksendefreiheit der Staaten," *Jahrbuch für Internationales Recht* (1954), Vol. IV, pp. 71 ff.

[12] A/574. *U.N. Yearbook*, 1947-1948, p. 301. A recent example of subversive propaganda is furnished by the Damascus radio following on Syria's separation from the United Arab Republic:

"The Arab people in Syria who were freed from oppression and domination by the nationalist movement of the Army, extend their hands to brotherly Arab peoples in Egypt who are fettered with chains, to free themselves from the dictatorial rule which caused separation between Egypt and Syria." *New York Herald-Tribune*, October 3, 1961.

although perhaps not as directly or immediately as the other two kinds. Nevertheless, when defamation and false news are sufficiently extreme and persistent, they tend to create hatreds, fears and passions whose predictable outlet is violence. For example, the "Azerbaijan Democratic Radio" asserted on February 15, 1950:

> The Shah has exterminated thousands of Azerbaijanies and Kurdish heroes and exiled tens of thousands of Azerbaijanies to southern parts of Iran . . . murderers like Hitler, Mussolini, and Chiang Kai-Shek acted in the same manner. They exterminated thousands of innocent workers . . .

Constant repetition over a period of years of a wide variety of similarly inflammatory statements by Communist radios beamed at Iran must plainly be regarded as a stimulus to physical violence.

In short, the subject of this book is, not what to do about propaganda in general, but what can be done with the kinds of propaganda—war-mongering, subversive, and defamatory—that imperil the peace.

Chapter II
Evolution of Propaganda
as a National Weapon

From the earliest times propaganda has been used by independent communities in both peace and war. But its elevation to the level of a major activity and even to a branch of government is a recent development.

For purposes of unfolding a full and consecutive account of the evolution of propaganda, it is useful to include mass persuasion in wartime along with propaganda in peacetime. This book, however, is not addressed to questions of "psychological warfare" during actual hostilities. This is not to say that all law has been suspended in wartime. On the contrary, a number of special rules have come into play, such as the international laws of war and neutrality and the Geneva Conventions on the treatment of prisoners. But when one considers that wholesale killing was legal in the active prosecution of a legal war,[1] one could hardly expect that peacetime legal limitations on verbal attack would apply. The real tragedy of the relation between psychological warfare and peacetime propaganda is that some nations do not seem to have sensed that techniques and tricks which they have developed and put to good use in wartime are out of place in peacetime— just as much in the verbal as in the physical realm.

Propaganda was utilized thousands of years before the term was invented or its meaning understood. When the early savage raised his fist and shouted defiance against his neighbor, he was using psychological pressure to overcome his enemy's will. Then as now propaganda was an effective and economical substitute for war. Hitler was not the first to prefer wherever possible to obtain his aims by methods "short of war." All governments have employed psychological pressures for this purpose.

Tribal warfare, like other warfare, is marked by various efforts to influence the mind of the enemy: hideous masks to frighten him, war

---

[1] There are still two kinds of legal use of force under the U.N. Charter: pursuant to a U.N. authorization, and self-defense. See Article 2(4) and Chapter VII, especially Article 51.

cries to weaken his resistance, and the promise of grace if he will give in without a fight. As Lasswell says in his work on propaganda in the First World War:[2]

> Small primitive tribes can weld their heterogeneous members into a fighting whole by the beat of the tom-tom and the tempestuous rhythm of the dance. It is in the orgies of physical exuberance that young men are brought to the boiling point of war.

Many instances of propaganda, both on the home front and in the realm of foreign affairs, can be cited from the history of Greece and Rome. Plato wrote instructions as to what should be told the youth of the ideal city-state to assure their devotion to truth and orthodoxy and their loyalty to the regime. For this purpose he even advocated censorship.[3] Aristotle, in his *Rhetoric,* left us specific principles for oratorical persuasion, emphasizing that the most forceful weapon for this kind of propaganda was the truth, for "the truth tends to win over the false."[4] The orations of Demosthenes were designed to warn the Athenians of dangerous aggression from Philip of Macedon.

The Romans, too, had poets to arouse the national spirit, and great leaders who understood, if only intuitively, the propaganda value of national festivities on the return of a victorious general to arouse the enthusiasm and loyalty of the populace.[5] Virgil's great poems, like the plays of Shakespeare many centuries later, served to create national unity and inspire the people with national pride.

Some of the methods then used have their modern counterpart. Thus Hannibal's message to the Italians after he crossed the Alps recalls tactics used by modern aggressors, for he assured the natives that he came not as an invader but as a friend and that his only object was to help them overcome the domination of Rome.[6] Many centuries later, in 1794, the French Revolutionary Army, approaching the Dutch frontier, assured the local population that the French came, not as

---

[2] Harold D. Lasswell, *Propaganda Technique in the World War,* London/New York, 1927, pp. 220-221. As an early example of war-mongering propaganda, we may cite the story spread by Attalus and the Rhodians in an effort to bring the Romans to fight on their side. The story had to do with an alleged secret treaty, supposed to have been signed about 202 B.C. by Philip V of Macedon and Antiochus III of Syria containing a promise to do away with the young King of Egypt, and to divide his lands between them. Although absolutely false, this story sufficed to bring the war-weary and reluctant Romans to fight on the side of Attalus. David Magie, "The 'Agreement' Between Philip V and Antiochus III for the Partition of the Egyptian Empire," reprint from *Journal of Roman Studies,* Vol. XXIX (1939), Part I.

[3] *The Dialogues of Plato* (Jowett translation), 5 vols., 3rd ed., New York/London, 1892, Vol. V, pp. 407-408.

[4] *Rhetorica,* Bk I, 2, 1354, ff.; *The Works of Aristotle,* (translation, W. A. Ross, ed.), 11 vols., Vol. 11, Oxford, 1924.

[5] Gaston Boissier, *Tacite,* 2d ed., Paris, 1904, pp. 239 ff.

[6] Frederick Elmore Lumley, *The Propaganda Menace,* New York, 1933, p. 57.

dominators, but as brothers with whom they could unite in all confidence.[7] Similarly, in 1948 the Communists advancing on Peking made similar assurances, with considerable success.[8] In the civil war between Octavian and Antony, each leader resorted to personal attacks on the other, and offered bribes through handbills promising rewards to those who would surrender—tactics used by American troops in World War II and in the Korean War. Reports from the front were falsified, and stories of Antony's alleged drunkenness circulated, together with attacks whose real object, although directed against Cleopatra, was to blacken the reputation of Antony. These accusations were met by countercharges which Antony issued in the form of a political pamphlet.[9] As St. Beuve has said, the "veritable Moniteur" of the Romans should be sought in the innumerable tables in marble and bronze whereon they engraved their laws and immortalized their victories.[10] It is not surprising to learn that these tables were carefully censored.[11] In their foreign propaganda the Romans merely had to adapt methods already evolved in the course of domestic policy; for Cicero, wishing to arouse public opinion against Catiline, had mobilized enough copyists to transcribe and distribute, in a short time, the depositions of witnesses in his favor and disseminate them from one end of Italy to the other.[12]

The Medieval Church set up what was probably the first official organization for the dissemination of religious convictions. We owe to it the very name of propaganda—the propagation of the Faith, although actually the Congregation established by Gregory XIII was designed mainly to handle the affairs of the church in non-Catholic countries. The Church used mass persuasion in war as well as in peace. In the 9th Century, Leo IV told the army of the Franks: "Now we hope that none of you will be slain, but we wish you to know that the kingdom of heaven will be given as a reward to those who shall be killed in this war."[13] Pope Urban II invited all those who had taken the vow and were headed for Jerusalem to carry the cross on their garments,

---

[7] Albert Sorel, *L'Europe et la Révolution Française*, 8 vols., Paris, 1889-1904, Vol. IV, p. 164.

[8] *Overseas Information Programs of the United States.* (Hearings Before a Subcommittee of the Committee on Foreign Relations, U.S. Senate, Washington, 1953, Part 2), p. 672.

[9] Lumley, *op. cit.*, pp. 58-59.

[10] Quoted by Boissier, *op. cit.*, p. 244. The *Moniteur Universal*, founded by Panckoucke, was the official journal of the French Government from l'An VIII to 1869.

[11] A modern parallel is the chipping out of the figures of discredited Soviet leaders in the mosaics in the Moscow subways, and the many other Soviet efforts to obliterate the names of fallen idols.

[12] Boissier, *op. cit.*, p. 272.

[13] O. J. Thatcher and E. H. McNeal, *A Source Book for Medieval History*, New York, c. 1905, pp. 511-512.

and declared that as a reward they would receive the forgiveness ot their sins.[14] In 1096 the Pope traveled throughout France personally spreading publicity for the first crusade, and was greatly aided by an amazingly successful propagandist, Peter the Hermit, who gathered up 15,000 pilgrims to follow him out of France and on to Constantinople.[15]

In the religious wars, handbills and placards, often plentifully illustrated, were widely used, despite pitiless repression by royal ordinance declaring such documents to be dangerous to the king's service, in part because they were sent to foreign lands and carried "calumnies and suppositions."[16] This same principle—danger to national security— is the *raison d'être* of several modern laws against propaganda, as we will see in later pages.[17] A recent scholarly work describes the role of psychological warfare in the Thirty Years War.[18] The pamphlets and sketches distributed during that terrible conflict were designed, like similar efforts in modern times, to steel the courage of the home forces and to break down the morale of the enemy. During this period the propaganda expert appears. The Protestants, in their campaign to prove the viciousness of the Jesuits, were led by Dr. Ludwig Camerarius, while the Catholics, for whom the enemy was worse than any Muslim, Turk or Pagan, had as their spokesman the Jesuit father Jakob Keller.[19]

At certain momentous periods of history, great political movements evolve after long ideological preparation, their leaders inspired by a vision of a new political, social and even economic order, and fired by the conviction that they have discovered ultimate truth. Uncertain at first whether this truth will spread of its own inherent force, or whether its advocates should go forth themselves and seek to spread it to the four corners of the earth, eventually the leaders frankly pose as missionaries or modern crusaders. The main tasks of such propaganda, according to Lasswell, are: "(1) to direct discontents, however caused, against the symbols and practices of the established order; (2) to organize favorable attitudes toward symbols which can be manipulated by a counter-elite during revolutionary crises; (3) to prevent

---

[14] Ferdinand Chalandon, *Histoire de la Première Croisade, Jusqu'à l'Election de Godefroi de Bouillon,* Paris, 1925, p. 39.

[15] *Ibid.,* pp. 54 ff.

[16] To curb such activities, a law passed in January 1561 provided that all printers, distributors of placards and defamatory libels would be punished, for the first offense with whipping, and by death in case of a second offense. Louis Eugène Hatin, *Histoire Politique et Littéraire de la Presse en France,* 8 vols., Paris, 1859-1861, Vol. I, p. 55.

[17] *Post,* pp. 111 ff.

[18] Elmer A. Beller, *Propaganda in Germany During the Thirty Years War,* Princeton, 1940.

[19] Robert Strausz-Hupé and Stefan T. Possony, *International Relations,* New York/Toronto/London, 1950, p. 368.

hyper-concentration of hostile influences until the probability of a successful revolutionary action is attained."[20]

What appears to have been the first instance of such a movement, although a relatively feeble one, was the Puritan Revolution in England. Cromwell was evidently moved by a naïve but resolute faith in the imminence of a revolution which, he believed, was bound to spread throughout the world. Thus his emissaries did not halt before the task of preaching the revolutionary gospel in foreign lands. One of these agents, on landing at Cadiz, said in a speech delivered in a public square:[21]

> With the example afforded by London, all kingdoms will annihilate tyranny and become republics. England has done so already; France is following in her wake; and as the natural gravity of the Spaniards render them somewhat slower in their operations, it will take Spain ten years to make the revolution.

During the Puritan Revolution, over 40,000 pamphlets were distributed, and incidentally the London government took action to outlaw "libellous and seditious pamphlets and discourses" sent from Scotland.[22] On the other hand, this agitation seems to have caused little alarm on the Continent, for at the time the cause of royalty there was particularly strong, and the English Republic was generally considered to be an isolated and purely local phenomenon, without risk of contagion even in states already subjected to civil dissension. Moreover, up to that time, so many years before the French Revolution, the word "republic" had few sinister connotations; the Swiss Republic, never of a nature to excite alarmists, was at the time one of the few examples of that form of government.[23]

French Revolutionary Propaganda

It was during the French Revolution that revolutionary propaganda first came into its own, to be used for both domestic and foreign ends. In the dynamic spirit behind the movement, the intensity of its propaganda, and the degree of alarm caused abroad, this revolu-

---

[20] Harold D. Lasswell and Dorothy Blumenstock, *World Revolutionary Propaganda*, New York/London, 1939, p. 21.

[21] J. W. Thompson and S. K. Padover, *Secret Diplomacy. A Record of Double-Dealing 1500-1815*, London, 1937, pp. 82-83.

[22] Quoted in Lumley, *op. cit.*, pp. 68-69.

[23] M. Guizot, *Histoire de la République d'Angleterre et de Cromwell 1649-1658*, 3 vols., new ed., Paris, 1864, Vol. I, pp. 206-207. Ferdinand Brunot, *Histoire de la Langue Française des Origines à 1900*, 12 vols., Vol. IX, Part 2, p. 628.

tion has many features in common with the Communist Revolution of our times.[24]

One striking characteristic of the early champions of the "new order" was the extraordinary zeal with which they were inspired. Thus Robespierre, one of the most impassioned of these "missionaries," believed in the "divine mission of France" to create liberty and overturn tyranny everywhere. Here is an example of his eloquence:[25]

> It is not for one people that we are fighting, but for the entire universe . . . Ah, may God grant that we have the power at this time to make our voices heard by all peoples, at the same instant that the torches of war are extinguished, the chains of the universe broken, and all peoples henceforth acting like one single nation of brothers. War to the limit against the kings, peace and fraternity with the people—there, in two words, is our entire diplomacy.

It was also during this period that the famous revolutionary song, the *Marseillaise*, was written, soon to be adopted by a whole army and an entire people, a song which ever since has inspired successive generations of Frenchmen in war and peace. This song was composed in a single night when the French Army, right after the declaration of war on Austria and the Allies, was faced with imminent danger of attack at Strasbourg.[26] So effective was this national anthem, that it was imitated throughout the world, and one general declared: just give him the Marseillaise and a thousand troops, and he would guarantee victory! Wherever the French Army marched, it carried with it its revolutionary symbols and slogans, to the dismay of many an absolute monarch and his entourage.

While Condorcet and others thought that the revolutionary doctrine would propagate itself by its own force,[27] without resort to arms,

---

[24] Crane Brinton, *A Decade of Revolution 1789-1799*, New York/London, 1934, pp. 186-189. Jacques Godechot, *La Grande Nation: l'Expansion Révolutionnaire de la France dans le Monde 1789-1799*, 2 vols., Paris, 1956 especially Chapters III-VI, XI and XX. For an exhaustive bibliography, see Vol. I, pp. 127-132. This author has given us this warning: "When one speaks of propaganda in the revolutionary period, it would be wrong to picture to oneself a vast governmental organization dependent, as is the case today, on a 'ministry' baptised modestly as 'of information' in democratic countries and carrying more cynically, in totalitarian countries, the title of 'ministry of propaganda.' If, after 1792, the French Government had supported a few agencies of 'propaganda' and assigned to them a certain budget, we may say that until then its propaganda had been strictly individual and spontaneous, and at times even unintentional [inconsciente.]." Also, pp. 159-160. And see, Jules Basdevant, *La Révolution Française et le Droit de Guerre Continental*, Paris, 1901, pp. 161-176.

[25] Francois Laurent, *Histoire de Droit des Gens et des Relations Internationales*, 18 vols., Paris, 1869, Vol. XV, p. 174.

[26] Jacques Bainville, *Histoire de France*, 2 vols., Paris, 1929-1930, vol. II, p. 75.

[27] Laurent, *op. cit.*, Vol. XV, pp. 161-169.

his more impassioned comrades fairly burned with a desire for armed propaganda.[28] But, as it turned out, the movement eventually lost its character as genuine ideological propaganda and become merely war propaganda. Although based at first on pure idealism, the Revolution deteriorated, giving way to the inexorable drive toward integral nationalism. A nation that began by renouncing all idea of conquest, ended by invading most of Europe. The metamorphosis of Revolutionary France is summarized by Lamartine as follows: "Militant enthusiasm for great generals replaced its admiration for its institutions; coups d'Etat with bayonet, military dictatorships, dynastic empires rose from the ambition so natural to the conquerors of foreign enemies."[29]

In the menaced countries the coalition formed to resist the Revolution, which at first waged a mere battle of propaganda, girded itself first for defense and finally for war and conquest.[30] This brings us to study another characteristic of the French Revolutionary propaganda which has its modern counterpart: the violent reaction produced in the foreign states exposed to ideological assault. This reaction took many forms, including an effort to spread counter-propaganda, a movement in which Russia, Spain, Sardinia and the Elector of Treves were engaged openly or as accomplices.[31]

Also Prussia sought in 1790 and 1791 to incite feudal Alsatians against France, disseminating pamphlets for this purpose.[32] On November 19, 1792, a decree later to become famous was voted by the Convention, reading as follows:[33]

> The National Convention declares in the name of the French nation that it will grant fraternity and aid to all peoples who desire to recover their liberty, and charges the executive power to give the generals the orders necessary to carry aid to these peoples and to defend the citizens who shall have been molested or could be molested for the cause of liberty.

This remarkable decree caused great consternation in foreign countries. This was especially true in Britain, where protests took the

---

[28] The French Revolutionists apparently believed that the idea of European federation was realizable only if the members all held similar ideas with respect to the sovereignty of the people. Similarly, Woodrow Wilson was later to maintain that the League of Nations could not succeed unless membership was limited to "democratic" states.

[29] Alphonse Marie Louis de Lamartine, *Histoire des Constituants*, 4 vols., Paris, 1855, Vol. IV, p. 375; Godechot, op. cit., p. 96.

[30] H. Lauterpacht, "Revolutionary Propaganda by Governments," *Transactions of the Grotius Society*, Vol. 13 (1928), pp. 150 ff.; Sorel, op. cit., Vol. III, Ch. IV, V.

[31] Summary in Van Dyke, op. cit., pp. 63-64.

[32] Ernest Lavisse, ed., *Histoire de la France Contemporaine, Depuis La Révolution jusqu'à la Paix de 1919*, 10 vol., Paris 1920-1922, Vol. I (by P. Sagnac), pp. 264-265.

[33] *Archives Parlementaires*, Vol. 53 (1792), 1st series, p. 474.

form of a paragraph in the King's Speech, which was followed by a long diplomatic quarrel between the two governments.[34] Lord Grenville, writing to Chauvelin, stated that in England the French decree was understood as intended to "encourage disorder and revolt in every country." Like Washington today in its dispute with Moscow, Grenville admonished the French to confine themselves to their own territory and to stop insulting other governments. He did not object to the French Republic *per se*, but to its aggressive claims, and above all, to its subversive propaganda.[35] In reply to the British, the French tried rather lamely and with no success to explain the decree away.[36] While the decree itself apparently had little effect on the British people, it served the British government well as propaganda for war, since at that time the British government was preparing to fight and was anxious to secure the support of the people behind it.[37] Nevertheless, the French did withdraw the decree, and in the constitution itself there was placed a declaration that France had no intention of interfering with the governments of other nations.[38] It is important to remember that Pitt, referring to the French disclaimer of any idea of fomenting insurrection in foreign countries, contended that this was done "upon the express ground . . . that such interference, and such attempts, would be a violation of the law of nations."[39]

Some of the objections made in England to the revolutionary doctrines are of special interest today. Certain orators protested vigorously against the egalitarian teachings of the Revolution, believing them not only dangerous, but even scandalous. The following remark by a 1798 historian is typical:[40]

> Here they were told, that every man, without exception, was on
> the clearest level with his richest and highest neighbor, and had as
> good a chance of rising to honors and preferments, through his
> courage and abilities, as any individuals whatsoever, however dis-

[34] *Annual Register,* Vol. 35 (1793), p. 128.

[35] Grenville to Chauvelin, December 31, 1792, *ibid.,* pp. 116 ff.

[36] Chauvelin to Lord Grenville, *ibid.,* p. 114; William Thomas Laprade, "England and the French Revolution, 1789-1797," *Johns Hopkins Studies in Historical and Political Science,* Vol. 28 (1909), p. 113.

[37] *Annual Register,* Vol. 35 (1793), p. 128.

[38] Decree of April 13, 1793. *Archives Parlementaires,* Vol. 62, 1st series (1793), p. 3. "The National Convention declares, in the name of the French people, that it will not interfere, in any manner in the government of other peoples." For article in the Constitution referred to here, see Constitution of 1793, Articles 118-119:

"118 The French nation is the natural friend and ally of free nations.

"119 It does not interfere with the affairs of government of other nations. It suffers no interference of other nations with its own." Henry C. Lockwood, *Constitutional History of France,* Chicago/New York, 1890, p. 313. For the Decree of 1793, see Basdevant, *op. cit.,* p. 164.

[39] *Annual Register,* Vol. 35 (1793), p. 46.

[40] *Ibid.,* Vol. 40 (1798), p. 20.

tinguished by their birth, their family connections, and their opulence!

Another curious statement heard in the House of Commons, and which recalls the "better Hitler than Stalin" sentiments of more modern times, was that made by Mr. Windham in 1793: "In his idea, the conquest of Britain by Louis XVI would by no means have been a calamity equal to the propagation of French principles."[41]

It is highly significant that then, as in recent times in a similar situation, the existing regime proceeded in alarm to protect itself by passing repressive legislation. In England, both before the execution of the French King and prior to the Terror, there existed various societies and clubs sympathetic to the cause of the Revolution which were circulating pamphlets, democratic treatises and placards. In an effort to curb such activities, the British passed anti-sedition statutes and other laws which threatened to make serious inroads on traditional doctrines of freedom of the press.[42] But the British invoked this same freedom of the press in answer to protests from Paris, made first by the Revolutionaries and later by Napoleon.[43] The latter was particularly upset by the propaganda coming from political refugees resident in Britain. Napoleon persisted in his claim that it was the duty of the British government to suppress such subversive propaganda on the ground that it menaced the interest and honor of foreign states. To the argument that since the British had to tolerate the hostile attacks of their own press, they expected foreign states to be similarly tolerant, Napoleon made the following cogent reply, which is pertinent to the present-day controversy over press freedom:[44]

> The particular laws and constitution of Great Britain are subordinate to the general principles of the law of nations, which supersede the laws of each individual state. If it be a right in England to allow the most extensive liberty of the press, it is a public right of polished nations, and the bounden duty of governments, to prevent, repress, and punish, every attack which might, by those means, be made against the rights, the interest, and the honor of foreign powers.

The British, however, denied that such a rule existed in international law.[45] This reply has a familiar sound at least to those who have

---

[41] *Ibid.*, Vol. 35 (1793), p. 53.

[42] Sorel, Vol. III, p. 212 ff.; Thomas Erskine May, *The Constitutional History of England Since the Accession of George Third 1760-1860*, 2 vols., New York, 1877, Vol. II, pp. 196-197.

[43] *Annual Register*, Vol. 45 (1803), pp. 660 ff.; Sorel, *op. cit.*, Vol. VI, p. 244.

[44] *Annual Register*, Vol. 45 (1803), p. 661. For American reply to Spanish protest in similar circumstances in 1885, see Moore, *Digest*, Vol. VII, pp. 980-981.

[45] *Annual Register*, Vol. 45 (1803), p. 665 (Dispatch by Lord Hawkesbury, August 28, 1802).

followed the debate in the United Nations between Moscow and Washington over freedom of information. According to Périvier, Lord Hawkesbury stated that if Napoleon's claim were accepted,[46]

> There would be no more liberty whatever for the press in any country. In fact, every writing, every paragraph in the journals on a foreign power's projects for aggrandisement, every protest against an injustice, could be considered by any power desiring to harm another as an injury to its interest and honor, assured that no one would be permitted even to refer to it.

Such arguments, difficult to answer then, are pertinent to present efforts to curb harmful propaganda.

It was not only in Britain, however, that nations were alarmed by French revolutionary propaganda, for attempts were made by the men of '89 to spread their doctrines all over Europe. Even Russia did not escape, although Catherine, perhaps somewhat optimistically, declared that she would make a mockery of this kind of propaganda. "All that is needed," she said, "is an order from the police to reduce to silence the few Free Masons who represent in these states the only agitation à la française."[47] In Switzerland, the people were much disturbed, fearing an immediate invasion from France in the wake of French propagandists.[48] This alarm was especially intense after the Convention voted the notorious decree already mentioned. As usual, however, the Swiss were prepared to stand up for their rights, and their newspapers replied with such fervor to the agitation from across the frontier that France felt impelled to protest.[49]

Fears were sown elsewhere, too. When, in 1792, King Gustave III was assassinated, many persons attributed this deed to the virus of French revolutionary doctrines.[50] In Germany, French propaganda at first claimed some successes, its most active agents being stationed at Munich, Ratisbonne and Stuttgart. But its effects waned after the Terror had discouraged the dreamers and idealists, the Revolution's best friends.[51] In Belgium, the French leaders, notably Lafayette, Brissot and Camille Desmoulins attempted to incite the people against their Austrian masters, and actually promised to help them create the United States of Flanders, a dream likewise dear to the Belgians. When, in 1792, the French armies were preparing to invade the Low Countries, Dumouriez turned to the propaganda arm as so many

---

[46] Périvier, *Napoléon Journaliste*, Paris, 1918, p. 218.

[47] Sorel, *op. cit.*, Vol. II, p. 217.

[48] *Annual Register*, Vol. 40 (1798), p. 21; J. B. Kaulek, *Papiers de Barthélemy, Ambassadeur de France 1792-1797*, 6 vols., Paris, 1886-1910, Vol. I, pp. 5, 433.

[49] Kaulek, *op. cit.*, Vol. I, p. 350; Godechot, *op. cit.*, Vol. I, p. 163.

[50] Sorel, *op. cit.*, Vol. II, p. 380.

[51] *Ibid.*. Vol. IV. p. 20.

21

other aggressors have done in similar circumstances, proclaiming to the people:[52]

> Our armies are at your frontiers; they bring war to tyrants, liberty to citizens. Take a stand! May the Belgian lion wake up! People of Belgium, we vow to make you free.

And to the soldiers:

> The French are free. Do you want to be free too? Come to France . . . Desert *en masse!* How are you fed? Worse than the dogs in France. Your leaders treat you like savage beasts they send to fight at will. Come, brave soldiers, taste the advantages of our laws, and divide up the lands and properties of the Artois, Condé and this band of rascals who share their crimes and misdeeds. Wipe them out first, purge the world of these monsters, and come live and die with your French brothers.

In Italy and Spain, too, the French agitators were busy. Joseph Bonaparte, the French Ambassador at Rome, made his house into a rendezvous for revolutionaries, patriots and intriguers, and all those plotting for change of regime.[53]

In looking back over all this feverish activity, it is clear—and this conclusion is of significance today—that revolutionary propaganda was only successful in countries where the soil was fertile. In lands with the fatal combination of weak government and a high level of expectation followed by frustration, the people, inspired and instructed by France's example, were ready to arise and follow the torch of 1789. No one has expressed this thought better than Sorel:[54]

> Wherever there was anxiety and misery, where the feudal regime was abusive, where the taxes were heavy or the charges unjustly distributed, wherever the great were odious and the governments detested, France found adherents, and imitators. The governments began to take account of this, but, affecting to see in such troubled spirits merely the sign of the meanness of peoples, instead of recognizing the effects of their own mediocrity, the only remedy they discovered was repression and violence.

Another major factor having to do with the success of French Revolutionary propaganda in foreign countries has its counterpart in the history of modern Communist propaganda. It is obvious that the Soviet agitation in our own day depends upon the backing of the Soviet army. The Communist regime would not last long in Hungary,

---

[52] *Ibid.,* Vol. II, p. 481, Vol. IV, p. 164.
[53] Sorel, *op. cit.,* Vol. V, p. 290.
[54] *Ibid.,* Vol. II, p. 411, Vol. IV, p. 2; *Annual Register,* Vol. 40 (1798), p. 20; Brinton, *op. cit.,* p. 187: ". . . it is pretty clear that where social and intellectual conditions favored it, the French Revolution propagated itself." See also Godechot, *op. cit.,* Vol. I, Ch. I, especially p. 32.

Poland or East Germany without the support of Russian bayonets. Similarly, radicals and revolutionaries in other countries were able to accomplish little without the active aid of the French revolutionary armies, as in the Netherlands and Italy. In Poland and Ireland, on the contrary, the revolutions failed, and the reason was clear. In short, French revolutionary agitation in foreign lands, when successful, was really a by-product of French invasion.

During the Napoleonic Wars, both the British and the French used against each other what today would be called psychological warfare, bitter and prolonged, and in this contest Napoleon actually took a personal part in writing for newspapers, especially against Pitt and other British ministers.[55] He himself was obliged to face the most virulent kind of attacks from England, where he was depicted as almost the devil himself.[56] As the first sovereign to talk to his subjects directly and frequently, and the first to employ governmental machinery systematically for the purpose, Napoleon can be considered the first modern propagandist.

REVOLUTION OF 1830

The 1830 Revolution was the occasion for a number of international incidents caused by the use of revolutionary propaganda. The French government was the target for many protests from states overrun by agents from France and bombarded with incendiary placards and other incitements to revolt sent from Paris, then a veritable center of subversive activity.[57] In 1830, for example, the Russian Ambassador urged King Louis-Philippe to reassure foreign powers "against the propagation of evil principles and the invasion of territories which are always their secret aim."[58] Although probably innocent of such agitation itself, and guilty if at all merely of a lack of zeal in repressing individual intrigue, the French government nevertheless declared it had no intention of disturbing the peace of other states; what is more, it admitted that such conduct would have violated the law of nations.[59] Furthermore, when a bill was introduced in Paris to repress agitation against their native states by political refugees living in

---

[55] Périvier, *Napoléon Journaliste*, Paris, 1918; Pierre Louis Roederer, *Oeuvres du Comte P. L. Roederer, 1754-1835*, 8 vols., Paris, 1853-1958, Vol. III, p. 429; Sorel, *op. cit.*, Vol. VI, pp. 244 ff.; Robert B. Holtman, *Napoleonic Propaganda*, Baton Rouge, 1950.

[56] *Annual Register*, Vol. 45 (1803), pp. 656-683 and *passim*.

[57] François Pierre Guillaume Guizot, *Mémoires pour Servir à l'Histoire de Mon Temps*, 8 vols., Paris, 1859-1870, Vol. II, pp. 80 ff., Vol. IV, pp. 33ff.; Vicomte de Guichen, *La Révolution de Juillet 1830 et l'Europe*, Paris, 1917, pp. 163 ff.

[58] de Guichen, *op. cit.*, p. 164.

[59] *Archives Parlementaires*, Vol. 81, 2d series (1833), pp. 614-617; Vol. 82, 2d series (1833), pp. 33-36.

France, the Minister of the Interior admitted that the government under international law was obligated to prevent the organization on its territory of plots against foreign territories.[60] This period of revolutionary activity, however, may be differentiated from the others here under review, first, because ideological considerations were of minor importance, and second, the agitation did not have the enormous advantage of direct governmental inspiration and direction.

THE COMMUNE, 1871

More characteristic of true revolutionary propaganda, however, was the agitation centering in the Paris Commune of 1871. During their brief reign, the Communards leaned heavily on the techniques of propaganda, their most effective weapon in the circumstances. Thus they stressed the "white terror," and the alleged iniquities of the bourgeoisie, and contrasted the evils of capitalism with the perfections of socialistic society, whose "first pale dawn" could already be perceived.[61] The address of the "Workers of Paris" to the "Workers of the Country" was distributed in the provinces from balloons equipped with a special releasing device. This manifesto stated "We are now and always have been, you and I, vassals of misery . . . The land to the peasant, the tool to the workers, and work for all."[62] This was not the first time that balloons were used by the French to distribute hostile propaganda. During the Revolution, Dumouriez, hoping to incite the enemy in Austrian Netherlands to desertion and treason, actually ordered the manufacture of fifty small balloons to carry propaganda leaflets across the frontier.[63]

The Commune's methods, however, were later held up by the Soviets as an example of how *not* to propagandize, and served as a lesson to Stalin. The main brunt of this criticism was the failure to suppress freedom of speech, for this permitted the continuance of dangerous "bourgeois" propaganda![64]

The new French Government, however, was not a party to these subversive measures. In fact it joined in the general resistance to them. Thus, at home, the government passed a law making it an offense merely to belong to the Internationale or similar organizations.[65] And abroad, it ordered its diplomatic agents to be on the alert, on this express ground: "Europe is faced with a work of systema-

---

[60] The Minister of the Interior admitted: ". . . it is our duty to forbid Frenchmen from engaging in propaganda; it is our duty, even more, to prevent refugees from doing such acts." *ibid.*, p. 36.

[61] See Edward S. Mason, *The Paris Commune, An Episode in the History of the Socialist Movement*, New York, 1930.

[62] Mason, *op. cit.*, pp. 265-266.

[63] *Ibid.*

[64] *Ibid.*, p. 357.

[65] *Archives Diplomatiques*, Vol. III (1874), pp. 241 ff.

tic destruction directed against each of the nations composing it, and against the very principles on which all civilizations rest."[66] Other powers, too, were taking various measures to resist dangerous doctrines. Spain, for example, proposed a general *entente* to engender universal and simultaneous protective action, and Portugal likewise favored a treaty of mutual aid. But the British played down the dangers of the Internationale in Britain, and refused to join in any kind of protective alliance.[67]

EARLY COMMUNIST PROPAGANDA[68]

The only example of propaganda at all comparable with the special kind developed during the French Revolution is the system adopted by the Soviets from the first and organized by them into a redoubtable machine of mass indoctrination at home and abroad. Although it is easy to overstress the analogy, with regard to underlying spirit, intensity, general character (especially the transformation from idealism-universalism to opportunism-nationalism) and finally, the nature of the reaction that ensued in exposed states, the two movements have some significant features in common. In both cases the original leaders and animators were fired with the same impassioned zeal, and were similarly convinced that they had discovered the ultimate truth which, if not carried round the world by its own force, was to be disseminated everywhere by the conscious efforts of the "crusaders." Also, both revolutions suffered a similar deterioration; the early renunciation of conquest (in the Russian case, regarding Manchuria and the Balkans especially) gave way to an open or occult drive for expansion, marked by a renaissance of integral nationalism. And since, in both cases, the propaganda employed was obviously intended to disrupt the internal order of foreign states, the threatened governments eventually reacted against the ideological assault by resorting to various protective measures, often invoking appropriate doctrines of self-defense. Domestic laws to repress political agitation were passed, although occasionally with reluctance when inconsistent with traditional liberties. In both cases the menaced powers acted together across frontiers in an effort to meet the danger (in modern times, through the Marshall Plan, Brussels Pact, North Atlantic Pact, etc.). The resistance of exposed states, both in the 1790's and the 1920's, resulted in a gamut of treaties which the propagandizing state was induced to sign, but not always to respect, grudgingly offering a formal promise to refrain thenceforth from interfering in the internal affairs of other states through propaganda

---

[66] *Ibid.*, pp. 85 ff.

[67] Mason, *op. cit.*, pp. 204-241.

[68] Harwood L. Childs and John B. Whitton, *Propaganda by Short Wave*, Princeton, 1942, pp. 4 ff.

or other methods. In both cases, too, the respective governments denied that their conduct had violated any duty under international law; the French attempted to explain away subversive designs and even officially denied them, while the Russians hid behind the alleged independent status of the Comintern, or invoked *tu quoque* arguments.

Despite these similarities, there were important differences. Above all, while from the first Soviet propaganda has been officially recognized and implemented as a regular weapon of state power, of equal rank with diplomatic, economic and military arms of statecraft, the propaganda of the Jacobins was sporadic and unorganized. Much of it, too, came in actual wartime and thus was to a degree the kind of propaganda engaged in by all nations at war. But Communism, in its use of psychological warfare, makes no distinction between war and peace. Class warfare, for the Soviets, is always going on.

Since the aims and nature of Communist revolutionary propaganda are today fairly well understood, only a brief review will be attempted here. World revolution was a major plank in the platform of Communist ideology from the very beginning, as is proved by the Communist Manifesto itself, in which we find this passage:[69]

> The Communists disdain to conceal their views and aims. They openly declare that their ends can be attained only by the forcible overthrow of all existing social conditions. Let the ruling classes tremble at a Communistic revolution. The proletarians have nothing to lose but their chains. They have a world to win.

Trotsky maintained that aid to world revolution was an "international duty." Even more striking was this grim declaration by Bukharin:[70]

> We must pursue the tactics of universal support of the international revolution, by means of revolutionary propaganda, strikes, revolts in imperialist countries, and by propagating revolts and insurrections in the colonies of these countries.

Lenin, admitting his debt to the French Commune of 1871, was a convinced believer in the power of agitation in foreign lands and its role in spreading the doctrines of the "new order." In 1920, among the 21 points drafted by Lenin to define the duties of the Internationale

---

[69] Karl Marx and Frederick Engels, *Communist Manifesto* (authorized English translation, annotated by Frederick Engels), Chicago, c. 1888, p. 58; Nathan Leites, *A Study of Bolshevism*, Glencoe, Illinois, 1953, pp. 368 ff.

[70] Nikolai I. Bukharin, *Programme of the World Revolution*, (No. 18 of a volume of pamphlets), New York, 1920, p. 63, quoted by Vera A. Micheles, in "The United States and Russia," *Foreign Policy Information Service*, Vol. IV (1928-1929), No. 25, p. 482.

in foreign countries, several specifically refer to the mission of Communist agitation abroad. Thus, in Point Three, he wrote:[71]

> In nearly every country of Europe and America the class struggle is entering upon the phase of civil war . . . It is their (the Communists) duty to create everywhere a parallel illegal machine for organization which at the decisive moment will be helpful to the party in fulfilling its duty to the revolution.

In Point Four, he stressed the necessity of "vigorous and systematic propaganda in the army," and in Point Five of "well-planned agitation in the country district." The Third Congress of the Communist International meeting in 1921 called upon the Communist parties in each country to utilize for purposes of political agitation the very institutions dear to free countries—free press, right of association, and parliamentary procedures.[72]

Meanwhile Bela Kun, head of the short-lived Communist regime in Hungary, was following Lenin's lead, making a great ado with his incendiary preachings. In fact one foreign observer remarked that "the one word 'Propaganda' sums up the whole foreign policy and diplomacy of the Soviet." In his proclamation of March 23, 1919, Bela Kun said, "We appeal to the Czechoslovak and Rumanian soldiers: refuse obedience, rise up and turn your weapons against your own oppressors . . . We appeal to the Proletarians of the world, to our French, English, Italian and German brother workers, and summon them to rise up in their own country in all their might against the capitalists."[73]

Radio was early adapted to the needs of the Soviet propagandists.[74] Beginning in 1926, Moscow, from its station in Odessa, began

---

[71] Walter Russell Batsell, *Soviet Rule in Russia*, New York, 1929, p. 763, see also p. 796. Note Stalin's speech of December 22, 1920, to the 8th Soviet Congress: "The dictatorship of the proletariat was successful because it knew how to combine compulsion with persuasion. . . .

". . . We must . . . see to it that the apparatus of compulsion, activised and reinforced, shall be adapted and developed for a new sweep of persuasion." Quoted by Leites, *op. cit.*, p. 375. But Lenin had in mind mainly propaganda to the "masses" rather than other elites. Leites, *op. cit.*, p. 368.

[72] *Theses and Resolutions Adopted at the Third World Congress of the Communist International*, New York, 1921, p. 39; Batsell, *op. cit.*, p. 773.

[73] Albert Kaas and Fedor de Lazarovics, *Bolshevism in Hungary: The Bela Kun Period*, London, 1931, pp. 327-328 and Ch. VII.

[74] "Convinced that the Russian Revolution constituted the first step in a movement which would soon engulf the world, the Bolsheviks, cut off from the West when they came to power, and still at war with the Central Powers, immediately turned to wireless telegraphy not only as a means of communicating with the world at large but also for purposes of propaganda proper. Their ambition in this respect is illustrated by the words, 'To all, all, all!' which initiated every one of their flashes. These messages were directed to the proletarian masses everywhere and admonished them to rise against their 'bourgeois and military

27

to attack the Rumanian government in nightly broadcasts accompanied by incendiary appeals for revolt. Rumania reacted by attempting to jam these broadcasts, but the Russians countered by setting up at Tiraspol, on the Russian-Rumanian frontier, a station with the same wave-length as Bucharest, but three times as powerful, and proceeded to deluge Bessarabia with messages inimical to Rumania.[75] And in 1930 Moscow began to broadcast in German, several times a week, messages berating political leaders in Germany and giving glowing accounts of life in Russia. The German government protested, but in vain. Russia's explanation, that the messages were directed to German settlers in Russia, especially in the Volga region, was not very convincing, for the programs called on Germans to revolt, and ended with the slogan, "Long live the German Soviet Republic!"[76]

At times these subversive attacks resulted in serious international incidents. Thus in 1923, Lord Curzon, Foreign Secretary, dispatched an ultimatum giving the Soviet government ten days in which to halt Bolshevik propaganda in various parts of the Empire, and within eight days Moscow responded with assurances that treaty promises would be fulfilled.[77] Again, in 1930, Moscow broadcast a letter from Maxim Gorky to workers in all states, especially England and France, urging them to support the Soviets and oppose foreign intervention. Foreign Secretary Henderson protested to Moscow against this action as a violation of the spirit, if not the letter, of provisions of the Anglo-Russian treaty against propaganda.[78] A similar incident occurred in 1935 between Washington and Moscow: Ambassador Bullitt protested when the Seventh All-World Congress of the Communist International approved a program of attacks on the economic and political system in the United States. This protest, claiming a violation of the Roosevelt-Litvinof accord, was met by a plea of confession and avoid-

oppressors' and to conclude a general peace without annexations, victors or vanquished; in this matter, the slogans of Wilson's Fourteen Points were invoked. During the peace negotiations at Brest-Litovsk the Russians used the radio as a medium of propaganda and, at the same time, as a weapon of pressure on the German leaders. Trotsky insisted on the textual broadcasting of the negotiations by telegraph and wireless, so that the Bolsheviks could appeal to world opinion over the heads of the enemy delegates. Thus, while negotiating, they at the same time exposed the annexationist aims of the Central Powers and incited German workers, soldiers and marines to strikes and insubordination." Childs-Whitton, *op. cit.*, p. 4.

[75] Sidney S. Biro, "The International Aspects of Radio Control," *Journal of Radio Law*, Vol. II (1932), pp. 60-61.

[76] *New York Times*, July 11 and 15, 1930. In those pre-Hitler days the Reich hesitated to answer the Soviet programs tit for tat for fear this would "savor of the use of the station for political purposes."

[77] Arnold Toynbee, *Survey of International Affairs, 1924*, Oxford, 1926, pp. 221 ff.

[78] Biro, *op. cit.*, p. 45.

ance—namely, that the USSR "cannot take upon itself and has not taken upon itself obligations of any kind with regard to the Communist International."[79] France, too, had similar difficulties with the Soviet regime. In 1927, along with China, its government protested strongly against the spread of Communist propaganda in their countries. France in fact temporarily recalled its Ambassador from Moscow and expelled the Soviet envoy from Paris.[80]

WARS OF THE UNITED STATES

Both sides in the American War of Independence employed techniques of mass persuasion, but the colonists showed themselves to be particularly adept in this field. The author of a leading work on this subject concludes that "Without their work independence would not have been declared in 1776 nor recognized in 1783."[81] An interesting example of such activities was the treatment of the "Boston Massacre," illuminated and enlarged beyond all semblance of the truth so as to yield the greatest propaganda value. Tom Paine, attacking the idea of reconciliation with England in *Common Sense*, used such fiery words as the following:[82]

> Hath your house been burnt? Hath your property been destroyed before your face? Are your wife and children destitute of a bed to lie on, or bread to live on? Have you lost a parent or child by their hands? . . . . if you have, and can still shake hands with the murderers, then you are unworthy the name husband, father, friend or lover, and whatever may be your rank or title in life, you have the heart of a coward, and the spirit of a sycophant.

During the American Civil War both sides resorted to tactics now familiar when they made use of the atrocity story to kindle the fires of war passion. The South played up the cruelty of Sherman's devastating march to the sea; the North stressed the horrors of Andersonville prison.[83] This was one of the first times that each belligerent used such methods to persuade a neutral, in this case Great Britain, of the justice of its cause.

As to the outbreak of the American war with Spain at the end of the century, it is generally agreed that propaganda stressing alleged

---

[79] *Department of State Press Releases*, August 31, 1935, pp. 149 ff.; *Am. J. Int. Law*, Vol. 28 (1934), *Off. Doc.*, pp. 3 ff.; C. C. Hyde, "Concerning a Russian Pledge," *ibid.*, Vol. 29 (1935), pp. 656 ff.

[80] *New York Times*, October 9, 14 and 16, 1927.

[81] Philip Davidson, *Propaganda and the American Revolution 1763-1783*, Chapel Hill, 1941, p. 410.

[82] *Ibid.*, p. 144.

[83] T. Cutler Andrews, *The North Reports the Civil War*, Pittsburgh, 1955; Charles A. Beard and Mary R. Beard, *Rise of American Civilization*, 4 vols., New York, 1927, Vol. II, pp. 85-88.

Spanish cruelties in Cuba (some of which existed only in the vivid imagination of newspaper writers) had much effect in arousing the American public to accept the burdens of war.[84] Considerable friction between Spain and the United States had existed, Spain protesting that the United States had been negligent in not repressing agitations on American soil in favor of the Cuban rebels. It is reported that on this occasion Hearst sent his notorious telegram to the painter, Frederic Remington, whom he had dispatched to Cuba as a correspondent: "You furnish the pictures and I'll furnish the war."[85]

WORLD WAR I

The great European wars were all preceded by campaigns of propaganda on both sides. The spark to set off the war of 1871 was the Ems Telegram, manipulated by Bismarck so as to ready both sides for war.[86]

We now know that the First World War was preceded by powerful campaigns waged by governments or individuals who desired the war or, in case war should come, wished to assure the leaders of strong popular support. The major part played by propaganda, in both Serbia and Austria-Hungary, before and after Serajevo has already been stressed.[87] In Germany many people, especially the Junkers, had been effectively indoctrinated with the myth of the "joyous war," and welcomed with song and dance the long-awaited "Der Tag."[88] In France, Barrès and Maurras, among others, had succeeded in implanting in the breasts of many persons, especially some influential leaders, a hope for revenge, and the French were never allowed to forget the sacred cause of Alsace-Lorraine.[89]

While in all previous wars more or less attention had been paid to psychological pressures directed to army and civilians both at

---

[84] G. W. Auxier, "The Propaganda Activities of the Cuban Junta in Precipitating the Spanish-American War 1895-1898," *Hispanic American Historical Review*, Vol. 19 (August, 1939), pp. 286-305; "Middle Western Newspapers and the Spanish-American War 1895-1898," *Mississippi Valley Historical Review*, Vol. 26 (March, 1940), pp. 523-534.

[85] Hearst later denied that his telegram was couched in this exact language, but it accurately expressed his hopes and sentiments, as reflected in the war-propaganda printed in his papers. John K. Winkler, *William Randolph Hearst, A New Appraisal*, New York, 1955, pp. 95-96. Marcus M. Wilkerson, *Public Opinion and the Spanish American War: A Study in War Propaganda*, Baton Rouge, 1932, p. 43.

[86] *Bismarck, The Man and the Statesman, Being the Reflections and Reminiscences of Otto, Prince von Bismarck*, translation by A. J. Butler, 2 vols., New York, 1898, Vol. II, Ch. 22, "The Ems Telegrams."

[87] *Supra*, p. 2.

[88] G. Lowes Dickinson, *The International Anarchy 1904-1914*, London, 1926, Ch. 16.

[89] Bernadotte E. Schmitt, *The Coming of the War*, 2 vols., New York, 1930, Vol. I, pp. 67-68.

home and in foreign lands, it was during the First World War that propaganda first received official recognition as a regular means of exerting power, a major instrument in the conduct of international relations, entitled to a place among established branches of government under the direction of trained specialists instead of amateur treatment by the army.[90]

Prior to 1914, propaganda was exploited mainly by revolutionaries, the fathers of modern methods of mass persuasion. But not long after World War I had begun, it became clear that modern warfare required the mobilization of the totality of the economic and industrial life of the nation, and that the traditional distinction between combatants and non-combatants no longer held good. Since the population was to be asked to make greater and greater sacrifices, civilian morale was obviously of vital importance, for without the unfailing support of non-combatants, the armed forces would eventually find themselves helpless. The morale of the nation in war is the sum total of the morale of the individual citizens; it depends on the loyalty and enthusiasm of the common man, who must be willing to be taxed, to enlist himself, to permit his sons to face the dangers of battle, and to accept many other privations. Hence the attention given by all belligerents to the importance of propaganda, for if armies are mobilized by orders, it is not too much to say that civilians are mobilized by propaganda. As regards the question of morale, there emerged a new conception of the importance of the morale of the individual soldier as well, especially when organized into vast conscript armies, which lack the trained and hardened resistance of the *soldat de métier*. Hence no means was neglected to stiffen his will and fire his ardor. In this effort propaganda was bound to play a most important part.

For all these reasons the belligerents were finally induced to coordinate the three main branches of state power into a coherent and integrated whole, using propaganda as a regular weapon alongside the economic and military arms. As early as 1914 the British established the War Propaganda Bureau.[91] The *Maison de la Presse* in France soon followed,[92] while the Germans left the waging of

---

[90] For propaganda in World War I, see Harold Dwight Lasswell, *Propaganda Technique in the World War*, New York, 1927; Hans Thimme, *Weltkrieg ohne Waffen*, Stuttgart/Berlin, 1932; George G. Bruntz, *Allied Propaganda and the Collapse of the German Empire in 1918*, Stanford/London, 1938; Oscar Butter, "La Presse et les Relations Politiques Internationales," *Hague Recueil*, Vol. 45 (1933), pp. 223-245; James R. Mock and Cedric Larson, *Words that Won the War*, Princeton, 1939; Alfred Vagts, *A History of Militarism*, New York, 1937, Ch. 8.

[91] James Duane Squires, *British Propaganda at Home and in the United States from 1914 to 1917*, Cambridge, 1935; Bruntz, *op. cit.*, pp. 18-30.

[92] George Huber, *Die französische Propaganda im Weltkrieg gegen Deutschland 1914 bis 1918*, Munich, 1928; Bruntz, *op. cit.*, pp. 8-18, 41-50 and *passim*.

propaganda to the army—a move much criticized later by Hitler, never one to underestimate the power of "scientific'" manipulation of the mind.[93] Finally, only eight days after the American declaration of war in 1917, President Wilson set up Mr. Creel's Committee on Public Information.[94] Wilson's persistent attack on German morale, especially in the last days of the war, is generally credited with contributing materially to the final disintegration and surrender of the Kaiser's armies.[95] Armed with highly-organized and generously-subventioned departments for psychological warfare, the belligerents carried on their work of mass persuasion with ever-increasing intensity. On the home front, where the task is always easier, "information bureaus" labored to strengthen the national morale, create confidence in the leaders, and establish faith in final victory. Lord Northcliffe in England and George Creel in America were the outstanding directors of war propaganda among the Allies. At the very outset, a great debate was waged between the respective belligerents over the question of responsibility for the outbreak of the war. (Later on Hitler was to resume this theme and use it cleverly to steel his people for a war of revenge.) Every effort was made to prove that the other side was the guilty party. So successful were they all that every soldier, whatever his uniform, could go into battle convinced that his cause alone had honor and justice, and even God, on its side.

In this contest for men's minds apparently any means were considered legitimate, not only the publication of scholarly-appearing but often incomplete or even inaccurate "color books," but even the issuance of false reports such as the claim in the German declaration of war that French airplanes had dropped bombs at Karlsruhe and Nuremberg. This affirmation was not only a complete fabrication but was even materially impossible in the light of the primitive state of aviation at that date.[96] (Similarly, at the outbreak of war in 1939, Hitler sought to justify his treacherous attack on Poland by alleging that the Poles had attacked first.) Throughout that First World War, the task of the British propagandist was considerably facilitated by the ineptitude of the Germans. Very helpful indeed was Bethmann-Hollwegg's cynical reference to Germany's promise to respect the neutrality of Belgium as a "scrap of paper." Similarly, the execution of nurse Edith Cavell, although legally justified in the circumstances,

---

[93] Thimme, op. cit.

[94] Complete Report of the Chairman of the Committee on Public Information, Washington, D.C., Government Printing Office, 1920; Lasswell, Propaganda Technique in the World War, pp. 18-19; George Creel, How We Advertised America, New York/London, 1920.

[95] Bruntz, op. cit., p. 60: "The most important producer of propaganda for America and the Allies was President Wilson. He had a knack of timing his speeches properly and of saying just the right thing." See also Mock and Larson, op. cit.

[96] Schmitt, op. cit., Vol. II, pp. 371-376.

was a great blunder, for it hardly needed any help from Lord North-cliffe, head of the Propaganda Policy Committee, to present this to the world as another crime of the "Lawless Hun."[97]

If the use of domestic propaganda grew by leaps and bounds during World War I, the same was also true of communication to foreign countries. Messages directed to the enemy camp were designed in the hope that they would spread defeatism and despair, and thus discourage the civilian population and demoralize the troops. Agitation by secret agents, and by means of leaflets dropped from airplanes or shot from guns, was calculated to cause distrust of leaders, disrupt national unity, and stir up minorities. Also, where possible, material of a defamatory or subversive nature was published in the press of foreign countries, but here the most fertile field was the press in neutral lands, where spies, sympathizers and venal newspapers susceptible to bribery were freely utilized.

Thus the Allies appealed to oppressed nationalities in German, Austro-Hungarian and Turkish empires; thus the Central Powers agitated in Ireland, India, and Tsarist Russia after the Kerensky revolution.[98] Other appeals were designed to preserve the close friendship and effective cooperation of an ally, by emphasizing community of interest, traditional friendship and common ideals, or, at times, by stressing the dangers of a separate peace. Other pressures had as their objective to create friction between a neutral and the enemy, or even to cause dissension among neutrals. Also the support of neutrals was earnestly and persistently solicited by arguments aiming to demonstrate that the interest of the neutral was identical with that of the propagandizing belligerent. Britain and Germany fought a pitched battle of words for the richest stake of all—the active belligerency or continued neutrality of the American nation, a battle the British finally won.[99] Of course, the American decision to fight was not due to propaganda alone, but propaganda did help materially. In this struggle the British enjoyed signal advantages. They could count on common language, traditions and way of life. In addition, most of the atrocities actually were on the German side. The British were fortunate in holding almost complete control over the oceanic cables, an advantage which, without modern radio broadcasting, the Germans were not in a position to overcome. In general, the German propaganda was inclined to be heavy-handed and naive, with its few successes confined to the home front. The allied efforts were remarkably effective, although some of their atrocity stories, especially those assembled in the Bryce Report, later were proved to be fabrica-

[97] Lasswell, op. cit., p. 32.
[98] Bruntz, op. cit., Ch. V and VI.
[99] H. C. Peterson, Propaganda for War: The Campaign Against American Neutrality 1914-1917, Norman, Oklahoma, 1939.

tions by over-zealous partisans, and boomeranged badly.[100] Partly as a result of Allied publicity, 400,000 Czechs deserted and joined the Russian forces.[101] It is not an overstatement to say that the final Allied victory was due to a skillful coordination of armed force, economic pressures, and effective propaganda.

As a contributing factor to the Allied victory, perhaps the most notable example of propaganda *par excellence*—although hardly conceived as such at the time—was Mr. Wilson's declaration of the Fourteen Points.[102] This offered the Germans the promise of a reasonably acceptable peace, and was in striking contrast with President Franklin D. Roosevelt's very different policy vis-a-vis the Germans of insisting on unconditional surrender. For inevitably the effect of an unconditional surrender policy was to induce the German leaders, and even the people and the army, to fight to the last ditch. In fact, some scholars cite this in proof of their view that President Roosevelt did not understand the systematic use of propaganda in total war. Nor in fact did he have much faith in it.[103]

BETWEEN THE TWO WORLD WARS

In the inter-war period the nations, after a slow start, continued to employ propaganda intensively in their mutual dealings as a weapon of power. Here the dictatorships showed the way. Each totalitarian regime, the Soviets in first place, found psychological methods of mass persuasion to be instrumental in its rise to power, and later adopted propaganda as an essential weapon in the international field. New methods were employed, and new media, with ever-increasing intensity. Finally, and very late, the free countries themselves found it necessary to reply in kind.

At first, most of such activity took place in Communist countries. As already indicated Soviet Russia, profiting from the experience of the belligerents in 1914-1918, proceeded to put into operation the most advanced methods of mass persuasion, first to gain complete political mastery and establish themselves firmly in the saddle, and then to spread the teachings of Communism to other countries, using propaganda not only for ideological purposes, but also for imperialistic expansion and power.[104]

Meanwhile the democracies had demobilized their war-time propaganda bureaus as quickly as they had relaxed their domestic economic controls. Not so the dictatorships. Mussolini from the first

---

[100] Lasswell, *op. cit.*, p. 19.
[101] Lumley, *The Propaganda Menace*, New York, 1933, p. 220.
[102] Bruntz, *op. cit.*, pp. 212 ff.
[103] Wallace Carroll, *Persuade or Perish*, Boston, 1948, p. 7; Edward W. Barrett, *Truth Is Our Weapon*, New York, 1953, Ch. III: "We Bumble Through."
[104] *Supra*, pp. 2, 25 ff.

made extensive use of propaganda both at home and abroad, a task facilitated by his dictatorial control of all media of information and communication.[105] Those two close students of Soviet and Fascist methods, Hitler and his propaganda chief, Goebbels, both at home and abroad, in war and in peace, devoted tremendous efforts to the molding of the minds of men.[106]

This development was highlighted by the advent of radio for propaganda purposes. An early case of radio warfare occurred between Berlin and Paris during the invasion of the Ruhr,[107] and another between Germany and Poland in their dispute over Upper Silesia.[108] In 1926 Moscow and Bucharest engaged in a propaganda war over Bessarabia, where the Russians resorted to both irredentist and Red revolutionary agitation.[109] Some such incidents occurred, too, between certain Danubian states.[110] And in Latin America radio proved handy to both sides in various boundary disputes.[111]

About this time the colonial countries inaugurated shortwave broadcasts to strengthen the bonds of empire. In this new development, Holland was a pioneer, commencing an experimental service to the Indies in 1927.[112] In this it was soon followed by the British, the French, and others. France began to broadcast to its colonies in 1931, during its Colonial Exposition, and inaugurated its foreign language programs in 1936.[113] Meanwhile, the BBC started its Empire Service in 1932, and Germany began its broadcasts to *Auslandsdeutsche* in 1933.[114] Italy was particularly interested in influencing Latin American countries, at first by reaching its own nationals there, in Italian (1935). By 1937 Italy was broadcasting to foreign peoples in eighteen languages. Many of these efforts, particularly in Latin America, were violently anti-American.[115] It should be added that "Radio Nations," broadcasting from Geneva, attempted to use the radio to

---

[105] Childs and Whitton, *op. cit.*, pp. 1-48, 153 ff.

[106] *Ibid.*, pp. 51-108; Lindley M. Fraser, *Germany Between the Two Wars: A Study of Propaganda and War-guilt*, Oxford, 1945, pp. 90 ff; Ernst Kris and Hans Speier, *German Radio Propaganda* (Report on Home Broadcasts During the War), London/New York/Toronto, 1944. For the role of propaganda in Nuremberg War Crimes Trials, *post.*, pp. 76 *et seq.*

[107] *New York Times*, March 6, and 9, 1923.

[108] John D. Tomlinson, *The International Control of Radiocommunications*, (thesis), Geneva, 1938, p. 226.

[109] Whitton, *op. cit.*, (*Hague Recueil*), pp. 560-561; L. John Martin, *International Propaganda, Its Legal and Diplomatic Control*, Minneapolis, 1958, p. 8.

[110] Whitton, *op. cit.*, p. 561.

[111] *Ibid.*

[112] George A. Codding, Jr., *Broadcasting Without Barriers*, The Hague (UNESCO), 1959, pp. 22-23; Arno Huth, *La Radiodiffusion, Puissance Mondiale*, Paris, 1937, p. 200.

[113] Childs-Whitton, *op. cit.*, pp. 8, 183 ff.

[114] Codding, *op. cit.*, pp. 22-23; Childs-Whitton, *op. cit.*, pp. 19 ff.

[115] Childs-Whitton, *op. cit.*, pp. 27 ff., 153 ff.

spread knowledge of the League of Nations and to increase international understanding, but without much success.[116] Meanwhile, Japan was sending over the airwaves its messages in support of its conquest of Manchukuo. Engaging in a propaganda war against the Chinese, it attempted to cut off the conquered Chinese masses from their homeland and to instill among them new loyalties. After 1935 Japan constructed short-wave stations to send propaganda to Hawaii, the western coast of America and the Latin American states.[117] Meanwhile, the United States did little or nothing to counter the hostile, even vicious propaganda issuing from Moscow, Berlin, Rome, and Tokyo. No forceful defensive measures were attempted by the U.S. government—not even the monitoring of such attacks—until after Pearl Harbor.

The first war in which shortwave radio was used by both sides on large scale was the Civil War in Spain. (True, radio was likewise a feature of the Italo-Ethiopian conflict, but Italy alone enjoyed the needed facilities to employ it effectively.) From the opening of hostilities both sides—the Loyalists from Madrid, the Rebels from Seville—sprayed their own partisans and the neutrals with their respective versions of the fighting, with great emphasis upon accusations of atrocities. Thus the world witnessed a real propaganda war. This war of words involved many other countries, notably Germany and Italy, for whom the Loyalists were "Reds," vying with the U.S.S.R., for whom they were "Patriots." Alleged anti-Nazi propaganda on the Moscow and Madrid stations was the basis for strong protests from Berlin.[118]

Mussolini, who, like Hitler, counted greatly on radio to maintain the loyalty of the home population, was sending beamed programs to the Arabs as a feature of his "cold war" with Britain, and, in an effort to gain prestige and power in Latin America, was broadcasting to this continent shortwave programs attacking the United States.[119] It was over two years before the British felt it necessary to reply to these maneuvers by establishing a service to the Arabs in the latters' own language, but the United States paid little attention to the Italian broadcasts sent to their southern neighbors until long after the war broke out. The reluctance of the democracies to engage in psycho-

---

[116] Pitman B. Potter, "League Publicity: Cause or Effect of League Failure?" *Public Opinion Quarterly,* Vol. II (1938), p. 404; G. F. Van Dissel, "League of Nations Wireless Station," *Proceedings of the Institute of Radio Engineers,* Vol. 22 (1934), pp. 430-448.

[117] Huth, *op. cit.,* pp. 295 ff.; Thomas Grandin, "The Political Use of the Radio," *Geneva Studies,* Vol. X (August, 1939), pp. 61-63.

[118] Childs-Whitton, *op. cit.,* pp. 24 ff.; O. W. Riegel, "Press, Radio and the Spanish Civil War," *Public Opinion Quarterly.* Vol I (1937), pp. 131-141.

[119] *Supra,* p. 35.

logical warfare at this crucial time is shown by the fact that as late as 1937, while Moscow was broadcasting in seven languages, Rome in sixteen, and Berlin in six, the British were still content to use English only.[120]

Hitler exploited the vehicle of propaganda with the usual Nazi ruthlessness,[121] as charged in the Act of Accusation of the war criminals at Nuremberg, and as amply proved by the evidence produced at the trial. One of his first acts on coming to power was to set up a National Ministry of Public Enlightenent and Propaganda, under Joseph Goebbels as its chief, with complete control over literature, the cinema, music, the graphic arts, commercial advertising and broadcasting.

Using the obligatory salute, "Heil Hitler," as a universal slogan, and the ever-present and easily designed Swastika as a dynamic symbol of power and loyalty, the Nazis neglected no propaganda trick in their drive for world power. Although the Russians were the first to use radio as a political weapon, for utter ruthlessness and scientific thoroughness in the adaptation of the new medium, no one could match the Nazis. As was brought out later at the Nuremberg trials, propaganda was found to be of enormous value in regimenting a nation of seventy million souls creating an atmosphere so thickly indoctrinated that occasionally American students spending a summer in Germany would come back favorably disposed, at least temporarily, toward the Nazi regime. At the start of his drive for power, practically the only weapon Hitler possessed was the force of persuasion, and for this purpose he turned to radio, which Goebbels made into a potent weapon to gain power. Once installed as Führer, Hitler relied on the same medium to consolidate his position, developing broadcasting into an all-pervading instrument of adult education and mass indoctrination. All other media of mass communication—platform, cinema, press —were, of course, directed to the same ends, and all were backed by material power—police, Gestapo, Elite Guards, and Storm Troopers, and the regular armed forces. Propaganda went hand in hand with the governmental censorship and the concentration camp. But while the effect of these other means must not be underestimated, radio, "total radio," undoubtedly played a predominant role. It enabled Hitler's voice to penetrate into every household. As anyone knows who visited Germany during the 'thirties, group listening was obligatory in restaurants and factories and other places of public assembly, while, in a continuing stream, indoctrination in Nazi and nationalistic principles was poured into every private home. One of the grimmest features of the extremely grim Germany of that day was the loud-

<hr>

120 H. Schuyler Foster, "The Official Propaganda of Great Britain," *Public Opinion Quarterly*, Vol. III (1939), pp. 263-271.
121 Grandin, *op. cit.*, pp. 11, 25, 46; Kris and Speier, *op. cit.*, pp. 51 ff.

speaker on many downtown street corners from which a hoarse voice —Hitler's or Goebbels' or some similar voice—kept up a continuous blast of poisonous persuasion.[122]

Thus did the Nazi leaders prepare the people morally for war. Thus were spread the vicious doctrines of common blood, master race, the *Führerprinzip,* and the glorification of brutality and warfare. In this way the smouldering resentments engendered by the Treaty of Versailles were fanned into flaming hatred against foreign nations marked for conquest. Having placed himself solidly in the saddle at home, Hitler turned his attention to foreign affairs, and here again radio had a major share in preparing and launching his vicious campaigns of aggression. The first test of the great Goebbels machine of thought control of the masses occurred in the Saar,[123] whose re-entry into the Reich was carefully prepared by psychological measures of a particularly virulent character, marked by terroristic intimidation to discourage dissident voters, and patriotic inspiration to instill loyalty to the Reich. Then from the Saar and elsewhere an irredentist attack was directed into Alsace-Lorraine; the French, curiously enough, made but a feeble reply. The next step came with the notorious vitriolic broadcasts of Habicht, picturing Austria as German and Nazi, oppressed by a "terroristic, separatist and treacherous minority backed by Germany's enemies." Alleged atrocities were recounted and the people summoned to revolt. On one such occasion Frauenfeld, exiled Vienna Gauleiter, bluntly called for the assassination of Dollfuss. In order to bring down Schuschnigg, radio for the first time was used in a way later to be applied to all countries marked for conquest—to carry the redoubtable strategy of terror. Propaganda was thus one of the mainstays in the drives for the conquest of Czechoslovakia, Danzig, Poland, and France.[124]

The British, on their part, finally found it imperative to counter the subversive campaign among the Arabs with programs of their own. And, after Munich, Britain and France began a counter-offensive against Berlin.[125] But not until it entered the war did the United States institute measures, by radio and otherwise, to counteract the tidal wave of hostile propaganda sent from Berlin, Rome, Moscow and Tokyo.[126]

Thus, between the two great wars, propaganda reflected with remarkable accuracy the foreign policies of the respective states. Aggressive states employed aggressive propaganda, revolutionary states subversive propaganda. The peaceful states either used no propa-

---

[122] Kris and Speier, *op. cit.,* pp. 59 ff.; Childs-Whitton, *op. cit.,* pp. 27 ff.
[123] Childs-Whitton, pp. 12 ff.
[124] For the above, *ibid.,* pp. 11-44, 51 ff.
[125] *Ibid.,* pp. 27 ff.
[126] Charles A. H. Thomson, *Overseas Information Service of the United States Government,* Washington, 1948, Ch. IV, Martin, *op. cit.,* pp. 22 ff.

ganda at all, or entered the psychological conflict only when forced into it, in self-defense, and often with too little and too late. However, as the powers were preparing for the great trial of arms, they already had commenced the struggle "by other means," after Munich, with an all-out radio war.

WORLD WAR II

During the Second World War governmental machinery to control men's minds was enormously expanded and systematized, so that for the first time in history the term "psychological warfare" became the proper term to describe such activities. It is well recognized that in the Second World War propaganda was an important auxiliary of the military and economic weapons. Some spectacular successes were: the magnificent effort of Winston Churchill to sustain British morale in the dark days of 1940 and 1941; De Gaulle's stirring messages to Occupied France, and his ability, mainly through propaganda (since he had little else in the way of power) to get his way despite lack of real support from Churchill and Roosevelt; and the remarkable success of Goebbels to keep the German population in the fight almost to the last despite Stalingrad, Normandy and the Battle of the Bulge.

One author, writing in the midst of the war, went so far as to assert that propaganda, especially by radio, "has become an arm in the hands of the belligerents who suppress, alter or falsify news . . . it is more dangerous in this war than gas or cannon. Upon its extent and quality may depend victory or defeat.[127] Actually the psychological warfare as waged by the aggressors long preceded the march of troops and the thunder of guns. This "indirect aggression" had been going on for years, so that in 1939 Germany, Italy and Russia merely had to expand departments of "enlightenment and information" already well established in peacetime and formally accepted as major instrumentalities of government. France, England and the United States, whose "information" departments had been demobilized shortly after the First World War, suffered at first a grave disadvantage, and were forced to rebuild almost from the ground up. In fact, the British Ministry of Information only came into existence after the war had commenced, and the British ideological effort did not really get under way until after Dunkirk.[128]

The United States too, came into the picture very late. It was only five months before Pearl Harbor that President Roosevelt set up the Office of Coordinator of Information, to channel news about the

[127] Raymond L. Buell, *Isolated America*, New York, 1940, p. 248, quoting from Thomas Grandin, "La Radio Pendant les Deux Premiers Mois de Guerre," *Politique Etrangère*, October, 1939.
[128] Charles J. Rolo, *Radio Goes to War*, New York, 1942, pp. 154 ff.; Childs-Whitton, *op. cit.*, pp. 111 ff., 214 ff., and *passim*.

United States to the outside world. But the OWI (Office of War Information) was not created until June 1942, with Elmer Davis as its
head. Its purpose was to send radio emissions and printed material
to allies, enemies and neutrals, while the OSS (Office of Strategic
Services) was charged with the undercover, subversive activities of
psychological warfare, such as espionage, false intelligence, aid to underground forces, sabotage, etc. As part of the OWI, the Voice of
America beamed its programs in 40 languages to all parts of the
world. A number of special services were developed by the OWI in
addition to radio. This included press services, libraries, exchange of
persons, film strips, and the distribution of literature to many countries of the world. Tactical activities were entrusted to the Psychological Warfare Branch of the Army, whose campaign of dropping leaflets to enemy troops is credited with certain outstanding successes,
notably in Africa to aid in the collapse of von Arnim's army, and in
Japan.[129]

In general, the techniques employed by the propagandist in this
war in an all-out effort to influence opinion at home, in enemy countries, and among neutrals, did not differ materially, except in degree,
from those found useful in the First World War. But there were certain notable innovations. In contrast with the situation in World War
I, when the use of propaganda on an organized scale developed only
gradually, the declaration of war in 1939 was preceded by a long
psychological build-up by the aggressors, but above all by Nazi Germany, who thus prepared for what was to follow. Goebbels, in a long
campaign of the most intensive character, using all possible media of
communication and the latest methods of mass persuasion, had carefully indoctrinated the German people with "hate-propaganda," designed to arouse them to fever-heat, not only against the Jewish
people, but also against Poles, French and British, in an effort to convince the German army and citizenry of the necessity to fight, and to
demonstrate the ease and sureness of victory.[130] In the chapter on
war-mongering propaganda we will have more to say on this subject,
stressing the Nuremburg Trial, where Nazi criminals were charged
with, and convicted of, the *preparation* for aggressive war.[131] At the
same time that the German people were being "prepared" for aggressive war, a psychological campaign, planned with equal care and carried on with even greater persistence, was designed to divide and

---

[129] Thomson, *op. cit.*, Ch. IV; Daniel Lerner, *Sykewar: Psychological Warfare
Against Germany*, D-Day to VE Day, New York, 1949, *passim*. See also Robert
T. Holt and Robert W. van de Velde, *Strategic Psychological Operations and
American Foreign Policy*, Chicago, 1960.

[130] Kris and Speier, *op. cit.*, pp. 3-22. For reference to Nüremberg War
Crime Trials, *post*, pp. 77 ff.

[131] Quincy Wright, "The Crime of 'War-Mongering,'" *Am. J. Int. Law*, Vol.
42 (1948), pp. 128-136.

conquer, to split allies from allies, and peoples from their governments. Propaganda was thus directed to Britain to spread the doctrine of appeasement, and to France to engender division and defeatism, and this campaign was stepped up to an ever-higher voltage as the moment for the "shooting war" approached.[132]

This degree of war-preparation propaganda was new, and so was the organization that inspired and directed it. Fifth column cadres and techniques and an efficient system of intelligence agents were all closely integrated with the war effort, and designed to operate at various places throughout the globe. The task of suavely and surreptitiously spreading poisonous words in foreign lands was confided particularly to agents and fifth-columnists, some of whom actually bought up foreign newspapers or bribed the latters' writers. Such activities proved especially successful in Poland and France. This work, which included spying, sabotage and bribery, was not considered too low a task for consuls and ambassadors, and not too refined for ordinary crooks. It was the most spectacular example of subversive propaganda in history. Due to the vast intelligence service, and the extensive research carried on by the Propaganda Ministry itself, Nazi broadcasters and political writers were kept fully informed of conditions and tendencies in all countries marked out for psychological operations. Thus "Paul Revere," speaking from Berlin to the farmer in Minnesota, could punctuate his insidious arguments with American slang, or references to early American hatred of the "Redcoats." Thus Zeezen was able to take advantage of every weakness in the American armor, needling the American public about the negro problem, anti-semitism or troubles between capital and labor. But as the studies of the Princeton Listening Center demonstrated, this campaign had little effect; few Americans, other than strong sympathizers, even listened to these programs.[133]

All the belligerents, however, including the Nazis, were in a position to profit greatly from invaluable lessons on propaganda learned during the first war. The Germans no longer left this subtle and extremely specialized task to the army, while the British now carefully avoided the grave mistake which, committed in the other war, had caused them no end of embarrassment—the fabrication of atrocity stories out of whole cloth. Furthermore, much more was now known about methods of mass persuasion, especially as many techniques had already been tried out in the great public laboratory by advertisers, public relations men and political parties. A vast literature on mass psychology, in particular works treating of mass attitudes in wartime, had appeared after 1918, and much new learning had resulted from the patient research carried on by social psychologists and by devotees

---

[132] Kris and Speier, *op. cit.*, Part I.
[133] Childs-Whitton, *op. cit.*, pp. 305 ff.

41

of that new discipline—the scientific study of pressure groups and public opinion.[134] When the war broke out these specialists were in great demand by all departments of psychological warfare, and were soon given ample opportunity for the practical application of their expert knowledge.

Another event which opened up an entirely new field for these specialists was the invention of radio. Thanks to radio, Goebbels could now talk to practically the entire world; no frontier could stop him.

On the other hand, the propagandist could hardly look upon the invention of radio as an unmixed blessing. In previous wars, the enemy's arguments, even if unanswerable, were not greatly feared when all media of communication were still in the control of the home government. Enemy or neutral newspapers could be stopped at the frontier, and harmful news or dangerous arguments kept from the public by censorship. True, toward the end of the First World War, tracts and leaflets were carried across enemy lines by airplane and balloons, but although many millions of such leaflets were dropped, their effect was limited. But the coming of radio brought with it an unprecedented and wholly unexpected means of checking the enemy's propaganda, especially when false news and such nefarious practices as the unrestrained use of the atrocity story were employed. The all-pervasive BBC could thus expose lies Goebbels might try to inflict on the Americans, or even on the Germans themselves. Similarly, a British desire to suppress embarrassing news, such as the loss of the "Prince of Wales," would inevitably be frustrated by the triumphant and cynical voice of "Lord Haw Haw." Also, the once-invaluable monopoly of the oceanic cables, a boon to the British in 1914, no longer played a role in 1939 since Zeezen, by short-wave, could now beam its news to the four corners of the earth.

No belligerent, however, suffered greater inconvenience as a result of radio broadcasting than the Nazis. Not only was Goebbel's hold on his own people loosened by broadcasts entering from enemy lands, but the efforts of the Nazis to control the occupied countries were partly stultified. Because of the BBC, it was impossible for the Nazis to prevent Wilhelmina from broadcasting comforting messages to the down-trodden Dutch, nor Haakon from stiffening the morale of the beleaguered Norwegians. And the BBC, with Churchill and de Gaulle as star performers, not only helped to keep the French in the war but gave continual inspiration—and transmitted daily orders—to the French Underground, many of whose members were enabled to listen to London's short-wave because of a gift from Soviet Russia, before the war,

---

[134] See excellent bibliographies in Quincy Wright, *The Study of International Relations,* New York, 1955, pp. 300-306, and under appropriate headings in Bruce Lannes Smith and Chitra M. Smith, *International Communication and Political Opinion* (A Guide to the Literature), Princeton, 1956.

of thousands of small receiving sets intended for listening to Moscow!

Another important development in this war, although not really an innovation, except in degree, was the use of propaganda on the field of battle. This was another phenomenon which, without the invention of radio and the loud-speaker, would have been impossible. The Nazis employed such tactics with remarkable success during the "Phony War" period, sending to the Maginot Line messages which had a wide audience among French troops. The futility of "fighting to save Danzig," and the alleged absence of British soldiers from the front lines were familiar themes of Nazi programs. The French soldiers were never allowed to forget that "England will fight to the last Frenchman," while a disparagement of the French Army was broadcast to the British. Propaganda was widely employed by the Nazis in actual conflict. Their defeatist and terroristic messages to front-line troops in battle were especially effective.[135] Somewhat similar methods were later adopted by the American Army, so extensively in fact that the operations conducted by the Psychological Warfare Board against the German troops prior to and during the Normandy invasion, so it is claimed, actually reduced the cost of that operation.[136] Similarly, allied front-line propaganda in Italy proved successful in inducing thousands of German and Italian troops to surrender.[137]

Radio during actual invasion proved to be a really lethal weapon when directed to the civilian population in time of defeat and retreat. This phenomenon, so graphically described by Edmond Taylor in his *Strategy of Terror*,[138] is the war of nerves carried to its highest pitch of intensity. First employed in the advance into Poland, it was again prominent during the retreat of the French Armies in 1940. A continuous barrage of terrifying messages in French was sent over the radio on French wave-lengths, bellowing the news of the approach of Nazi tanks and bombers, and warning the people to flee for their lives. This the people proceeded to do, jamming the roads to the great embarrassment of the Allied armies, and offering a ready target to the very planes from which they were attempting to flee. This formidable weapon served also to give false orders and "black propaganda"[139] to the Allied troops, and in general played an important role in all German advances. In Britain, however, such tactics had little effect.

---

[135] Edmond Taylor, *The Strategy of Terror, Europe's Inner Front*, Boston, 1940.

[136] James P. Warburg, *Unwritten Treaty*, New York, 1946, p. 122.

[137] "The Italian people were knocked out of the war at least as much by psychological factors as by military defeat. . . . Both strategic and front-line propaganda were highly effective." *Ibid.*, p. 122. See Holt and van de Velde, *op. cit.*, Ch. V.

[138] *Supra*, n. 135, and see Leland Stowe, *Conquest by Terror*, New York, 1952.

[139] *I.e.*, messages falsely purporting to come from the listeners' own country.

Before the war ended, combatants and most of the neutrals were sending broadcasts almost around the world. More than 360 transmitters, divided among 55 states, were broadcasting in more than 40 languages.[140]

SINCE WORLD WAR II

Although the belligerents laid down their weapons after 1945, psychological warfare did not abate, except temporarily in the camp of the democracies. Quickly the Western Powers, very much as after the victory in 1918, not only materially reduced their armed forces, but even beat their propaganda swords into ploughshares. Nor did they re-convert them until the outbreak of the Cold War had destroyed their illusions as to the possibility of Great Power accord, the assumed basis for the U.N. Charter.

It would be impossible to do justice here to the great propaganda contest which has characterized the years since World War II. This would require not one volume but many volumes. We can merely suggest the general nature of that conflict and, for purposes of illustration, say a word about the propaganda organizations of the chief protagonists in this struggle, the Soviet Union and the United States. We cannot describe the parallel organizations and activities of other countries vitally engaged in this contest, notably Britain and France in the Western camp, experienced although not always consistent propagandists, nor, in the other camp, Communist China, a newcomer but rapidly becoming a formidable adversary. Other governments, too, because of their heavy reliance on agitation in foreign countries, for instance, Egypt, Yugoslavia and Cuba, also deserve special mention.

Soviet Russia,[141] unlike the Western Democracies after 1945, never relaxed its weapons of psychological and political warfare, nor its military power either. The end of the war found Moscow equipped with the greatest organization for mass pressures ever known. This was Agitprop, or Administration of Agitation and Propaganda of the Communist Party Central Committee, with 1,400,000 trained employees.

---

[140] Codding, op. cit., p. 23.

[141] George H. Bolsover, "Soviet Ideology and Propaganda," International Affairs, Vol. 24 (1948), pp. 170-180; Jean-Marie Domenach, "Leninist Propaganda," Public Opinion Quarterly, Vol. 15 (1951), pp. 265-273; Frank Bowen Evans, ed., Worldwide Communist Propaganda Activities, New York, 1955; Harold D. Lasswell, "The Strategy of Soviet Propaganda," Proceedings of the Academy of Political Science, Vol. 24 (1951), pp. 66-78; U.S. Senate, The Soviet Propaganda Program (Staff Studies, Subcommittee on Overseas Information Programs of the United States, Staff Study No. 3, Senate, 82nd Congress, 2d Session), Washington, D.C., 1952; Martin, op. cit., pp. 46-54. See also, John B. Whitton (ed.), Propaganda and the Cold War, Washington, 1963, especially Ch. 2, 3, 4.

Its director ranked high in the Soviet hierarchy, for it was his responsibility to manipulate public opinion, after receiving basic policy decisions from the Politburo. Aiding these well-trained public servants was the Cominform, set up in October, 1947, to replace the defunct Comintern, apparently dissolved in 1943 to placate public opinion in the West. (The Cominform itself was abolished in 1956). While in operation, these agencies assured to Communism a great world-wide agency for subversion, dominated by Moscow despite assurances to the contrary.

Agitprop is assisted by the All-Union Committee on Radio Information and the Ministry of Cinematography. The program of world-wide radio propaganda is prepared by the psychological warfare department of the Foreign Office, with its 250 experts. Radio is only one cog, although a major one, in the Soviet propaganda machine. There is a vast program which includes the distribution of books and pamphlets in many foreign countries in local languages, and even local dialects, and the publication and distribution of periodicals, news and films.[142] An important advantage enjoyed by the Russians is the possession of a well-organized and widely-experienced propaganda apparatus which dates back to 1917 and has been tried out in many emergencies. Also, in many foreign lands spies and fifth-columnists, and embassies and consulates serving as illegal centers of expionage and subversion, complete the picture. This formidable machine which no free country, not even the United States, has felt impelled to match is generously financed, and is aided by foreign newspapers of leftist tinge. In a sense it is even "aided" by great free newspapers like the *New York Times* which, in the interest of news value and complete coverage, print entire speeches of Soviet leaders, despite their obvious propagandistic character and intention. There is also a major cultural exchange program, under the direction of VOKS, the All-Union Society for Cultural Relations with foreign countries. Soviet radio propaganda has been markedly increased in recent years. The U.S.S.R. as of December 1962, was broadcasting weekly to foreign countries approximately 1,200 hours a week, including more than 250 hours to Western Europe alone.[143] An important development is the increasing attention now given by Communist regimes to Latin America. There are Communist radio programs of one kind or another in at least 10 Latin American countries. Time is bought by local Communist parties or by

---

142 Don Wharton, "Poison from Red Printing Presses," *Readers Digest*, November 1961, pp. 299-302. The author states the Soviet Union printed 40 million books in non-bloc languages in 1960, an increase of ten million over 1959. India alone received 4 million in 1960, but only 17,000 in 1955. Cuba has become a major center for dissemination of Soviet publications for all of Latin America.

143 *New York Times*, March 4, 1962, Sec. E, p. 3.

bloc diplomatic missions. Some television time is also purchased.[144]

On December 6, 1962, the U.S.I.A. issued the following release:

Total USSR international broadcasting output as of December 1 amounts to 1,205 hours per week, a 13 per cent increase since the start of the year and the highest rate of expansion noted since 1956, a U.S. Information Agency survey revealed today.

Most of the increase occurred in the current winter schedule starting in October and coinciding with the Cuban crisis, the USIA report said.

There were three major components to the increase.

First was an increase of almost 60 per cent in broadcasts to Africa, from 73:30 hours to 112 hours per week.

Second was a more than 50 per cent increase in broadcasts to the Far East, from 117 to 180 hours, most in Mandarin, Vietnamese and English.

Third was a more than 100 per cent increase in Spanish language broadcasts to Latin America—from 45:30 to 101:30 hours per week, of which 70 hours were beamed specifically at Cuba for the first time.

The new USSR total puts it further in the lead of international broadcasting, with Red China second at 780 hours per week and the Voice of America, broadcasting arm of the U.S. Information Agency, third with 740 hours per week.

Lately Radio Moscow has been seconded by Radio Peking, which apparently is trying to outdo its mentor in the virulence of its programs. Its major target is, of course, the United States, although South Korea and Taiwan come in for heavy attack. Japan is either cajoled or calumnied according to the changes in the international situation. The expansion attained by Communist China lately in this field is shown by the fact that while in 1953 it was broadcasting abroad less than 100 hours a week, by 1962 this had grown to 780 hours. The programs in Arabian, Persian and Turkish were extended greatly during this period. Emissions to the Far East from the entire Communist Bloc also rose. North Korea virtually blanketed South Korea, with 100 hours a week, contrasting China's "peacefulness" with the "aggressive and imperialist intentions of the West," especially the United States, and extolling the industrial rehabilitation of Northern Korea.[145]

---

[144] Simon Costikyan, *Twelve Years of Communist Broadcasting, 1948-1959*, (Office of Research and Analysis, U.S. Information Agency), Washington, 1960, pp. 1 and 30, and Charts, pp. 54 ff.; John B. McConaughy, "A Review of Soviet Psychological Warfare," *Military Review*, Vol. 11, No. 9 (December 1960).

[145] *Enc. Britt., Book of the Year 1960*, p. 352; Costikyan, *op. cit.*, pp. 9, 75. "The time of broadcasts and the transmitting facilities of Communist China have been greatly expanded since the early days, so that at the end of 1959,

According to a report based on a study of twelve years of Communist radio propaganda, issued by the USIA on January 8, 1961, Communist countries broadcast for about 3,000 hours a week in fifty-five languages, a five-fold increase since 1948. It was reported that after the Suez crisis in 1956 the Arab world became a prime target of Communist political communication by radio, and for the first time broadcasts were directed to Africa.[146]

UNITED STATES EFFORTS

The first year following the World War II saw the United States abandon most of its wartime apparatus of political communication. The disintegration of America's great wartime effort in the field of propaganda went forward even more rapidly than the demobilization of the armed forces. As early as August 31, 1945, only sixteen days after the Japanese surrender, President Truman by executive order abolished the Office of War Information, merely leaving in its place an interim international information service.[147] This agency, ordered to cut the wartime program to the bone, reduced the number of its employees from 11,000 to 3,000. Expenditures amounting to $71 million in 1945, fell to $45 million in 1946 and to a mere $20 million in 1948.[148]

The interim program also replaced a number of other wartime services having something to do with propaganda, among others, the Office of Inter-American Affairs, the Special Assistant to the Secretary for Press Relations, and the Division of Cultural Cooperation. Meanwhile, the Fulbright Act in 1946 set in motion an important program of cultural and student exchanges.[149] In January, 1947, the interim agency became the OIC (Office of International Information and Cultural Affairs.)

Thus was born the United States' first venture, in peacetime, into the field of international political communication, with William Benton as the first director. The title was changed again in 1947, becoming the OIE (Office of International Information and Educational Exchange.) This was the low point for the information effort, and in fact the service was actually threatened for some time with abolition by Congressional action. Fortunately a Senatorial sub-committee, after

---

Communist China was broadcasting 512 hours per week in its international services, compared with 16 hours per week in 1948." *Ibid.*, p. 10. For the "hate campaign" by China against the United States, see Denis Warner, *Hurricane from China*, New York, 1961.

146 *New York Times*, Jan. 9, 1961.

147 Executive Order 9608, August 31, 1945. Report of the Committee on Foreign Relations, "Overseas Information Programs of the United States," 83rd Congress, 1st Session, Senate, Report No. 406, June 15, 1953, p. 138.

148 *Ibid.*, p. 79.

149 Public Law 584, 79th Congress, *ibid.*, p. 63.

a world-wide investigation, reported such a need for a vital information service abroad that Congress was convinced, and voted another reorganization. This took the form of the Smith-Mundt Act of 1948,[150] which today still constitutes the basic charter of the services of international information and cultural exchange.

Senator Smith, co-author of the Smith-Mundt Act, described the purposes of this act as follows:[151]

> The United States Information Service must be the voice of America and the means of clarifying the opinion of the world concerning us. To be effective it must (1) tell the truth; (2) explain United States motives; (3) bolster morale and extend hope; (4) give a true and convincing picture of American life, methods and ideals; (5) combat misrepresentation and distortion, and (6) aggressively interpret and support our foreign policy.

He also said:

> We have nevertheless been too preoccupied in the past with feeding the stomachs of people, while the Soviets have concentrated on feeding their minds.

Through the Smith-Mundt Act the information-exchange services were given a new lease on life, with the acquisition of permanent legislative status. The OIE was divided into the OII (Office of International Information) and the OEX (Office of Educational Exchange), each with an Advisory Commission appointed by the President. The OII and OEX were merged into the IIA, (International Information Administration) in 1952, but each kept its own advisory committee. Despite this important step, an information service in peacetime still seemed strange to the American people and the Congress, and their apathy was reflected in the budget, which allotted to this work only $31 million in 1949; and even in 1950, despite the shock caused by the Korean War, this item amounted only to $47 million.[152]

Nevertheless 1950 was a year of awakening. Even before the outbreak of the Korean War, an aroused National Security Council had called for a more aggressive use of propaganda and in response President Truman, in April 1950, made an appeal for a "Great Campaign of Truth."[153] When the war broke out the emphasis was changed in

[150] Public Law 402, 80th Congress, *ibid.*, p. 64.

[151] Report of the Committee on Foreign Relations, "The United States Information Service in Europe," 80th Congress, 2nd Session, Senate, Report No. 855, January 30, 1948, pp. 3-5.

[152] Report of the Committee on Foreign Relations, "Overseas Information Programs of the United States," 83rd Congress, 1st Session, Senate, Report No. 406, June 15, 1953, pp. 48 ff., 78.

[153] *New York Times*, April 21, 1950.

favor of a more dynamic program designed to answer the Soviet campaign of defamation and false charges.[154]

The information service was subjected to a number of investigations and reports.[155] One was made by the Jackson Committee, appointed *ad hoc*, another by the official Advisory Commission on Information, headed by Dr. Mark A. May, and a most exhaustive investigation by a sub-committee of the Senate, headed first by Senator Fulbright and then, with a change of administration, by Senator Hickenlooper. Meanwhile Senator McCarthy was conducting his own inquest, which hardly was of a nature to permit healthy, unimpeded growth of the agency.[156] As a result of these various investigations and studies, the agency was again reorganized in 1953, by a Presidential order (Reorganization Plan 8 of 1953) which was approved by Congress and went into effect on August 1st of that year.[157]

The voluminous testimony before the Senatorial sub-committee is of great interest. Pervading the Senators' questions was an obvious feeling of doubt as to the value and effectiveness of the foreign information program, which was gone over with a fine tooth comb. Part of this doubt was due to the lack of any reliable means of evaluating foreign propaganda, a formidable problem to this day. There was also difference of opinion whether to confine the message to a "campaign of truth," or to extend this to comment and argument of a more positive nature. Many felt that the United States had neglected the "propaganda of the deed," and had failed to do more than react to more imaginative Soviet initiatives. Some programs were attacked as being too boastful, causing resentment and even enmity. Other criticism was directed at the lack of full cooperation both between policy-making and information services, and between these two and the armed services. It was claimed also that the State Department had never given more than a grudging support to the propaganda effort. Many experts expressed the view that to give the service essential prestige, and to assure effective coordination between it and the other weapons of governmental power—the military, economic and diplomatic—it was imperative to give the director of the USIA Cabinet status. In this connection there was much argument over whether the service should be a part of the State Department, or be established outside as a separate agency. The USIA was finally established as an independent

---

154 See Rowland Ludden, "Development of Informational Activities," Ch. 18 in Stephen D. Kertesz, *American Diplomacy In A New Era*, Notre Dame, 1961.

155 Dizard, *Strategy of Truth*, New York, 1961, p. 40.

156 Report of the Committee on Foreign Relations, "Overseas Information Programs of the United States." 83rd Congress, 1st Session, Senate, Report No. 406. Also, Final Report of same Committee, 83rd Congress, 2nd Session, Senate, Report No. 936.

157 Reorganization Plan 8 of 1953.

agency in 1953.[158] It was to receive its foreign policy guidance from the State Department, but it was responsible for its own information policy.

The first director of the USIA was Theodore C. Streibert, who served until September 15, 1956, when he was replaced by Arthur Larson, former Under Secretary of Labor. The position at this point was described as a Cabinet level appointment, the Director having direct access to the President and attending all Cabinet and National Security Council meetings. Mr. Larson was succeeded by Ambassador George V. Allen, who directed the agency from October 16, 1957 until the appointment in 1961 of Edward R. Murrow, the well-known television commentator and producer.

A chief instrument of the U.S.I.A. is radio, particularly the Voice of America, although the radio station in Berlin, so often attacked by the Russians, RIAS, is also under its direction. VOA broadcasts around the clock over a network of 87 transmitters, 32 of them in the U.S., the others strategically located around the globe.[159] Its work is supplemented by several privately-owned radio stations: the World Wide Broadcasting System, operating for the past 25 years from Boston, the Committee for Free Asia, Inc., sending programs to Asia from San

---

[158] For an excellent short history of the U.S.I.A., see Steven R. Brown, "United States Information Agency," *Freedom of Information Publication No. 70.* School of Journalism, University of Missouri, 1961, and Wilson P. Dizard, *Strategy of Truth,* pp. 43-47. For a summary of the current criticisms of the American program of international communication, see Ch. 1, "The American Effort Challenged," in Whitton, *Propaganda and the Cold War,* and the answer to these criticisms by Thomas C. Sorensen, Deputy Director, U.S.I.A., in *ibid.,* Ch. 7: "New Directions Under the Kennedy Administration."

[159] A good example of how the U.S.I.A. reacts to a particular crisis is this account of its program during the Cuba crisis, as related in its release of October 24, 1962:

"The Voice of America, global radio network of the U.S. Information Agency, is alerting listeners behind the Iron Curtain to stand by tomorrow for a saturation broadcast that will surmount Communist jamming and spread as widely as possible the truth about the U.S. quarantine of Cuba.

"Fifty-two VOA transmitters totalling 4,331,000 watts in power—the equivalent of more than 86 of the strongest U.S. radio stations broadcasting simultaneously—will be used for the eight-and-a-half-hour crash radio barrage, starting at 10 a.m. EDST.

"Iron Curtain listeners, denied the truth by Communist censorship and distortion, will hear on some 80 different frequencies a full report of United States actions, the reasons therefor, and a summary of related developments. These broadcasts will reach their target areas during the night hours when reception is best, supplementing regular VOA reporting to eastern Europe.

"To build up a maximum listening audience for tomorrow's broadcasting, pre-announcements have been made in the 10-language programs of VOA repeatedly during the past 24 hours. This proclamation tactic was determined because Communist jamming is so developed that a maximum of only three unjammed minutes could be gained by a surprise move. Since jamming, at best, is never completely successful, the advantage of alerting the prospective audience

50

Francisco and Manila, Radio Liberation, operating from Munich, and Radio Free Europe.

During the fiscal year 1962, the U.S.I.A. budget for salaries and operational expenses totaled $111,500,000. The agency had a personnel of 2,365 in the United States, and 8,291 abroad, 6,775 of whom were nationals of host countries. There were 219 field posts abroad, responsible to diplomatic missions in 99 countries. Services were made available from the United States in the fields of radio, television, press, cinema, libraries, translations, exhibits (including two exhibits that toured the Soviet Union under terms of a U.S.-USSR Agreement of November 1959—"Plastics-USA" and "Transportation-USA"). It had other cultural activities. The VOA was broadcasting daily in thirty-seven languages. Pamphlets and other publications were distributed in 69 languages, and books were translated in 50 languages. 176 libraries, and 85 reading rooms were operated in 80 countries. In addition, support was provided for 128 bi-national centers in 35 countries.

Another major instrumentality for communication from American sources to foreign lands, with concentration on the satellite countries, is Radio Free Europe. The non-governmental status of this chain per-

---

outweighs the advantage of a possible few unjammed minutes of the programs.

"The half-hour program will be broadcast seven times in Russian, twice in English, and once each in Armenian, Georgian, Ukrainian, Estonian, Latvian, Lithuanian, Hungarian and Czech. Regular VOA programming to the areas will be suspended during the concentrated radio campaign.

"Only once before have Voice of America transmitters been similarly massed. This was for the "Sunday Punch" on November 5, 1961, when Edward R. Murrow, USIA Director, ordered an all-out effort to tell people behind the Iron Curtain of world reaction to Soviet secret and protracted high-megaton nuclear testing. Subsequent reports indicated that Soviet jammers were routed by the VOA effort and that the broadcasts were successful beyond expectation. The Communists employ some 2,000 interference transmitters to try to blot out free world broadcasts. To operate such a jamming complex would cost the U.S. in excess of $150 million annually, more than the entire USIA appropriation. . .

"Other USIA efforts to tell the world the truth about the Cuban crisis:

"Spanish-language short-wave broadcasts to Cuba have been tripled to 24 hours a day. Number of frequencies employed have more than doubled from five to 11.

"Ten private US radio stations, in an unprecedented link-up with the Voice of America, are carrying VOA Spanish-language programming nightly from dusk to dawn and thus providing additional frequencies, eight of them standard-wave, on which the Cuban people can hear the truth.

"Russian-language broacasts, half an hour each morning and each evening have been initiated to Cuba for the Soviet technicians assigned there.

"The Agency's radio-teletype network is carrying some 10,000 words daily to 107 posts overseas—official texts, commentaries and background material—for rapid translation and delivery to local officials and newspaper editors.

"USIA films and television programs, dubbed in multiple foreign languages, have been air-expressed to posts around the world for showing to audiences numbering in the hundreds of millions."

mits it greater flexibility and freedom (especially from Congressional interference) in its objectives and their implementation, than would be possible for the VOA. It was started in 1949 under the initiative of three former members of the American Foreign Service, George Kennan, Joseph C. Grew and DeWitt C. Poole, with the collaboration of Dean Acheson. The organization embarked on a number of ambitious enterprises, including the Free University in Exile, set up at Strasbourg, France, later discontinued. But its major effort was the institution and operation of RFE. It is supported by funds raised through another independent agency, Crusade for Freedom.

Powerful transmitters are operated from Munich, which has 21 studios. The headquarters, and the director, are located in New York City, with a European director at Munich.[160]

RFE is unique in its major reliance on exiles speaking to their native land. For this purpose it operates five semi-autonomous stations which purport to be attuned to the climate and atmosphere of the peoles with whom they are communicating.

Both Radio Free Europe and Radio Liberation[161] have as their objective the keeping alive of the hope of eventual freedom in satellites and in the Soviet Union respectively. However their policy, like the policy of the United States Information Agency,[162] has for some years been to rely upon objective truth and factual reporting as the principal means of reaching listeners.

---

[160] See Robert T. Holt, *Radio Free Europe*, Minneapolis, 1958, and Lewis Galantière, "The Role of Radio Free Europe", in Whitton, *Propaganda and the Cold War*, Ch. 10.

[161] Radio Liberation is the voice of the Coordinating Center of Anti-Bolshevist Struggle, formed in October, 1952. One of its major tasks is to train Soviet political emigres to work together democratically.

[162] See Appendix: *USIA Basic Guidance Paper*. The B.B.C. has from the beginning followed a similar line. *The Story of the BBC* (published by BBC for the Brussels Universal and International Exhibition), 1958.

PART II

THE LAW

Chapter III

The Pattern of the Law of Propaganda

The purpose of this chapter is to present an outline of the pattern that will be followed in analyzing the law of propaganda.[1]

---

[1] On the international law of hostile propaganda, see: *Broadcasting and Peace* (International Institute of Intellectual Cooperation), Paris, 1933; Gerhard Dambmann, *Propaganda im Friedensvölkerecht* (mit ausfuhrlichem Literaturverzeichnis), Frankfurt a/M, 1953; Edwin D. Dickinson, "The Defamation of Foreign Governments," *Am. J. Int. Law*, Vol. 22 (1928), p. 840-844; Charles G. Fenwick, "The Use of the Radio as an Instrument of Foreign Propaganda," *ibid.*, Vol. 32 (1938), pp. 339-343, and "Intervention by Way of Propaganda," Vol. 35 (1941), pp. 626-631; Sidney Hyman, "State Responsibility for the Hostile Utterances of Its Officers," (unpublished M. A. dissertation, University of Chicago), Chicago, 1938; Von Johann Joeden, "Die Funksendefreiheit der Staaten," *Jahrbuch für Internationales Recht*, Vol. III (1954), pp. 85-128, Vol. IV (1954), pp. 71-119; Günter B. Krause, *Beiträge zum Rundfunkrecht*, Hamburg, 1960 and "Der Rundfunkfriedenspakt von 1936," *Jahrbuch für Internationales Recht*, Vol. IX (1960), pp. 33-57; H. Lauterpacht, "Revolutionary Propaganda by Governments," *Transactions of the Grotius Society*, Vol. 13 (1928), pp. 143-164 and "Revolutionary Activities by Private Persons Against Foreign States," *Am. J. Int. Law*, Vol. 22 (1928), pp. 105-130; L. John Martin, *International Propaganda: Its Legal and Diplomatic Control*, Minneapolis, 1958; Manuel R. Garcia-Mora, *International Responsibility for Hostile Acts of Private Persons Against Foreign States*, The Hague, 1962; Lawrence Preuss, "La Répression des Crimes et Délits contre la Sûreté des États Étrangers," *Rev. Gén. de Droit Int. Pub.*, Vol. 40 (1933), pp. 606-645; and "International Responsibility for Hostile Propaganda Against Foreign States," *Am. J. Int. Law*, Vol. 28 (1934), pp. 649-668; Arnold Raestad, "Les Ondes Hertziennes et le Droit International," *J. des Télécommunications*, (1935), p. 213, and "Le Projet de Convention sur la Radiodiffusion et la Paix," *Rev. de Dr. Int. et de Lég. Comparée*, Vol. 62 (1935), pp. 289-298; Walter Rudolph, "Informationsfreiheit und Rundfunk im Völkerrecht,"*Jahrbuch für Internationales Recht*, Vol. V (1955), pp. 256-288; William Schwartz, "The Reign of the Verbal Tyrant in the Domain of International Law," *Boston Univ. Law Rev.*, Vol. 40 (1960), pp. 196-209; Seymour N. Siegal, "Radio and Propaganda," *Air Law Review*, Vol. X (1939), pp. 127-145; J. S. Brabner Smith, "Subversive Propaganda, the Past and the Present," *Georgetown Law Journal*, Vol. 29 (1941), No. 7; René Sténuit, *La Radiophonie et le Droit International*, Brussels/Paris, 1932; Julius Stone, *Legal Controls of International Conflict*, New York, 1954, pp. 318-334; Fernand Terrou and Lucien Solal, "Legislation for Press, Film and Radio," (Vol. II of Miscellaneous Pamphlets, Publication No. 607 of UNESCO), Paris, 1951; Vernon Van Dyke, "The Responsibility of States

The major division will be into three chapters corresponding with the three principal kinds of hostile propaganda already described: war-mongering propaganda; subversive propaganda; and defamatory propaganda.

Each of these chapters will open with actual examples showing the nature of the factual problem giving rise to the need for legal rules and remedies. Of course, the historical account in the last chapter contains many such examples, drawn from each of the three types of propaganda. The illustrations to be used at the beginning of the forthcoming chapters will be largely contemporary rather than historical, to show the reality and the immediacy of the legal problem.

Each chapter will then analyze existing law of the particular kind of propaganda. The law falls under two main headings, international and domestic. While the greater part of the relevant law is international law, it should not be forgotten that one important source of propaganda control is the legal restraint imposed within particular countries by their own laws.

In the discussion of the law, and particularly of international law, three kinds of responsibility have to be kept in mind. The first and most important is the *responsibility of a state for the state's own act*. The obvious example of this kind of responsibility would be the liability of a state for propaganda broadcasts by a state-controlled radio. The liability of a state for its own act will be dealt with as a part of the basic discussion of the substantive illegality of the various kinds of propaganda. The second kind of responsibility, less important but more troublesome as a matter of legal doctrine, is the *liability of the state for the acts of private individuals and corporations*. An example of this kind of question would be the issue whether Country A is responsible for pamphlets distributed by private persons from within its borders to people in Country B, with a view to overthrowing the government of Country B. The third category of liability is *that of a private actor for his own act*. An example of this category would be the problem of what action could be taken against the agitators themselves in the last illustration. The most obvious source of control here

in Connection with International Propaganda," (unpublished doctoral dissertation, University of Chicago), Chicago, 1937, and "The Responsibility of States for International Propaganda," *Am. J. Int. Law*, Vol. 34 (1940), pp. 58-73; John B. Whitton, "Propaganda and International Law," *Hague Recueil*, Vol. 72 (1948), pp. 545-659, and "The United Nations Conference on Freedom of Information and the Movement Against International Propaganda," *Am. J. Int. Law*, Vol. 43 (1949), pp. 73-87, and "An International Right of Reply," *ibid.*, Vol. 44 (1950), pp. 141-145, and "Cold War Propaganda," *ibid.*, Vol. 45 (1951), pp. 151-153, and "Radio Propaganda—A Modest Proposal," *ibid.*, Vol. 52 (1958), pp. 739-745; Quincy Wright, "The Crime of 'War-Mongering,'" *ibid.*, Vol. 42 (1948), pp. 128-136 and "Subversive Intervention," *ibid.*, Vol. 54 (1960), pp. 521-535. For response to this last article, see Whitton, "'Subversive Intervention' Reconsidered," *Am. J. Int. Law*, Vol. 55 (1961), pp. 120-122.

would be domestic law, but since the trial of the war criminals at Nuremberg and Tokyo for crimes including fostering war by propaganda, there is also the question of liability of the individual under international law.

The next main division is between the five principal sources of international law. For each of the three kinds of liability just described, an attempt will be made to find as much law as is available under these sources. The most authoritative statement of the sources of international law is that contained in Section 38 of the Statute of the International Court of Justice. According to this Statute, the three primary sources of international law are: (a) treaties; (b) custom; and (c) "general principles of law recognized by civilized nations." Two additional sources are described as subsidiary. These are (d) the writings of the most highly qualified publicists; and (e) judicial decisions.

Treaties, where they are available, are by their nature, one of the most trustworthy sources of international law. Treaties may be bilateral or multilateral. Sometimes they take the form of conventions signed by so many nations that they have been loosely termed "international legislation." The Charter of the United Nations, the Statute of the International Court, and other constitutional instruments of international organizations are other important examples of treaties.

International *customary law* is both an ancient and a versatile source of rules. It is made up of a vast mosaic of practices, protocols, habitual and accepted conduct of states, diplomatic usage, and the like extending over hundreds of years.

The *"general principles of law recognized by civilized nations"* is the least developed and least exploited of the three major sources of law.[2] Although there has been some disagreement among scholars on exactly what this phrase implies, the only interpretation which gives the phrase any substantial meaning and pays respect to the obvious

---

[2] From the vast literature on this subject—general principles of law as a source of international law—we especially recommend the following: L. Oppenheim, *International Law*, 2 vols., (8th ed. Lauterpacht), 1955, Vol. I (Peace), pp. 29 ff.; H. Lauterpacht, *Private Law Sources and Analogies of International Law*, London, 1927, *passim;* Alfred von Verdross, "Les Principes Généraux du Droit dans la Jurisprudence International," *Hague Recueil*, Vol. 52 (1935), pp. 195-250; Bin Cheng, *General Principles of Law as Applied by International Courts and Tribunals*, London, 1953; Manley O. Hudson, *The Permanent Court of International Justice 1920-1942*, New York, 1943, pp. 610-612, sec. 550; Lazar Kopelmanas, "Quelques Réfléxions au Sujet de l'Article 38, 3° du Statut de la Cour Permanente de Justice Internationale," *Rev. Gén. de Dr. Int. Pub.*, Vol. 43 (1936), pp. 285-308; Myres S. McDougal and Associates, *Studies in World Public Order*, New Haven, 1960, *passim;* C. Wilfred Jenks, *The Common Law of Mankind*, London/New York, 1958, pp. 106-123; Paul Guggenheim, *Traité de Droit International Public*, 2 vols., Geneva, 1953-1954, Vol. I, pp. 149-153; Arthur Larson, *When Nations Disagree*, Baton Rouge, 1961. See bibliography in Oppenheim, *op. cit.*, Vol. I, Sec. 19.

meaning of the words is this: if there can be found within the internal legal principles of the major civilizations a common element, this common element can be elevated to the status of binding international law.[3] Note the stress on the word "internal." This stress is deliberately designed to bring out the fact that the "general principle" need not be one referring to international conduct. Indeed, if the only principles referred to by this phrase were principles governing international conduct, a set of such principles recognized by civilized nations would presumably already have the force of law as a matter of customary international law. If the "general principles" phase meant nothing more than this, it would be surplusage, and it is a well-known principle of legal interpretation that a phrase should not if possible be so construed as to convert it into surplusage and meaninglessness. What the "general principles" phrase obviously means, then, is that if, for example, in all major civilizations there is found to exist the rule of estoppel, this principle would be entitled to the status of a principle of international law.

This preliminary explanation of the nature and validity of the "general principles" source of international law is stressed at this point because the "general principles of law recognized by civilized nations" have only recently begun to be incorporated into the analysis of major fields of international law on equal terms with the other

---

[3] See F. J. Berber, *Rivers in International Law*, pp. 185-195, in which the author examines the interpretation of "General Principles of Law" by a number of leading publicists including Oppenheim, Rousseau, Guggenheim, Verdross, Moller, Ross, Kaufmann, Habicht, Politis, Scelle, Ruck, Kopelmanas, Brierly, Gihl, Spiropoulos, Sorensen, Lauterpacht, Ripert, McNair, Märle, Gutteridge, and Mann. On the strength of this survey, he reaches the following conclusions:

(1) The general principles of law recognised by civilised nations in the sense of the Statute and of the coinciding state practice apart from the Statute can only be extracted from private law and not from international law itself by way of analogy and generalisation . . . .

(2) Legal rules of municipal law cannot as such be taken over into international law, but only general principles derived from such rules of law.

(3) It does not suffice that such general principles are found in the national law of one or more states, it must be possible to demonstrate their existence in all or at least most of the main legal systems of the world . . .

(4) Not all general principles which are consistently found in the main legal systems are helpful for international law, but only those which provide a solution for a problem analogous to the international law problem requiring solution. There are many institutions in private law which have no analogy in international law, and vice versa . . .

(5) The main differences between the general principles of law recognised by civilised nations and rules of customary international law are as follows: The general principles of law are more general, more abstract, more vague than rules of customary law, they are only principles which indicate the prescribed conduct in large and rough outlines, and not in detailed technical arrangements . . .

sources of law.[4] One reason this source has been neglected in the past is that an adequate examination of all systems around the globe in today's world would be a task of staggering difficulty and complexity. Since some kind of limitation had to be put on this part of the study, it was decided to concentrate on the four legal systems accepted by the countries most directly involved in the problem of international propaganda. These systems are: the common law, the civil law, Islamic law and Soviet law.

The fourth source of international law, the *writings of publicists*, although a subsidiary source for obvious reasons, is frequently helpful in filling out the gaps left by the other sources and in drawing together the component parts of international law into patterns of principle.

The fifth source, *judicial decisions*, includes not only decisions of the International Court of Justice and its predecessor, the Permanent Court of International Justice, but also decisions of the various arbitral tribunals that have produced hundreds of decisions in the last century and a half, as well as decisions of other assorted tribunals that have had occasion to pass upon questions of international law. It may surprise a person familiar with the Anglo-American common law tradition to discover this source in the subsidiary category. Indeed, the Statute of the International Court specifically goes on to say that its decisions are binding only between the parties. In this respect the Statute departs from Anglo-American practice and follows the practice prevailing in civil law countries and in most of the rest of the world. However, this theoretical difference should not be allowed to disguise the well-known fact of human nature and history that when a court has decided a case in a particular way once it will probably decide a similar case the same way the next time one arises.

As we attempt to fit together the various sources of law with the three kinds of liability for the three kinds of propaganda, there will unavoidably be many missing pieces in the pattern. In some instances, perhaps only one or two sources of law will have anything significant to say on a particular kind of liability. The important thing is to identify where the strong points and weak points are. Only in this way will we have workable guides to remedial action.

At this point there ought to be inserted once and for all a general statement that the international law of propaganda has many weaknesses and deficiencies. No one should be led to look for anything approaching the comprehensiveness, the definiteness, and the enforceability that one is accustomed to find in a major legal field under the domestic laws of a modern state. With this *caveat* once issued, it

---

[4] Berber, *op. cit., supra,* is an outstanding exception. See also Jenks, *op. cit.,* p. 57, n. 1, and Larson, *op. cit.,* for an application of this technique to the great principles underlying world peace and order.

should not be necessary to issue it again and again throughout the discussion to ward off the charge of excessive optimism. The state of the law will be allowed to speak for itself. Moreover, it is dangerous to generalize about the law of propaganda as a whole, since some parts of the law are far more important than other parts. Existence of a well-established rule on one important point may well offset weakness in the law at several less important points. One generalization on this matter of relative importance may be kept in mind throughout the ensuing discussion. It will be observed that international law is at its strongest when dealing with the liability of a state for the state's own act. The strength and definiteness of the law begins to diminish, and various problems such as freedom of speech begin to multiply, as the law approaches the responsibility of a state for an individual's act. As to the third category of liability, that of an individual for his own act, international law appears to be at its weakest and least developed. The significant point for present purposes is that this descending scale of effectiveness of international law is paralleled by a similar descending scale in the importance of the three kinds of liability to the problem of propaganda as a threat to international peace. Plainly it is the propagandistic activities of states themselves that hold the greatest potential peril for international relations. Acts of an individual of the kind which might engage state legal responsibility may also be a threat to peace, but by no means as often or as seriously on the whole. And acts of an individual which would engage the individual's own responsibility, while still a matter of serious concern, would even less often figure as major contributing causes of war. One other *caveat* on this matter of importance may be worth mentioning. The amount of writing, argument, and conference-holding on a given point of law is not necessarily a reliable index of its importance. An important point of law may be already reasonably clear, and therefore evoke comparatively little discussion. The less important point of law may be quite evenly balanced, and may therefore continue to produce abundant literature.

In addition to international law, domestic law will be relied upon at certain points. Domestic law comes into play in two ways. The first has already been mentioned. When a principle of domestic law is sufficiently widely accepted it may become a principle of international law. In additon, domestic law may act directly upon certain kinds of propaganda activities. This would normally be possible only when the actor is an individual or corporation. Here again, with over one hundred nations now having independent status, the discussion can obviously only adduce selected examples of such laws.

This completes the outline of the substantive law analysis. There will follow in Part III a discussion of the remedies available through international law, domestic law and the United Nations, to back up the substantive law, and a consideration of possible ways to improve both the substantive law and the remedies available through the techniques of law and diplomacy. At this point there is also included a treatment of the pervading question of how values of freedom of speech can be reconciled with the necessities of restraint of propaganda, and a suggestion of a code for communicators which might be put into service in the form of private voluntary agreements, treaties, or a United Nations draft covenant or declaration.

Chapter IV

War-Mongering Propaganda by a State

The Nature of War-Mongering Propaganda

War-mongering propaganda is propaganda calculated to implant in the minds of peoples a disposition or desire to engage in an international armed conflict. It does this by means of communications that stir up bad blood, resentment, fear, hatred, perhaps a desire for revenge, or perhaps a hope of glory and loot. At times its object is to produce a conviction that a nation must fight in self-defense, or fight a preventive war. Or the theme may be that war is necessary to serve some high moral cause, such as the need to save helpless people from oppression. The message may be the necessity of a great "civilizing mission," as in the case of colonial war.

War-mongering propaganda, then, refers in general to a direct attempt, usually by organized and concerted pressures, to shape the minds of the masses in the direction of international war. Pressures may be intended at the same time for the leaders as well as the civilian population. War-mongering propaganda was defined in 1935 by a special legal committee at the Disarmament Conference of the League of Nations for inclusion in a treaty on moral disarmament. This draft goes further than merely to prohibit propaganda for "war," narrowly defined; it would have obliged the signatories to adopt, in their local or domestic laws, legislation calculated to penalize:[1]

> Direct public propaganda urging the state to be the first to commit, contrary to its international understandings, any one of the following acts: a) declaration of war upon another state; b) invasion by its armed forces, even without declaration of war, of the territory of another state; c) attack by its land, naval or air forces, even without declaration of war, upon the territory, vessels or aircraft of another state; d) naval blockade of the coasts or parts of another state; e) assistance, given to armed bands, organized in its territory, which have invaded the territory of another state, or refusal, in spite of the request of the invaded state, to take in its territory all possible steps to deprive the aforesaid bands of all assistance or protection.

[1] L. O. N., IX Disarmament (1935), 1935 1-4, p. 702.

It will be noted that this definition includes, as part of war propaganda, agitation in favor of any armed bands invading a foreign territory. This bears out the contention made by some that subversive propaganda, especially when it proceeds from the state itself, can be interpreted as propaganda for war. One jurist, Quincy Wright, has contended that revolutionary propaganda should be considered as an act of war, rather than mere interference with sovereign rights.[2] No one can deny that such measures may lead to serious disorder, and even to war itself. For, if successful, they engender civil war. Also, it is conceivable that they may so weaken the victim of the subversive movement as to tempt a neighbor to attack it, especially a power favoring the cause of the insurgents. Further, the menaced state may consider itself forced to adopt material measures to clean up the sources of the subversive agitation, measures taking the form of military acts of counter-intervention or of self-defense. However, it has seemed preferable to treat subversive propaganda here as a separate problem, since its aims are usually more limited than those of propaganda for war, and since for such situations considerable separate law has already developed.

War-mongering propaganda is found in several distinct types.[3] Some such campaigns are directed by the government to its home population, in an effort to provoke them to war against a foreign state. At other times the pressure is directed, not to the home front, but to a foreign people or its leaders. The Machiavellian statesman may attempt to improve the position of his state in the world balance of power by inciting a second state to make war on a third, or even against his own state. Another distinction is possible, based on the identity of the author of the campaign for war. The responsible party may be the government itself, as when the Nazis spurred the Germans on to an aggressive war with Poland. Or it may come from a pressure group, such as the entourage of President McKinley which wanted the United States to embark on war against Spain as part of a career of empire-building. Finally, the promoter may be a private individual, such as Hearst, whose newspapers strove to provoke a war against Spain and later propagandized for war against Mexico. The commonest kind of war-mongering propaganda is that directed by a government to its own people. The most prolific current source of examples is the Middle East. Innumerable examples can be culled from Arab press and radio. A few of these can be offered here for illustrative purposes.

Nasser, in the introduction to the book, *This is Zionism*, Cairo, 1955, wrote:

---

[2] Quincy Wright, "The Crime of 'War-Mongering,'" *Am. J. Int. Law*, Vol. 42 (1948), pp. 131-132.

[3] Whitton, *Hague Recueil*, Ch. II.

The war between us and Zionism has not yet ended, and perhaps has not yet even begun. For us, the war of tomorrow or of the near future means the ending of a disgrace, the realization of a hope and the regaining of rights.

Also, the *Cairo Radio,* in a broadcast on January 12, 1956, said that

peace between us and the Jews is impossible. As far as we are concerned, the problem is a matter of life and death and not a dispute over frontiers or interests.

According to a B.B.C. News Broadcast of May 15, 1948, Assam Pasha, Secretary General of the Arab League, actually said:

This will be a war of extermination and a momentous massacre which will be spoken of like the Mongolian massacres and the Crusades.

Other Arab states have resorted to similar methods. See the "Fatwa" (religious ordinance) of Abdullah Kalkili, Mufti of Jordan:

Both Moslem law and religion forbid peace with Israel because the Koran says: Moslems are obliged to fight until the enemy capitulates to Moslem rule. It is forbidden to Moslems everywhere to make peace with Israel . . . Peace with Israel is treason to Islam.

Hatred against the Jews of Israel was poured out on November 15, 1956, by *Sayaad,* a Beirut weekly:

The crime perpetrated by Egypt against humanity along the lines described by Hitler in his book "Why I Fought the Jews" is that Egypt let them out instead of annihilating them and thus relieving the world of their evils. If the free world still remembers Hitler, it is for one deed—namely, the purification of the world of the Israeli plague. The world has begun to regret that Hitler died before he had accomplished his *humanitarian mission.* (Italics supplied)

Another example is provided by *El-Massa* (Lebanese evening daily), according to *Falastin* (Jordan), of October 14, 1956: "Only the sword will decide between us—either we annihilate them or they annihilate us." Syria, earlier, had added her voice to the chorus, as the Syrian Minister of Education, quoted by *Al-Ayam* (Damascus, June 7, 1951), declared: "The Syrian people will take revenge for the shame that besmirched the honor of all Arabs. We swear that we men of the pen and men of the sword together will liberate Palestine."

At times, Egypt even appears to threaten war against the United States[4]:

We know how to inflict heavy losses on the enemy. We know how to counter demolition of one simple house in any Syrian village with the demolition of many millions of dollars worth of American

_____

[4] *Radio Cairo,* October 26, 1957.

installations in the extreme south of the Arabian peninsula. We know how to counter the killing of one Syrian soldier on Syrian territory with the destruction of American bases and airfields in Dhahran or Morocco. We always welcome a fight with imperialism. Today we are confident of our strength. Let America come and we will put an end to American imperialism forever.

Russian war-mongering in the Arab world is exemplified in the following excerpt from *The State of Israel—Its Position and Policies.*[5]

> The Zionist movement represents a form of the nationalistic ideology of the rich Jewish bourgeoisie, intimately tied to imperialism and to colonial oppression of the people of Asia. Zionism has tied itself to American and other Western capitalism and, with Jewish terrorist tactics, attacked its Arab neighbors. The national liberation movement of the people of the Middle East, spearheaded by its native leaders (such as President Nasser, King Ibn Saud, of Saudi Arabia, and King Iman Ahmad, of Yemen) is constantly threatened by naked Jewish aggression. The clear duty of all Marxists and Communists in this situation is to help the Asian and African people crush the reactionary Jewish forces.

In the definition of the scope of war-mongering propaganda, two exclusions should be noted. First, this term does not apply to wartime propaganda or psychological warfare between combatants. It is intended here only to include the kind of propaganda that *leads* to war. Second, the term would not apply to preparing people for use of force when under the United Nations Charter the use of force is a legitimate one. This can occur generally in only two cases: genuine self-defense and use of force under actual authorization by the United Nations.

The concept of war-mongering propaganda does include one particularly vicious and effective kind of communication: false news. For example, the Nazi preparations for the attack on Poland included a series of false atrocity stories calculated to justify the attack. It even involved a carefully staged attack by German soldiers in Polish uniform following a faked offer of peace sent over the radio, all to convince the Germans that they had to fight in self-defense.[6]

WAR-MONGERING PROPAGANDA UNDER INTERNATIONAL LAW

War-mongering propaganda carried on officially by a state or its agencies is a violation of accepted principles of the law of nations. This is a direct corollary of accepted rules against aggression. Like the rules against aggression, the rules against war-mongering propaganda

---

[5] Soviet State Publishing House, 1958.

[6] *Trial of the Major War Criminals before the International Military Tribunal,* 42 vols., Nuremberg, 1947, Vol. I, pp. 39, 202, Vol. III, pp. 233 ff.

are of comparatively recent development. The main difficulty here is not to establish the existence of the rule, but to arrive at a sufficiently detailed workable definition of the offense, and to enforce the available sanctions in case of violation. In close cases, the line between justified criticisms (including scandalous but truthful reports) and actual agitation for use of force may not be easy to trace.

Treaties

The illegality of war-mongering propaganda rests upon two propositions, both amply supported by international law: generally with the two exceptions of self-defense and taking part in an authorized United Nations action, the use of armed force is an international crime. Second, incitement by words to commit a crime is in itself illegal.

The illegality of aggressive war is firmly established by the United Nations Charter. Article II, Paragraph 4 of the Charter states that "members shall refrain in their international relations from the threat or use of force against the territorial integrity or political independence of any state." There are other provisions of the Charter that would be violated by the waging of war. The Preamble of the Charter states that the members of the United Nations are determined "to practice tolerance and live together in peace with one another as good neighbors." Waging war is a direct violation of the stated purposes of the organization which include "to maintain international peace and security" and "to develop friendly relations among nations based on respect for the principle of equal rights and self-determination of peoples."

The outlawing of war through treaty is generally associated with the Briand-Kellogg Pact under which the signatory nations in 1928 solemnly renounced war as an instrument of national policy and agreed to settle all their disputes by peaceful means.[7] Prior to that time there had been a number of efforts in the same general direction which, as a matter of law, could not on the strength of any one document be used as proof of the existence of a definite legal prohibition of war at that time, since the documents were either unratified treaties or mere resolutions. These included the Draft Treaty of Mutual Assistance (1923),[8] the Geneva Protocol (1924),[9] the League of Nations Assembly Resolution (1927)[10] and the Havana Resolution (1928) of the Pan American Union.[11] This is not to say that these documents are of no

---

[7] *Foreign Relations of the United States*, 1928, Vol. I, pp. 153-157.

[8] L. O. N., Doc. A.35.1923. IX.

[9] L. O. N. Doc. C.708.1924.IX, p. 363.

[10] L. O. N., O. J. Spec. Suppl. No. 54 (1927), p. 155.

[11] *Report of the Delegates of the U. S. of A. to the 6th International Conference of American States* (held at Havana, Cuba, 1928), Washington, 1928, p. 320.

relevance to international law. As will be noted later, they may cumulatively help to establish the existence of a rule of customary law.

The Briand-Kellogg Pact, however, was treated by the Nuremberg Tribunal as definitely creating a rule of international law. There has been considerable controversy over the application of this rule of law to the individual defendants in the Nuremberg Trials, but even the critics of this feature of the Trials generally agree that nations as nations were bound by the Briand-Kellogg Pact both in 1939 and in all the period down to the present time.[12]

The proposition that direct provocation to commit a crime is illegal is familiar to all students of criminal law and hardly requires argument and documentation. If an aggressive war is an international crime, as declared at Nuremberg, then propaganda directed to the provocation, promotion or incitement of such a war must likewise be considered to be a criminal act, and it was indeed held to be a criminal act at Nuremberg. Supporting law on this point will be adduced below under the "judicial decisions" and "general principles" headings.[13]

Since the treaty basis for the illegality of war rests mainly on the United Nations Charter, and since the Charter recognizes two exceptions to the illegality of use of force,[14] there remains the practical difficulty that a nation accused of war-mongering propaganda might well try to claim the benefit of one of the exceptions. As to the exception in cases of military action specifically authorized by the United Nations, this is not apt to cause many such problems since in a given case the United Nations either will or will not have authorized the action. Authorization was given in the case of the Korean conflict. But as to the exception of self-defense, more concern is warranted. It has become almost routine for aggressors to assert that they are acting in self-defense. The problem of defining the difference between aggression and self-defense has plagued both writers and international organizations for years.[15] On the other hand, this difficulty of framing an all-purpose generalized definition of either aggression or self-defense should not be construed to mean that aggression or self-defense cannot be identified when a given specific set of facts is presented. This

---

[12] Stone, *op. cit.*, pp. 324 ff.

[13] See *infra* p. 70 ff. See also *infra* p. 124 ff., for discussion of treaties generally bearing on various kinds of propaganda.

[14] Julius Stone, *op. cit.*, pp. 302-304; and his *Aggression and World Order*, Berkeley/Los Angeles, 1958, Ch. V.

[15] *Ibid.*, Introduction, Ch. I and *passim;* D. W. Bowett, *Self-Defense in International Law*, New York, 1958; C. A. Pompe, *Aggressive War, An International Crime*, The Hague, 1953, Ch. II. "It is supremely in the area where States claim to act in self-defense, that is, where they conceive their vital interests to be involved, that national versions of 'truth' flourish like jungle growth to hide the outlines of the landscape of truth." Julius Stone, *Aggression and World Order*, p. 144.

situation is not a unique one in the story of law. It may sometimes happen that the problem of wrapping up an entire concept or doctrine of law in a neat package of words appears insuperable. Nevertheless, the law of that subject continues to operate on specific cases as they arise, since the understanding of the concept is sufficiently developed to support judgment when a particular set of facts is in question. On this question of aggression, although the pages of the Official Journal of the League of Nations are filled with doubts about the possibility of defining aggression, that organization had no difficulty in finding Italy to be the aggressor when it attacked Ethiopia.[16] And although similar expressions about the problem of definition have marked the United Nations, Communist China was readily branded as the aggressor by the General Assembly of the United Nations in the Korean War.[17] Similarly, in the Nuremberg Trials, the Nazi defendants raised the plea of self-defense to justify the German attacks on Poland and other countries, and this plea was definitely rejected.[18]

Although there may be some definitional and even practical difficulties, a considerable proportion of instances of war-mongering propaganda appear to be so flagrant that the claim of self-defense would be clearly unavailable. For example, the violently aggressive war propaganda from the Middle East, of which examples were given at the beginning of this chapter, is hardly the language of a state whose only purpose is to hold its own ground against outside attack.

The difficulty presented by the possible claim of self-defense is diminished further by the addition of a well-established principle that a unilateral claim of the necessity for self-defense is not in itself conclusive. One of the central principles of the Nuremberg Trials was the doctrine that such a claim must be subject to impartial third-party determination. The principle of independent third-party judgment is itself an elementary one without which a true system of the law could hardly exist. It is obvious that a rule banning aggressive war would be a nullity if any nation could make on its own behalf a conclusive and unreviewable assertion that it was acting in self-defense—just as any rule of law, international or domestic, would be a nullity if the actor could make a unilateral unreviewable finding of the justifiability of his conduct. This means, then, that the mere fact that a nation engaging in war-mongering propaganda may claim to be acting in self-defense is no reason for despairing about the legal approach to the problem. As necessity arises, independent determinations have

---

16 For the report of the committee of the Council of the League holding that the hostilities constituted "war" in the sense of the Covenant, see L. O. N., *Off. Journal*, 16th Year, No. 11, November, 1935, pp. 1223-1226.

17 Gen. Ass. Res. 498 (V), February 1, 1951, *U. N. Yearbook 1952*, pp. 224-225.

18 *Trial of the Major War Criminals, op. cit.*, Vol. I, pp. 208.

been made and can be made in the future on the question whether the self-defense exception is available in a particular case.

Customary International Law

Customary international law supports the specific proposition that war-mongering propaganda is illegal.

It confirms the legal conclusion reached by putting together the two propositions that war is illegal and that incitement to commit an illegal act is also illegal.

The best evidence of customary international law as to the illegality of war-mongering propaganda is the repeated, consistent, and unanimous affirmation of this proposition by the members of the United Nations. It is true that the passage of a resolution by the General Assembly of the United Nations does not in itself create international law in the same way that the passage of a statute by a domestic legislature does, or as the agreement under the treaty process to the charter and statutes of the United Nations does. Nevertheless, such resolutions are evidence of customary international law, and when they are sufficiently clear, universal, and sustained over a long period of time, they may become almost incontestable evidence to establish a rule of customary international law.[19]

When to this is added confirmatory expressions in other international organizations, and the complete absence of objection or challenge to the principle by any nation, the case for the existence of the principle becomes even more solid.

A review of some of the international expressions relevant to customary international law will give an indication of the cumulative effect of these sources. In May, 1931 the League of Nations Assembly, in the Preliminary Draft of the General Convention to Improve the Means of Preventing War, took up the problem of war propaganda, declaring "there are circumstances in which aggressive propaganda against a foreign power may take such offensive forms, and assume such a threatening character as to constitute a real danger to peace."[20] The prohibition of war propaganda was also strongly recommended by the Legal Committee of the abortive League of Nations Conference for the Reduction and Limitation of Armaments.[21] The International Bureau for the Unification of Criminal Law, at its meeting in 1930 attended by fourteen governments, recommended the punishment under the municipal law of each state of private individuals conducting propaganda favoring wars of aggression.[22]

---

[19] Leland M. Goodrich, *The United Nations*, New York, 1959, pp. 206-210, 282 ff.
[20] L. O. N., *VII Political* (1931), Doc. A.14.1931.VII.8, pp. 32, 43.
[21] L. O. N., *IX Disarmament* (1933), 1935, 1-4, p. 702.
[22] L. O. N., *Quarterly Bulletin*, Vol. II, No. 8 (1930), p. 375.

In September, 1936, the Convention Concerning the Use of Broadcasting in the Cause of Peace was completed. Twenty-two states became parties to it, thirteen by ratification and nine by accession. The Convention came into force on April 2, 1938. Article II of this Convention bound the parties "to insure that their transmissions do not constitute an incitement to war, or to acts likely to lead to war."[23] This Convention will be discussed in more detail in connection with the liability of states for individual acts. Presumably this treaty, recently revived by the United Nations, is still binding on the nations that ratified it, and for this reason could be listed above under the heading of treaties as a source of law on this topic. Germany, Italy and Japan, who were among the principal offenders at the time, did not sign. The United States also declined to ratify, not on the ground that it doubted the illegality of war propaganda, but on the ground that the United States did not control its private broadcasters, and that broadcasting to foreign countries was rare.

For present purposes, the strongest evidence of customary international law is the amassing of repeated condemnations of war-mongering propaganda since World War II. In 1947 the General Assembly of the United Nations adopted an anti-war-mongering resolution. The resolution was first introduced by the Soviet delegate, and an amended text proposed by Australia, Canada, France and Venezuela was unanimously adopted. It reads in part:[24]

> The General Assembly: . . . (1) condemns all forms of propaganda, in whatever country conducted, which is either designed or likely to produce or encourage any threat to the peace, breach of the peace, or act of aggression.

In 1947, also, the Fifth International Congress on Penal Law at Geneva passed a strong resolution in favor of "an international law to give penal protection to peace by scrupulous repression of acts of propaganda for aggressive war."[25]

In 1948, the United Nations Conference on Freedom of Information and of the Press listed as one of its basic objectives "to combat forces which incite to war, by removing bellicose influences from media of information." Resolution Number Two, adopted by the Conference by an overwhelming majority,[26]

> Condemns solemnly all propaganda either designed or likely to provoke or encourage any threat to the peace, breach of the peace, or act of aggression, and all distortion or falsification of news through

---

[23] Krause, *op. cit.* ("Der Rundfunkfriedenspakt von 1936"), for a thorough study of this treaty.

[24] General Assembly Resolution 110 (II).

[25] *Rev. Int. de Droit Pénal*, Vol. 18 (1947), p. 44.

[26] U. N. Doc. E/Conf. 6/C.1/19. Whitton, "United Nations Conference on Freedom of Information and the Movement Against International Propaganda," *op. cit.*, p. 75, n. 9.

whatever channels, private or governmental, since such activities can only promote misunderstanding and mistrust between the peoples of the world and thereby endanger the lasting peace which the United Nations is consecrated to maintain.

The General Assembly passed another resolution against this kind of propaganda in 1950[27] reaffirming the earlier resolutions and condemning all propaganda against peace, declaring that the latter included incitement to conflicts or acts of aggression.[28] On the strength of these repeated and unanimous expressions, and in the absence of any protest or challenge, it seems justifiable to conclude that there exists a rule of customary international law making war-mongering propaganda illegal.

"General Principles"

The main function of "general principles" as a source of law at this point is to bolster the proposition that incitement or solicitation of an illegal act is itself illegal. It has been shown that aggressive war is now illegal under international law. The general principles of law recognized by the four major legal systems used in this study will now be analyzed to see whether there is acceptance of a general principle that the use of words to incite or solicit violence or illegal action is itself illegal.

The common law position has been summarized as follows: "The word 'solicitation,' in the sense of 'criminal solicitation' is employed in the law as a general label to cover any use of words or other device by which a person is requested, urged, advised, counseled, tempted, commanded, or otherwise enticed to commit a crime."[29]

Solicitation is a distinct common law misdemeanor in which the act forbidden consists of the accused person's parol or written efforts to activate another to commit a criminal offense.[30]

The offense of solicitation received its first recognition in 1801 in *Rex v. Higgins*,[31] where it was held a misdeameanor to solicit a ser-

---

[27] *U. N. Yearbook 1951*, pp. 203-204.

[28] In the Third Committee, during the discussions on the Covenant and Declaration of Freedom of Information, and on the Draft Covenants of Human Rights, the Soviet Union has repeatedly argued in favor of provisions outlawing propaganda for war. *United Nations Review*, May 1960, p. 48. This quest attained a measure of success in October 1961, when the Third Committee adopted Articles 19-26 of the Covenant and Civil and Political Rights. Article 26 thereof purports to prohibit all war propaganda as well as "any advocacy of national, racial or religious hatred that constitutes incitement to discrimination, hostility or violence." *General Assembly, Official Records,* 16th Session, 3rd Com., 10171st Meeting, October 12, 1961.

[29] Perkins, *Criminal Law,* p. 505 (-1957).

[30] Clark and Marshall, *Law of Crimes,* p. 194 (6th Ed.).

[31] 2 East 5, 102 Eng. Rep. 269. In this case Lord Kenyon, C. J. noted:

But it is argued that a mere intent to commit evil is not indictable, without

vant to steal his master's goods although no other act was done.

As to civil law: In Germany a person who intentionally induces another by threats, promises, gifts, abuse of authority, trickery, or any other means to commit a crime is punishable as an instigator (Anstifter). His punishment is geared to punishment for the offense which he has successfully instigated.[32] Instigation under this section can be committed by any acts designed to bring about the desired effect, including words.[33] Such words need not be expressed in violent tones, but can consist of "good advice" or a "wish coming from the heart."[34]

> an act done; but is there not an act done when it is charged that the defendant solicited another to commit a felony? The solicitation is the act; and the answer given at the Bar is decisive, that it would be sufficient to constitute an overt act of high treason . . . it would be slander upon the law to suppose that an offence of such magnitude is not indictable. I am also of the opinion, that it is indictable at the Quarter Sessions, as falling in with the class of offences, which, being violations of the law of the land, have a tendency, it is said, to a breach of the peace. 102 Eng. Rep. 274.

A much quoted passage from the opinions rendered in this case is that of Lawrence, J.:

> The whole argument for the defendant turns upon a fallacy in assuming no act is charged to have been done by him; for a solicitation is an act. The offence does not rest in mere intention; for in soliciting Dixon to commit the felony, the defendant did an act towards carrying his intent into execution. The doctrine laid down by Lord Mansfield in *Rex v. Scofield*, which comprises all the principles of the former decisions entirely governs the present case; that so long as an act rests in bare intention it is not punishable by our laws; but immediately when an act is done, the law judges not only the act done, but of the intent with which it is done; and if accomplished with an unlawful and malicious intent, though the act itself would otherwise have been innocent, the intent being criminal, the act becomes criminal and punishable. Id. at 275.

The reasoning in *Higgins* proved sufficiently persuasive that, more than a century later, it could be stated:

> Although there are a few cases expressing a contrary view, in general it may be said that mere solicitation of another to commit a felony or a misdemeanor of an aggravated character, or one tending to a disturbance of the peace or detriment of the public welfare, is a substantive offense at common law . . . Solicitation to crime as substantive common-law offense, 35 A. L. R. 961 (1923).

Thus, in *State v. Avery*, 7 Conn. 266 (1828), which referred to the *Higgins* case, it was held a misdemeanor to write a letter seeking to entice a married woman to commit adultery; in *State v. Bowers*, 35 S. C. 262, 14 S. E. 488 (1892), it was held indictable to offer someone money to burn down a certain house; and in *Commonwealth v. Wiswesser*, 134 Pa. Super. 488, 3 A. 2d 983 (1939), solicitation to commit embracery was deemed a crime—even though embracery was not a felony. For further cases see 35 A. L. R. 961; Curran, "Solicitation: A Substantive Crime," 17 Minn. L. R. 499 (1933); Blackburn, "Solicitation to Crimes," 40 W. Va. L. R. 135 (1933).

[32] German Penal Code, Section 48.

[33] See 1 Maurach, *Deutsches Strafrecht*, 537 (2d. ed. 1958); Schönke, *Strafgesetzbuch, Kommentar*, 252 (9th ed. Schroder 1959).

[34] See generally 37 *Entscheidungen des Reichsgerichts in Strafsachen*, 402,

Instigation to commit crimes is likewise punishable under other European penal codes, such as those of Belgium, the Netherlands and France.[35]

As to the Islamic system: The Egyptian penal code provides that:

Whoever by speeches or cries uttered in public . . . has directly provoked the author or the authors to commit an action qualified as a crime or misdemeanor is punished as an accomplice of this action, if the provocation was put in effect. The speeches or cries are to be considered public when they are uttered or reproduced by mechanical means in a public assembly . . . or when they are broadcast by radio-electric means or in any other way.[36]

The penal code goes on to provide that incitement to certain serious crimes is punishable whether the provocation is put into effect or not.[37]

404-405 (1903). Section 49a of the German penal code, as amended, similarly provides for the punishment of persons who attempt to cause another to commit a crime. However, this section is only applicable if the crime attempted to be instigated is a felony. The instigator is punished as one who attempts to commit a felony.

See generally Maurach, *op. cit.*, 548-558. This section was originally adopted by Law of February 26, 1876, [1876] which followed the Belgian law of July 7, 1875.

Words which neither successfully incite to commit crimes, nor unsuccesssfully incite to commit felonies, can nevertheless be punishable under sections 110, 111 of the German penal code. The former makes it a misdemeanor, punishable by jail up to two years or with a fine, to publicly request an assembly of persons not to obey laws or validly promulgated ordinances and administrative regulations. The latter section provides for a like punishment of persons who, by the same means, successfully or unsuccessfully request an assembly of persons to commit crimes.

See generally Schröder, *op. cit.*, 528-532; 2 Maurach, Deutsches Strafrecht 581-583. Thus, a Communist campaign slogan to "beat the Fascists wherever you find them" was considered sufficient to constitute a violation of Section III.

Maurach, *op. cit.* at 583, citing 65 *Entscheidungen des Reichsgerichts in Strafsachen*, 200.

[35] Art. 66, paragraphs 4, 5 of the Belgian penal code; Art. 60, paragraph 1 of the French penal code, and Art. 47, number 2 of the Netherlands penal code.

See 1 Ancel, *Les Codes Pénaux Européens* 181, 187-188; 2 *ibid.* 633, 642; 3 *ibid.* 1375, 1393 (1958). With respect to Art. 47(2) of the Netherlands penal code, see also Pompe, *Handboek van het Nederlandse Strafrecht*, 253-266 (5th ed. 1959).

[36] Title II; Chapter 14, Crimes and misdemeanors executed by means of press, etc. Article 171.

[37] *Id., Article 172.* Whoever, by the means annunciated in the preceding Article, incites directly to commit the crimes of murder, plunder and arson, or crimes against the security of the State, without the said provocation being put into effect, will be punished by imprisonment.

Article 177. Whoever incites by any of the same means the disobedience of laws or advocates acts qualified as crimes or misdemeanors by the law will be punished by the same punishments.

The Sudanese penal code has an elaborate set of rules on "Abetment" which includes any case in which a person "instigates any person to do that thing." The code then provides various kinds of punishment depending on the gravity of the crime abetted, the degree of success in the principal crime, and so on.[38]

The Libyan penal code states that: "Anyone is considered to be an accomplice who:

1) Incites to the commission of the act constituting the offense if the act is done as the result of the incitement."[39]

The Lebanese penal code states:

> Whoever incites or attempts to incite by any means whatsoever, another person to commit an infraction, is considered an instigator. The responsibility of the instigator is independent of that of the person whom he engaged to commit the infraction.[40]

As to the Soviet legal system: The principle of incitment is summed up in the Soviet Legal Dictionary as follows:

> Instigator (Podstrekatel')—one of the kinds of accomplices whose criminal activity consists in the persuading of another person or of several persons to commit a crime (see *Complicity*). The methods used by the instigator in order to provoke in the other person the determination to commit the crime may be of the most manifold nature; persuasion, bribery, compulsion, request, etc. The instigator always acts intentionally. He not only is conscious of all factual circumstances of that particular crime which will be committed, but he also wishes the occurrence of the criminal consequences as a result of his activities (for instance, in the case of instigation to murder, he wishes the death of the victim). This will also determine the criminal responsibility of the instigator whose criminal acts will, as a rule, be evaluated according to the same section of the special part of the Criminal Code as the acts of the perpetrator of the committed crime, however, with a reference to Sec. 17 of the Criminal Code. . . .[41]

The Soviet law specifically makes incitement criminal, as a matter of general principle.[42]

It is abundantly clear, then, that the use of words to incite, solicit,

---

[38] Chapter VI, of Abetment. Sections 82 to 91.

[39] The Libyan Penal Code (Unofficial translation by Judge G. A. Good, C. B. E., former President of the Court of Appeals of Cyrenaica). *Article 100.*

[40] The Lebanese Penal Code. Title IV, of the Responsibility; Section I, Responsible Persons; Chapter 2, Criminal Participation; The Instigator. *Article 217.*

See also The Transjordanian Penal Code, Chapter II, of Criminal participation; The Abettor, *Article 71.* Iraquian Penal Code, *Article 54.*

[41] I Uridicheskii Slovar' [Legal Dictionary], 2nd ed., v. 2(1956). Moscow, Government Publishing Office of Legal Writings, p. 143.

[42] Law of December 25, 1958 Concerning Approval of the General Principles of Criminal Legislation of the USSR and Constituent Republics. Vedomosti, 1959, item 6. *Sec. 17. Parties in Crime.* Two or more persons who inten-

or instigate a criminal act is in itself a criminal act under the general principles of law recognized by common law, civil law, Islamic law and Soviet law systems.

Writings of Publicists

The writings of publicists confirm the conclusions drawn from the sources already cited.[43] As early as 1933 Pella asserted that since the Covenant of the League of Nations and the Pact of Paris had obligatory force for the nations, war propaganda constituted a direct provocation to violate the stipulation of these accords.[43a] Recently a similar view was expressed by a German author, arguing that since the UN Charter makes war unlawful, an official organ of the government engaging in war propaganda is acting contrary to international law.[44] During the last forty years there has been much argument among leading writers on two controversial matters: 1) whether war propaganda by an individual is a *délit du droit des gens* and 2) whether a state is under an obligation to suppress war-mongering on the part of an individual over whom it has jurisdiction. But the important point for us here is that apparently these writers never questioned that an act of war propaganda, if committed by the *state*, was a violation of the law of nations.[45] The

---

tionally participate in the commission of a crime shall be considered parties in crime.

Organizers, instigators, and accomplices shall be considered parties in crime along with the perpetrators.

Whoever incites to a crime shall be considered its instigator.

[43] "Propaganda which instigates or encourages aggression as other crime against international law has been considered a crime, not in itself, but because of its relationship to the international delinquency or crime which it incites . . ." Quincy Wright, "The Crime of 'War-Mongering,'" *Am. J. of Int. Law*, Vol. 42 (1948), p. 131.

"In so far . . . as such propaganda provokes or encourages aggression or other international crime it becomes a crime itself." *Ibid.*, p. 132.

"If such propaganda (war-mongering propaganda) originates with official organs of the government, the latter is acting contrary to international law since it incites to a forbidden war. The Charter of the United Nations has made a blanket prohibition of war, even in the preamble the member states declare their determination to assure that force of arms shall be used only in the common interest. And Article 2, paragraph 4 of the Charter expands on this basic principle of the United Nations." Von Johann Joeden, "Die Funksendefreiheit der Staaten," *Jahrbuck für Internationales Recht*, Vol. IV (1954), p. 94.

See also: Quincy Wright, "The Outlawry of War," *Am. J. Int. Law*, Vol. 19 (1925), pp. 80-93; E. S. Rappaport, "Propagande de la Guerre d'Agression comme Délit du Droit des Gèns," *Revue Pénitentiaire de Pologne*, Annexe No. 13, Warsaw, 1939; Pompe, *op. cit.*, p. 350; Report of Congrès International de Droit Pénal (1933), *Rev. Critique de Droit International*, Vol. 29 (1934), pp. 556-558.

[43a] Pella, *op cit.*, (R.G.D.I.P., 1933), p. 466

[44] Joeden, *op. cit.*, (JIR, 1954, IV), p. 94.

[45] *Infra*, pp. 134, 158.

basis for state liability for this type of "ideological aggression" as it has often been called[46] has been summarized by Quincy Wright. Liability has been deduced, he says, 1) from the general principle that states are bound to employ due diligence to prevent, within their jurisdiction, all acts which are disrespectful to other states or which constitute a danger to their domestic order, as well as acts calculated to instigate or encourage aggression or other offenses against the law of nations; 2) from the existence in many states of laws for the punishment of such actions; and 3) from the recognition of such acts as international crimes by international conferences, tribunals, and international conventions.[47]

Judicial Decisions

The Nuremberg Trials are the most direct source of decisional law on the illegality of war-mongering propaganda. The Nuremberg judgments support several points of law directly relevant here: the illegality of aggressive war; the parallel illegality of incitement to war through propaganda; and, as noted earlier, the necessity of submitting to third-party judgment on a claim of self-defense.

The Nuremberg Trials took the form of trials of individuals for war crimes, of which the use of propaganda to incite war was recognized as one. Because of the controversy surrounding this specific question of the liability of individuals, it is easy to make the mistake of supposing that the conclusions of the Nuremberg Trials are controversial throughout. However, on the questions of propaganda and self-defense, even the critics of the Nuremberg Trials generally agree that the conclusions of the Trials are valid as applied to states.[48] There has also been considerable criticism of the finding that a rule of customary international law was in force in 1939 making aggressive war an international crime. Here again the controversy, while of historic interest, is of little importance to the present case, since the illegality of war has now been firmly established by the provisions of the United Nations Charter.[49]

When the application of these rules effectively comes into play only after a war has been caused, it may be that the most effective way punishment can be imposed for the crime is to impose it on in-

---

[46] Julius Stone, *Aggression and World Order*, Berkeley and Los Angeles, 1958, pp. 54, 54-60, 66 ff., 85.

[47] Quincy Wright, "The Crime of 'War-Mongering'", *Am. J. of Int. Law,* Vol. 42 (1948), p. 129.

[48] There is a vast literature on this subject. See bibliography in Oppenheim, Vol. II (7th ed., Lauterpacht), London, 1960, Sec. 257.

[49] See discussion *supra,* pp. 67 ff.

dividuals. The guilty state could presumably be punished also by being made to pay damages and reparations for the consequences of its illegal act, and this is often done in peace treaties. In earlier peace treaties the fact of victory was sufficient reason for imposition of reparations obligations. But since the waging of war has become illegal, reparations can certainly be justified, at least in law, not as spoils or the vindictive fruits of military success, but as the partial undoing of damage illegally caused.

For present purposes, however, we are more interested in the preventive value of the outlawing of war propaganda. For this purpose, it is of primary importance to convince states as such that warmongering propaganda is forbidden by law. The value of the Nuremberg judgments is that they support this rule, regardless of the special questions raised by the individual character of the defendants.

The Nuremberg judgments are entitled to weight both because of what preceded them and because of what followed them. The trials were preceded by many months of investigation, which brought to light a mountainous assembly of documentary evidence. Oral testimony of scores of witnesses, including that of the accused themselves, was adduced. The tribunal was one of considerable distinction, and many eminent lawyers and authorities were involved on both sides.

The principles of Nuremberg have subsequently been given approval through a number of official channels. They were affirmed by the General Assembly of the United Nations in a resolution passed unanimously on December 11, 1946.[50] And the United Nations Commission on the Codification and Progressive Development of International Law, at a meeting held at Geneva June 19, 1950, reaffirmed the Nuremberg rule against aggressive war, defining the crime against the peace as the "planning, preparation, initiating or waging of a war of aggression or a war in violation of international treaties, agreements, or assurances."[51]

The Nuremberg Trials had to establish the illegality of war without benefit of the provisions of the United Nations Charter. For our purposes, the principal value of the Nuremberg judgments, then, is not so much the holding that war is a crime as the holding that propaganda in aid of producing war is itself a crime. On this key point,

---

[50] U. N. Yearbook 1947, p. 254. This, according to Pompe, "was the affirmation of the existence of an international criminal law as case law inaugurated by the International Military Tribunal," op. cit., p. 316.

[51] See the International Law Commission report for its Second Session (1950). A.1316, pp. 11-14, and the discussion in Pompe, pp. 321 ff. Further substantiation of the Nüremberg principles is found in the Draft Code of Offences against the Peace and Security of Mankind, adopted by the ILC at its Third Session (May 16 to June 27, 1959). For the Report on Third Session, see Doc. A/1858.

there is repeated support in the indictment, evidence, and judgments.

The indictment, in Count One, sets forth the charge of a common plan or conspiracy, alleging that "the defendants planned, prepared, initiated, and waged wars of aggression."[52] But before resorting to outright war, they first, in preparation, used such "opportunistic methods"[53] as "fraud, deceit, threats, intimidation, fifth column activities, and propaganda." Direct reference in the Indictment to the use of propaganda is likewise made under the caption, "Doctrinal Techniques of the Common Plan or Conspiracy," where it is alleged that the defendants disseminated and exploited certain doctrines, i.e., the myth of "German Blood" and the master race; the Leadership Principle (Führerprinzip); and the concept "that war was a noble and necessary activity of Germans."[54] By promoting beliefs and practices incompatible with Christian teaching, the Nazi conspirators sought to subvert the influence of the churches over the people. Annihilation of the Jews "became an official State policy, carried out both by official action and by incitements to mob and individual violence."[55] The use of warmongering propaganda was underlined in the charge that "In order to make the German people amenable to their will, and to prepare them psychologically for war, the Nazi conspirators reshaped the educational system and particularly the education and training of the German youth." They also "imposed a supervision of all cultural activities, controlled the dissemination of information and the expression of opinion within Germany as well as the movement of intelligence of all kinds from and into Germany, and created *vast propaganda machines*." (Emphasis added.)[56]

In the Judgment these accusations were held to have been proved by the evidence presented at the trial. The condemnation of the use by the defendants of hostile propaganda appears in various parts of the Judgment. The efforts to destroy the influence of the church are described, and the long campaign of atrocities against the Jews was meticulously reviewed.[57]

Also, the many actions taken by the Nazi government in order to increase its power over the German population are stressed. "In the field of education," states the Judgment, "everything was done to ensure that the youth of Germany was brought up in the atmosphere of National Socialism and accepted National Socialist teachings."[58] Particularly significant are the following passages:[59]

---

[52] *Trial of the Major War Criminals, op. cit.,* Vol. I, p. 29.
[53] *Ibid.,* p. 30.
[54] *Ibid.,* p. 31.
[55] *Ibid.,* p. 33.
[56] *Ibid.,* p. 34.
[57] *Ibid.,* p. 180.
[58] *Ibid.,* p. 181.
[59] *Ibid.,* p. 182.

The Nazi Government endeavored to unite the Nation in support of their policies through the extensive use of propaganda . . . The greatest emphasis was laid on the supreme mission of the German People to lead and dominate by virtue of their Nordic blood and racial purity; and the ground was thus being prepared for the acceptance of the idea of German world supremacy. Through the effective control of the radio and the press, the German People, during the years which followed 1933, were subjected to the most intensive propaganda in furtherance of the regime. Hostile criticism, indeed criticism of any kind, was forbidden, and the severest penalties were imposed on those who indulged in it.

The Tribunal also stressed the role of *Mein Kampf.* Here was warmongering *par excellence,* for many of its passages extolled the use of force as an instrument of foreign policy and called for acts of aggression. "The very first page of the book," said the Tribunal, "asserts that 'German-Austria must be restored to the great German Motherland,' not on economic grounds, but because 'people of the same blood should be in the same Reich.' "[60]

Even more specific are instances of hostile propaganda as charged against several of the defendants, and for which most of the latter were convicted. In several of the individual judgments the tribunal singled out propaganda as constituting an integral part of the crime in question. Rudolph *Hess,* "an active supporter of preparation for war," was convicted of Crimes against the Peace (Count 2) in part because of his close relations with the illegal Nazi party in Austria, to which he gave instructions during the entire period, from the assassination of Dollfuss to the Anschluss. "On 27 August, 1939 when the attack on Poland had been temporarily postponed in an attempt to induce Great Britain to abandon its guarantee to Poland, Hess publicly praised Hitler's 'magnanimous offer' to Poland, and attacked Poland for agitating for war and England for being responsible for Poland's attitude."[61]

Rosenberg, the Party's ideologist, was convicted on all four counts. The Tribunal found him guilty of developing and spreading Nazi doctrines in numerous books and periodicals, some of which he wrote himself, and of having been "in charge of the organization whose agents were active in Nazi intrigue in all parts of the world." His book, *Myth of the Twentieth Century,* had a circulation of over a million copies.[62]

An interesting case for our purposes is that of *Streicher,* although, strictly speaking the crime for which he was convicted was incitement to mass murder rather than incitement to war. This defendant was sentenced to death on Count 4 (Crimes against Humanity)

[60] *Ibid.,* p. 187.
[61] *Ibid.,* pp. 283-284.
[62] *Ibid.,* p. 294.

although he took no administrative or military part in the crimes for which he was convicted. His role was almost wholly that of a propagandist. His acts of anti-Semitic incitement, notably as publisher and editor of *Der Stürmer,* the vitriolic anti-Jewish weekly, and through other media, were considered to be incitements to murder and extermination. The Judgment stated: "With knowledge of the extermination of the Jews in the Occupied Eastern Territory, this defendant continued to write and publish his propaganda of death." He injected poison "into the minds of thousands of Germans which caused them to follow the National Socialist policy of Jewish persecution and extermination." He also advocated his evil doctrines in foreign countries.[63]

Von Shirach, long the Youth Leader of the Nazi Party and eventually raised to Cabinet rank as Reich Leader of German Youth, was indicted on Count 1 (Conspiracy) and 4 (Crimes against Humanity) but was convicted on the latter count only, for participation in the deportation and extermination of the Jews. It was found that he had "used the Hitler Jugend to educate German youth 'in the spirit of National Socialism' and subjected them to an intensive program of Nazi propaganda." Apparently his connection with the Nazi leadership was considered to be too vague to substantiate a charge of preparing wars of aggression under Count 1.[64] The prosecution made a determined effort to connect von Shirach, under Count I, with the conspiracy to initiate, prepare and wage an aggressive war. This proof could only be based on the defendant's intensive efforts to control the minds of German youth, through his speeches, writings, songs and pre-military training. But the prosecution could not quite establish a case on the facts, although the Tribunal apparently had no doubt of the legal rule against propaganda for aggressive war.

A similar view led to the much-criticized acquittal of *Fritsche* despite the fact that he was ministerial head of the Radio Division of the Reich Ministry of Propaganda and Enlightenment and Director of the Home Press Division, through which he supervised 2300 daily papers. Utilizing these media, "a vigorous propaganda campaign was carried out before each major act of aggression." Best known as a radio commentator, he was charged with inciting German nationals to wage aggressive war, the rendering of false assurances to interested nations, and the fabrication of excuses to initiate war, all extreme types of hostile international propaganda.[65] The majority of the judges, however, voted to acquit Fritsche. They found that he was in the main only a go-between, or "conduit," merely following instructions coming from Goebbels; that while there was undoubtedly

[66] *Ibid.,* pp. 302-303.
[64] *Ibid.,* p. 318.
[65] *Ibid.,* Vol. I, p. 337.

much propaganda material in his personal broadcasts, this was not of a nature to incite the Germans to commit atrocities. "His aim was rather to arouse popular sentiment in support of Hitler and the German war effort."[66] His propaganda, therefore, was not intended to incite to crimes against the peace. And given his subordinate position, he could not affect, alter or help the planning of the propaganda.

This disposition of the Tribunal to lean over backwards seems questionable, as was pointed out in a strong and lengthy dissent by the Russian judge.[67] On the other hand, for our purposes the crucial point is that in the cases of both Von Shirach and Fritsche the Tribunal entertained no doubts of the existence of a rule against propaganda for a war of aggression; it merely found that in the circumstances the acts of these defendants did not come within this rule.

Two conclusions offered by the Tribunal with respect to hostile international propaganda, which are both rather questionable, but which may turn out to be of importance, remain to be noted. One was the distinction established in the case of Fritsche between propaganda designed to incite the population to illegal acts against foreign peoples, and propaganda as a tool to arouse "popular sentiment" in favor of the government, namely, Hitler's government. Here is the excerpt of the Judgment making this point:[68]

> It appears that Fritsche sometimes made statements of a propagandistic nature in his broadcasts. But the Tribunal is not prepared to hold that they were intended to incite the German people to commit attrocities on conquered peoples . . . His aim was rather *to arouse popular sentiment in support of Hitler.* (Italics added.)

This distinction would appear to be tenuous, for to determine in this case whether a type of propaganda is designed to arouse popular support, or whether it is aimed to incite to violence, is not an easy task. At any rate, the Tribunal here definitely recognized the criminality of international propaganda which incites a population to commit illegal acts.

The second case concerns the acquittal of von Papen on Counts 1 and 2, as follows:[69]

> The evidence leaves no doubt that von Papen's primary purpose as Minister in Austria was to undermine the Schuschnigg regime and strengthen the Austrian Nazis for the purpose of bringing about Anschluss. To carry through this plan he engaged in both intrigue and bullying. But the Charter does not make criminal such offenses against political morality, however bad these may be. Under the

[66] *Ibid.,* p. 338, and Vol. 19, pp. 312 ff., for defense of this defendant.
[67] *Ibid.,* Vol. I, pp. 350-353.
[68] *Ibid.,* Vol. I, pp. 337-338.
[69] *Ibid.,* p. 327.

Charter von Papen can be held guilty only if he was a party to the planning of aggressive war . . . But it is not established beyond a reasonable doubt that this was the purpose of his activity, and therefore the Tribunal cannot hold that he was a party to the common plan charged in Count One or participated in the planning of the aggressive wars charged under Count Two.

So the propaganda in this case was held merely a violation of "political morality." But if an official representing State A is urging the people in State B to revolt, while it may not constitute "planning aggressive war" under the specific terms of Nuremberg Indictment, it might still be illegal as subversive propaganda, which is the concern of the next chapter.

———

In summary, as to war-mongering propaganda by a state, the cumulative weight of treaties (including the U.N. Charter), customary international law, the general principles of law recognized by civilized nations, the writings of publicists, and the decisions of tribunals, establishes the proposition that such propaganda is a violation of international law.

Chapter V

Subversive Propaganda by a State

THE NATURE OF SUBVERSIVE PROPAGANDA

Subversive propaganda consists of communications calculated to overthrow the existing internal political order of a state.[1] Unlike war-mongering propaganda, it is not directly designed to facilitate or incite war between state and state. Yet it has probably caused more trouble between states than any other kind of propaganda. The illegality of war, as we have seen, is a comparatively recent concept. But the illegality of subversive interference in the internal affairs of another country is a concept of long standing. Accordingly, rules against subversive propaganda have a much longer history than rules against war-mongering propaganda. Because of the newness of the law on illegal war and war-mongering propaganda, the principal source of such law is in treaty form, notably the Briand-Kellogg Pact and the United Nations Charter. But since the law of subversion and subversive propaganda is of much greater antiquity, there has been time to build up most of the necessary international law in the form of custom and practice, so far as subversive acts by states themselves are concerned.

As noted earlier, while the avowed purpose of subversive propaganda may not be war between state and state, this is apt to be its natural result. The reason for retaliation is one of elementary self-defense and survival. Any regime which finds its internal affairs being subject to sinister attempts to undermine its political structure, produce conflict between classes, and foment ultimate violent action to overthrow the government, will itself presumably stop at nothing to ward off its own destruction.

---

[1] Lauterpacht, "Revolutionary Propaganda by Governments," *op. cit.;* Whitton, *op. cit.,* (Hague Recueil), pp. 579 ff.; Joeden, *op. cit.,* pp. 91 ff.; Van Dyke, *op. cit.,* ("The Responsibility of States for International Propaganda"); Ellery C. Stowell, *Intervention in International Law,* Washington, D.C., 1921, p. 378; Fedor Fedorovich Martens, *Traité de Droit International,* translation from Russian by Alfred Léo, 3 vols., 1883-1887, Vol. I, Sec. 74; William Edward Hall, *A Treatise on International Law,* 8th ed., 1924, (ed. by A. Pearce Higgins), p. 339; Dambmann, *op. cit.,* pp. 43 ff.

Indeed, it is a familiar fact of international life that nations react to even minor interferences in their internal affairs with a violence bordering on the pathological, so deep-seated and intense is the emotional insistence on the national right to be free from interference. For example, in 1898, when Lord Sackville, British Minister at Washington, privately advised an American citizen how he should vote in a presidential election, the United States Government lost no time in terminating his mission.[2] Certainly more forceful measures of defense or even of retaliation must be expected if the interference takes the form of psychological warfare threatening the very existence of the government and perhaps of the state itself.

How such attacks engender retaliation in kind is demonstrated by the radio campaigns originating in Cuba and Venezuela and directed against Trujillo in Santo Domingo. Whatever one's views may have been about the Trujillo regime, it must be admitted that he could hardly have remained indifferent when, for example the "Union Radio" on successive broadcasts of March 2, 10, and 12, 1959, said in part:

> Forward, friends, a step forward! The Dominican people need your help in the death struggle against Trujillo . . . Spare neither the sweat nor the blood necessary for attaining your liberty. In Cuba we are all at your side ready to die also for the liberty of Santo Domingo . . .
>
> You have to rebel against Trujillo's tyranny because you have sworn to defend the country and not Trujillo. You are Dominican, and you are duty bound to prevent Trujillo's infamy through the Foreign Legion.

From Venezuela, on March 2, 1959, on the "Continental Radio," this message came:

> Dominican people: However powerful a tyranny may appear, it cannot withstand the action of a people united and determined to recapture their freedom; do not let yourself be awed by the military power of which Trujillo boasts so much; in Venezuela and Cuba it has been proved that war tanks, arms and planes of a dictatorship represent nothing against a people determined to recapture their freedom.

As might have been anticipated, such vitriolic messages did not go unanswered. Santo Domingo replied to radio attacks from Venezuela with a campaign of its own marked by subversive messages of extreme violence. Here are two examples:

From the "Dominican Voice," on August 24, 1959:

---

[2] *Foreign Relations of the United States,* 1888, Part I, xi-xii; Moore, *Digest,* Vol. IV, pp. 536, 537.

Attention, officers and non-comms of the armed forces! Attention, danger. The 'rat of Miraflores' will not ease up a moment in his intentions of destroying you. Join the revolution and the officers and non-comms who conspire against the Communist penetration into ill-fated Venezuela. Venezuelans: Down with the tyrant Betancourt who will expropriate your land, down with the deserter who bleeds and robs you, down with Romulo Betancourt!

Earlier, on the 23rd of August:

Attention, officers and non-comms of the armed forces! Attention, free spirits of Venezuela! The die is cast. Join the revolutionary groups who are combating dictatorship. Use sabotage in conjunction with lead fire, and ignite the 'rat of Miraflores,' Romulo Betancourt. Throw down the tyrant who keeps the country of Bolivar enchained . . . Because you are Venezuelans, do your duty. Go down to Caracas. Go down to Caracas, attack Miraflores, evict the rat who has his lair there. When you have done your civic duty, your pains and calamities will be ended. [3]

On close analysis, three categories of subversive propaganda appear to exist, although a certain amount of overlappping is unavoidable. These are:)1 ordinary subversive propaganda;)2 irredentist propaganda; 3) social-revolutionary propaganda.

The first type—ordinary subversive propaganda—is employed by a state to advance its cause in a power struggle by an effort to effect the disruption, and above all the downfall, of a foreign regime. Sometimes the object is to threaten, in order to break down the resistance of the victim when some concession had been demanded. By such coercion a rival may be weakened, and the international position of the propagandizing state may be advanced in the struggle for power. Or it may enable a state to obtain some valued prize—control of certain strategic territory, or an alliance with a government grateful for help in a successful struggle to seize control over the nation.

An early case of such propaganda occurred in 1815-1825, when Russia was giving its support to *Le Hétairie,* a revolutionary organization collecting money and arms and distributing manifestoes in preparation for the revolution of the Serbs against Turkey. This was a typical case of a great power employing propaganda as a weapon of foreign policy. The Tsar, himself a member of this body, in his drive for Constantinople was profiting from the labors of sincere patriots who were expected to pull his chestnuts out of the fire for him. Metternich later persuaded Alexander I to repudiate publicly all sym-

---

[3] The Dominican Republic was rebuked for its propaganda campaign against other American Republics by the Inter-American Peace Committee, at its meeting June 8, 1960. *New York Times,* June 9, 1960.

pathy with the insurgents in the interest of European peace and in accordance with the principles of the Protocol of Troppau.[4] So, as has been so often the case, the propaganda was disavowed—which may at times constitute an admission that it is opposed to proper international practice or even of international law, although it may also be interpreted as a mere bowing to the political exigencies of the moment.

Between 1880 and 1885 the Tsarist government brazenly disseminated propaganda hostile to the Bulgarian government, sending agents into Bosnia and Herzegovina and enlisting volunteers at Russian consulates. Russian agents also founded newspapers in Bulgaria to spread subversive doctrines. An idea of the character of such tactics is shown by the following telegram sent by the Director of the Asiatic Department to the Russian Consul at Roustchouk on June 2, 1883:[5]

> Please inform of the decisions of the liberal party and secretly direct their activity, either directly or indirectly. You must instigate meetings, blaming the governmental measures and demanding that the prince give up his *pleins pouvoirs*. Report by telegram on this subject . . . Act with prudence and do not give away the Russian initiative.

Any number of instances of ordinary subversive propaganda could be cited from the history of the half-century of political agitation originating abroad and aimed at Balkan countries in an effort to undermine the authority of the Ottoman Empire. During this period the deplorable misgovernment of Abdul Hamid offered a rich opportunity for the official propaganda of Bulgaria, Greece, Rumania and Serbia, whose governments competed for many years in Macedonia.[6] And in 1877, Turkey protested on the ground that Greece was permitting the formation of armed bands on its territory; that this menace to Turkish authority was a "flagrant violation of international law . . . while the official press in Greece does nothing to calm public opinion already worked up by the unofficial organs of the press."[7]

The period between the two world wars was marked by many instances of aggressive propaganda whose aim was to cause internal troubles in foreign states, serving thus the national interest of the aggressors. Such propaganda was particularly effective in France,

---

[4] Grégoire Yakchitch, *L'Europe et la Résurrection de la Serbie*, 2nd ed., Paris, 1917, pp. 377, 421.

[5] R. Léonoff (ed.), *Documents Secrets de la Politique Russe en Orient, 1881-1890*, Berlin, 1893, p. 52.

[6] Reviewed in Van Dyke, *op. cit.*, pp. 64 ff.

[7] Viktor Bruns, ed., *Fontes Juris Gentium*, Series B, Sec. 1, Vol. II, part 2, p. 366.

and even in Britain it may have served to reinforce the sentiment expressed by some: "Better Hitler than Stalin."

Since the shooting in World War II ended, the potentialities of such subversive propaganda have not been overlooked by certain states in their drive for power. Thus, at a meeting of the United Nations, the representative of Turkey complained against the Soviet press and radio, which he said were seeking to incite Turkish citizens against one another, and to persuade the Turkish Army and Turkish soldiers to rebel against the state. He also claimed that Moscow was fomenting movements against the territorial integrity of Turkey, and that it had attempted to incite the Turkish people against their neighbors, Turkey's neighbors against Turkey and the Soviet people against the Turks.[8] Furthermore, as noted earlier, the United Nations Commission of Investigation concerned with Greek border troubles reported Yugoslavian and Bulgarian governmental action, through official speeches and articles, to promote separatism.[9]

Speaking before the Commission, Mr. Alex Kyrou, the Greek representative, made grave accusations against the three Balkan countries, reviewing their subversive propaganda in the following paragraph:[10]

> The psychological campaign against Greece is a typical example of a "war of nerves" exercised through sustained diplomatic pressure and an incessant propaganda disseminated by the press and the radio. The volume of this propaganda is enormous, its sources are not limited to the Balkans, and its funds seem to be inexhaustible. The method used is the familiar one of pre-war days. A few simple but false formulas are repeated with unvarying regularity and undiminishing intensity in the hope that the public will believe them in the end. The psychological principle involved is one that has been employed before; the bigger the falsehood, the greater the chance that it will be believed, if iterated and reiterated with persuasive emphasis. Those who wish to refresh their memories will find a replica of the Sudeten crusade in today's campaign on the subject of Slavophobes residing in Greek Macedonia. The method is identical; so is the end in view: the Sudetenland in 1938-1939; so called "Aegean" Macedonia in 1947; the political subjugation of Czechoslovakia then; of Greece today.

Even after the defeat of the Communist guerillas in 1949, Soviet Russia continued its subversive campaign in Greece. An example of the kind of messages sent in the course of this campaign is the following, an excerpt from the Greek language broadcast of Radio Moscow on September 6, 1949:

---

[8] *U. N. Weekly Bulletin,* Vol. III, No. 19 (1947), p. 582.

[9] *U. N. Yearbook 1950,* p. 245, A/935 and A/981.

[10-14] *The Conspiracy Against Greece,* (Greek Under-Secretary for Press and Information), Athens, 1947, pp. 155-156.

The Monarcho-Fascist hangmen of Athens who have bathed the country in blood, are executing people without any semblance of trial. . . It is difficult to find a historic parallel for the servility of the Athens Government which falls over its own feet in its haste to surrender the management of the country's affairs into the hands of a foreign power . . . The Americans control all units of the monarcho-fascist Army and the entire machinery of government, indeed they have reduced the country into an American colony . . . The Greek people will defend their freedom. Despite the "assistance" of the Anglo-American imperialists and the treason of the monster Tito, Free Greece is alive and fighting.

The inflammatory propaganda campaign against the present Greek government has continued. The effort to discredit Greece abroad as a "police state" reached its climax in 1959 on the occasion of the trial and conviction in Athens of an espionage ring which counted among its members a prominent Communist leader, Manolis Glezos, editor of the Communist daily AVORI. Together with a group of other Greek Communists who entered the country illegally from the neighboring satellite states, Glezos was tried for espionage and for the organization of a subversive underground ring. After a public trial he was condemned to five years imprisonment, four years exile, and eight years loss of civil rights. International Communism clamored that the judicial proceedings constituted a "terroristic orgy" which demonstrated that an "anti-democratic regime" had secured control of the country and was preparing to proceed with "unconstitutional measures." In the Communist daily AVGHI for February 3, 1959, Premier Khrushchev condemned the "judicial prosecution" of Manolis Glezos, and wrote: "The Soviet Government fully shares your fears as concerns the massive arrests of Greek patriots who are threatened with harsh punishment in Greece."

In connection with the dispute over Kashmir, the Representative of India in January, 1948 complained to the Security Council, citing a protest from the Government of Kashmir against Pakistan radio as follows:[15]

Pakistan radio appears to have been licensed to pour out volumes of malicious, libellous, false propaganda. Smaller feudatory states are prompted to threaten and even intervene with armed interference in Kashmir State . . .

On the other hand, Pakistan protested against a broadcast by Pandit Nehru for his "highly provocative attacks on the Pakistan Government."[16]

Subsequently the two governments agreed to refrain from further propaganda against each other's interest and promised to curb their

---

[15] Security Council, *Official Records*, 3rd Year, 1948, p. 16.
[16] *Ibid.*, p. 91.

own information media to this end. And representatives of the newspaper associations of the two countries later agreed to ban propaganda against either country from the columns of their publications.[17] That this agreement has not been entirely successful is shown by the following, from *Milap,* New Delhi (Urdui Daily,) December 11, 1958:

> It is said that General Ayub Khan and General Azam Khan are using martial law for usurping other people's wealth and have become multi-millionaires in a few weeks. Their relatives and friends too have accumulated much wealth. But this loot based on military might and aggression cannot last long. If Nadir Shahi and Hitler Shahi did not last long, how can this Ayub Shahi stay, which is based on aggression and compulsion?

Another example is a news story appearing on December 26, 1958, in *Basumati,* a Bengali Daily of Calcutta, under this headline:

> Oppression, injustice and corruption in East Pakistan: miseries of common people reached climax due to shortage of essential commodities: controlled democracy has miserably failed.

In the body of this news story it is reported that

> Wise and intelligent persons are being arrested everywhere. Students are no exception. Now almost all the progressive students are in jail . . . The majority of arrested persons are Hindus who constitute from 80 to 85% of the arrested persons. In this way controlled democracy is being established in East Pakistan through martial law administration.

In the drive for the unification of the Arab States, propaganda originating in Cairo and even issuing from the mouth of Nasser himself has violently attacked other Arab States, particularly Lebanon, Jordan and Iraq. A few examples may serve to typify this campaign.

Against Lebanon:

During the crisis over Lebanon in 1958, *Radio Cairo* addressed many virulent subversive appeals to the people of that troubled country. Thus a commentator on that station, on July 23, 1958, declared that the rulers of Lebanon, particularly Chamoun, al-Sulh and Charles Malik were the black sheep who had strayed from the fold, and that it remained for their peoples to "get rid of them" in the same way the people of Egypt and Iraq had rid themselves of their former leaders. On July 28, 1958, *Radio Voice of the Arabs* said:

> Any ruler in the Arab countries who enters into treaties or opens the door of his country to pacts will be considered a traitor, for pacts mean colonialism and occupation. The people in such a country will

---

[17] *New York Times,* May 7, 1950

not allow that ruler to remain in power, but will fight him. The people must liberate their countries.[18]

Incidentally, referring to John Foster Dulles, the commentator charged that "he wants to kindle the fire of war in the Middle East. He does not care about peoples or peace; he cares only for oil, cheap raw materials, cheap labor, and markets for American arms merchants who trade in destruction and death."

Against Jordan:

The *Voice of Iraq*, a clandestine station, broadcasting in Arabic on May 7, 1958, was particularly subversive:

> Will the ruler of Jordan continue to hang free people and will he continue to throw them in jails and detention camps? And will terrorism and corruption prevail in the country? No, by the God of the Arabs. By the hands of the free people of Jordan, darkness will be dispelled and the sun of freedom will rise. The people of Jordan will recover all their rights, and they will eliminate the traitors. They will impose their will on the oppressors, and that will be soon. God Almighty has promised victory to the patient.

Particularly remarkable is the following excerpt from the *Middle East Review* (FBIS), July 18, 1958 which cites a message going even to the extreme of suggesting assassination:

> Damascus, Cairo and Baghdad radios are heard calling on the Jordanian people to overthrow King Hussein and his regime, and put an end to imperialist intervention. A statement by Abdullah at-Tall, described as a "prominent Jordanian political refugee," is carried by Damascus, exhorting the Jordanian people to rise and end "imperialist intereference."A Damascus commentary says the "little ruler" of Jordan forgets the Hashimite union was formed by two kings who did not represent the will of their people, while at Baghdad talk calls for Jordanians to emulate Abdullah's assassinator, and to "revolt against the puppet of the British and Zionism."

Along similar lines, let us note the message of July 20, from the *Baghdad, Iraqi Home Service*:

> Revolt against the tyrant and imperialist agent, the traitor and grandson of a traitor! Revolt against the criminal who desecrated our soil! Revolt against the puppet of the British and Zionism and break the shackles with which you were fettered by the man king! Revolt, like your fathers and forefathers did before you, against the oppressors and tyrants!

Salah al-Bitar, UAR Minister of State, as quoted by *Al-Amal*, Beirut daily, August 22, 1958, said:

---

[18] Egypt itself was the target of subversion when in October 1961 the newly-independent Syrian radio called on the peoples of Egypt to revolt against Nasser. *New York Times,* October 3, 1961.

We are waiting for the British forces to quit Jordan in order to give the free Jordanians the signal to proclaim a revolt, oust King Hussein and annex Jordan to the UAR . . . The Socialist Renaissance Party (in Jordan) is making the necessary preparations to carry out the revolution with the departure of the last British soldier from Jordan.

It would be impossible to prove that the assasination of Premier Hazza Majali of Jordan, with the death and injury of many others, was a direct consequence of such terroristic propaganda, which has continued almost without interruption. But it can be said that in the success of this assassination the undoubted purposes of such vicious communications were fully achieved and their natural end result realized[19]

Against Iraq:

Voice of the Arabs (Cairo, May 9, 1958):

The Iraqi people are bound to shatter these hopes and frustrate these dreams. They have achieved a passive victory in their boycott of the Iraqi elections. Nuri cannot claim that the newly returned National Assembly is truly representative of the Iraqi people when no elections were held in more than three quarters of the constituencies. *The Iraqi people will not stop at this limited victory; they should not be momentarily blinded and lose sight of their ultimate goal—the removal of Nuri and the liberation of Iraq.* (Italics supplied)

An excellent example of a campaign of subversion is found in the Soviet radio broadcasts to Iran. Particularly since February 1959, *Radio Moscow's* foreign language broadcasts to Iran have been violently hostile. They have sharply criticized the government of that country, personally vilified the Shah and stressed the possibility of the violent overthrow of the Iranian government. These broadcasts have attacked the international and domestic policies of Iran as being treacherous, threatening to the safety of Iran and a betrayal of the interests of the Iranian peoples. Thus on February 19, 1959, *Radio Moscow* predicted that

the fury and indignation of the Iranian people against the rotten and hated monarchy will, like a sweeping fire, reduce to ashes all abomination, egotism and immorality which now prevent the prosperity of the Iranian people.

On June 19, *Radio Moscow* accused the Shah and Iranian government of plundering the country, killing innocent people, and "employing any type of guile and atrocity." The broadcast cited the

---

[19] *New York Times,* August 30, 1960. For an account of Nasser's renewed propaganda campaign against King Hussein, see "United States Foreign Policy: Middle East," (Staff Study prepared for the use of the Committee on Foreign Relations), U.S. Senate, No. 13, June 9, 1960, Washington, D.C., Government Printing Office, 1960.

fate of Nuri as-Said and asserted that the fate of the Iranian regime was unavoidable. The Soviets in periods of particularly extreme hostility to Iran have preferred to speak over a clandestine radio. One such began operations on April 27, 1959, as the "Azerbaijan Democratic Radio." On July 8th, this station called for the unity of all national forces against the Iranian government. It said, "We fully associate ourselves with the freedom-loving officers and patriots and their desires to get rid of the coup d'état regime." It urged "Anyone and everyone—worker, student, peasant and all—to join in one line to realize this sacred national aim."

A recent example of subversive propaganda is noted by the *Manchester Guardian Weekly* for May 19, 1960:

> Six weeks ago a broadcasting station in East Germany broadcast a message in Persian from the Central Committee of the Tudeh, or Persian Communist party. The Committee admitted that its organizations were still scattered, its members "distracted," and their ideas confused. But it went on to urge "every revolutionary individual" to revive the party in Persia, to "establish contact with trusted party elements," and to form cells. The following day "all patriotic elements" were invited (in an East German broadcast once more) to co-operate with the revived party to achieve "victory over colonialism and reaction, to establish a national, free government, and to overthrow" the government of Mohammed Reza.

On November 15, 1961, the following news story appeared in the *Washington Star*:

> Iranian Ambassador Ardeshir Zahedi said today that if there is any doubt about the Soviet Union's ultimate intention in Iran, that doubt has been resolved by Moscow Radio's broadcast yesterday urging the people of Iran to revolt against the Shah.
>
> Mr. Zahedi pointed out that this is Radio Moscow's first open proposal that the Iranian people revolt against the Shah, that heretofore such propaganda has been of clandestine origin attributed, for example, to East German radio broadcasts.
>
> Soviet-controlled radio stations in East Berlin and the Russian Caucasus have been pouring around-the-clock radio propaganda daily into Iran. The broadcasts are in Persian and regularly warn Iran that it faces nuclear destruction "in the not too distant future" unless it pulls out of the United States-backed Central Treaty Organization, the envoy said.[20]

The second type of subversive propaganda is irredentist propaganda. The term "irredentist" originated in pre-1914 Italy, referring to Italians living in Trentino and the Tyrol under Austrian rule—as *Italia Irredenta* (unredeemed).

Psychological warfare of an irredentist character is particularly

---

[20] For a number of other examples from 1949 to 1959, see *infra*, p. 107 *et seq.*

dangerous to the course of healthy international relations. Given the natural affinities of blood, and the strong susceptibility of racial minorities to nationalistic appeals, such messages can be extremely effective. They are admirably adapted to the objectives of foreign powers or even of individual groups bent on mischief, for they permit clandestine operations through underground channels in ways difficult to unmask and not easy to check. And since such propaganda may result in grave injury to the interested state, and even cause it to lose valuable territories together with important sources of national power, such attacks are bound to be keenly resented and vigorously resisted.

A few examples of irredentist propaganda will serve to illustrate its peculiar dangers. One of the most successful was the campaign made by Cavour as part of the *risorgimento* which finally led to the unification of Italy. On every side Cavour, through his secret agents, spread nationalistic fervor as a preliminary to the general uprising of Italians under the banner of Victor Emanuel II. When the "legitimate" regime fell, to be succeeded by Italian insurgents, it was apparent that the *coup* had been prepared long in advance. The most effective work in the matter was done by secret patriotic associations, above all, the *National Society,* together with numerous collaborators, known and unknown, unified by La Farina, its founder and director. This society was secretly aided by Cavour, who once said to La Farina, "Come and see me whenever you wish, but always at the break of day, and let no one see you!"[21]

Another irredentist movement was that initiated by Greece in the 1860's when it backed the insurrectionists in Crete. Here again, propaganda was widely used, as is shown by the note of protest sent in 1866 by Turkey to Greece:[22]

> When a press systematically hostile spurs itself to propagate atrocious calumnies every morning against a neighboring state; when it seeks to incite the people of this state against their legitimate sovereign; when men prominent in the country and even government civil servants form committees in order to send aid to a people they are trying at any price to incite to revolt, and when all this takes place in the capitol and under the very eyes of the government which is on friendly terms with the neighboring state concerned, the latter cannot remain indifferent.

The most damaging of all irredentist maneuvers, that of the Serbs in Bosnia and Herzegovina before World War I, has already been mentioned at the beginning of the book as an example of the direct causal connection between propaganda and war.

---

[21] Paul Matter, *Cavour et l'Unité Italienne* 1848-1856, (3 vols.), Paris, 1925-1927, Vol. III, p. 35.

[22] *Archives Diplomatiques,* Vol. III, 8th Year (1868), p. 908.

Although this may come as a shock to some Americans, the official sponsorship of "Captive Nations Week," proclaimed on July 17, 1957, has been considered by some authorities to be an example of subversive and irredentist propaganda. "Captive Nations Week," with a program to be observed "with the appropriate ceremonies and activities", was the result of a joint resolution voted unanimously by both houses of Congress. Supporting proclamations were issued by the governors of fifteen states and the mayors of twenty cities. It was keenly resented by the Soviet government, and Prime Minister Khrushchev protested that it was "direct interference in the Soviet Union's internal affairs."[23] We will return to the legal implications of this event in connection with a discussion of the law of subversive propaganda.

The third category of subversive propaganda is revolutionary propaganda. A number of illustrations of this kind of propaganda are afforded in the historical sketch given in Chapter III. These include not only early examples from French Revolution and other revolutions, but also current revolutionary propaganda by the Communists. At this point, it may simply be noted that the problem of subversive intervention through revolutionary agitation still exists. The Bucharest Declaration, issued by the International Communist Conference on June 27, 1960, although couched in terms of "peaceful co-existence," actually contains a directive to Communist leaders throughout the world to work for the violent overthrow of any government in appropriate and feasible cases.[24] Reiterating the statement made at a similar International Communist Conference held in Moscow in 1957, the Bucharest Declaration, after discussing the possibility of a "peaceful" socialist revolution in some countries, goes on to say: "At the same time, it is also necessary to proceed from the possibility of the working class gaining a victory for the Soviet Revolution by non-peaceful means." Commenting on this statement, a *New York Times* editorial said:[25]

> It is hard to read this statement as meaning anything other than a directive to Communist leaders throughout the Free World to work for violent overthrow of the governments of their countries wherever they think they have a chance to accomplish that purpose. This is playing with fire in an inflammable world. It also represents clear intervention in the affairs of other countries by the nations of the Communist bloc, since the Bucharest Declaration was issued by the Communist parties which hold power monopolies in twelve nations.

It has become quite clear that Castro, or more precisely Moscow through its Cuban outpost, is using every possible means to subvert

---

[23] Quincy Wright, "Subversive Intervention," *Am. J. Int. Law*, Vol. 54 (1960), p. 522, quoting ACEN News, July-September, 1959, pp. 8, 23-26.
[24] *New York Times*, June 28, 1960, p. 12.
[25] *Ibid.*, June 29, 1960, p. 32.

other Latin-American countries. Radio Havana and the mass of subversive books and pamphlets exported from Cuba provide the media for incitement to revolution. This development was officially denounced by the American government in a formal document issued by the State Department on April 3, 1961. The following excerpt is particularly significant:[26]

> The present strategy of Fidelismo is to provoke revolutionary situations in other republics through the indoctrination of selected individuals from other countries, through assistance to revolutionary exiles, through incitement to mass agitation, and through the political and propaganda operations of Cuban embassies. Cuban diplomats have encouraged local opposition groups, harangued political rallies, distributed inflammatory propaganda, and indulged in a multitude of political assignments beyond the usual call of diplomatic duty . . . . The regime is now completing construction of a 100,000-watt radio transmitter to facilitate its propaganda assault on the hemisphere.

During the great crisis of October 1962 over Soviet missile bases in Cuba, the Cuban government stepped up its campaign of subversive propaganda to other American republics. Then followed numerous riots in various countries, and enormous damage, through sabotage, to oil installations in Venezuela.[27]

Subversive State Propaganda under International Law

In regard to subversive propaganda designed for the population of a foreign "friendly" state (which merely means one with which one is legally at peace), the rule of law is clear if the offender is a state. The government of a state is under a legal duty to refrain from spreading subversive propaganda hostile to a foreign country in time of peace. Few rules are more firmly established; in fact, at one time such machinations were considered to be illegal even in wartime, although this thesis would never be advanced today.[27a]

---

[26] *New York Times,* April 4, 1961.

[27] The *New York Times,* October 29, 1962, reported as follows:
"*Washington,* Oct. 28. Instructions to pro-Castro elements in Latin America urging terrorism and agitation against United States property have been broadcast from Havana within the last 24 hours, reliable sources reported here tonight.
"It was understood that monitors here have interpreted messages in an 'amateurish code' sent by Havana radio stations calling for agitation, terrorism and 'Algeria-type plastique' activities.
"The last was a reference to the plastic explosive bombs used during the Algerian war.
"It was believed here that last night's sabotage in the Venezuelan oil fields may have been the first direct result of such instructions to Premier Castro's followers in the hemisphere."

[27a] Oppenheim, *op. cit.,* Vol. II, Sec. 162a.

Authority for this rule is not difficult to discover; the writers are in accord on the subject. Vattel wrote: "It is unlawful for Nations to do any act tending to create trouble in another state, to stir up discord, to corrupt its citizens, to alienate its allies."[28]

More specifically he declared: "It is in violation of the laws of nations to call on subjects to revolt when they are actually obeying their sovereign, although complaining of his rule."[29] Subversive activities by the state are considered particularly grave because they constitute illegal intervention in the internal affairs of a friendly power.[30] Fauchille in fact calls such maneuvers *"intervention de propagande."*[31] As such, they constitute a violation of the right of sovereign independence, or, to put it differently, the duty to refrain from such measures is a corollary of the obligation to respect the independence of other states. Thomas and Thomas, in their book, *Non-Intervention,* which devotes an entire chapter to the subject, "Intervention by Propaganda," demonstrate through numerous examples the significance of this matter in modern times. In one key paragraph, the authors state:[32]

> The question of how a change in government is being sought is no longer of major significance. The important points are what ends are desired, and who is controlling the direction of the propaganda to obtain these ends. If the ends desired are hostile to the present form of government in a state, and if efforts to obtain these ends are directed by an agency of another state—whether such agency be a local citizen, an organization dependent upon foreign government, or a political party which is in reality the foreign government—then such actions are actions of a foreign state, and are prohibited by international law.

One striking recent illustration of such intervention is furnished by these authors. This was the action of the government of India in supplying money, advice, encouragement and leadership to Portuguese of Indian origin in Goa who were engaged in a movement to

---

28 Vattel, Bk II, Ch. I, Sec. 18.

29 Vattel, Bk II, Ch. IV, Sec. 56: "But no power will fail to protest, as for an atrocious injury, if someone attempts, through its emissaries, to provoke its subjects to revolt."

30 Stowell, *op. cit.*, page 378; Manuel R. Garcia-Mora, *International Responsibility for Hostile Acts of Private Persons Against Foreign States,* The Hague, 1962, pp. 80 ff.

31 Paul Fauchille, *Traité de Droit International Public,* Paris, 2 vols., 1921-1926, Vol. I, Sec. 300(3): "This is what the Russian Soviet government has been using since its coming to power in November 1917, to destroy the political and social organizations of different states of Europe, America and Asia in order to substitute therefor the Communist regime and the anarchy which characterizes it."

32 Ann Van Wynen Thomas and A. J. Thomas, Jr., *Non-Intervention, The Law and Its Import in the Americas,* Dallas, 1956, p. 276.

rebel against the colonial power, Portugal, and go over to India.[33]

As to the "Captive Nations Week" program of the United States, a leading American authority has this to say:[34]

> Whatever may be the responsibility of governments in regard to libelous and seditious utterances by private agencies, it seems clear that such action by official agencies is violative of existing international law . . . It is difficult to see what is the purpose of the President's Proclamation of Captive Nations Week if it is not to encourage and incite revolt by the people in those states against the governments recognized by the United States. It may be that those governments are so firmly established that there is no clear and present danger that such revolt will actually occur, but this would not excuse official action intended to have that effect. It, therefore, seems impossible to reconcile the approval by Congress and the Proclamation by the President of "Captive Nations Week" with the international obligation of the United States to respect the independence of other states.

Customary International Law

In their diplomatic practice the nations in the past have demonstrated their *convictio juris* that the rule in question existed as law. On numerous occasions it has been invoked in support of diplomatic protests against alleged violations, and the defendant state in the course of the resulting diplomatic exchanges has not denied the existence of the rule. The latter's rejoinder has taken the form of a denial of the basis of the charge, or some other excuse or defense (i. e., non-responsibility in the special circumstances of the case), but the existence of the norm itself has been generally acknowledged or recognized, either expressly or by implication.

The 1792 Decree of the French Convention promised aid to all peoples disposed to "throw off the yoke" and establish the "new order" under French revolutionary inspiration. Evidence that such conduct admittedly violated an accepted rule of international law may be found in the vigor, universality and consistency of the protests made by exposed states, and the willingness of the French government, under pressure it is true, to withdraw the decree and even to make a formal declaration of an intention not to interfere in the internal affairs of other states.[35] Other evidence of the same character appears in the widespread protests made by other states exposed to revolutionary propaganda. Again and again in the diplomatic exchanges during this period we find assertions, never denied, that the conduct of the French government and its agents was an infraction of accepted

---

[33] Thomas and Thomas, *op. cit.,* p. 285.

[34] Wright, *op. cit.,* p. 533. Discussed also by John B. Whitton, " 'Subversive Propaganda' Reconsidered," *Am. J. Int. Law,* Vol. 55 (1961), pp. 120-122.

[35] Jules Basdevant, *La Révolution Française et le Droit de la Guerre Continentale,* Paris, 1901, pp. 163 ff.

principles and norms of the law of nations. Thus, Pitt claimed that the French disclaimer against any idea of exciting insurrection in foreign countries was made "upon the express ground (stated in the paper) that such interference, and such attempts, would be a violation of the law of nations."[36]

The Russian government in the years following 1816 was undoubtedly behind *Le Hétairie,* the notorious Greek association working for a general insurrection of Christians in the Balkans, but the Emperor himself felt it necessary to disavow Ipsilant, his secret agent. In this dangerous double game, in which the Russians were assuring Turkey of their friendship while the Tsar was sending subsidies to the revolting Serbs, all sides nevertheless paid grudging homage to the rule of law.[37]

After the Revolution of 1830, when many nations were protesting vehemently against subversive agitation centering in Paris and spreading to outlying lands, the French government declared it would do nothing of a character to disturb the domestic peace of nations. All parties concerned appear to have considered that this French disavowal, as well as the subsequent repression by the government of subversive activity in various parts of France, was in conformity with accepted rules of law.[38] It is notable, too, that during the half century preceding the Balkan Wars, when many powers were working to undermine the authority of the Ottoman Empire, it was considered prudent to proceed by underground methods, and when the secret maneuvers were brought out into the open, to deny the charges and disavow the agents. This cautious and often hypocritical conduct was of course prudent astuteness, but it was also evidence of a conviction that a rule of law existed.[39]

In the feverish days after Sarajevo, already mentioned, the historic and tragic Austrian ultimatum was in large part a tirade against subversive propaganda from Serbia, and the latter, in its response, agreed to undertake a number of extreme measures to end it. In this exchange of notes, as well as in the general conduct of the parties, there can be perceived a clear acceptance of the view that no nation is legally permitted to indulge in propaganda hostile to the very existence of a friendly government.[40]

The diplomatic exchanges between the two world wars offer many examples of protests against subversive propaganda spread by foreign governments. The protest against Soviet propaganda made by

---

[36] *Annual Register,* Vol. 35 (1793), p. 46.

[37] *Supra,* p. 85.

[38] Van Dyke, *op. cit.,* p. 62.

[39] *Supra,* p. 86.

[40] Jonathan French Scott, *Five Weeks: The Surge of Public Opinion on the Eve of the Great War,* New York, 1927, pp. 20-98; Sidney B. Fay, *The Origins of the World War,* 2d ed., New York, 1931, Ch. VII.

the United States is an example. In its protest to the Soviet Union, the American government based its opposition to subversive propaganda on accepted rules of the law of nations. It was stated that the United States for sixteen years had withheld its recognition of the Soviet government "mainly for the reason that the Soviet government had failed to respect the right of this nation to maintain its own political and social order without interference by organizations conducting in or from Soviet territories activities directed against our institutions."[41] In taking this stand, the American government was merely following a well-established tradition. Earlier President Jackson, referring to Mexico, had declared that "any act on the part of the government of the United States, which would tend to foster a spirit of resistance to her government and laws, whatever may be their character or form . . . would be unauthorized and highly improper."[42]

Britain, France, China, Germany and other states likewise protested against various manifestations of Soviet propaganda. A review of the correspondence in these cases will show that the Soviets did not deny the existence of a rule of law condemning subversive propaganda although they were never at a loss for an answer to the specific charges complained of. The same was true of the Nazi replies to the many protests against German propaganda during the period preceding the Second World War. When the Austrian government, reacting against incendiary German broadcasts as well as compromising Nazi documents seized within Austria, charged that "The threads of these actions, of this conspiracy, lead back over the frontier,"[43] Hitler replied with denials and countercharges, but did not attempt to refute the contention that the law of nations prohibited such acts. Berlin made a similar reply when the Governing Commission in the Saar imputed to the Nazi government the responsibility for violent and subversive attacks on the administration of the territory, and for alleged acts of political terrorism. In none of these cases did the German government deny that the rule, as set forth above, was a reality in international law.[44]

Further evidence, if any were needed, is found in a number of

---

[41] Charles Cheney Hyde, *International Law*, 3 vols., 2d rev. ed., Boston, 1947, Vol. I, p. 175, n. 2, Secretary of State Hughes had stated in 1923: "Recognition is an invitation to intercourse. It is accompanied on the part of the new government by the clearly implied or express promise to fulfill the obligations of intercourse. These obligations include, among other things, the protection of the persons and property of the citizens of one country lawfully pursuing their business in the territory of the other and abstention from hostile propaganda by one country in the territory of the other." *Ibid.*, p. 171.

[42] Cited by Van Dyke, *op. cit.*, p. 63.

[43] Preuss, *op. cit.* ("International Responsibility for Hostile Propaganda Against Foreign States"), p. 664; Childs-Whitton, *op. cit.*, pp. 16 ff.

[44] Preuss, *op. cit.*, pp. 665-666; Childs-Whitton, *op. cit.*, pp. 12 ff.

the deliberations of various organs of the United Nations. These resolutions, although most of them are still in the form of mere projects or unratified conventions, are so numerous and so consistent as to be remarkably probative. There is, for example, Article 22 of the Draft Declaration of the Rights and Duties of States, drawn up in 1948 by the U.N. International Law Commission:[45]

> It is the duty of every state to ensure that, within its territory, no activities are organized for the purpose of fomenting civil strife within the territory of another state.

Equally general is the 1947 General Assembly resolution, voted unanimously, which condemns all propaganda "either designed or likely to provoke or encourage any threat to the peace, breach of the peace, or act of aggression."[46]

More specifically, the General Assembly, in its resolution on the *Essentials of Peace,* adopted in 1949 by a vote of 53-5, with one abstention, called on all nations "To refrain from any threats or acts, direct or indirect, aimed at impairing the freedom, independence or integrity of any state, or at fomenting civil strife and subverting the will of the people in any state."[47] And one may read in the Draft Code of Offenses Against the Peace and Security of Mankind, formulated in 1952, the inclusion as one of the offenses the fomenting of civil strife and acts of terrorism:

> The undertaking or encouragement by the authorities of a state of activities calculated to foment civil strife in another state, or the toleration by the authorities of a state of organized activities calculatted to foment civil strife in another state.[48]

What is even more significant for our purposes is the meaning of Article 2(12-ii), which condemns "Direct incitement to commit any of the offenses defined in the preceding paragraphs of this article."[49]

---

[45] A/CN.4/2, December 15, 1948, p. 123. At the conference of lawyers from 23 nations of the Americas, convened in San Jose, Costa Rica, in June 1961, the delegates declared their dedication to certain principles of international law as essential to an effective international system. Principle No. 9 read as follows:
"All nations must abstain from the unlawful use of armed force, political
subversion, economic aggression or defamatory propaganda."
They also recommended the development of international law to deal with subversion and political propaganda. Consensus of San Jose, Approved June 14, 1961.

[46] *Yearbook of the United Nations, 1947-1948,* pp. 91-93, Res. 110 (II).

[47] *Yearbook of the United Nations, 1950,* p. 344, Res. 290 (IV).

[48] Article 2(5). *Yearbook of the United Nations, 1952,* p. 842.

[49] *Ibid.*

Treaties

Further evidence of the disposition of the states to be bound, at least in principle, by a rule against official subversive propaganda is found in the numerous treaties, both bilateral and multilateral, designed to curb such communications. Several such treaties date from the period of the French Revolution and the subsequent Napoleonic period, and contain an obligation, either express or implied, to refrain from this type of agitation. Other accords of this nature are scattered throughout the nineteenth century, for instance, the treaty between Serbia and Austria-Hungary in 1881, prolonged in 1889.[50] As early as March, 1918, in the ill-fated peace treaty of Brest-Litovsk, Russia and the Central Powers agreed to refrain from official propaganda.[51] After the First World War, Soviet Russia entered into over a score of such agreements. Of these, the treaties with Britain, France and the United States are the best known.[52] Germany, too, both before and after the rise of the Nazis to power, signed several such conventions.[53] We should note, too, the 1923 accord on Tangier between Spain, France, and Britain, notably its Article 10 which states: "Any agitation, *propaganda* or conspiracy against the established order in the French or Spanish zones of Morocco is forbidden from the zone of Tangier. *Similar agitation against any foreign state is also forbidden.*"[54]

Several Pan American conventions include similar provisions. Article 8 of the Montevideo Convention of 1933 states: "No state has the right to intervene in the internal or external affairs of another."[55] This obligation, properly interpreted, must cover subversive propaganda. Also in point is the Charter of the Organization of American States, signed at Bogota in 1948, which stipulates, in Article 15: "No State or group of States has the right to intervene, directly or indirectly, for any reason whatever, in the internal or external affairs of any other State. The foregoing principle prohibits not only armed force but also any other form of interference or attempted threat against the personality of the State or against its political, economic and cultural elements." And Article 16 contains this admonition: "No State may use or encourage the use of coercive measures

---

[50] A. F. Pribram, *The Secret Treaties of Austria-Hungary*, 2 vols., Cambridge, 1920-1921, Vol. I, pp. 51, 137.

[51] Leonard Shapiro, ed., *Soviet Treaty Series*, Vol. I, 1917-1928, Washington, D.C., 1950, p. 4.

[52] Martin, *op. cit.*, pp. 90 ff.

[53] *Ibid.*, pp. 95 ff.

[54] de Martens, *Nouveau Recueil Général de Traités*, 3rd series (Triepel, ed.), Leipzig, 1925, Vol. 13, pp. 246, 249. (Italics added).

[55] *U.S. Dept. of State, Conference Series*, No. 19 (1934), p. 167—Article 8 of Convention on Rights and Duties of States.

of an economic or political character in order to force the sovereign will of another State and obtain from it advantages of any kind."[56] Under this Charter and the Rio Treaty of 1947, intervention by propaganda would be considered as an aggression, although not armed aggression. If of such a nature as to affect the inviolability or the integrity of a member's territory, or its sovereignty or political independence, such propaganda would be characterized as an act of aggression against all American states. In such event the Organ of Consultation is expected to meet immediately for the purpose of agreeing on measures to be taken to assist the victim of aggression. In actual practice, however, such guaranties may encounter grave difficulties. For example, if a *coup d'état* results in a change of government, it may not be easy to determine whether this came as a result of hostile foreign propaganda, or as a consequence of a genuine domestic movement, perhaps based on legitimate grievances.[57]

Further collective efforts to meet the ever-growing menace of Communist propaganda in Latin America were taken at the Tenth Inter-American Conference, held at Caracas in March, 1954. There a "Declaration of Solidarity for the Preservation of the Political Integrity of the American States Against the Intervention of International Communism" was approved by a vote of 17-1, Guatemala voting no and Mexico and Argentina abstaining. The Declaration condemns the activities of the international Communist movement as constituting intervention in American affairs, and expresses the determination of the American states to take the necessary measures to protect their political independence against such intervention. It declares that the domination of the political institutions of any American state by the Communist movement would constitute a threat to the sovereignty and political independence of all the American states. It also recommends to each American state certain specific measures to be taken to counteract subversive Communist activities.[58]

Finally there may be mentioned the general provisions of the United Nations Charter which were cited under the heading of Treaty Law in the discussion of war-mongering propaganda. In view of the direct connection between subversive activities and dis-

---

[56] Pan-American Union, *Law and Treaty Series No. 23*, Charter of the Organization of American States, Washington, D.C., 1948, pp. 26-27.

[57] *Ibid.*, p. 28.

[58] 10th Inter-American Conference, Caracas, 1954, *Report of the U.S. Delegation* (Dept. of State Publ. 5692), Washington, D.C. 1955, pp. 9, 156. See Charles G. Fenwick, "Proposed Control over Radio as an Inter-American Duty in Cases of Civil Strife," *Am. J. Int. Law*, Vol. 48 (1954), pp. 289-292. It was reported in September, 1961 that Latin-American diplomats were planning a new conference to expand traditional concepts of aggression "embodied in the 1947 treaty so that a mechanism could be devised to deal with the growing pattern of Cuba-inspired subversion." *New York Times*, October 1, 1961. See additional discussion of treaties on propaganda, *infra* at p. 124 *et seq.*

turbance of peaceful relations between nations, it could well be concluded that the agreement of the signatories to the United Nations Charter to live together in peace as good neighbors would be violated by efforts, through propaganda or other means, to disrupt and overthrow the government of another country.[59]

"General Principles"

The domestic law counterpart of subversive propaganda may be found in the general use of words to cause or incite harm.

As has been shown by actual examples of subversive propaganda, the action called for is sometimes the actual assassination of the head of the state, or at any rate physical violence sufficient to dislodge the government. It has been shown earlier that there is a common principle among civilized nations forbidding the use of words to bring about murder, physical harm, and other illegal consequences.[60] This general principle should therefore be applied to the corresponding acts of nations contributing to subversion.

Judicial Decisions

The Nuremberg Judgments, already discussed under the heading of War-Mongering Propaganda, may be considered to condemn subversive propaganda as well. The indictment refers to "fifth-column activities." The activities for which Rudolph Hess was convicted included subversive activities in Austria, and the propagandistic activities of such defendants as Rosenberg and Streicher involved activities in other countries which were of a subversive character.[61]

As to subversive propaganda by a state, then, there is an impressive degree of consensus among the sources of international law establishing the illegality of such propaganda. The difficulty here is not to establish the existence of the legal principle. The difficulty is rather to bring international conduct into closer conformity with accepted law. As a first step toward this end, it is hoped that this effort to marshal present law will be helpful.

---

[59] *Supra*, p. 66 *et. seq.*
[60] See Chapter IV, under "General Principles", subsection.
[61] *Supra*, p. 76 *et. seq.*

Chapter VI

Defamatory Propaganda by a State

The Nature of Defamatory Propaganda

Defamatory propaganda consists of those communications which tend to degrade, revile and insult foreign states, or their institutions, leaders or agents, especially when such attacks are of a nature as to disturb peaceful relations between the states concerned. Some such publications, depending on their underlying purpose or natural tendency, could be considered also within the categories of subversive or war-mongering propaganda. As an illustration of the subversive type, we could mention name-calling whose object is to incite a foreign people against its leader, and of the war-mongering type, scurrilous remarks about a foreign king against whom it is hoped to stir up hatred in preparation for war.

Often, however, the motive behind such attacks may be difficult or impossible to ascertain. As a matter of fact, the intent of the author may be immaterial if the natural consequence is to cause mutual misunderstanding and bad blood among nations or otherwise to lead to a disturbance of international relations. This is the vital question—the degree of harm caused to a major international interest, the maintenance of peace. In 1853, discussing the problem raised by propaganda sent by political refugees in England to other lands, the Lord Chancellor formulated this principle with unusual clarity:

> The reason why libellers in such cases were prosecuted was not simply on the ground of their having libelled foreign sovereigns, but because such libels were calculated to create a hostile feeling in foreign states, and to *cause a breach of the peace.*[1] (Emphasis added)

In this matter, a study of domestic laws of libel can be useful. Under the common law, words spoken, however maliciously, are not considered to offer grounds for conviction for criminal libel unless calculated to cause a breach of the peace and harmony within the community.[2]

---

[1] *Hansard*, 3d series, Vol. 124, 1853, p. 1060.
[2] *Corpus Juris Secundum*, Vol. 53, Sec. 282; W. Blake Odgers, *A Digest of the Law of Libel and Slander*, London, 1896, pp. 443-444.

Before proceeding to consider the attendant legal problems, it may be helpful at this point to give a few cases to illustrate the special character of libellous attacks in the international field. An early instance, strictly speaking one of wartime rather than of peacetime propaganda, has already been referred to: the circulation by Octavian of scurrilous stories about the alleged drunkenness and revelry of his enemy Antony.[3] An even better illustration for our purposes is that given by Vattel, who writes that "Certain medals and offensive jests irritated Louis XIV against the United Provinces and brought on his attack upon them in 1672, which proved the destruction of the Republic."[4]

Somewhat later, in 1787, Lord Gordon was convicted of defaming Marie Antoinette,[5] and Peltier was convicted of libelling Napoleon. Here the Court is reported as saying ". . . any publication which tends to degrade, revile, and defame persons in considerable situations of power and dignity in foreign countries may be taken and be treated as a libel, and particularly where it has a tendency to interrupt the pacific relations between the two countries."[6] And on this side of the Atlantic one Cobbett was prosecuted in Philadelphia for inserting in local newspapers certain scurrilous attacks on the French nation.[7]

After the First World War, an American paper published documents harmful to the Mexican Government which later proved to be forgeries.[8] With the rise of the dictatorships in the 'thirties, and their resort to unrestricted propaganda in their home and foreign policies, the frequency and intensity of libellous attacks increased. Not all the attacks eliciting protest came from the totalitarian states. Thus Secretary of the Interior Ickes made certain statements about Nazi Germany against which the latter protested,[9] and Japan reacted in a similar fashion against uncomplimentary remarks about Emperor Hirohito which had appeared in the Conde Nast publications.[10] Meanwhile the American Government complained officially of articles published in Nazi newspapers, for instance, objectionable comments appearing in the controlled press about American women.[11] Such charges and counter-charges became so frequent during

---

[3] *Supra*, p. 14.

[4] Vattel, Bk. II, Ch. I, Sec. 19.

[5] 22 *Howell State Trials*, p. 175 (1787).

[6] 28 *ibid.*, pp. 529, 617 (1803); Oppenheim (8th ed., Lauterpacht), Vol. I, Sec. 121.

[7] Moore, *Digest*, Vol. II, pp. 161-162.

[8] Dickinson, *op. cit.* (*Am J. Int. Law*, Vol. 22 (1928), p. 842), This author remarks that such publications "would seem adequately characterized only as the grossest abuse of the freedom of the press."

[9] *New York Time*, December 23, 25, 31, 1938.

[10] Hyde, *op. cit.*, Vol. I, Sec. 217.

[11] *Ibid.*, Sec. 217, n. 8.

the years just prior to the Second World War as almost to blot out all distinction between peace and war, causing jurists to despair of restoring any respect for moral or legal rules in the premises. Thus Lauterpacht felt impelled to write in 1937:[12]

> The series of statements and speeches made in the years 1936 and 1937 by representatives of Germany, Italy and Russia, and containing violent attacks on the governments and institutions of the countries concerned, must be regarded as exceptional and as evidencing a suspension, in this matter, of the operation of an accepted rule of international law in the relations of these states.

But the period just referred to was certainly no worse in this respect than that which followed the end of the shooting in the Second World War, once the Cold War got under way. In fact, a complete account of international defamation occurring during this period would fill many volumes. Only a few examples need be given here. At Lake Success, at a meeting of the Subcommission on Freedom of Information and of the Press, in answer to Russian charges of "war-mongering" by American newspapers, Professor Chafee, the United States delegate, cited Soviet press attacks on Senators Vandenberg and Connally, who were represented as planning to extend American rule over the entire world.[13] And while the Turks were complaining of vilifications coming into their country over the Soviet shortwave, the official American Military Government radio was labelling Communism in Europe as a "combination of wickedness, insincerity and irresponsibility."[14] On July 19, 1948, the United States government protested sharply to the Czech Foreign Office, demanding a retraction of grave allegations that American forces in Germany had engineered a plot to kill the Czech Minister of National Defense.[15]

In a pamphlet issued by the Kennedy administration on April 3, 1961, denouncing the Castro regime in Cuba, grave charges of defamatory propaganda were laid at the door of the Cuban government, as follows:

> Thus the Cuban Foreign Minister has applied unprintable language to President Frondizi of Argentina. Government broadcasts have denounced President López Mateos as "the betrayer of the Mexican revolution," President Alessandri as "the corrupter of the faith of the Chilean people," President Lieras Camarego of Colombia as "the

---

[12] Oppenheim (5th ed., Lauterpacht), London, 1937, Vol. I, p. 231, n. 1.

[13] *New York Times*, January 23, 1948. Defamation in the U. N. reached perhaps its lowest point on September 17, 1961, when Ahmad Shukairy in the General Assembly called Israel a "Nazi incarnation," "another Eichmann" and "barbarism seated in gangsterism rooted in Naziism!" *New York Herald-Tribune*, October 18, 1961.

[14] *New York Herald-Tribune*, February 6, 18, 1948.

[15] *New York Times*, July 20, 1948.

intimate friend of exploiting imperialism," President Betancourt of Venezuela as the "revolutionary of Mercurochrome Bandaids," President Eisenhower of the United States as "decrepit" and "bottle-fed," and so on.[16]

It is only too obvious that false and slanderous charges by radio and press directed by one state against another are of frequent occurrence today. There is ample proof of both their existence and their dangers to peace. This can be illustrated by examples from one single campaign: the attacks directed to Iran from Moscow since the Second World War. Moscow not only uses its own radio, but also speaks occasionally through clandestine stations or the radio of a satellite, notably East Germany. The following are taken from broadcasts heard during the 1949-1959 period. Some of these programs, as will be obvious, are designed to weaken the regime in Iran, while some are aimed indirectly at the United States:

Radio Moscow, October 8, 1949:

> By smuggling Iranian foodstuffs out of this country, American officials have brought starvation to many parts of Iran . . . The refusal of the American Government to assist the hungry Iranian people once again shows American imperialism in all its repulsive ugliness. From experience, the Iranian people are convinced that the American imperialists and their servile Iranian lackeys have thrown Iran into the grips of a horrible famine.

Radio Moscow, in Persian, January 19, 1950:

> While the colonizers reap large profits from oil resources and pearls, the inhabitants live in a state of appalling destitution and misery. The barbarous activities of the monopolists have brought unemployment, hunger and disease to the inhabitants.

Pravda (Moscow) article on "Mysterious Happenings in Iran," March 18, 1951:

> On March 7, the Iranian Premier, General Ali Razmara, was murdered in Tehran. The murder was committed in broad daylight, in the courtyard of the mosque in which the Premier was to have assisted at a special religious ceremony . . .
>
> It is easy to understand that Razmara's holding the post of Premier in no way served the interests of U.S. ruling circles, who had for years been striving to establish their predominant influence in Iran. The conclusion is evident that men closely connected with "American influence" in Iran were interested in eliminating Razmara.

Radio Moscow, in Persian, June 23, 1951:

> As we know this year the locusts came to Iran from Arabia, British Sudan, Egypt and Pakistan . . . The scientists and local peo-

---

[16] "Cuba," *Department of State Publication 7171*, April, 1961.

ple of these countries know the breeding grounds of locusts, but the British and U.S. imperialists who influence these countries do not worry about helping the local population . . . Besides, if a miracle occurred and the locusts died out, they would try to breed more in their laboratories and turn them loose in the wheat fields of the eastern countries. Not long ago they dropped Colorado beetles in various parts of Europe . . . The imperialists have sunk so low in the slime of corruption that they openly consider famine, shortage, war and oppression necessary in the world.

Radio Moscow, in Persian, May 28, 1952,
based on New Times article:

The U.S. imperialists are pursuing malicious aims in which a very dangerous and ugly role has been assigned to Iran. They are trying to bring Iran under their full control, depriving her of national independence and grabbing her oil.

"Azerbaijan Democratic Radio," in Azerbaijani, August 6, 1952:

As soon as Qavam, the notorious American agent, assumed power, the youth intensified their struggle against American imperialism and the royal regime. For, like the workers, the sober students knew that the treacherous Shah and criminal Qavam wanted to implement rapidly the sinister plans of the American war-mongers by creating an atmosphere of terror in the country and to turn the Iranian oil fields over to the American imperialists. The struggle conducted against Qavam was also directed against the Shah and American imperialism.

Radio Moscow, based on Pravda article by "Observer",
August 19, 1953:

To the intrigues of the American agents, the Iranian people have replied by holding mass demonstrations under such slogans as "Death to the Conspirators!" and "The Iranian people demand that American spies be thrown out of the country." Numerous inscriptions such as "Yanks, Go Home!" and "Long Live the People!" appeared in Tehran. Thus, the policy of rough interference in the internal affairs of other states, pursued by the ruling circles of the U.S., has once again suffered an ignominious failure.

Radio Moscow, in Persian, February 19, 1959:

Who among our listeners would deny that as the living standards of the Iranian people worsen, the deposits of the Shah and his retinue in foreign banks rise proportionately? But the inevitable course of the history of our time shows that those rulers who plunder their people and rely on foreign bayonets and dollars cannot play with the fate of their country for long.

Radio Moscow, in Persian, May 14, 1959:

. . . We know that the Shah's clique and Mohammed Reza Pahlevi have personally caused the bloodshed of hundreds of honest army officers and thousands of patriotic Iranians. How then can there be peace for the widows and orphans? How can these people love those executioners and murderers? How can Iranian toilers, the creators of the country's riches, have love and affection for those who let these riches be plundered by foreigners?[16a]

Increasingly over the past few years the Arab Press and radio, particularly in Cairo, have been disseminating charges that the United States is conspiring or plotting against the Arabs and attempting to oppose Arab nationalism by the subversion of nationalist regimes.[17] The charges have sometimes been imaginative undocumented deductions. For example, in an editorial of Akram Hawrani in *al-Baath* of April 28, 1957, the writer suggested that in view of the discovery that the United States was not opposed to the objectives of the triparite aggression against Egypt but only to the feeble means used, it was logical to expect that the United States might resort to armed aggression in the Middle East to liquidate the problems in the area quickly. Sometimes the propaganda has taken the form of the exaggeration and forced interpretation of minor events, such as the preposterous story accusing the United States of killing Egyptian scientists studying in America, recounted by Saleh Dessouki in *al-Bulis* magazine of March 24, 1958. The practice of employing sensational "revelations" of "conspiracies and plots" against the Arabs is not confined to Arab propaganda of only the last few years. Such charges have been common ever since the Palestine war. Perhaps the outstanding "conspiracy" charge was the attempt to implicate members of the American diplomatic mission to Syria in the assassination of the Syrian Deputy Chief of Staff, Adnan Malki, in April 1957.[18] Such allegations have been commonplace in the Arab press and on the radio in order to provide the Arab audience with sensational "facts" on which to base emotional predilections.

It would be supererogation to present here further illustra-

[16a] See also examples given *supra*, p. 91.

[17] Similarly, on September 21, 1961, Britain made a strong protest to Ghana over "disgraceful allegations" in the Ghanian *Times* which charged Britain with "history's number one international murder of U.N. Secretary-General Dag Hammarskjold." *Manchester Guardian Weekly*, September 28, 1961.

[18] *An-Nur*, Damascus, April 26, 1957. "In 1953, when Cairo Radio began its foreign programs, it beamed only 164 hours weekly in eight languages. In 1961 Cairo was beaming 766 hours a week of international short wave propaganda broadcasts—second only to Radio Moscow's 1,045 hours. By contrast, the Voice of America broadcasts only 633 hours. Cairo uses 122 studios, talks in 28 languages, including many African tongues, and has two short wave frequencies capable of reaching all five continents." *Near East Report*, October 2, 1961, p. 39.

tions of these incidents of the current international situation.[19] They are especially prevalent whenever grave disputes arise between nations, and are characteristic of the recent controversies between Israel and Arab states, India and Pakistan, Algeria and France, Cuba and the United States, Venezuela and Santo Domingo, and naturally, of every stage of the Cold War. The dangers incident to such a deterioration of international conduct are only too evident. Such accusations are keenly resented and provoke retaliation. Their cumulative effects are often lasting, and may contribute markedly to the outbreak of war. Thus it is important to determine whether any remedy is to be found in existing rules of international law and, in later chapters, what reforms, either international or local, have been proposed or are now available, so as to discourage such incidents in the future and, where they have occurred, to attenuate their repercussions and effects.

DEFAMATORY STATE PROPAGANDA UNDER INTERNATIONAL LAW

Writings of Publicists

Defamatory propaganda by one state against another is generally considered to be a violation of international law. A leading authority has stated the law as follows:[20]

> International law clearly forbids the higher officials of a state to indulge in uncomplimentary or insulting comments upon the personality of another state or its rulers . . . While the character of the officer and the circumstances in which his remarks were made, as well as the substance of their remarks themselves, have been considered elements in determining the state's responsibility, it appears that if the utterance is public, is attributable to one's state, and is insulting to the personality of another state or its ruler, the first state is legally bound to apologize.

---

[19] Many examples could be given from current press reports. Thus on December 27, 1961, Assistant Secretary of State Mennen Williams stated that much of the opposition to the UN operations in the Congo was fomented by a well-financed propaganda machine which among other questionable activities had fabricated "horrendous lies of indiscriminate mayhem by the United Nations troops". *New York Times,* December 28, 1961. Also see the recent attack on the United States in a monarchist newspaper in Spain, "a string of the most vitriolic accusations at (sic) the United States that diplomats and observers can recall in recent times." *Ibid.,* January 21, 1962.

[20] Hyde, *op. cit.,* Vol. I, p. 709; Quincy Wright, "The Denunciation of Treaty Violators," *Am. J. Int. Law,* Vol. 32 (1938), p. 528; Oppenheim, Vol. I, Sec. 121. During a discussion of measures to curb hostile propaganda, in the First Committee of the General Assembly, a majority of the delegates argued that defamation of leaders of foreign governments was a form of war propaganda. *General Assembly,* 2nd Session (1947) *First Committee,* 79th Meeting, pp. 184-188.

Customary International Law

The statement quoted above from Hyde on the illegality of defamatory propaganda by a state is based to a considerable degree on the cumulation of international diplomatic custom and practice. The obvious problem here is the question: at what point does the repeated violation of the rule of customary international law begin to place in question the existence of the rule itself? In view of the prevalence of international verbal abuse, this question must be squarely faced.

First, it is a rather obvious observation that a rule of law should not lightly be considered destroyed even by a considerable amount of battering in practice.[21] The world is full of deadbeats who do not pay their bills, but we do not for that reason conclude that the common law principle of the binding force of contracts has lost any of its vigor.

Another consideration is this: as the factual description of the problem of defamatory propaganda points out, while defamatory state utterances have been common, official protests have also been common. In some situations, where the stream of defamation is almost continuous, as in the case of the Moscow radio campaign aimed at Iran, one would hardly expect each particular defamation to bring forth an individual specific official protest. The fact that official protests were lodged even during the period of the worst excesses of fascist propaganda, and are still being regularly lodged in such instances as the attacks by Castro on the United States, is an indication of determination to keep the standard of international practice in force, in spite of violations.

Finally, although a rule established by practice can presumably be discredited by practice, the rule of international law forbidding state defamatory propaganda is drawn not only from practice but from other sources of international law, discussed both before and after this subsection. It is therefore of a special importance that these sources, particularly the general principles of law recognized by civilized nations, be exploited to the full.

"General Principles"

The obvious counterpart of defamatory propaganda in domestic law is libel and slander.

---

21 "The best evidence for the existence of international law is that every actual State recognizes that it does exist and that it is itself under an obligation to observe it. States may often violate international law, just as individuals often violate municipal law, but no more than individuals do States defend their violations by claiming that they are above the law." J. L. Brierly, *The Outlook for International Law*, Oxford, 1944, p. 5.

The Principle of the Illegality of Defamation

The first principle in this field recognized by civilized nations is the underlying principle that defamation in the form of libel and slander is illegal, particularly when it has a tendency to cause a breach of peace.

Under the common law:

> Libel is the malicious publication of durable defamation. It is a misdemeanor at common law and also under modern statutes unless it has been made a felony, which is not common.[22]

One of the earliest trials for criminal libel was the *De Libellis Famosis*, which was tried before the Star Chamber in 1605.[23]

---

[22] Perkins, *Criminal Law*, pp. 351-2 (1957).

[23] 5 Co. Rep. 125a, 77 Eng. Rep. 250 (1605). See Perkins, supra, p. 353, n. 86. Because of the important points of law decided in this leading case, it deserves some quotation at this point:

"Every libel (which is called *famosus Libellis, seu infamatoria scriptura),* is made either against a private man, or against a magistrate or public person. *If it be against a private man it deserves a severe punishment,* for although the libel be made against one, yet it incites all those of the same family, kindred, or society *per consequens* to quarrels and breach of the peace, and may be the cause of shedding of blood and of great inconvenience: *if it be against a magistrate or other public person, it is a greater offence;* for it concerns not only the breach of the peace but also the scandal of Government; for what greater scandal of Government can there be than to have corrupt or wicked magistrates to be appointed and constituted by the King, to govern his subjects under him? And greater imputation to the State cannot be than to suffer such corrupt men to sit in the sacred seat of justice, or to have any meddling or concerning the administration of justice."

"*Although the private man or magistrate be dead, at the time of the making of the libel, yet it is punishable;* for in the one case it stirs up others of the same family, blood, or society, to revenge, and to break the peace, and in the other the libeller traduces and slanders the State and Government, which dies not".

"It is not material whether the libel be true, or whether the party against whom it is made, be of good or ill fame; for in a settled state of Government the party grieved ought to complain for every injury done him in an ordinary course of law, and not by any means to revenge himself, either by the odious course of libelling, or otherwise: he who kills a man with his sword in fight is a great offender, but he is a greater offender who poisons another; for in the one case he, who is openly assaulted, may defend himself, and knows his adversary, and may endeavour to prevent it: but poisoning may be done so secretly that none can defend himself against it; *for which cause the offence is the more dangerous because the offender cannot easily be known*: and of such nature is libelling, it is secret, and robs a man of his good name, which ought to be more precious to him than his life, & *difficullimun est invenire authorem infamatoriae scripturae;* and therefore when the offender is known he ought to be severely punished. Every infamous libel *aut est in scriptis, aut sine scriptis;* a scandalous libel in scriptis is, when an epigram, rhime, or other writing is composed or published to the scandal or contumely of another, by which his fame and dignity may be prejudiced. And such libel may be published, 1. *Verbis aut cantilenis*: as where it is maliciously repeated or sung in the presence of others. 2. *Traditione,* when

Statements in this case would seem to support the observation that "preventing breaches of the peace was the historical justification for criminal libel."[24] It was perfectly consistent with the rationale to punish defamation even of a dead person. As one court put it: "A libel even of a deceased person is an offense against the public, because it may stir up the passions of the living, and produce acts of revenge."[25]

As to the law of the United States: Today every American jurisdiction—the 50 states, the District of Columbia, and Puerto Rico—punishes libels directed at individuals.[26]

As to the civil law: the German penal code distinguishes several degrees of insult: simple insult by word or deed;[27] asserting or disseminating statements of fact which are not demonstrably true and have a tendency to subject a person to public scorn and contempt,[28] assertion or dissemination of statements known to be untrue and having a tendency to subject a person to scorn and contempt.[29] There seems to be little difference between the various European penal codes in this respect.[30]

As to Islamic law: Although ". . . the most cursory glance at the law that prevails in the Middle East today reveals the fact that it is a hotchpotch, part Islamic and indigenous and part secular and Western,"[31] the principles of Islam, even when they are not sanctioned by legislation, are still respected in the Middle Eastern countries. Governments as well as individuals are supposed to abide by the general principles of Islam, particularly the undisputed preaching of the Koran. This is why it is always valid in Middle Eastern jurisprudence to support a legal argument by the instructions of the Koran.

A pertinent verse in the Koran for present purposes is No. 11

---

the libel or any copy of it is delivered over to scandalize the party. *Famosus libellis sine* scriptis may be 1. *Picturis,* as to paint the party in any shameful and ignominious manner. 2. *Signis,* as to fix a gallows, or other reproachful and ignominious signs at the party's door or elsewhere." 77 Eng. Rep. at 251-2.

[24] "Developments in the Law—Defamation." 69 *Harv. L. R.* 875, 946, n. 510 (1956). But see 3 Burdick, *Law of Crime,* §785 (1946).

[25] *Comm. v. Taylor,* 5 Binn. (Pa.) 277. *Cf. State v. Haffer,* 94 Wash. 136, 141, 162 Pac. 45, 47 (1916).

[26] *Beauharnais v. Illinois,* 343 U.S. 250, 255 (1952).

[27] German Penal Code, (Sec. 185).

[28] *Id.* (Sec. 186).

[29] *Id.* (Sec. 187).

[30] See, *e.g.,* Belgium, Arts. 443-452; France, Art. 29 of the Press Law of July 29, 1881; Netherlands, Arts. 261-271. See generally Liepmann, Die Beleidigung, 4 Vergleichende Darstellung des deutschen und ausländischen Strafrechts 217, 279-310 (1906), with comparative survey; von Lilienthal, Üble Nachrede und Verleumdung, *ibid.* 375, 413-449 with comparative survey.

[31] J. N. D. Anderson, *Islamic Law in the Modern World,* New York, 1959, Ch. 2, p. 18.

of the Sura (chapter) of "The Private Apartments" which reads:

> 11. O ye who believe! Let not a folk deride a folk who may be better than they (are), nor let women (deride) women who may be better than they are; neither defame one another, nor insult one another by nicknames. Bad is the name of lewdness after faith. And whoso turneth not in repentance, such are evil-doers.

The codes of various Islamic countries specifically make defamation a criminal offense, as in the codes of Egypt,[32] the Sudan,[33] Libya,[34] Lebanon,[35] Transjordan[36] and Iraq.[37]

---

[32] *The Egyptain Penal Code.* Chapter 7; Title III, Defamation and insults. *Article 302.* Whoever by the means indicated in Article 171 of the present Code, imputes to any individual whomsoever, facts which if there existed would expose the person against whom they were uttered to the application of legal punishments or to the despise of the citizens, will be guilty of the misdemeanour of defamation.
Article 306. In the circumstance envisaged by Article 171, all insults not containing the imputation of a precise fact but which breach in any way the honour or the esteem of the person, will be punishable by imprisonment not exceeding one year and a fine not exceeding LE100 or either of these punishments.

[33] *The Sudanese Penal Code,* Chapter XXVII, of Defamation. 436. Whoever by words either spoken or reproduced by any mechanical means or intended to be read or by signs or by visible representations makes or publishes any imputation concerning any person, intending to harm or knowing or having reason to believe that such imputation will harm the reputation of such person.
437. Whoever defames another shall be punished with imprisonment for a term which may extend to two years or with fine or with both.
443. Whoever intentionally insults and thereby gives provocation to any person, intending or knowing it to be likely that such provocation will cause a breach of the peace or the commission of any other offence, shall be punished with imprisonment for a term which may extend to two years or with fine or with both.

[34] *The Libyan Penal Code,* Offences against honor.
Article 438. Insult. Whoever offends against the honor or dignity of a person in his presence shall be punished by a penalty of detention for a period not exceeding six months or a fine not exceeding twenty-five pounds. The same penalty shall apply to anyone who commits the offence by means of telegraph or telephone or writings or picture directed to the person injured.
Article 439. Defamation. Due regard being taken to the provisions of the preceding Article, whoever injures the reputation of another by publication to several persons shall be punished by a penalty of detention for a period not exceeding one year or a fine not exceeding fifty pounds.

[35] *The Lebanese Penal Code,* Title VII, of Crimes and misdemeanours against persons; Chapter II, of Crimes against liberty and honor; of Defamation and insult.
Article 582. A defamation against an individual which is committed by any of the means stated in Article 209, will be punished with imprisonment up to 3 months and with a fine up to LL100 or with either punishment. The punishment will only be a fine in a case where the defamation is not public.

[36] *The Transjordanian Penal Code,* Of Crimes against public authority; No. III, of Defamation and insult.
Article 180. (i) Defamation is to impute a certain act to a person, even in doubtful or questioning manner, which would injure the person's dignity or

114

As to Soviet law: The Russian criminal code contains the following provisions:

> *Slander,* that is, the spreading of fabrications (*izmyshlenii*) which are known to be false and defamatory (*pozoriashchikh*) to another person shall be punished by deprivation of liberty for a period of up to one year, or by corrective labor for the same period of time, or by a fine of up to fifty rubles, or by public censure, or it entails application of measures of public compulsion (*obshchestvennoe vozdeistvie*).
>
> *Libel* in a work printed or published in any other form of manifold production, as well as committed by a person who has been tried previously for slander shall be punished by deprivation of liberty for a period of up to three years or corrective labor for a period of up to one year.
>
> *Slander* coupled with the accusation of the perpetration of a crime against the State or another grave crime shall be punished by deprivation of liberty for a period of up to five years.
>
> *Sec. 131. Insult.* Insult, that is, intentional degrading of the honor or dignity of a person, expressed in an improper form shall be punished by corrective labor for a period of up to six months, or by a fine of up to fifty rubles, or by public censure, or entails application of measures of public compulsion (*obshchestvennoe vozdeistvie*)
>
> Insult in print, as well as insult inflicted by a person who has been previously tried for an insult, shall be punished by corrective labor for a period of up to one year or a fine of up to one hundred rubles.[38]

It is thus quite clear that the illegality of defamation is one of the general principles of law recognized by civilized nations. *

The Principle of Fair Comment

These general principles, in addition to bolstering the existence of the underlying prohibition of defamatory utterances, are helpful in the drawing of certain troublesome lines between illegal abuse and legitimate criticism. Before anyone throws up his hands and despairs of the possibility of ever drawing such a line for purposes of international conduct, let him recall that the domestic law of libel and slander has had to face this problem for centuries, and has managed to arrive at reasonably workable solutions which are being applied to particular cases daily. If, for purposes of domestic law, a balance can be struck between free speech and fair comment on the

---

honour or expose him to the hatred or despise of people, whether such act is a legal crime or not. (ii) Insult is an offence against the honour, dignity or respect of another person, even in a doubtful or questioning manner, without spefying a particular act.

[37] The Iraquian Penal Code follows the same pattern as the Lebanese Code.

[38] *RSFSR Criminal Code of 1960*, Section 130.

one hand and the actionable defamation on the other, eventually this may become possible with respect to international law.

Probably the doctrine of most immediate relevance is that which sanctions "fair comment on a matter of public interest."

As to the common law: the defense of fair comment on a matter of public interest is well established. As Dean Burdick has expressed it:

> The official acts of public officers, the character and fitness sof candidates for public office, the publications of authors, and public dramatic or other entertainments are matters of public interest, and, therefore, are the subject of fair comment and fair criticism by people generally.[39]

Apparently, comment is "fair" when based on facts truly stated which are the honest, reasonably based belief of the person speaking or writing.[40]

As to the civil law: The Netherlands penal code provides that there is no defamation if the utterance was evidently made in the public interest or in necessary self-defense.[41]

The German penal code provides that the expression of negative judgments on the academic, artistic, or business activity of others, as well as statements made in the pursuit or defense of rights or in the exercise of legitimate interests are only punishable as simple insults if the form of the utterance or the surrounding circumstances show that there has been an insult.[42]

As to Islamic law: the Sudanese penal code contains one of the most carefully worked out set of exceptions in the general area of fair comment to be found anywhere.

> First Exception.—It is not defamation to impute anything which is true concerning any person, if it be for the public good that the imputation

---

[39] Burdick, *Law of Crime.* §799a (1946).

[40] *Ibid.* See also "Developments in the Law—Defamation," 69 *Harv. L. R.* 875, 925-8 (1956).

[41] Article 261, par. 3. Simple defamation becomes calumny, with greatly increased penalties, where proof of truth is permissible, such proof is not forthcoming, and the offender knew the falsity of his statements. (Art. 262). Proof of truth, finally, is admissible only (1) where the judge deems it necessary in passing on the defendant's assertion that he acted in the public interest or in necessary self-defense; or (2) where defamation concerns a public official in the exercise of his official functions (Art. 263).

[42] *German Penal Code* Sec. 193. As this clause establishes a defense against actions for simple insult only, it does not apply to reckless (Sec. 186) or knowingly mendacious defamation (Sec. 187). See generally Schönke, *op. cit.*, 753-759; 2 Maurach, *op. cit.*, 141-146. Art. 449 of the Belgian penal code provides that even if at the time of the offensive utterance there existed legal proof of the facts imputed, the calumniator shall nevertheless be punished if it is established that he has made the imputation without any motive of public or private interest, and for the sole purpose of inflicting harm.

116

should be made or published. Whether or not it is for the public good is a question of fact.

Second Exception.—It is not defamation to express in good faith any opinion whatever respecting the conduct of a public servant in the discharge of his public functions or respecting his character so far as his character appears in that conduct and no further.

Third Exception.—It is not defamation to express in good faith any opinion whatever respecting the conduct of any person touching any public question and respecting his character so far as his character appears in that conduct and no further.

Fourth Excepton.—It is not defamation to publish a substantially true report of the proceedings of a Court of Justice or of the result of any such proceedings.

Fifth Exception.—It is not defamation to express in good faith any opinion whatever respecting the merits of any case civil or criminal which has been decided by a Court of Justice or respecting the conduct of any person as a party, witness or agent in any such case or respecting the character of such person as far as his character appears in that conduct and no further.

Sixth Exception.—It is not defamation to express in good faith any opinion respecting the merits of any performance which its author has submitted to the judgment of the public or respecting the character of the author so far as his character appears in such performance and no further.

Seventh Exception.—It is not defamation in a person having over another any authority either conferred by law or arising out of a lawful contract made with that other to pass in good faith any censure on the conduct of that other in matters to which such lawful authority relates.

Eighth Exception.—It is not defamation to proffer in good faith an accusation against any person to any of those who have lawful authority over that person with respect to the subject matter of accusation.

Ninth Exception.—It is not defamation to make an imputation on the character of another, provided that the imputation be made in good faith for the protection of the interests of the person making it or of any other person or for the public good.

Tenth Exception.—It is not defamation to convey a caution in good faith to one person against another provided that such caution be intended for the good of the person to whom it is conveyed or of some person in whom that person is interested or for the public good.[43]

As to the Soviet Union: The Constitution of the Soviet Union states:
In conformity with the interests of the working people, and in or-

---

[43] Sudanese Penal Code, Chapter XXVII, Section 436.

der to strengthen the socialist system, the citizens of the USSR are guaranteed by law:

    a) freedom of speech;

    b) freedom of the press;[44]

The following commentary has been applied to this guarantee:

> In our state, naturally, there is and can be no place for freedom of speech, press, and so on for the foes of socialism. . . Freedom of speech, press . . . [are] fully guaranteed by the state upon the single condition that they be utilized in accord with the interests of the toilers and to the end of strengthening the socialist order. (*Ibid.* p. 617.)[45]

In a sense, this might add up to "fair comment in the public interest," once Vyshinsky's definition of the public interest is conceded.

Thus, although there are many variants on the theme, and although, even in a particular system, the concept leaves a wide range of discretion within which the standards of the community can operate, it appears to be a fair statement that the general principles of law recognized by civilized nations include an exception to the principle of defamation when a comment is made non-maliciously with an honest regard for the public interest.

This principle of fair comment, and particularly of fair criticism of actions contrary to principles of law or humanity, has been recognized in international law. As Holtzendorf wrote as long ago as 1891, the foreign press and the foreign state have the right publicly to disapprove any action contrary to the law of nations or in violation of the principle of humanity.[46] If a given state has violated its treaty obligations, or has transgressed an accepted norm of customary international law, other states are entitled to enter a protest or express their disapproval. The principle underlying this rule was voiced at a meeting of the International Federation of League of Nations Societies in 1936. Commenting on the Geneva conference to be held to consider restrictions on radio propaganda, the conference passed a resolution in the following terms: "The Twentieth Plenary Assembly . . . is of the opinion that these restrictions ought not, under any circumstance, to interfere with transmissions which conform to the spirit of the Covenant, even if they include criticisms of nations for failing to fulfill their international obligations."[47] Some authors have gone further, and have maintained that such criticism is not only permissive, but even mandatory, in case of a breach of an undoubted

---

44 Article 125 of the Constitution of the Soviet Union.

45 A. Y. Vyshinsky, *The Law of the Soviet State*, New York, 1954, p. 617.

46 Franz von Holtzendorff, *Elements de Droit International Public*, Paris, 1891, p. 81.

47 L.O.N., *Bulletin of Information on the Work of International Organizations*, Vol. VIII, 1936, p. 84.

duty to refrain from aggression such as is set forth in the San Francisco Charter.[48]

To close the mouths of nations in the presence of grave encroachments on rules of law would be an unwarranted restriction on their liberty, and would endanger the best interests of the international community. A principle useful as a guide here is that formulated by Huddleston, J., in *Whistler v. Ruskin.*

> Liberty of criticism must be allowed. . . Fair discussion is essentially necessary to the truth of history and the advancement of science. That publication, therefore, I shall never consider a libel, which has for its object, not to injure the reputation of any individual, but to correct misrepresentations of fact, to refute sophistical reasoning, to expose a vicious taste in literature, or to censure what is hostile to morality.[49]

In practice the interpretation of the rule permitting fair criticism may not be easy. In fact, few of its consequences or refinements seem to have been thought through. Suppose, for example, that after one state had criticized another for an alleged violation of a treaty, it should appear on further investigation that the criticism had not been well founded. Must the criticizing state then make reparation? But suppose, in the special circumstances of the case, the latter had reasonable grounds to believe that an actual violation had taken place? Such cases are bound to cause difficulty because it may be impossible to prove whether such criticism is well founded or not. This is

---

[48] Wright, *op. cit.*, "The Denunciation of Treaty-Violators," pp. 531-532, citing Elihu Root, "The Outlook for International Law," *Proc. Am. Soc. Int. Law,* 1915, pp. 2-11, esp. pp. 8-9. Professor Wright suggests that a state is under a *moral* duty to protest against breaches of ordinary treaties, but under a *legal* duty to protest against the violation of a treaty to refrain from aggression.

One author, searching for the correct distinction between permissible criticism of a foreign state and illegal calumny, argues that there is a substantial difference between stating as a fact that State A has broken X Treaty, and referring to State A as a "race of treaty-violators." Sidney Hyman, *State Responsibility for the Hostile Utterances of its Officers* (unpublished study, University of Chicago Library, 1938), pp. 95, 157. See Odgers, *A Digest of the Law of Libel and Slander,* London, 1896, pp. 34-35: "A true critic never indulges in personalities, or recklessly imputes dishonourable motives, but confines himself to the merits of the subject matter before him." W. Averell Harriman, testifying before the Senate Committee on Foreign Relations, stressed the truth that in policy as in law, there is a substantial distinction between honest reprehension and the reckless hurling of epithets. Criticism of the Soviet Union and its policy was justified, he believed, but added: "I do not think that a policy of calling names is a useful one." He also said: "I do know and I do believe that we command the respect of the people of the free world more if we deal with our conflict with the Soviet Union in sober, serious terms, not in exaggeration or of vindictive expressions." "Hearing before the Committee on Foreign Relations, United States Senate, January 31, 1961, on the nomination of W. Averell Harriman as Ambassador at Large," Committee Print, pp. 7, 9.

[49] *London Times,* November 27, 1878, cited by Odgers, *op. cit.,* p. 35.

particularly serious, given the absence of a duty among states to submit legal disputes to arbitration or adjudication. That the rule should be applied with particular caution has been recognized; it has been suggested that before lodging a protest a complaining government would do well to await the result of international procedures of inquiry, conference and adjudication, and should be guided by the results of such procedures in formulating its own criticism or denunciation. At all events, it seems evident that in connection with such charges and counter-charges, any accepted law could be considerably strengthened in practice by provision for a right of reply, discussed later in Chapter XII. Otherwise, in the dynamic conditions of our present international society, such a rule may easily fail of its object, or become a dead letter.[50]

The Principle of Group Libel

Another category of domestic law with an obvious carry-over by analogy to the international scene is the relatively new area of group libel.

As to the common law countries: Legislative recognition of the potentialities for discord or breach of the peace arising out of defamation directed at a group, class, or race has led to the enactment of group libel statutes. These statutes have raised various problems

---

[50] The foggy limit between permissible though severe criticism, and impermissible charges of scandalous misconduct on the part of a foreign state or its leaders, is illustrated by the *Kämpfer* affair of 1934, which concerned criticism of the Nazis by a Communist paper in Switzerland. This is described as follows by Hartmann in his study of the Swiss press:

The *Kämpfer* was a Communist Newspaper which had published an article containing the following: "We accuse Chancellor Hitler of murder; we accuse the Prime Minister of Prussia, Hermann Goering, of murder; we accuse the ruling class of Germany of murder." Upon the protest of the German government, action was taken against the newspaper. The Minister of Public Affairs of the Confederation considered the excerpt in a decree. He recognized that the recent executions in Germany had aroused much feeling among the Swiss working class, and that "a severe criticism can consequently, be understood. However, the terms went beyond the limits of what is permissible in form." But on July 4, 1934, the commission unanimously concluded that no measures should be taken against the *Kämpfer* in the light of the events which took place in Germany from June 30 to July 2, 1934. It added: "The entire Swiss press condemns the frightfully bloody form of the repression ordered by the German government. Our public opinion would not understand an action taken against a newspaper because of an accusation which the conduct of the foreign government itself justifies . . . ." Frederick H. Hartmann, "The Swiss Press and Foreign Affairs in World War II," *University of Florida Monographs*, Social Sciences No. 5 (Winter, 1960), p. 32.

which have been analyzed in scholarly articles.[51] The Supreme Court of the United States in *Beauharnais v. Illinois*[52] upheld a conviction under the Illinois group libel statute of a defendant who distributed handbills which attacked the Negro race.[53] In a recent British case, a conviction was had under a group libel statute. The leader of the neo-Nazi movement in Britain was convicted for having addressed a public rally with insulting words which the court considered likely to cause public disorder. The defendant's invocation of the doctrine of free speech was denied, and he was sentenced to prison under the Public Order Act of 1936. The two vital facts proved at the trial were the following: first, the violent abuse of the Jewish race by the accused, including the charge that the Jews had caused the Second World War and rejoiced when it broke out, and second, the fact that the meeting ended in actual disorder of a serious nature.[54]

As to civil law countries: Until quite recently, there were no express provisions in the German penal code generally dealing with the defamation of groups of persons. The insult and defamation provisions (secs. 185-187) were generally thought and held to apply to individuals only, since their purpose was the defense of personal honor. There always were, however, some statutory exceptions to the rule that groups of persons were not as such protected from insult and defamation: section 166 proscribes vituperations in public against recognized religious communities and their customs; and section 196 contains a somewhat indirect reference to the defamation of government agencies. In time, the strictly individualistic interpretation of the general insult and defamation provisions was increasingly relaxed.

---

[51] See, *e.g.*, David Riesman, "Democracy and Defamation: Control of Group Libel," *Columbia Law Review*, Vol. 42 1942), pp. 727-780; Tanenhaus, "Group Libel," 35 *Corn. L. Q.* 261 (1950). One such problem inheres in the circumstance that, unlike the "fighting word" of the libel of an individual, utterances defamatory of groups often bear some relation to true discussion. Tanenhaus, id. at 277. Therefore, it is difficult to draft a statute which will punish group libel and yet not infringe on free speech and be vague. A New Jersey group libel statute was struck down as unconstitutional on such grounds. *State v. Klapprott*, 127 N.J.L. 395, 22 A. 2d 877 (1941).

[52] 343 U.S. 250 (1952).

[53] As has been pointed out in a law review note, the majority opinion in *Beauharnais* does not directly indicate whether the application of group libel statutes is limited by the clear and present danger doctrine. 69 Harv. L.R. 875, 900 (1956). However, it would seem, when one views the opinion as a whole, that the Court considered group libel to lie beyond the ambit of constitutionally protected free speech, and so not to be subject to the clear and present danger test. As of 1956, it appeared true that:
"The *Beauharnais* decision has not led to the enactment of any new group libel statutes, and apparently no new prosecutions have been initiated under existing acts." 69 Harv. L. R. 875, 901 (1956).

[54] *New York Times*, August 21, 1962.

First, the old Supreme Court extended protection from insult and defamation to organizations fulfilling a public function. Then, in a leading decision, the present Supreme Court held that all organizations of persons with a sufficiently distinguishable membership and with an autonomous will and sense of honor were so protected.[55] Protection under sections 185-187 was later extended to cover German Jews who had survived Nazi persecution in Germany and were still resident there; the Supreme Court reasoned that such persecution had established a common bond and sufficient marks of distinction although the number of those affected was very large.[56] Nevertheless, many persons who took part in the anti-Semitic disorders which suddenly erupted in 1959 were punished under an extensive interpretation of secs. 185-187. This practice, and the unusually severe penalties inflicted, came in for vigorous criticism.[57] In response to public pressure, Parliament then enacted a statute expressly proscribing group libel. This new law, which replaces the obsolete provision, "incitement of classes of the population to acts of violence in disturbance of the peace," previously contained in sec. 130 of the penal code, reads as follows:

> Whosoever in a manner suited to disturb public tranquillity attacks the human dignity of others by
> 1. inciting hatred against parts of the population;
> 2. advocating violent or arbitrary measures against the same; or
> 3. curses, maliciously exposes to contempt, or calumniates the same shall be punished by imprisonment not less than three months. In addition, a pecuniary penalty may be imposed.[58]

In France a decree-law dating from 1939 proscribes hostile attacks against groups, i.e., a race, profession or religion, allowing any member thereof to sue provided the group is sufficiently defined and restricted so that the plaintiff can consider himself to be personally maligned.[59] The defamer may also be subjected to criminal sanctions.[60] The Italian penal code forbids incitement to hatred among social classes and punishes anyone who engages in propaganda in favor of the violent suppression of a social class.[61] In all of these

---

[55] 6 *Entscheidungen des Bundesgerichtshofes in Strafsachen* 186, 190-191 (1954); (corporation owning a newspaper). For prior developments, see *ibid.*, 187-190; Schönke, *op. cit.*, 735-737.

[56] 11 *Entscheidungen des Bundesgerichtshofes in Strafsachen* 207, 208-209 (1958). This decision, however, was criticized by eminent authority as going rather far. Maurach, *op. cit.*, at 121.

[57] Baumann, "Justiz und Politik," [1961] *Juristenzeitung* 18.

[58] Law of June 20, 1960, [1960] 1 *Bundesgesetzblatt* 478.

[59] Tardu, *infra*, note 62, p. 123.

[60] *Recueil Dalloz*, 1953, p. 342.

[61] *Italian Penal Code, Section 272.*

codes,[62] the main consideration is the danger to the public peace which such defamation is liable to engender.

As to Islamic countries: The Egyptian penal code provides:

> Whoever by the same means (enunciated in Article 171) excites hatred or contempt against one or many classes of persons, will be punished with imprisonment not exceeding one year or with a fine from twenty to one hundred Egyptian pounds, or by one of the two punishments, when the excitations are of the nature of breach of public peace.[63]

Similarly, the Sudanese penal code states:

> Whoever seeks to incite hatred or contempt against any class of persons in the Sudan in such a way as to endanger the public peace, shall be punished with imprisonment for a term which may extend to two years or with fine or with both.[64]

As to Soviet Law: Article 123 of the Constitution provides:

> Any direct or indirect restriction of the rights of, or, conversely, the establishment of any direct or indirect privileges for, citizens on account of their race or nationality, as well as racial or national exclusiveness or hatred and contempt, are punishable by law.[65]

The criminal code contains the following provision:

> *Violation of National and Racial Equality*. Propaganda and incitement with the purpose of exciting racial or national enmity or discord, as well as direct or indirect restriction of rights or establishment of direct or indirect privileges for citizens depending on their racial or national affiliation, shall be punished by confinement for a period of from six months to three years or exile for a period of from two to five years.[66]

It seems a reasonable conclusion, so far as the four systems represented here are concerned, that either through judicial interpretation or legislation (or both) the principle of the illegality of group libel has become a general principle of law recognized by civilized nations. The applicability of this principle to the international scene was well expressed by one observer:

---

[62] Hurwicz, "Beleidigung Sozialer Einheiten," 31 *Zeitschrift für die Gesamte Strafrechtswissenschaft* 873; De Naurois, "Diffamation et Injures Envers les Collectivités," (1948), *Revue de Science Criminelle et de Droit Pénal Comparé* 1; Tardu, "La Protection Juridique des Groupes Sociaux Contre la Propagande d'Hostilité," 26th year, (1956) *Revue Internationale de Droit Pénal* 59.

[63] *The Egyptian Penal Code, Article 176.*

[64] *The Sudanese Penal Code, Article 106.*

[65] *Article 123* of the Constitution of the Soviet Union of 1936.

[66] Law Concerning Criminal Responsibility for Crimes Against the State of December 25, 1958, Sec. 11.

There is no direct danger to tne community in which the speaker or writer issues his mischievous statements or appeals. The danger is to international peace, via the resentments or fears of another country, or the hatreds of his own. And there is no antecedent danger; the danger is made by the statement, as it becomes a general hue and cry.[67]

Treaties

Most of the treaties that have dealt with propaganda have not been limited to any one of the three kinds of propaganda into which our legal discussion is divided. Since the law of war-mongering propaganda by states rests so firmly on the United Nations Charter and other legal sources, and since the law of subversive propaganda by states has such a wealth of support in customary international law and other sources, we have saved the general review of propaganda treaties for the area of defamatory propaganda by states, where additional legal bolstering can be used to the best advantage. In the summary of treaties that follows, it will be noted that most of the treaties have binding force only between limited numbers of states, although in some instances the number is quite large. Quite a few are expressly addressed to radio propaganda, but this does not greatly diminish their importance, since radio propaganda is the largest single part of the international propaganda problem. Some of the treaties may seem to be more concerned with the obligation of a state to control propaganda by private individuals than with utterances by the state itself, but in most of these instances it seems clear that the treaty would also expressly or impliedly operate upon communications by the state as such. One reason why some of the treaties have taken this form is that in earlier years the part played by private media in international communications was relatively larger than it is now, and the part played by state radio and propaganda services was relatively smaller.

A number of treaties designed to avoid the evils of international propaganda were signed and ratified between the two world wars. An early treaty of considerable historical significance, since it ushered in the movement to induce states to attenuate by joint action the menace of radio propaganda, was that signed on March 31, 1931, between the Reichs-Rund-Funk Gesellschaft and the Polskie Radio. It bound the parties to take all reasonable steps to prevent the broadcasting over their respective stations of material prejudicial to the spirit of cooperation and good understanding "necessary if broadcasting is to fulfill its mission of drawing nations together," in respect to politics, religion, economics, and intellectual or artistic matters. Special attention was to be devoted to programs sent out by either side

---

[67] William E. Hocking, *Freedom of the Press: A Framework of Principles,* New York, 1947, p. 35, n. 20.

in the language of the other.[68] This, it will be noted, was an agreement between more or less independent broadcasting companies. It is significant that after the Nazis assumed power, they immediately got their hands on radio as well as on all other media of communication. So it was the German government that, in February 26, 1934, as a reflection of the short-lived *détente* between it and the Polish government, agreed to work in continous cooperation with the latter in all matters relating to public opinion, press and propaganda. As a result of this understanding, for some time press comment in each of the two states on events and tendencies in the others was unusually restrained.[69]

In this same year (1934) the independent Austrian radio "Ravag," and the Czech "Radio-Journal," entered into an agreement whereby each party promised to abstain from all propaganda directed against the other, and likewise to exclude anything calculated to wound the feelings of the population or government of the other party.[70] And in July, 1936, Austria and Germany agreed to refrain from all aggressive use of wireless, films, news services and the theater, but this agreement was not destined to last very long.[71] Also, Poland and Lithuania agreed in November, 1938 not to permit their press to make use of propaganda unfavorable to the other.[72]

Up to the present time the most all-embracing treaty against propaganda, either by radio or any other medium, is that completed at Geneva in September 23, 1936, as the "Convention Concerning the Use of Broadcasting in the Cause of Peace." Twenty-two states became parties to it, thirteen by ratification and nine by accession. The convention came into force April 2, 1938.[73]

A study of the 1936 deliberations at Geneva throws much light on the entire problem of international propaganda and should be considered in connection with the long and arduous efforts made toward the same end since the Second World War by various organs and agencies of the United Nations. The obligations set forth in the 1936 treaty may be summarized as follows:

1) The parties promise: To prohibit, or stop without delay within their territories the broadcasting of transmissions of a nature to incite the population of any territory "to acts incompatible with the internal

[68] L. O. N., Doc. 602 M 240. 1931. IX-IX Disarmament 1931 IX. 19. Howard S. LeRoy, "Treaty Regulation of International Radio and Shortwave Broadcasting," *Am. J. Int. Law,* Vol. 32 (1938), pp. 719-728.

[69] Arnold Toynbee, *Survey of International Affairs 1935,* Vol. I (1936), p. 204.

[70] *Rev. Int. de la Radioélectricité,* (1934), p. 96.

[71] Arnold Toynbee, *op. cit.,* 1936, pp. 450-452.

[72] Martin, *op. cit.,* p. 95, citing Ignaz Rothenberg, *The Newspaper,* London, 1946, p. 5.

[73] L. O. N. *Treaty Series,* 1938, Vol. 186, pp. 303-317; *Am. J. Int. Law,* Vol. 32 (1938), Supp., p. 113.

order or the security" of any signatory state (Art. 1);

2) To ensure that their transmissions do not constitute an incitement to war, or to acts likely to lead to war (Art. 2);

3) To prohibit, or stop without delay all transmissions likely to harm good international understanding on account of an inaccuracy which the broadcaster knew, or ought to have known; also, to rectify such statements at the earliest possible moment by the most effective means, even if the inexactitude became apparent only after the broadcast had taken place (Art. 3);

4) In time of crisis especially, to see that no information on international relations be broadcast unless its accuracy has been properly verified by all means within the power of the persons responsible for the emission (Art. 4). This excellent provision is almost unique in the annals of such treaty efforts.

Furthermore, the parties were strongly urged to "take into account the influence that may be exercised on good international understanding by transmissions of such a character as to harm the interests or offend the national, political, religious, or social sentiments of other peoples." Special vigilance was recommended in regard to transmissions in a foreign tongue (a matter early recognized, and still a matter of special urgency). In times of international tension, the parties were urged to employ broadcasts of a nature to lessen the tension and restore a peaceful atmosphere.

The United States took part in the 1936 deliberations but declined to ratify the finished treaty. The Secretary of State informed the Secretary-General of the League of Nations that the United States preferred to rely on "voluntary and patriotic cooperation of the broadcasting companies," pointing out that "under its present laws, this government does not control the content of or censor radio programs broadcast in the United States."[74] To show how times have changed, it is interesting to read in this same note the explanation that the broadcasting of programs in the United States intended for the population of another state was "rare," since the American broadcasting stations "depend for their support largely upon the sale of time to sponsors who desire to sell products to persons within the service range of the stations."[75] One significant and quite valid objection made was that such treaties were not likely to interest the very states whose broadcasting was the most objectionable and the most dangerous to world peace. This result had been foreseen by the Finnish government which, prior to the conference, remarked:[76]

> . . . it is extremely probable that the signatory states would be among those which, even without being committed by such a conven-

---

[74] L. O. N., Doc. C. L. 44.1936. XII. Annex, p. 22, n.
[75] Ibid.
[76] Ibid., p. 5, n. 1.

tion, do not adopt in the matter of broadcasting, an attitude contrary to the proposed stipulation.

Polish and Hungarian governments expressed similar views.[77] Significantly and ominously, Germany, Italy and Japan did not sign.

After the Second World War, the United Nations took note of the existence of this treaty and brought it to the attention of the members. The General Assembly, by resolution December 17, 1954, decided to ask the member states whether they desired to transfer to the United Nations the functions under this treaty formerly entrusted to the League, and to elicit this information directed the Secretary General to circulate a protocol to the contracting states. This protocol was in three parts. 1) It provided for the transfer already mentioned; 2) it permitted the accession of members and non-members which had not signed the original convention; 3) it suggested the addition of new articles providing that each Contracting State "shall refrain from radio broadcasts that would mean unfair attacks or slanders against other peoples anywhere and in so doing conform strictly to an ethical conduct in the interest of world peace by reporting facts truly and objectively, and to provide that each High Contracting Party shall not interfere with the reception, within its territory, of foreign radio broadcasts."[78]

By June, 1957, 14 of the 26 states parties to the Convention had replied. Fourteen expressed approval of the proposed transfer of functions, three (Burma, Denmark, Ireland) expressed approval of the entire draft protocol, while one (Switzerland) considered itself not bound by the new articles.[79]

From what has been said so far, it is evident that the most advanced treaties relating to the use of radio can be expected from those states already having achieved the greatest degree of mutual cooperation, and among whom relations are already of a more or less amicable nature, Consequently, it is not surprising to observe that the Latin American republics have entered into more treaties in this field than any other group of states. The conventions between these nations are notable not only for their negative proposals aimed at the suppression of objectionable broadcasts, but also for their many practical suggestions for the use of radio for the promotion of international understanding and good will.

The Seventh Pan American Conference, held at Montevideo in December, 1933, made a number of general recommendations for the positive use of radio to promote better international relations, and

---

[77] *Ibid.*, p. 20 ff., and L. O. N., Conf./E.R.P./1st Session, P.V. 1/(1)-9 (1), Minutes, pp. 16-17.

[78] U.N. General Assembly Res. 841 (IX), December 17, 1954, *U. N. Yearbook 1954*, pp. 241-242.

[79] U. N., *Annual Report of the Secretary-General*, June 16, 1956 to June 15, 1957, G.A.O.R., 12th Sess., Supp. 1, 1927, p. 83.

directed the Pan American Union to prepare a plan along such lines. No definite action against propaganda was taken at this time, but there was a growing sense of appreciation of the ominous possibilities of broadcasting.[80] To deal with this problem a special agreement was signed at Buenos Aires on April 10, 1935, known as the "South American Regional Agreement on Radio Communications." This accord contained a pledge by the parties to control the sources and accuracy of information broadcast, avoid defamatory transmissions, and abstain from participation in political and social movements taking place in other adhering states.[81]

In December, 1936, at the Inter-American Conference for the Maintenance of Peace, held in Buenos Aires, three major resolutions concerning broadcasting and peace were approved.[82] Resolution XIV recommended, among other things, that the American states adhere to the Geneva Radio Treaty of 1936 and the South American Regional Agreement of April 10, 1935. Resolution XV proposed measures for the positive use of radio to promote international understanding, and warned the parties to avoid messages likely to disturb peaceful relations or wound the national susceptibilities of foreign listeners. A third (Resolution XXI) offered suggestions for the establishment of a Pan American Radio Hour, administered by the Pan American Union, and again warned that comment upon the local political affairs of American nations, as well as subversive propaganda, should not be permitted on this hour. This agreement was revised at Rio de Janeiro in 1937. There it was specifically suggested that the contracting powers should adopt measures to assure that the international political news broadcasts concerning contracting states should be made with full disclosure of authorized and unimpeachable sources; that all emissions should be avoided which might put a strain upon international relations, offend the national sentiments of other peoples, or disturb international activities designed to promote peace. Further recommendations concerned the positive use of radio in the service of peace.[83] A still more detailed plan for such positive use of radio was voted at the Eighth Pan American Conference, held at Lima in December, 1938. [84] A further revision took place on January 17, 1940, when the South American Radio Communications Agreement was signed at Santiago. [85] Among other stipulations, it was stated that the administrations of the signatory countries were

---

[80] Dept. of State, *Conference Series*, No. 19 (1934), pp. 279-280.
[81] Manley O. Hudson, *International Legislation*, Vol. VII (1941), No. 407.
[82] Dept. of State, *Conference Series*, No. 33 (1937), pp. 218-223.
[83] Hudson, *op. cit.*, Vol. 7 (1941), No. 486.
[84] Dept. of State, *Conference Series*, No. 50 (1941), pp. 154-155; Charles G. Fenwick, "Intervention by Way of Propaganda," *Am. J. Int. Law*, Vol. 35 (1941), pp. 626-631.
[85] Hudson, *op. cit.*, Vol. VIII (1949), No. 576.

to ensure that the dissemination of news or of commentaries which might disturb the good relations between States, offend national sentiment of other countries or injure the work of the organization and consolidation of peace, as well as all which might offend the officially designated authorities of States, shall be avoided."

As might have been expected, the emerging international crisis put a halt to this movement. In June, 1940, at the meeting of the Inter-American Neutrality Committee at Rio de Janeiro, it was recognized that since the International Convention for the Use of Broadcasting in the Cause of Peace and the South American conventions on radio communications, had been designed for times of peace, each state should now be left free to decide to what extent the application of such obligations would be in accord with the duties of neutrality.[86] And at Havana, on July 21-30, 1940, when the Foreign Ministers met in their second session, the vital problem was then how to find appropriate means of resisting subversive and disruptive propaganda from Axis countries. So the American states were urged to adopt all necessary measures to prevent and suppress activities of foreign source tending to subvert their domestic institutions or foment disorder in their internal political affairs.[87] Secretary Hull, commenting on these measures, declared that they were directed at "propaganda designed on the one hand to stir up dissension in the Western Hemisphere by beguiling and misleading the people, and, on the other hand, to intimidate them by express or implied threats of what may happen if the American republics fail to recognize and to take into account the foreign purposes and policies of certain foreign governments."[88]

Action taken at the Bogota Conference (1948) should be noted here, although in form aimed mainly at non-American propaganda. While the end of the Second World War relieved Latin American states of the worst dangers of Nazi and Fascist indoctrination originaating in Europe, the Western Hemisphere still remained exposed to the now universal and all-pervading menace of Communist propaganda. This redoubtable menace became clear with the worsening of the international situation, so that by 1948 the American republics apparently had become convinced of the necessity of concerted defensive measures. Consequently, at the Conference of Bogota, held in that year, the American republics pledged themselves to take the necessary measures to deal energetically with subversive propaganda coming from abroad and dangerous to American institutions and public order. In Resolution 32, Par. 3, the American republics voted "To adopt, within their respective territories and in accordance with their respective constitutional provisions, the measures necessary to eradicate and

---

[86] Charles G. Fenwick, "The American Neutrality Committee," *Am. J. Int. Law*, Vol. 35 (1941), pp. 12, 34 ff.

[87] Text in *Am. J. Int. Law*, Vol. 35 (1941), Supp., p. 1.

[88] *Dept. of State Bulletin*, August 3, 1940, Vol. III, No. 58, p. 66.

prevent activities directed, assisted, or instigated by foreign governments, organizations or individuals tending to overthrow their institutions by violence, to foment disorder in their domestic political life, or to disturb, by means of pressure, subversive propaganda, threats or by any other means, the free and sovereign right of their peoples to govern themselves in accordance with their democratic aspirations."[89]

In 1949, a dispute arose between the Republic of Santo Domingo and Haiti, the latter claiming to be a victim of "moral aggression." One of its former colonels, taking refuge in Santo Domingo, had made broadcasts of an "extremely vulgar and provocative nature offensive to the President of the Republic of Haiti," aimed at the overthrow of the Haitian government, thus constituting "moral aggression."[90] After the matter had been submitted to the Council of Consultation of the Organization of American States, the two states settled the matter amicably, agreeing not to

> tolerate in their respective territories the activities of any individuals, groups, or parties, national or foreign, that have as their object the disturbance of the domestic peace of either of the two neighboring Republics or of any other friendly nation.[91]

In April, 1950, the OAS Council called upon the governments of "Haiti and the Dominican Republic to avoid any systematic and hostile propaganda against one another or against any American country."[92]

From another part of the world, the April 1948 agreement between India and Pakistan, already mentioned in another connection, should be noted again here for the sake of completeness. In that agreement the two governments promised to "insure that their respective organizations handling publicity, including publicity through radio and film, refrain from and control" propaganda against the other dominion, or news "likely to inflame, or cause fear or alarm to, the population or section of the population of either dominion."[93]

In a recent accord, Tunisia and the United Arab Republic agreed not to use their radios to attack each other. In Tunis it was generally believed that the main object of this agreement was to curb attacks on President Bourguiba by the Voice of the Arabs from Cairo. It was

---

[89] 9th International Conference of American States, Bogota, Colombia (*Report of the United States Delegation*), Dept. of State Publ. 3263, International Organization and Conference Series II, American Republics, 3, p. 266 ff.; *Annals of the Organization of American States*, Vol. I (1949), p. 134.

[90] See Charles G Fenwick, "Proposed Control Over the Radio as an Inter-American Duty in Cases of Civil Strife," *Am. J. of Int. Law*, Vol. 48 (1954), pp. 289-292. *Annals of the Organization of American States*, Vol. I (1949), pp. 217-219.

[91] *Ibid.*, p. 326.

[92] *Ibid.*, Vol. III (1951), p. 23.

[93] *Supra*, p. 88

likewise agreed that political refugees from one Arab country could be granted asylum in another, but that such refugees would be prevented from engaging in any political activity.[94]

So far as action under United Nations auspices is concerned, with the exception of the revival of the League of Nations Treaty, activities have taken the form of draft resolutions and unratified conventions. For this reason, although these actions are not without legal significance and are of first rank importance in the overall story of propaganda control, they will be reserved for discussion in Part III under the heading of Remedies and Improvements.

To sum up the treaty situation: between certain groups of countries, notably those adhering to the League of Nations Treaty and the Latin American countries, restraints imposed by treaties give added strength to other sources of law forbidding defamatory as well as other kinds of harmful propaganda. The fact that more universal conventions have not been adopted should not be interpreted as detracting in any way from the basic rule drawn from other sources condemning defamatory propaganda. This is particularly so since the objection which has prevented acceptance by states like Great Britain and the United States of more universal treaty coverage of the subject has not been disagreement with the substantive rule condemning such propaganda, but reluctance to assume responsibility for controlling private utterances. Whatever problems this reluctance may raise for the restraint of private expressions, it does not call in question the obligation of states themselves to refrain from defamatory propaganda.

Judicial Decisions

While judicial decisions on the specific question of defamatory radio propaganda by states do not appear to have arisen, there have been decisions establishing the general liability of states for comparable wrongful acts.

In the famous Trail Smelter case[95] the damage in question took the form of allowing fumes produced by the smelter to escape and travel from British Columbia to the State of Washington. The matter

---

94 *New York Times*, Feb. 8, 1961.

95 Arbitration between the United States and Canada, Decision of Tribunal reported March 11, 1941, *Am. J. Int. Law*, Vol. 35 (1941), pp. 684, 716; Dept. of State Publication 1649, Arbitration Ser. 8, pp. 31-32. C. C. Hyde, citing this case, writes: "The underlying principle would seem to be that what a State claims the right exclusively to control, such as its own territory, it must possess the power and accept the obligation to endeavor so to control as to prevent occurrences therein from becoming by any process the immediate cause of such injury to a foreign State as the latter, in consequence of the propriety of its own conduct, should not be subjected to at the hands of a neighbor." *Op. cit.*, Vol. I, pp. 723-725.

was submitted by mutual agreement to an arbitral tribunal. The tribunal decided that

> Under the principles of international law, as well as of the law of the United States, no state has the right to use or permit the use of its territory in such a manner as to cause injury by fumes in or to the territory of another or the properties or persons thereon, when the case is of serious consequence and the injury is established by clear and convincing evidence.

Assuming that damage is demonstrable, it is not much of a step from harmful fumes to harmful words caused by electronic impulses across national boundaries. And there is ample historical evidence for the proposition that defamatory propaganda has caused damage to particular states and to international relations in general.

Also, in the Corfu Channel Case[96] which concerned heavy damage done by mines to British warships passing through the Channel, the International Court of Justice held that in view of "every state's obligation not to allow knowingly its territory to be used for acts contrary to the rights of those states," the Albanian authorities were bound to give warning of the presence of a mine field in Albanian waters. This is an example of the basic doctrine known as "abuse of rights," reflected in the famous maxim, *Sic utere tuo ut alienum non laedas.* This principle, which has been in some form familiar to both the civil and the common law, and to other systems as well, comes into play in international law when a state, acting by virtue of a right enjoyed under international law, nevertheless proceeds in an arbitrary manner causing unreasonable damage to another state or its nationals.[97] For example, a nation is permitted in principle to grant its nationality to an individual or to withdraw it at will. But if it exercises this right in an unreasonable manner the aggrieved state is entitled to make a complaint.[98]

To summarize the law on defamatory propaganda by a state: in spite of the admitted prevalence of breaches of the rule, the cumulative effect of customary international law, the writings of publicists, the existing treaties between certain nations, decisions on broad principles of state liability for harmful acts, and the general principles of law on libel, slander, and particular kinds of verbal attacks of special relevance to international affairs, appears to be the establishment of an international rule of law making defamatory propaganda by a state illegal.

---

[96] *I. C. J. Reports,* 1949, pp. 4, 26.

[97] Nicolas Politis, "Le Problème des Limitations de la Souveraineté et la Théorie de l'Abus des Droits," *Hague Recueil,* Vol. VI (1925), pp. 1-121; Oppenheim, Vol. I, Sec. 155a.

[98] *Ibid.,* Sec. 293.

Chapter VII

State Responsibility for
Private Propaganda

NATURE OF THE PROBLEM

The legal analysis up to this point has been designed to establish, first, the substantive wrongfulness under international law of warmongering, subversive, and defamatory propaganda, and second, the legal responsibility of states for their own acts when engaging in any of these three kinds of wrongful conduct.

The legal discussion from this point on is primarily concerned, not with the substantive illegality of particular kinds of propaganda, but with the question of the extent to which the law has imposed responsibility going beyond the state's responsibility for its own act. The present chapter and the one which follows deal with two problems under international law: the responsibility of the state for acts of individuals, and the responsibility of individuals (as a result of official conduct) for the acts of the states. There will then be considered the responsibility of individuals for their own acts as individuals, both under international law and domestic law.

Since many examples of private propaganda have been intermingled with the earlier discussion of both the history and the law of propaganda, and since a number of other examples will be used in the legal discussion which follows, it will not be necessary here to set forth a special array of illustrative exhibits to show the nature of the problem. It will be sufficient to recall a few of the most conspicuous types of situation in which the problem arises. In the warmongering category, we may recall the private agitation in the Hearst newspapers preceding the Spanish-American War. In the subversive propaganda category, we have noted the agitations of irredentist groups preceding World War I. And in the defamatory propaganda category, we have seen examples of newspaper attacks by private individuals which have elicited official protests from governments.

The Law of State Responsibility for Private Acts of Propaganda

Before we look into the various sources of international law, it might be well to indicate the pattern around which the law will be discussed, since it is somewhat different from the pattern of the preceding chapters and also from the pattern of other discussions of this subject. The thread that runs through the analysis is this: as in any question of the liability of one legal entity for the acts of another, the degree of control which the first entity has to exercise over the act in order to become liable is of primary importance. The other principal variable is the seriousness or dangerousness of the conduct involved. It is the interplay of these two variables that should be watched for in the ensuing attempt to trace the outlines of the law on this subject.

Since the *writings of publicists* are so closely connected with *customary international law* as a source, the two sources will be brought together here. Moreover, there will be some reference to domestic statutes (or the lack of them) as bearing on the question of customary international practice. The primary operative effect of these domestic statutes is to act directly upon offending individuals within particular countries, and in this aspect of their function they will be discussed in the chapter on individual responsibility for private propaganda. In the present chapter these statutes are of interest as throwing light on the question whether states, by passing such statutes, have shown that they believe that they are under an international obligation to restrain certain kinds of conduct by individuals.

Subversive Propaganda

Let us look first at the question whether the state is under any obligation to protect foreign states from individual subversive propaganda. Two doctrines appear to have grown up, and there is a considerable divergence between them. These may be called the broad responsibility school (insurance) and the narrow responsibility school (neutrality).

Broad Responsibility School

According to this concept, called by some the "mutual insurance school," each state would be held to strict accountability in case private individuals under its jurisdiction should attempt to foment political troubles in a friendly foreign state. Proponents of this view hold that the nation should be quick to protect not only its own security, but also that of its neighbors. Such action, it is said, is commanded by enlightened self-interest; if a state disregards entirely those acts which, although they do not menace its own interests, are harmful or even dangerous to other states, it may become a repair for unscrupulous individuals. In addition, tolerance of such conditions may actually provoke reprisals on the part of some foreign power. Such internal disorders instigated from abroad are a grave menace to peace and security. Consequently, the adoption by the nations of a policy of mutual insurance against subversion from abroad is recommended by certain higher considerations, notably the welfare of the internaional community.[1] The *rationale* underlying such views is authoritatively stated as follows in the *International Law of the Future*:[2]

> If States are to live together as good neighbors in the Community of States, it is not enough that they be obligated to refrain from official intervention in the internal affairs of other States. It is necessary also that each State be assured of its internal security, free from subversive influence due to *non-official* activities in other States.

Much respectable authority can be assembled in support of this school of thought. It is not surprising that much of it originated in Germany, where the power of the state over the individual has always been great. German writers attribute to the state a heavy responsibility in relation to political agitation caused by private individuals and injurious to foreign nations. Thus Von Liszt considers contrary to international law "every enterprise directed against the existence or security of another state. Each state has a duty to see that no enterprise of this kind is prepared or executed on territory submitted to its authority, either by its nationals, or by foreigners."[3] Several French writers, including Despagnet, Pradier-Fodéré, and Fauchille, have expressed similar views.[4] According to Rivier, "Agita-

---

[1] The matter has been admirably summarized recently by a member of this school of writers. After reviewing the authorities, he says: "These persuasive recitals would seem to be conclusive as to the obligation of a state to prevent revolutionary activities and hostile propaganda by private individuals against foreign states. In default of such a duty, the state has incurred an international responsibility. It is therefore concluded that the view that international law is not violated by private hostile actions against foreign governments may well have become an archaic hangover not at all consonant with international morality and must probably be regarded as unsound. It may be said to be a principle emerging from the international conventions here reviewed that a state's tolerance of private revolutionary activities and hostile propaganda against foreign nations is not only illegal under modern international law but it is also a disservice to the cause of international peace and security." Garcia-Mora, *op. cit.*, p. 108.

[2] *Am. J. Int. Law*, Vol. 38 (1944), Supp., p. 78 ff., discussion under Principle 4: "Each State has a legal duty to prevent the organization within its territory of activities calculated to foment civil strife in the territory of any other State." Italics supplied.

[3] Franz von Liszt, *Le Droit International, Exposé Systématique*, (Gidel translation), Paris, 1927, p. 69.

[4] Frantz Despagnet, *Cours de Droit International Public*, 2d ed., Paris, 1899, pp. 179 ff.; Pradier-Fodéré, *Traité de Droit Public Européen et Américain*, 8 vols., Paris, 1885-1906, Vol. I, Sec. 238; Fauchille, *op. cit.*, Vol. I, Secs. 245, 255, 256.

tions fomented, undertaken, even tolerated in one country against the integrity of the territory of another, under color of nationality, revenge, religious solidarity, etc., are directly contrary to the right of conservation and constitute, as such, positive violations of international law."[5] See also DeLouter, who asserts that "every state is obliged to see that its territory does not serve those planning an attempt against neighboring governments, and that it does not become in any manner a danger for any other state."[6]

These views are not entirely confined to the writers. A certain amount of domestic legislation is similarly oriented. Thus in Belgium, ever since 1858, a prison term awaits anyone aiming at the destruction or modification of the form of government of a foreign state, or inciting the inhabitants thereof to arm themselves against their leaders.[7] The 1928 Spanish Code outlaws attempts against the internal or external security of a foreign country. Similar laws have been passed in Czechoslovakia, Greece, Switzerland, Finland and Yugoslavia. Liechtenstein, Belgium and Israel provide for the punishment of anyone instigating rebellion and endangering the security of foreign states.[8]

Thus there is considerable authority to substantiate the view advanced by the broad responsibility school. But the states are far from being in accord on this matter. Britain and the United States, for example, have maintained an entirely different point of view.[9]

Before leaving this discussion of the broad responsibility or insurance school, it should be remarked that even those who favor this concept do not hold the state responsible in case of mere moral support given by individuals to a subversive movement in another country.[10] But we must admit that to draw a line between mere "moral support" and psychological pressures which risk grave injury to a foreign state is becoming more and more difficult in modern times, due to the invention of redoubtable techniques of mass persuasion, and to the skill of clever agitators in the pay of some dictatorship bent on world conquest.

Nevertheless, the rule as stated as to mere moral support apparently still stands. Vigorous moral support was given by individuals

---

[5] Alphonse Rivier, *Principes du Droit des Gens*, 2 vols., Paris, 1896, Vol. I, p. 266.

[6] Jan De Louter, *Le Droit International Public Positif*, 2 vols., Oxford, 1920, Vol. I, p. 244.

[7] Act of March 12, 1858, Art. 5, cited by Pella, "La Protection de la Paix par le Droit Interne," *Rev. Gén. de Dr. Int. Pub.*, Vol. 40 (1933), p. 446.

[8] See compilation of local laws aimed to curb propaganda causing international unrest, in Pella, *op. cit.*, pp. 801-803, Martin, *op. cit.*, pp. 237 ff., and Fernand Terrou and Lucien Solal, *Legislation for Press, Film and Radio*, Paris (UNESCO), 1961, pp. 314 ff.

[9] See discussion of *Narrow Responsibility School* in following subsection.

[10] Stowell, *op. cit.*, p. 378.

or groups of individuals in foreign lands on the occasion of the Greek War of Independence, the Polish insurrections of 1832 and 1863, the Hungarian uprising of 1848, and the Boer War of 1898-1899. It is believed that so long as such demonstrations are merely the expressions of popular feeling, the state where they occur is not bound to do anything about it.[11] Thus in 1898, when Italians on Swiss soil staged a popular demonstration in support of an insurrection in Milan, and paraded with placards urging Italians to aid their oppressed brothers, the Federal report on the incident stated: "From the international point of view, there was no reason to act; the fact that the Italians worked themselves up with indignant speeches on what was going on at home and against the government of their own country could not constitute for us a motive for intervention."[12]

Narrow Responsibility School

A second concept of the proper rule applicable to subversive propaganda by individuals may be called the Narrow Responsibility School, known to some as the Neutrality Doctrine. The latter term is taken from an analogous rule, applicable in time of war, which requires the neutral state to abstain from conduct harmful to a belligerent, but ordinarily without any obligation to intervene if an individual under its jurisdiction indulges in similar conduct.[13] There are indications, however, that this view, so far as subversive propaganda is concerned, has been somewhat weakened by the deleterious effects, even in "free" states, of Communist propaganda sparked from abroad. This doctrine of narrow responsibility, to which Britain and the United States, despite some inconsistencies, are devoted, is based on several major considerations. In part it is a reflection of the special position of its proponents which, as self-confident democracies, do not fear the possible effects of subversive propaganda originating abroad. Another reason underlying this concept is the fear that the adoption of a contrary rule would lead the state to adopt measures inconsistent with traditional freedoms of speech, press and assembly. The reason just given was set forth in the reply of the Secretary of State in 1911 to protests from Mexico against private propaganda in the United States.[14]

> . . . the carrying on of a mere propaganda either by writing or speaking does not constitute an offense against the law of nations nor does it constitute an offense against the local law since freedom of speech

---

[11] Ibid., p. 378, n. 84.

[12] "Chronique des Faits Internationaux," Rev. Gén. de Dr. Int. Pub., Vol. V (1898), pp. 480, 483.

[13] Lauterpacht, "Revolutionary Activities by Private Persons Against Foreign States," Am. J. Int. Law, Vol. 22 (1928), p.113; Moore, Digest, Vol. VII, p. 980.

[14] Hackworth, Digest, Vol. II, p. 142.

and of the press is, under the Constitution of the United States, absolutely assured to those dwelling within its jurisdiction.

In these states the comforting and over-optimistic opinion has also been voiced that the best way to meet the dangers inherent in such maneuvers is to assure a wider hearing for all views, in the hope that the common sense of the people will triumph over foreign agitation.[15] Finally, it has been asserted that

> A state must not be forced into the impossible position, dangerously approaching intervention, of a guardian of other states' constitutions and tranquility. Foreign governments themselves should secure this end, either by adequately enforcing their own laws or else by creating reasonable conditions for their firm establishment.[16]

Such counsels of perfection, however, cannot be expected to impress the leaders of weak states exposed to conflagrations started by powerful, well-subventioned incendiaries on the other side of the frontier.

American practice is reflected in a statute passed in 1917.[17] The United States has refused energetically to restrain the liberty of speech or press guaranteed by the Constitution, even when the use of this liberty was giving foreign nations considerable trouble. Thus Bayard, Secretary of State, in reply to a complaint from the Spanish Minister that American soil was being used as a base for hostile agitation in Cuba against the Spanish government, states as follows:

> The Executive of the United States has no authority to take cognizance of individual opinions and the manifestations thereof, even when taking the shape of revolutionary or seditious expressions directed against our own government, and it is no less incompetent to pass upon the subversive character of utterances alleged to contravene the laws of another land.[18]

Great Britain has had many occasions to announce officially a

---

[15] Archives Diplomatiques, Vol. II, (1876-1877), p. 298; *U. N. Weekly Bulletin, November* 1947, p. 4.

[16] Lauterpacht, *op. cit.,* p. 129. This position has been attacked boldly in a recent study by García-Mora. "It must be added," he writes, "that it is most questionable on grounds of public policy whether the United States can remain totally passive in the presence of activities calculated to create hostile feelings in foreign states and, more specifically, to cause a breach of peace between nations." García-Mora, *op. cit.,* p. 89.

[17] Act of June 15, 1917, 40 Stat. 223, Title V. See Moore, *Digest*, Vol. VII, pp. 908-934, for development and application of an earlier statute. See also, Hackworth, *Digest,* Vol. VII, pp. 394 ff.

[18] Mr. Bayard to Mr. Valera, July 31, 1885, *For. Rel.* (1883), pp. 776-778, at p. 776. On the other hand anti-anarchist laws in the United States would seem to offer some protection against subversive propaganda by individuals against foreign states. (Martin, *op. cit.,* p.130). Thus, a New Jersey law originating in 1902 states that "Any person who, in public or private, by speech, writing, printing, or otherwise, advocates the subversion or destruction by force of any and all government, or attempts by speech, writing, printing, or otherwise to incite or abet, promote, or encourage hostility or opposition to any and all government, is

similar doctrine.[19] Thus when the French complained of seditious publications sent to France by political refugees resident in England, the British refused to accept the French thesis that governments must repress or punish publications of a nature to cause injury to the interests and honor of foreign states.[20] True, the British are disposed to take action against individuals whose publications constitute criminal libel against a foreign sovereign, but even here their attitude is less certain today than in former times, as, for instance, when Peltier was convicted for a libel on Napoleon.[21] In 1852, when foreign powers were again demanding that British do something about the subversive activities carried on by refugees resident in England, again the latter refused to take action, invoking its traditional liberties of freedom on the press.[22] Similarly, in 1856, Britain refused to associate itself with the efforts of other powers to curb injurious attacks appearing in the Belgian press, but admitted that action would be justified if the attacks took the form of incitements to assassination.[23] Gladstone, in 1873, expressed similar views.[24]

But even the British and the Americans join the proponents of the broad responsibility school in two exceptional cases: 1) when the maneuvers hostile to a friendly state take the form of an "overt act," and 2) when they constitute incitement to murder.[25]

---

guilty of a high misdemeanor. . . ." (*N. J. Statutes Annotated*, permanent ed., 1953, Title 2A: 148-7.) The law of that state punishes anyone who incites, promotes, encourages or attempts an assault on any "ruler, governor, or other chief executive of any state, or heir apparent or heir presumptive to the throne of a foreign state." (Ibid., 2A: 148-6) And the following furnishes a precedent which, for our purposes, is particularly significant: "If any person, organization, society or order brings, introduces, or circulates, or aids, assists, or is instrumental in bringing, introducing or circulating within this state any printed or written paper, pamphlet, book or circular with intent to incite, promote or encourage hostility or opposition to, or the subversion or destruction of any and all government, such person or the members of such organization, society or order in any way responsible therefore, shall be guilty of a high misdemeanor. . . ." (*Ibid.*, 2A:148-9).

[19] British laws and cases reviewed by Preuss, "La Répression des Crimes et Délits contre la Sûreté des Étrangers," *Rev. Gén. de Dr. Int. Pub.*, Vol. 40 (1933), pp. 631 ff.

[20] *Annual Register*, Vol. 45 (1803), pp. 656 ff.

[21] *Rex. v. Peltier*, 28 St. Trials, 530, 617 (1803).

[22] *British and Foreign State Papers*, Vol. 42 (1852-1853), London, 1864, pp. 401 ff.

[23] *Ibid.*, Vol. 46, pp. 124 ff.

[24] *Hansard*, 3rd series, Vol. 215 (1875), p. 634. W. F. Craies, "Le Droit d'Expulsion des Étrangers en Angleterre," *J. de Dr. Int. Privé, Vol.* 16 (1889), pp. 357, 379.

[25] The principle is illustrated by the British case of *Reg. v. Most*, L. R., 7 Q. B. Q. 244 (1881), in which the court declared that the fact of plotting in England against the peace of a foreign State did constitute a crime, when it amounted to preparation for murder or incitement to murder. Defendant published in a British newspaper an article exulting over the recent murder of the Emperor of Russia, commending it as an example to revolutionists throughout the world.

The "Overt Act"

If private individuals are engaged in organizing an expedition on domestic soil with the intention of giving aid and support to a subversive movement in a foreign country, then the state must use the means at its disposal to repress such activities or, if it cannot prevent them, must punish the perpetrators. If the act is the actual preparation, organization, or setting on foot of an armed expedition with subversive designs on another power, then the responsibility of the state is engaged. It should follow, therefore, that propaganda employed as part and parcel of such unlawful hostile preparations should equally come under the ban of the law as an "overt act." To illustrate: if in State A a group of riflemen is being organized with the intention of crossing the frontier into State B, there to take part in a revolt against the latter's government, and a private newspaper or independent radio chain puts on an organized campaign for recruits, or solicits financial support in aid of the expedition, then the responsibility of State A is clear. If, on the other hand, this uncontrolled press or radio in State A is merely making a demonstration of moral support in behalf of the rebels in State B, but with no direct connection with the armed expedition, then such expressions of opinion may be tolerated by the latter government without giving State B a legal right to demand reparation.[26] This, it would seem, is the proper interpretation of the American statute dating back to 1794,[27] which punishes anyone for beginning a military or naval expedition against a friendly foreign state, including anyone who "provides or prepares a means for," or "furnishes the money for," such an expedition.[28] But this statute does not seek to prohibit mere moral agitation.[29] The British practice is to refuse to take action in case of a conspiracy, plot or other treasonable practices against a foreign state unless it amounts to levying of war (the overt act), or, as mentioned below, is related to incitement to

---

[26] Whitton, op. cit. (Hague Recueil), p. 590.

[27] Am. J. Int. Law, Vol. 11 (1917), Supp., p. 186.

[28] 18 U.S.C.A. 906, re-enacted most recently in 1948. See application of this statute to the Cuba invasion in Arthur Larson, "The Cuba Fiasco and the Rule of Law," Saturday Review, Vol. 44 (May 13, 1961), pp. 28, 53.

[29] See reply of Secretary of State Knox to a protest made by the Mexican Government against the toleration of the activities of Madero, who was agitating, from American soil, for the overturn of the Mexican Government: "The Department of State has the honor again to suggest to the Mexican Ambassador for his consideration the fact that under the Constitution of the United States free speech is absolutely assured, and that therefore in order to bring inflammatory speeches or propaganda within the statutes of the United States it will be necessary that some *definite act or acts* of which the mind can take cognizance be proved in addition to the mere word, written or spoken, which, even though indicative of the strongest desire and the most determined purpose to do the forbidden act, will not constitute the offense." (Italics supplied) U.S. For. Rels., 1911, p. 393.

murder.[30] Similarly, the French government has admitted that it is under obligation to prevent the organization of local plots against foreign territories, or the continuance by refugees of war against the home country.[31] In short, while revolutionary propaganda ordinarily does not fall within the scope of hostile acts which a state feels that it is bound to prevent, if an "overt act" has taken place, the responsibility of the state is engaged. The same is true with regard to a second exceptional situation, now to be discussed.

Terroristic Propaganda

If the subversive propaganda carried on by private individuals takes the form of terroristic incitement, here again the case is considered to be of such gravity that the state involved must take appropriate action if it is not to be held strictly accountable. Thus, if individuals are making plans to murder or assassinate the representative of a foreign state, even if the act is to take place on foreign soil, the local government is under a duty to employ all reasonable means of suppression or punishment, or both. Such acts are considered so heinous that even in time of war they are held to constitute a violation of international law.[32] Since the responsibility of the state is engaged if it is informed that one or more individuals under its jurisdiction plan to assassinate an official representative of a foreign state, the same rule must logically apply in case such persons are using the media of information to promote such plans, or to incite persons to commit such acts, as Habicht did in his broadcasts against Dollfuss. This follows as a corollary from the international rule with respect to terrorism, as set forth in the resolution of the Council of the League of Nations on December 19. 1934:[33]

> The Council recalls, that it is the duty of every State neither to encourage nor tolerate on its territory any terrorist activity with a political purpose; That every State must do all in its power to prevent and repress acts of this nature and must for this purpose lend its assistance to governments which request it.

---

[30] Preuss, op. cit., ("La Répression des Crimes," etc.) pp. 631 ff.

[31] Archives Parlementaires, Vol. 82 (1833), pp. 32 ff. See statement in Chamber of Deputies by the Duc de Broglie, Minister of Foreign Affairs, declaring that the refugee has no immunity, and in the interest both of France and his own country must not "provoke among friendly governments revolt, sedition or disorders, nor compromise the security of the country by what is called propaganda, the very propaganda you have condemned at this tribune." Ibid., p. 33.

[32] Fauchille, op. cit., Vol. II, Sec. 1081[1], Art. 23, Hague Conventions of 1899 and 1907.

[33] L. O. N., Official Journal, Minutes of Council, 15th year, No. 12 (Part II), December 1934, p. 1759.

The United Nations, in its Draft Code of Offenses Against the Peace and Security of Mankind, included as No. 6 of such offenses:[34]

> The undertaking or encouragement by the authorities of a State of terrorist activities in another State, or the toleration by the authorities of a State of organized activities calculated to carry out terroristic acts in another State.

Renvoi Doctrine

A certain number of states deal with the problem of political agitation by individuals by reference to some "higher law." In other words, such acts are not considered illegal *per se*, but only if they transgress a principle whose object is to protect some major interest. This system of reference is known as *renvoi*.[35] There are several types of such higher laws. Some domestic statutes outlaw all acts by individuals against a foreign state (and this includes propaganda) which "violate international law," but this merely begs the question. Nevertheless such a rule is found in Swiss law.[36] Another higher law to which reference is made is the law of treason; thus some states, notably Germany, Austria, and Tsarist Russia, considered to be unlawful any act committed to the detriment of an outside power if the same act, committed against the local sovereignty, would have amounted to treason.[37] The rule in the United States and Britain, however, is definitely *contra*.[38] Other domestic laws treat as illegal any acts which, injurious to a foreign state, are such as to endanger the international relations of the home government.[39] Underlying this latter rule one may perceive some trace of a veritable international point of view, since the object of the law is to maintain peace. Although in actual fact the basic purpose here may be selfish, since the maintenance of peace is in the national interest, nevertheless the good resulting to international society as a whole is just as genuine as if the lawmakers had been inspired by the purest altruism. However, the world is still a long way from the principle formulated by

---

[34] *General Assembly. Official Records, IX, Supp.* 9 (A/2693) c.iii, p. 2.

[35] Lauterpacht, *op. cit.,* (supra p. 55), p. 118.

[36] Bourquin, *op. cit.,* p. 219.

[37] German law discussed by Bourquin, *ibid.*.

[38] Lauterpacht, *op. cit.,* p. 117.

[39] See Belgian Law of March 12, 1858, discussed by Bourquin, *op. cit.,* p. 220. Articles 84 and 85 of the French Penal Code have been cited as examples of *renvoi*, but it is doubtful whether they can be interpreted to cover this type of propaganda. Garraud, who considers this law to be "inapplicable, dangerous, insufficient," maintains that it only applies to an overt act such as organizing an armed expedition or opening up a subscription in favor of a faction revolting against a foreign State. But it "leaves outside the range of repression, mere plots tending to overturn a foreign government or modify its form, associations having the same end, offenses by words and by writing." R. Garraud, *Traité Théorique et Pratique du Droit Pénal Français,* 2nd ed., Paris, 1899, No. 835.

Garraud during his discussion of crimes against the law of nations: "The mere fact of belonging to the community of those nations which have reached the same stage of civilization creates in each State the duty to repress and to punish all attempts directed against other states by individuals."[40]

Subversive Propaganda by Political Refugees

Propaganda by political refugees has probably caused more ill-feeling among the nations than any other type of subversive propaganda by individuals, and thus deserves special mention. Political refugees have often proved to be a thorn in the flesh of their native land, and in the country where they have taken refuge they occasionally wear out their welcome by engaging in political agitation of a nature to embroil the latter with other states, particularly the state of origin. Some refugees have been guilty of biting the hand that fed them, although this is more frequent among fake refugees planted by hostile governments. Just before World War II, Poland in a series of notes protested to Czechoslovakia against the agitation then being carried on by Polish refugees, against their "mother country." The Czech government, admitting most of the charges, promised to take remedial measures, but apparently with little success.[41] It is not surprising, then, that the country of origin often demands and occasionally obtains from the state of refuge the acceptance of broad obligations to repress incendiary propaganda. The problem is a particularly delicate one because the state consenting to harbor refugees must conciliate its devotion, on the one hand, to the right of asylum and its fidelity to freedom of speech, with, on the other hand, its obligations toward friendly powers or with the exigencies of national security.

Given these difficulties, it is not surprising that there is considerable difference of opinion as to the proper policy to be adopted in this matter by the state of asylum. There is no general acceptance, either in theory or practice, of the rule as stated by Wheaton: ". . . if the hospitality of a State is so abused by such refugees, that the safety of its neighbors becomes imperilled, it then becomes its duty to adopt such measures as will control them, and make their residence harmless to other states."[42] But while the duty of the state of refuge in this situation remains undetermined, its right in international law to repress refugee activity harmful to a friendly foreign nation, or even to use the remedy of expulsion, is free from doubt.

---

[40] Garraud, *op. cit.*, No. 1160.

[41] Martin, *op. cit.*, p. 178.

[42] *Wheaton's Elements of International Law*, 5th ed., (Phillipson), London, 1916, p. 193.

Thus the European Convention for the Protection of Human Rights and Fundamental Freedoms (November 4, 1950) states that the signatories may impose any restrictions they desire on the political activities of aliens.[43]

The peculiarly grave dangers incident to refugee agitation have led a number of states to enter into *treaties* calling for strict measures of repression. Many such treaties could be cited, some of them of very early date. In the middle of the 17th century, Britain and Denmark agreed that they would neither "harbour, or suffer . . . the enemies or rebels of the other."[44] In their treaty of October 8, 1801, France and Russia agreed that "every subject of one of these powers inhabiting the states of the other, who shall do anything to menace its security, shall be removed from the said country and transported beyond its frontiers without any claim to the protection of its own government."[45] Some fifteen states of Central and South America have made agreements to prevent political refugees from living in border regions or engaging in activities of a nature to disturb the peace in their country of origin.[46] After World War I many such treaties appeared. See, for example, Article 5 of the Treaty of June 1, 1922, between Soviet Russia and Finland, in which the parties agree to expel from the frontier zone on request all nationals of the other power "whose actions appear likely to disturb the neighborly peaceful relations existing at the frontier."[47] And Saudi Arabia and Iraq agreed, on April 2, 1936, that if refugees from one of the parties came to the territory of the other, the latter had to disarm them and remove them to an area where they could do no harm.[48]

A study of *domestic laws* dealing with this problem reveals some interesting facts. British practice has varied considerably. In 1793 the Aliens Act provided for rigorous supervision of the activities of refugees.[49] Its more severe provisions soon fell into disuse, although in 1848 the executive received for a limited period the right to send away any stranger considered a danger to the country.[50] Lord Lyndhurst, it is true, once declared in the House of Lords that "the offense of endeavoring to excite revolt among the subjects of a neigh-

---

[43] *Am. J. Int. Law,* Vol. 45 (1951), Supp., p. 24, discussed in Oppenheim, *op. cit.,* 8th ed., Sec. 340 (o).

[44] Treaty of February 13, 1660-1661, Lewis Hertslet, *Treaties and Conventions,* Vol. I, London, 1840, p. 180; Whitton, *op. cit.,* (*Hague Recueil*), p. 594.

[45] De Martens, *Recueil des Principaux Traités,* Gottingen, 1831, Vol. VII, pp. 386-388.

[46] Van Dyke, *op. cit., p.* 59.

[47] L. O. N. *Treaty Series,* Vol. 16, 1-4 (1923), p. 343. For impressive list of other similar treaties made during this period by Soviet Russia, see Martin, *op. cit.,* p. 255, n. 129.

[48] L. O. N., *Treaty Series,* Vol. 174 (1937), pp. 131, 134 (Art. 5).

[49] 33 Geo. III, c. 4, (repealed 1871).

[50] 11 and 12 Vict., c. 20 (repealed 1875).

boring state is an offense against the law of nations,"[51] and after the Orsini Plot against Napoleon III the British Parliament passed a law increasing the punishment for conspiracy so as to permit more effective action against refugees.[52] But the British policy in general has conformed to Palmerstone's statement in 1853, namely, that "The British government has never undertaken to provide for the internal security of other countries; it is sufficient for them to have the power to provide for the internal security of their own."[53] It is significant that Nesselrode protested to the British that foreign nations were not so much afraid of "overt acts" committed by refugees, which the British did outlaw, as of the troubles caused by seditious proclamations, subversive agents, the raising of money, and offensive manifestations.[54] The British have been disposed at times to resort to the expulsion of refugees whose agitations have proved embarrassing, and in fact forced King Carol, in 1928, to leave the country after he addressed an inflammatory message to his former subjects, sending planes to Rumania to drop handbills claiming his right to the throne of King Michael.[55]

This remedy of expulsion has been employed by other powers, too, for instance by Belgium, when it expelled General Boulenger in 1889,[56] and by the Swiss on numerous occasions.[57] Switzerland has been particularly troubled by protests from other powers in this matter, one case occurring as early as 1795, and the Swiss government has shown a disposition to deal severely with refugees in many ways, both by criminal prosecutions and by restriction on their liberty of action.[58] In 1834, the Swiss yielded to the demand of the Powers that foreigners guilty of hostile enterprises against neighboring states be expelled.[59] In 1879 the Swiss Government expelled a German journalist for publishing in a socialist paper an article which reproached German Socialists for their inactivity and exhorted the latter to more energetic propaganda.[60] And in the years just prior to the Second World War, political refugees were expelled from the

---

[51] He added, "No writer on the law of nations states otherwise." *Hansard,* 3rd series, Vol. 124 (1853), p. 1048.

[52] 24 and 25 Vict., c. 100, sec. 4. *The Statutes* (3rd rev. ed.), London, 1950, Vol. VII, p. 254.

[53] *Hansard,* 3rd series, Vol. 124 (1853), p. 805.

[54] *British and Foreign State Papers,* Vol. 42 (1852-1853), pp. 429-433, and Vol. 46 (1855-1856), pp. 124 ff.

[55] *Parl. Debates,* 5th Series, Vol. 217 (1928), pp. 175-178.

[56] Fauchille, *op. cit.,* Vol. I, sec. 450, citing a large number of similar cases of expulsion.

[57] Reviewed by Preuss, *op. cit., (Rev. Gén. de Dr. Int. Pub.),* pp. 622, 628 ff.

[58] Sorel, Vol. IV, p. 164; Lauterpacht, *op. cit.,* (Transactions of Grotius Society), p. 124; Preuss, *op. cit.,* pp. 622 ff.

[59] *British and Foreign State Papers,* Vol. 24 (1835-1836), p. 999.

[60] Preuss, *op. cit.,* p. 624.

Republic for incendiary articles against Nazi Germany and other powers.[61]

France, too, has been involved in such difficulties, both on the sending and on the receiving end. In the Revolutionary period and under Napoleon, many protests were lodged by the French government against hostile propaganda sent into France by émigrés, operating especially from Britain and Switzerland.[62] After the Revolution of 1830, as already remarked, many political refugees from different parts of Europe were using Paris as a center of agitation against their own lands. Louis Philippe took severe measures against refugees from abroad,[63] and prevented the Pepe revolutionary expedition from leaving Marseilles to carry the revolt into the Two Sicilies.[64] In the United States, the government has not varied from its usual policy of refusing to intervene in cases of political refugee activity unless there is evidence of an overt act.[65]

No one will deny that hostile propaganda when persistently carried on against a given state by refugees therefrom living abroad may constitute a grave problem of international relations. To the state granting the asylum, it means serious friction if not dangerous controversy certain to plague its relations with the refugees' home country. To the target state such agitation may be a mere pinprick which can safely be ignored; on the other hand, it may cause dissatisfaction among the populace or even serve to incite the latter to revolt; thus it is highly resented. As we have seen, important measures have been taken, both in local and in international fields, to curb these evils. Diplomatic protest has been followed by apology,

---

[61] Martin, *op. cit.*, p. 174. The Institute of International Law affirmed the right of a state to expel "foreigners who, on the territory of the state, are guilty or strongly suspected of attacking, in the press or otherwise, a foreign state or its sovereigns, or the institutions of a foreign state, provided that these infractions are punishable if, committed abroad by nations, they were directed against the state itself." The criticism of this project by the Rapporteur, de Bar, is interesting: "At this rate," he said, "if a journalist took the risk of doubting the credit of a foreign nation, he would suffer expulsion, under the pretext of an attack or outrage against the nation; this would end by forcing journalists to be forever optimistic." *Annuaire, Inst, de Dr. Int.*, Vol. 12 (1892-94), pp. 213 ff. See also Ch. de Boeck, "L'Expulsion et les Difficultés Internationales qu'en Soulève la Pratique," *Hague Recueil*, Vol. 18 (1927), p. 568.

[62] A. Périvier, *Napoléon Journaliste*, Paris, 1918; *Annual Register*, Vol. 45 (1803), pp. 656 ff. A recent example is the refusal of West Germany and Portugal to allow Bidault to carry on anti-deGaulle agitation from within their boundaries.

[63] *Archives Parlementaires*, 2d series, Vol. 81 (1831), pp. 613 ff.; De Guichen, *op. cit.*, pp. 163 ff.

[64] César Vidal, *Louis-Philippe, Metternich et la Crise Italienne de 1831-1832*, Paris, 1931, pp. 55-58.

[65] Hackworth, *Digest*, Vol. II, pp. 140 ff. As to overt acts, note the official U.S. action restricting raids by Cuban refugees in 1963, and the deep resentment of these restrictions by the refugees.

promises of legal and political remedial measures, and even expulsion of the unwanted refugees. Treaties covering the matter have been signed and ratified, some of them bilateral agreements, others impressive multilateral conventions. But despite these developments, it is impossible to deduce therefrom any uniform rule of international law governing the agitation of refugees, as such, acting on their own, without the control of a government.

Defamatory Propaganda

The next question is: to what degree does there exist already a rule among nations holding the state responsible for non-official or non-governmental libellous communications issuing from its territory? As usual, in making such an inquiry, one must rely on the familiar sources of international law, namely, treaties, custom, general principles of law, judicial decisions and the writing of authoritative scholars.

A few treaties exist which rule out propaganda of a nature to cause international friction or cause bad feeling between two or more nations, and certainly a libellous attack by individuals on the resident ambassador of State A in State B, or on the ruler or president of State A, could be considered to come within this category. For example, the Geneva Convention Concerning the Use of Broadcasting in the Cause of Peace, which came into force April 2, 1938, ruled out radio transmissions "likely to harm good international understanding or statements the incorrectness of which is or ought to be known to the persons responsible for the broadcast."[66] A similar obligation of a very general nature which might be construed to encompass the making of libellous attacks on foreign states or their official representatives is found in the April, 1948 treaty between India and Pakistan which calls on the parties to refrain from and to control propaganda, and to avoid news "likely to inflame, or cause fear or alarm to, the population of either Dominion."[67] Poland and Lithuania agreed in November 1938, not to permit their press to make use of propaganda

---

[66] *Supra*, p. 125.

[67] E/CN.4/Sub. 1/105, p. 29. One of the most recent accords of this nature was an oral agreement made in 1957 between the Emperor of Ethiopia and the visiting President of the Legislative Assembly and the Prime Minister of Liberia. The two governments agreed to do their utmost to prevent the dissemination within their borders of propaganda hostile to the interests of the other or calculated to foment mistrust or create misunderstandings between their peoples (Press Release, Ministry of Foreign Affairs, Addis Ababa, July 25, 1959.) Also, note the accord between Tunis and the United Arab Republic of February 7, 1961, whereby they agreed not to use their radios to attack each other. It was reported that this agreement was aimed specifically at attacks on President Bourguiba of Tunis by the Voice of the Arabs in Cairo. *New York Times*, February 8, 1961.

147

unfavorable to the other.[68] The South American Regional Agreement on Radio Communications, signed at Buenos Aires on April 10, 1935, pledges the parties to *"avoid defamatory emissions."* This is one of the few treaties which specifically cover defamatory international propaganda.[69] But we also have the South American Radio Communications Agreement signed at Rio de Janiero on June 6, 1937, which called on the parties to "ensure that the dissemination of news or of commentaries which might disturb the good relations between States, offend national sentiment of other countries or injure the work of the organization and consolidation of peace, as well as all which might offend the officially designated authorities of States, shall be avoided."[70] Such treaties are too few in number, and their stipulations too vague, to permit us to deduce therefrom any rule of customary international law creating a general international obligation, beyond the treaty obligation of the parties themselves. It may be, however, that the duty forbidding calumny against at least foreign diplomats, and perhaps also against foreign sovereigns, was so well accepted that states felt no necessity to include such obligations in international conventions.

Attacks on Diplomatic Agents

The responsibility of the state for defamatory attacks made on foreign personalities by persons under its jurisdiction appears to depend on the official status of the person maligned. If a *foreign diplomat* is the object of such libels, the law in the matter is reasonably clear. This is not surprising, given the fact that from time immemorial diplomatic agents have been considered worthy of special protection. Thus as early as 1794, when an American publication referred to the British Minister at Philadelphia as "The British Solomon," a contemptible person, and an incendiary jack-in-office, this was considered by the United States Attorney General as a proper case for an action of criminal libel. He said: "The law of libel, which protected the citizen, was, in the case of a foreign minister, strengthened by the law of nations, which secures the minister a peculiar protection, not only from violence, but also from insult."[71] And in 1898, Mr. Day, Secretary of State, in a letter to the United States Attorney General, stated that a publication charging the diplomatic representative of one country with operating a spy system in the interest of another constituted sufficient ground for the prosecution of the author for

---

[68] Ignaz Rothenberg, *The Newspaper*, London, 1946, p. 5, cited by Martin, *op. cit.*, p. 95.

[69] Supra, p. 127.

[70] Supra, p. 128.

[71] Moore, *Digest*, Vol. IV, pp. 629-630.

criminal libel.[72] An American scholar who in 1940 studied the legislations of fifty-one states reported that all or practically all of them give legal protection to foreign diplomats against defamatory attacks. He concluded that "the tentative conclusion may therefore be drawn that protection of resident foreign diplomats from libel is so generally afforded by municipal law as to indicate a response to a requirement of international law."[73] This view is supported by no less an authority than C. C. Hyde.[74] Since these works appeared several more legislatures have added laws to protect foreign diplomats from slanderous attacks.[75] Also, in 1938 the United States Court of Appeals of the District of Columbia held, in *Frend et al. v. U. S.:*

> The law of nations . . . requires every government to take all reasonable precautions to prevent the doing of the things which the resolution makes unlawful.[76]

The resolution referred to is a federal statute making it unlawful within 500 feet of an embassy, legation, or consulate in the District of Columbia to display "any flag, banner, placard or device designed or adapted to intimidate, coerce, or bring into public odium any foreign government, party or organization" or its diplomatic or consular representative.

In 1961 the United Nations Conference on Diplomatic Intercourse and Immunities adopted the following statement in the final "Act of Vienna":

> *Article 29:* The person of a diplomatic agent shall be inviolable He shall not be liable to any form of arrest or detention. The receiving state shall treat him with due respect and shall take all appropriate steps to prevent any attack on his person, freedom or dignity.[77]

Attacks on Heads of State

Thus there appears to be a general consensus among the nations that a state must take appropriate measures to prevent or suppress libellous publications directed by individuals against foreign diplomats. But no concordance of domestic legislation exists with respect to attacks by individuals against *the head of a foreign state.* According to Van Dyke, the authority already cited,[78]

---

[72] *Ibid.,* p. 630.

[73] Van Dyke, *op. cit.,* p. 70.

[74] Hyde, *op. cit.,* Vol. II, pp. 1249-1250.

[75] Martin, *op. cit.,* pp. 126 ff.

[76] 100 Fed. (2d) 691 (1938), certiori denied in 306 U.S. 640 (1938).

[77] Final Act, U. N. Conference on Diplomatic Intercourse and Immunities, Vienna, March 2-April 14, 1961. See also Art. 17 and Comment thereon, in Draft Convention on Diplomatic Privileges Immunities, prepared under direction of Harvard Law School. *Am. J. of Int. Law.,* Vol. 26 (1932), Section Two, Official Documents, pp. 90-97.

[78] *Op. cit.,* p. 69.

Of the fifty-one states whose legislation was studied, twenty-eight give protection from libel to foreign sovereigns or heads of states, three protect sovereigns only, and the remaining twenty ignore the subject altogether. Of the seven Great Powers, Japan and the Soviet Union apparently give the heads of foreign states no protection at all from libel; Germany gives protection to sovereigns, but not to presidents of republics; and Great Britain and the United States in the common law (enforceable in American state courts, but not in the Federal courts) apparently grant protection only if the libel involves a threat to the public peace. Only France and Italy seem willing to grant thorough protection.

Since this survey was made, however, a number of states have passed laws to outlaw such offenses.[79] But the United States and Britain, although not always consistent, still remain outside the fold. And Soviet Russia only protects "toiler states."[80] We must conclude, therefore, after a review of the authority available, that it is not possible to deduce from domestic legislation any rule of international law obliging the state to protect sovereigns or other heads of foreign states from libellous attacks by individuals. The evidence from treaty law and from the writings of jurists is equally inconclusive.

In fact, both Britain and the United States appear to be less disposed to afford complete protection to heads of foreign states than formerly. Certain early British cases, for instance those involving libels against the Emperor of Russia, Marie Antoinette and Napoleon Bonaparte, resulted in convictions of the defendants.[81] Lord Gordon was convicted for imputing tyranny and oppression to Queen Marie Antoinette, disparaging her character and that of her chargé d'affaires in London.[82] The crucial consideration in the eyes of the court was the fact that the defendant had attempted to rekindle animosity between France and England. John Vint was convicted for publishing in a British newspaper the charge that the Emperor of Russia by various acts of tyranny was rendering himself obnoxious to his subjects and ridiculous in the eyes of Europe.[83] Here again, the court was most impressed by the fact that such a charge risked embroiling the two interested countries. The question put by the defense, (Thomas Erskine, later Chancellor) invoking the doctrine of freedom

---

[79] Particularly interesting is the law of the Dominican Republic which prohibits any public entertainment or radio broadcast that may "hold up to international scorn or defame friendly nations or nationals or foreign heads of State." (Act No. 5906 of July 5, 1949, Art. 31) This law is curious, both because of the excellence of the principle therein reflected and because it has been so dramatically disregarded by the government in question. Martin, *op. cit.*, p. 127.

[80] Penal Code, Art. 58; Harold J. Berman, *Justice in Russia, An Interpretation of Soviet Law,* Cambridge, Mass., 1950, p. 276.

[81] *Supra*, p. 105.

[82] 22 *Howell's St. Tr.* 175 (1787).

[83] 27 *Howell's St. Tr.* 627 (1799).

of speech, is worthy of quotation here: "Is every writing necessarily to be adjudged a libel, which questions the wisdom or integrity of a foreign prince, or which condemns his counsels as weak, capricious, and unjust, though manifestly injurious to our own people . . . ?"[48] The court in the case of Jean Peltier, convicted for a libel on Napoleon, was likewise impressed by the danger caused by such publications to relations between Britain and France, although a still more grave element in the case was the fact that it contained certain incitements to assassination.[85] A more recent case, although referring approvingly to earlier convictions for criminal libel, gives such a narrow interpretation of the laws against seditious libel as to throw considerable doubt on the principles set forth in former decisions. In the case of *Rex v. Antonelli and Barberi,* decided in 1900, the court said: "Seditious libels are such as tend to disturb the government of this country, and in my opinion a document published here, which was calculated to disturb the government of some foreign country is not a seditious libel, nor punishable as a libel at all . . . To hold otherwise . . . would be to hold that all the strong language used against the government of Turkey at the time of the Bulgarian rebellion was seditious libel, and it would make many of our great statesmen guilty."[86] But the court found defendant guilty of incitement to murder, and did not need to rely on the charge of seditious libel. Furthermore, the court reaffirmed the important principle according to which the vital consideration is whether the publication is of a nature to disturb international relations: "Libels which bring persons into hatred or contempt may apply to persons outside the dominions of the king, *because they are liable to bring the peaceful relations existing between states to an end.*"

In the United States, formerly such offenses, if directed against the head of a foreign state, could be prosecuted in the Federal courts, as was expressly asserted in 1794 by the Attorney General with respect to a libel against the British Minister.[87] Twenty years later this rule was set aside in the case of *United States v. Hudson.*[88] But the state courts are still available for the prosecution of such offenses, as already mentioned.

In France the tribunal at Tunis in 1896 convicted the printer

---

[84] *Ibid.,* at p. 631.

[85] 28 *Ibid.,* p. 530 (1803)

[86] 70 J. P. 4 (1906)

[87] Moore, *Digest,* Vol. II, p. 163.

[88] 7 Cr. 32 (1812). There has been little disposition to follow the principle set forth in Chief Justice McKean's charge to the grand jury in Philadelphia in 1791, with respect to certain violent statements concerning the French nation and its leaders which had appeared in Philadelphia newspapers: "Every nation ought to avoid giving any real offense to another." Referring to the conduct of the publisher, he said: "The Government that will not discountenance, may be thought to adopt it, and be deemed justly chargeable with all the consequences." Moore, *Digest,* Vol. II, p. 162.

of a newspaper who had called the King of Italy a *sombre et sinistre soudard,* of an offense against the person of a foreign sovereign. Such a publication came within the terms of Articles 36 and 37 of the law of 1881, which deals with offenses publicly committed against sovereigns and heads of foreign states. Article 36 was later modified by decree so as to extend its protection to heads of governments and foreign ministers.[89] It should be added that theoretically libels against the heads of foreign states fall within the purview of Articles 84 and 85 of the French Penal Code, permitting prosecution of acts which are of a nature to subject France to a declaration of war, or its citizens to reprisals, although very few cases have come up under this law and in the opinion of some leading French jurists the law is unworkable.[90]

The Swiss law is worth mention because it punishes outrages against the foreign *nation* as well as those aimed at the head of the state.[91] A number of incidents of this kind have been caused by political refugees resident in Switzerland, but the government usually prefers expulsion over criminal prosecution as the best remedy in such cases.[92]

Thus although some legislations repress libellous attacks undertaken by an individual against the head of a foreign state, in general such acts do not as a consequence engage the international responsibility of the government under whose jurisdiction they take place. But there is an exception to this rule. If such scurrilous statements are connected with a terroristic campaign, in other words have as their objective the incitement of certain individuals to assassinate the head of a foreign state, then in such case the state is under a heavy responsibility. Assassination of foreign sovereigns, even in time of war, is frowned on by international law.[93] Hence incitement to commit such crimes is equally unlawful. Thus a commission of jurists, meeting at The Hague in 1923 on rules of aerial warfare, agreed that it was unlawful to drop leaflets from planes in wartime if their intent was to incite to

---

[89] Garraud, *op. cit.,* No. 837.

[90] Garraud, *op. cit.,* No. 835 ff.

[91] Paccaud, *Régime de la Presse en Europe,* Lausanne, 1887, p. 187, discussing the case of Karl Schill, who was convicted under Swiss law for having distributed, during the Basle Carnival, a number of brochures entitled "Vive la France!" directed against Germany, particularly with respect to the cause of Alsace-Lorraine, See also, "Chronique, Offenses Publiques contre un Gouvernement Étranger," *J. de Dr. Int. Privé,* Vol. 15 (1888), pp. 638 ff.

[92] *Supra,* pp. 6, 145.

[93] Already discussed, *supra* p. 141. And see case of *Reg. v. Tchorzewski,* 8 St. Tr. (N.S.) 1091 (1858), where the defendant was let off after he expressed regret and promised to desist from such act in the future; his offense was the publication of a pamphlet recommending in express terms the assassination of Louis Napoleon as a tyrant, and lauding the attempt by Orsini on the life of the latter and lamenting that the attempt had failed. But the Court reaffirmed the rule that it was a crime to plot and conspire on British soil for the commission of a crime in a foreign country.

murder or assassination.[94] In other words, as discussed under "subversive propaganda" above, a state must use the means at its disposal to prevent terroristic propaganda, or, if it has taken place, must see that the case is followed up and the offenders punished.

Thus after the French government in 1857 had protested violently against certain propaganda by terrorists in Britain alleged to have been partly responsible for the attempt on the life of Napoleon III, the British government admitted the validity of the protest and passed a law to strengthen its domestic laws applicable to such offienses.[95] In 1881 the British court upheld the conviction of a man who had published in Britain a pamphlet exulting over the assassination of the Tsar of Russia and commending the idea to others.[96] This was held to be a scandalous libel at common law and an offense under a statute for conspiring, confederating or agreeing to murder any person within or without the realm.[97] In 1883, when the British protested to the American government against publications alleged to have prompted the commission of assassination and arson in England, the legal problem received no definite solution since Secretary of State Frelinghuysen believed that the best solution in the circumstances was a policy of silence, on the assumption that if unnoticed by the government such maneuvers would remain impotent.[98] Another case in point occurred in 1875, when certain Belgian bishops sent to the clergy in Prussia writings of a nature to incite them against the authority and laws of the state, and one person had actually written to a French archbishop offering to assassinate Bismarck. The Prussian government declared in its protest to the Belgian government, apropos of both libellous and subversive propaganda:[99]

> It is an uncontested principle of the law of nations that a State cannot permit its nationals to trouble the interior peace of another State and that it is bound to assure that its laws are sufficient to satisfy this international obligation . . . The common duty of all states is not to tolerate that their territory should become a center for aggressions directed against the security of neighboring states.

It is significant that Belgium, in its response, invoked the principle of freedom of the press, claiming that such freedom had proved to be the best way to overcome the propaganda of the Internationale

---

[94] *Am. J. Int. Law,* Vol. 32, (1938), Supp., pp. 22-28.

[95] *Hansard,* 3rd series, Vol. 148 (1857-1858), pp. 1741-1847.

[96] *Queen* v. *Most,* 7 Q. B. Div. 244 (1881).

[97] In accordance with 24 and 25 Vict. c. 100. *The Statutes* (3rd. rev. ed.), London, 1950, Vol. VII, p. 254.

[98] Moore, *Digest,* Vol. II, p. 170. But actually in that case there was an absence of any direct incitement to assassination. *Ibid.,* p. 171.

[99] *Archives Diplomatiques,* 1876-1877, Vol. II, p. 298.

"whose doctrines, produced in the open, have succumbed before the good sense of the populations."[100]

Attacks on a State

Suppose that it is not the diplomat nor the head of a foreign state who is the object of derogatory attacks by an individual, but *the state itself*—its institutions, constitution, policies. Is the government under whose jurisdiction such an act takes place under any duty to use due diligence to prevent such acts or at least to punish the offender? The question is important, for independent publications have always indulged freely in criticism of other nations, and the practice has never been more widespread than during the present period. From earliest times such attacks have led to serious international incidents, as when Dumouriez complained in 1792 of unfriendly statements in Swiss papers in which, he said, "are propagated the sentiments which suggest to our most cruel enemies a hatred of our constitution and the hope of a counter-revolution."[101] Mutual charges of similar characters are frequent features of the present Cold War. We have already cited sufficient examples of such tactics.

There is a widespread opposition to any attempt to throttle criticism by outlawing articles of this kind, although some states, as mentioned below, have attempted to do so. To interfere in this manner with the prerogatives of the independent journalist would constitute a grave inroad on the freedom of the press, guaranteed by many national constitutions and now accepted as a fundamental international right.

According to the great weight of authority, private individuals may write or publish articles derogatory of foreign states without engaging the responsibility of the government under whose jurisdiction the act takes place. Here the governmental duty of prevention is not identical with the duty of abstention; even where the particular act may not be done legally by the state, it does not follow that the failure of the state to supress the same or similar act, when done by an individual, creates an international responsibility. The law in this matter is so certain that even in time of war the right of individuals in a neutral state to criticize a foreign state is upheld; "unneutral" sentiments may be expressed by individuals without giving the interested belligerent a right to protest. The United States has long denied that as a neutral it is under any obligation to control the expression by private individuals of opinions adverse to the cause of a belligerent, despite the fact that in the first years of the First World War President Wilson urged his people to be neutral even in spirit.[102]

---

[100] *Ibid.*, p. 308.
[101] *Papiers de Barthélemy, op. cit.*, Vol. I, p. 164.
[102] Hackworth, *Digest*, Vol. VII, pp. 372 ff.; Moore, *Digest*, Vol. VII, p. 980.

In actual fact, however, such attacks in peace and in war may be very dangerous to the course of peaceful relations. And some authorities, especially those of German origin, have insisted that the state in these circumstances is under a broad legal as well as moral responsibility to suppress publications derogatory of foreign states.[103] One American authority has asserted that "The existence of an international obligation to protect foreign governments locally against defamation seems amply supported by principle and analogy."[104] Furthermore, certain states have taken it upon themselves to pass laws designed to repress such propaganda. Even the United States government, while denying any such duty exists under international law, has occasionally expressed regrets for statements made by individuals under American jurisdiction and considered objectionable by foreign countries.[105] Some twenty-seven states in their domestic legislation prohibit attacks by individuals on foreign states of such a nature as to endanger peaceful relations with the foreign nations attacked.[106] One of the best known of such statutes is the French law (Articles 84 and 85 of the Penal Code) which provides penalties against anyone whose hostile action against a foreign country exposes France to a declaration of war, or French nationals to the danger of reprisals.[107] And in Switzerland, by a law passed in 1934, a newspaper considered guilty of endangering international relations by means of extravagant criticism of foreign countries is first given a warning, and if it does not desist, may be suspended.[108] In Denmark, Section 108 of the Penal Code provides for the punishment of anyone insulting a foreign state.[109] A new law now under consideration in Finland would penalize the defamation of a foreign power, if of a nature to jeopardize Finland's relations with that power.[110] This law is readily understandable when one considers Finland's special geographical position. The Swedish law resembles the proposed Finnish statute.[111]

In the field of radio, we find laws of this character in Mexico, Peru and Uruguay. Mexico has forbidden the broadcasting of messages opposed to "international good will."[112] The object of such legis-

---

[103] Franz von Liszt, *Das Völkerrecht systematisch*, 12th ed. (Fleischman), Berlin, 1925, p. 118.

[104] Dickinson, *op. cit.*, pp. 840-844.

[105] Hyde, *op. cit.*, Vol. I, Sec. 217.

[106] Van Dyke, *op. cit.*, p. 70.

[107] *Supra*, p. 142.

[108] Resolution of the Federal Council, March 26, 1934, *Feuille Fédéral*, 86th year (1934), Vol. 1, p. 867; *Freedom of Information* (UN Sales No. 1950, XIV, 1), Vol. I, pp. 135-136.

[109] *Ibid.*, p. 207.

[110] *Ibid.*

[111] *Ibid.*, pp. 213-214. Martin, *op. cit.*, pp. 232 ff.

[112] For Mexico: Arthur W. Scharfeld, "Changes in Mexican Law of Radio-communications," *J. of Radio Law*, Vol. II (1932), p. 433, n. 127. For Peru:

lation is the prevention of hostile reactions, to avoid international incidents and to obtain the benefits of reciprocal protection. Other laws of this nature have a different *raison d'être*: an old German law penalized verbal attacks on foreign states if such action, directed against a member of the German federation, would have amounted to treason,[113] and a Soviet law penalized the dissemination of propaganda against a workers' state even if the latter is not a member of the USSR.[114] These citations are impressive as far as they go; nevertheless there is not a sufficient consensus to engender a rule of customary international law.

WAR-MONGERING PROPAGANDA

Some authors maintain that any state having accepted the Pact of Paris, the United Nations Charter and other restrictions on the right to go to war, is under a legal duty to see that those under its jurisdiction do not commit acts likely to involve it in an illegal war. There are numerous local laws for the suppression of acts which might weaken the resistance of a state in war, or interfere with preparations for it. Other laws seek to prevent acts so grave as to compromise the foreign relations of the state or expose it to a charge of violating its international obligations.[115] According to Martin, a "fairly large group" of states already provide in their domestic laws for the prosecution of individuals urging a state to go to war against a foreign state and he lists twenty-five such states.[116] A Polish law is directed against communications inciting the Polish state to an act of aggression, and even goes further by outlawing propaganda tending to incite *any* state to such acts.[117] Article 141 of the Brazilian Constitution reads "propaganda for war . . . shall not be tolerated."[118] And war propaganda is outlawed under Article 6 of the Constitution of the Democratic Republic of Germany.[119] Under the Defense of Peace Law (1951), in the USSR, war propaganda is characterized as "the

Francis Déak and Philip C. Jessup, *A Collection of Neutrality Laws, Regulations and Treaties, Washington,* 1938, p. 872. For Uruguay: L. O. N., Doc. C. L. 44. 1936. XII, p. 5; Order of June 18, 1928 of the Law No. 8380, amended June 15, 1935; this law actually forbids all transmisions of a nature to disturb public order or peace, either in Uruguay, or in *other states.*

[113] Penal Code, Art. 102.

[114] *Supra*, p. 150, n. 80.

[115] For compilation of such laws, see Martin, *op. cit.*, Ch. 6.

[116] Martin, pp. 134, 238. He also states that "a number have had laws since the turn of the nineteenth century making it a crime for any citizen or alien to engage in activities that might provoke a war against the state, or to furnish grounds to some foreign state for a declaration of war." *Ibid.*, p. 133.

[117] Defense of Peace Act of December 29, 1950, Arts. 1, 2; Penal Code, Arts. 1, 2; Penal Code, Art. 113

[118] Brazilian Constitution, Article 141, No. 5.

[119] Constitution of the Democratic Republic of Germany, Art. 6.

gravest crime against humanity," and punishment is prescribed for it as "a most grave criminal offense." This law applies to all persons wherever they may be, and irrespective of the state which is the object of the incitement.[120]

---

[120] U.S.S.R. Criminal Code, Art. 58 (1), discussed in Martin, *op. cit.*, p. 134.

Law on the Defense of Peace of March 12, 1951, *Vedomosti*, No. 5 (662), March 21, 1961. The Supreme Soviet of the Soviet Socialist Republics, guided by the high principles of the Soviet peace policy which seeks to strengthen peace and friendly relations between the peoples, recognizes that the [human] conscience and concept of right of the peoples who during one generation suffered the calamities of two wars, cannot accept that the conduct of war propaganda remain unpunished, and approves the proclamation of the Second World Congress of the Partisans of Peace, who expressed the will of entire progressive mankind concerning the prohibition and condemnation of criminal war propaganda.

The Supreme Soviet of the U.S.S.R. decrees:

1. to recognize that war propaganda under whatever form it is made, undermines the cause of peace, creates a threat of a new war and, because of this, is the gravest crime against humanity.

2. to bring to court persons guilty of war propaganda and to try them as having committed a most grave criminal offense. Law Concerning Criminal Responsibility for Crimes Against the State of December 25, 1958 (*Vedomosti*, 1959, item 8).

Sec. 8, Propaganda of War. Propaganda of war, regardless of the form in which it is carried on shall be punished by confinement for a period of from three to eight years. (*Note*: this section is identical with Section 8 of the RSFSR Criminal Code of 1960.)

Commentaries. "The laws on the protection of peace, adopted in the countries of the people's democracy, stressing to the full extent the public danger of propaganda of war, decree heavy penalties for this crime.

The significance of these laws exceeds the limits of internal criminal policy." (Morozov, G. I., "Responsibility for War Propaganda," *Sovetskii Exhegodnik Mezhdunarodnogo Prava* (Soviet Yearbook of International Law), 1955, p. 323.)

"According to its legal nature war propaganda is very close to incitement to commit a crime, however, it does not coincide with it.

"Incitement as a kind of complicity, as a general rule, entails criminal responsibility only when the call to crime materializes in the criminal result, the commission of a crime. War propaganda as one kind of crime against humanity entails criminal responsibility also in the case where aggression did not take place.

"In addition, the incitement presupposes a direct call to commit a crime, as for instance, murder, arson, etc. Similarly, war propaganda may not contain a direct call to war. . . .

"Finally, incitement presupposes the call to a particular crime, for instance, the murder of a certain person. The propaganda of aggression will take place also where there is no direct call to war against a specific state; a general call to aggression is enough for the notion of propaganda" (*Sovetskoe Ugolovnie Pravo* [Soviet Criminal Law]. Special Part. V. D. Men'shagin and P. S. Romashkin, gen. eds., Moscow, 1957, pp. 536-537.)

"The consideration of all these factors leads to the conclusion that war propaganda constitutes an independent crime expressed in the dissemination by the aggressive forces using all means at their disposal of calls for war, and also of ideas and views which in any form pursue the aim of undermining peaceful co-existence and of drawing the peoples into aggressive war; the encouragement of such criminal activities should also be considered as war propaganda." G. I. Morozov, *op. cit.*, p. 325.

Some writers contend that war-mongering by individuals already constitutes a crime at international law, *a délit du droit des gens*.[121] Such acts, actually characterized as crimes in international law by some legislations, are those which, although committed by individuals, nevertheless violate a fundamental interest protected by international law, so that any state having possession of the accused is entitled to prosecute him. Such exceptional acts committed by individuals are piracy, counterfeiting, and traffic in women, children and slaves. Prosecution in such cases is universal, in the sense that any state may assume jurisdiction over the offense. War-mongering propaganda, it is claimed, lies within this category, and should be dealt with by means of a convention obligating each signatory to introduce appropriate laws in its domestic legislation. As in the case of piracy, such exceptional jurisdiction would be justified, it is claimed, on the ground that although the act is a crime against the whole human race, no adequate remedy is to be found today in normal criminal procedures. In fact some advanced thinkers have proposed that war-mongering be governed by an international penal code, and judged in an international tribunal empowered to try individuals for such offenses.[122]

Such proposals, however, have not as yet found a place in positive international law, or *lex lata*, and even as *lex ferenda* have encountered great opposition. The analogy to the law of piracy, we admit, is not impressive. Some authorities actually deny that piracy itself is correctly considered a *délit du droit des gens*. The *Rapporteur* of the authoritative Harvard Research study of the international law of piracy so maintains, "since there is no international agency to capture them (i.e., the pirates) and no international tribunal to punish them and no provision in the laws of so many states for punishing foreigners whose piratical offense was committed outside the state's ordinary jurisdiction."[123] But even if piracy, as maintained by the great majority, is a veritable crime by an individual against the law of nations, this does not necessarily follow for the crime of war-mongering. For, in marked contrast with the alleged international crime of war propaganda, there are many precedents, extending over hundreds of years, for the national and international suppression of piracy. And while most legislations provide for the punishment of piracy "as defined by the law of nations," there is almost nothing similar in the local laws outlawing propaganda for war, and few as-

---

121 This matter should not be confused with the case of acts of aggressive war committed by a state for which the leaders are prosecuted as individuals for crimes against the peace, etc., as at Nuremberg. *Supra*, pp. 76 ff.

122 Sténuit, *op. cit.*, pp. 142 ff.; Pella, *op. cit.* (*Rev. Gén. Dr. Int. Pub.*), p. 493.

123 Research in International Law, Harvard Law School, "Piracy," discussion in the Introduction. *Am. J. Int. Law*, Vol. 26 (1932), Supp. p. 756. Garcia-Mora, *op. cit.*, p. 132 ff.

sertions in such laws that the offender is an enemy of the human race. It is important, too, to note that such prominent members of the Free World as the United States, Britain, Sweden and Switzerland have no laws against war propaganda as such. The day may come, of course, when the war-monger will be generally characterized as a *hostis humani generis,* for if one who seizes a ship on the high seas is so considered, surely anyone who in this day and age strives to promote and incite aggression among the nations is at least equally guilty.

Some believe it would actually be dangerous to obligate a state to suppress as criminal the act of individual war-mongering under its jurisdiction. According to Donnedieu de Vabres, the great French expert on criminal law, this would "open the door to inequality, arbitrariness, vexatious pursuits and blackmail." Not only would such a concept interfere with freedom of the press, but it would soon become a dead letter. It would place on the same plane "the vulgar culprit and the honest man who in a moment of patriotic exaltation forgets himself." Consequently de Vabres doubts the wisdom of elevating "this neophyte to the mysterious and romantic circle of the *délits du droit des gens.*"[124]

From this brief review of the law, it is evident that, despite many proposals to this end, there is no general international law at present requiring a state to repress war-mongering when the author is an individual (newspaper, radio, television, private person) acting on his own. The attitude of the American government in this matter was reflected, in 1948, in the answer to a Soviet protest against an article in Newsweek discussing possible bases for an attack on the Soviet Union. Washington invoked the constitutional guarantee of freedom of the press in denying any obligation to suppress such articles when appearing in an independent journal.[125] In 1948, at the Geneva Conference on Freedom of Information and of the Press, the American delegation firmly took a similar stand.[126]

THE RELATION BETWEEN CONTROL AND RESPONSIBILITY: RADIO

So far we have taken note of the extent to which the gravity of individual action, such as incitement to assassination or actual overt preparation for subversion, might affect the responsibility of the state

---

[124] Donnedieu de Vabres, "Pour Quels Délits Convient-il d'Admettre la Compétence Universelle?" *Rev. Int. de Dr. Pénal,* 9th year, (1932), pp. 315, 322.

[125] *New York Times,* June 11 and 30, 1948.

[126] Whitton, *op. cit.* ("The United Nations Conference on Freedom of Information," etc.), pp. 83 ff. But see Chapter XIII for an account of the new American position and the reversal of the Soviet position when an actual agreement was at stake.

tor the acts of an individual. There remains to be considered the factor of degree of control by the state over the individual.

The thread that has run throughout the positions taken by the United States, Great Britain, and other countries resisting governmental liability for individual propaganda has been the idea that the governments of such countries simply do not control the press, periodicals, and books published on their soil.

However, when we come to the problem of international radio, we encounter some new considerations. As to control: since private broadcasters must have a license from the government in order to use their assigned wave lengths, the relation of the government to the broadcaster is necessarily different than the relation of the government to the newspaper or publisher. But a broadcaster has a license which is conditioned on his using it in the public interest. No such public interest condition attaches to the right to publish newspapers, periodicals or books.

Coupled to this is the fact, already stressed, that the inherent danger of radio in the realm of international propaganda is so conspicuously greater than that of the printed word that different rules can well be justified. If a foreign government objects to propaganda in printed form issued by individuals, it can at least partially protect itself by stopping the materials at the border. But when the international radio channels are used, and when foreign government has no practicable way to defend itself from the private broadcasts, there is much more cogency in its contention that the country of origin should assume responsibility for restraining the harmful emissions. When to this is added the other factors, such as the peculiar potency of the actual human voice, that have been discussed earlier, it is not difficult to justify a broader rule of responsibility of the state when the medium involved is international radio.

This broader responsibility cannot be disclaimed by merely invoking the phrase "free speech." Freedom of speech is not absolute in any country. As Justice Holmes observed, it gives no one the right to shout "Fire" in a crowded theatre.[127] As to radio and television in particular, these media have habitually been subjected to a degree of interference with freedom of speech which would never be tolerated for printed media. Many chapters of current novels could not be read over the radio, so different are the controls over offensive or obscene language. The amount and to some extent the tone and charac-

---

[127] *Schenck v. United States,* 249 U. S. 47 (1919). "The most stringent protection of free speech would not protect a man in falsely shouting fire in a theatre and causing a panic. It does not even protect a man from an injunction against uttering words that have all the effect of force. . . . The question in every case is whether the words used are used in such circumstances and are of such a nature as to create a clear and present danger that they will bring about the substantive evils that Congress has a right to prevent." Pp. 51-52.

ter of advertising on radio and television is also controlled, while printed media can carry twenty columns of advertising for every one column of news if they think they will get away with it commercially. This being so, when we come to the far graver questions of warmongering, subversion, and international defamation tending to produce war, it becomes more difficult to assert that the government's lack of effective control, or the traditions of free speech, make it impossible to assume responsibility for preventing these dangerous effects.

The rule that certain types of radio messages issuing from a given state engage its responsibility under international law has the backing of high authority. Cavaglieri, in his report to the Institute of International Law in 1927, stated that

> it is certain that a state cannot tolerate, without incurring the gravest international responsibility, the transmission from its territory of messages containing phrases offensive to a foreign state, for its head or its representatives; or which propose as their object a work of propaganda, false news, or defamation against other governments; or which are addressed to the citizens of any state to incite them to revolt.[128]

Furthermore, the Institute of International Law, in 1927, declared that the state is responsible

> if it does not employ the means at its disposal to prevent radio-telegraphic emissions which, by their contents, are of a nature to disturb the public order of another state, when similar emissions have already been called to its attention by the latter.[129]

But Lauterpacht writes:

> It is believed that this article is only so far expressive of existing international law as it applies to broadcasting stations managed by the State itself . . .[130]

Hyde maintains that

> the failure of a state to employ the means at its disposal to prevent uses of radio stations . . . from causing injury to a foreign state by radio communications

constitutes a failure to perform an international obligation.[131] The Swiss government took a similar stand during a discussion of a proposal for a radio-telegraph station designed to insure for the League of Nations independent communications in time of emergency. In an

---

[128] *Annuaire*, I. D. I., Vol. I (1927), p. 152.

[129] *Ibid*, Vol. III, p. 294. Arrigo Cavaglieri, "Principes de Droit International Régissant la T. S. F.," *Rev. de Dr. Int.*, Vol. II (1928), pp. 860 ff.

[130] Lauterpacht, *op. cit.* ("Revolutionary Propaganda by Governments"), p. 162, n. (i).

[131] Hyde, *op. cit.*, Vol. I, Sec. 192.

official note addressed to the League it affirmed that by virtue of its territorial sovereignty, a

> State is responsible to the other members of the international community for certain acts which may take place in its territory . . . This axiom applies to the case of a radio-telegraphic station, and no state can therefore disregard the activities of an establishment of this kind on its territory.[132]

These authorities, it will be noted, consider that the responsibility of the state is engaged even if a private individual (i. e., an independent broadcasting station) is sending out the objectionable message. Most writers who have considered this problem hold the same view[133] despite Lauterpacht's above-cited contrary opinion.[134] Sténuit thinks the responsibility of the state for harmful broadcasts by an independent radio devolves from the fact that the government may grant or withdraw the concessions.[135] Similarly— to take an analogy from the law of neutrality—while ordinarily the duty of the neutral state is one of abstention but not of repression, nevertheless, this is not so when a particular act by an individual assumes an unusually grave character; thus the neutral must take appropriate action if a private individual or corporation under its jurisdiction is recruiting soldiers for a belligerent, or is outfitting a warship at the latter's behest. Here the duty of the state becomes active and positive. It requires actual repression—prevention or punishment, and sometimes both. Similarly, radio propaganda of the pernicious type, whether defamatory, subversive or war-mongering, represents such a danger to world peace that the law may fairly be considered to require the sending state, in such circumstances, to take the means at its disposal either to prevent or to suppress it.

This relation between the facilities within the control of a state and the extent of its duty is reflected in the broad principle of liability imposed by international law for harmful acts emanating from a state. For example, Judge John Bassett Moore stated in his dissenting opinion in the *Lotus Case:* "It is well settled that a State is bound to use due diligence to prevent the commission within its do-

---

[132] L. O. N. *Official Journal,* Vol. 9, 8-12 (1928), p. 1974.

[133] Carlo Cereti, "La Radiotelegrafia e la Radiotelefonia nei Rapporti Internazionali," *Rivista di Diritto Internazionale,* Vol. 18 (1926), pp. 1-23; Arnold Raestad, "Les Ondes Hertziennes et le Droit International," *J. des Télécommunications,* 1935, p. 213; S. S. Biro, "The International Aspects of Radio Control," *J. of Radio Law,* Vol. II (1932), pp. 45 ff.; Hyde, *op. cit.,* Vol. I, Sec. 192; René Sténuit, *La Radiophonie et le Droit International Public,* Brussels/Paris, 1932, pp. 134 ff.; Günter B. Krause, "Der Rundfunkfriedenspakt von 1936," *Jahrbuch für Internationales Recht,* Vol. IX (1960), pp. 43 ff.

[134] *Supra* p. 161. Also, Joeden, *op. cit.,* (JIR [1954] Vol. IV) pp. 98 ff.

[135] Sténuit, *op. cit.,* p. 146.

minions of criminal acts against another nation or its people."[136] For authority Judge Moore cited with approval the case of *United States v. Arjona*[137] and particularly Mr. Justice Waite's declaration that

> The law of nations requires every national government to use "due diligence" to prevent a wrong being done within its own dominion to another nation with which it is at peace, or to the people thereof; and because of this the obligation of one nation to punish those who within its own jurisdiction counterfeit the money of another nation has long been recognized.

Implicit in the concept of "due diligence" is a recognition that there may be variations between political systems with respect to the amount of state control that can be expected within the context of due diligence. Certainly international law does not expect various countries to revolutionize their constitutions and political systems in order to be able to discharge their international duties. But if, as in the case of radio, a government through its licensing power and through its tradition of exercising some control over standards of content, has shown that a considerable degree of control is readily within its power, then it is not asking too much of the rule of due diligence to require the government to use that available control to minimize threats to peace through propaganda. This theme of "using the means at its disposal" runs throughout most of the statements quoted above summarizing a government's duty, and will also be found to characterize many of the treaties on broadcasting described earlier in the chapter on Defamatory Propaganda. Many of those treaties, it will be recalled, operate not only upon utterances by the state, but also upon state's responsibility to control utterances by individuals. These treaties are good traditional law as between the parties, although they may not be of sufficient universality to add up to a rule of customary international law of themselves.

There is a Latin maxim which states: "*Cessante ratione cessat lex.*" (When the reason ceases, the law ceases). Like all maxims, this one is less than literally reliable. However, the general idea behind it has an important application to the present argument. There is, as we have seen, an impressive body of customary law, authoritative opinion of jurists, treaties, and general principles of law supporting the broad principle that a state ought to be considered responsible for certain dangerous kinds of propaganda by individuals. The United States, England, and other countries have resisted acceptance of this principle, except in two or three extreme cases. However, the reason for this resistance has been that these countries, under their traditions of free speech, do not control the private media involved. As indi-

---

[136] P. C. I. J., Series A, No. 10, Manley O. Hudson, ed., *World Court Reports*, 4 vols., Washington, 1934-1943, Vol. II, p. 80.
[137] 120 U. S. 479 (1887).

cated above, when we come to international radio, this reason cannot be maintained. Since the reason fails, and since these countries have objected on no other grounds, it might well be concluded that their objection does not extend to situations in which their governments can in fact exercise effective control over the particular medium—and can do so without endangering the traditions of free speech any more than they have already been endangered.

The Relation Between Control and Responsibility: Identification of "Private" Entity or Person with State

In some instances the degree of state control over or identification with a theoretically "private" entity may be so great that the case is properly treated as one of state activity. This applies to the cases of the *presse officieuse,* and of the radio chain owned by the state, and of those communicators over whose news and editorial policy the state exerts substantial control—e.g., through subsidies, or the appointment of the governing body. This is likewise true of propaganda issuing from a political party or political organization whose policies are directly controlled by the government. Thus to the impartial observer there can be no doubt of the responsibility of the Soviet Government for subversive messages sent out by the Comintern, although Moscow, in 1935, replying to American protests against such propaganda, replied that "U.S.S.R. cannot take upon itself and has not taken upon itself obligations of any kind with regard to the Communist International." And naturally when the Nazi Party in Germany yesterday, and the Communist Party in Soviet Russia today, are guilty of subversive foreign propaganda, the government cannot evade responsibility, for, in such cases, the *party is the state.*

This may seem to place upon the authoritarian regime a particularly heavy responsibility. But, as Lauterpacht writes, "A State which has chosen this particular form of government may, by this very fact, find itself compelled to follow a considerably higher standard of formal and substantive respect for the dignity, susceptibilities and interests of its neighbors." But some may argue that this difference under the existing rules of law between authoritarian and free countries with respect to the ownership of the media of communication appears to put the former in a disadvantageous position as compared with "free" states. A verbal attack on a foreign nation by the authoritarian press will engage the responsibility of the state while, in the free state, a similar attack by independent newspapers can be made with impunity. From the legal point of view this difference in responsibility seems justified, for a word from Moscow will

164

stop attacks on foreign states, while Washington has no such power over the American press engaged in berating Russia. Nevertheless Soviet Russia has bitterly complained of attacks on it by individuals, and can hardly be expected to be entirely satisfied with the response that the American government possesses no legal means of throttling the press, whose freedom is actually guaranteed by the Constitution, nor by the argument that Washington is under no obligation in international law to take repressive measures.

An individual, even if employed by the government, does not necessarily bind the government by his utterances. When a corporation acts, some individual or individuals are taking action which is attributed to the corporation. But acts they perform in their private capacity do not bind their superior. The same distinction obtains with respect to the national entity, or state, except that when the national executive, for instance, the President of the United States, says something offensive to some foreign country or its leaders, it is difficult for the latter to consider that he is speaking only in his private capacity. Minor officials are in a different category. In fact, the United States has denied any legal responsibility for the hostile utterances of minor officials, although it has at times voluntarily apologized to the aggrieved government. Thus, in 1937, when the German Embassy complained of certain aspersions on the Nazi Government made in a public address by the Mayor of New York City, the Secretary of State, invoking the doctrine of freedom of speech, denied federal responsibility but nevertheless expressed regrets.[138]

In this connection the matter of "privilege" may be mentioned. The messages of the President to Congress are claimed to be immune from protest, on the ground that such a message, not being addressed to foreign governments, is a mere internal transaction. Nevertheless, nations offended by something appearing in a message of the President to Congress have been known to object officially. France protested against President Jackson's message of December 1834, in which reprisals were threatened. Also, Austria protested against President Taylor's comments on the Kossuth Revolution of 1848. The analogy invoked here to the rule of the common law according to which communications between officers of a corporation cannot be made the basis of a suit for libel is not in point, for such messages are, unlike the President's messages, kept within the family. Our government has likewise maintained that debates in Congress are not open to objection by foreign governments, although if the debate leads to the passage of a law inimical to the latter, protest is considered legitimate. In 1920, when Spain objected to certain remarks in the House of Representatives alleged to be derogatory to the Spanish nation and government, the United States pointed out

---

[138] *New York Times,* March 4, 5, 6, 1937.

that under the Constitution Senators and Representatives are not to be questioned in any other place for speeches or debates in either House. It must be admitted, however, that untactful remarks made, even off the cuff, by some Congressman protected by the rule of privilege may be deeply resented by one or more foreign countries and do real harm not only to the national interest but likewise to the cause of good international relations.

Summary of Law on State Responsibility for Private Propaganda

The law on state responsibility for private propaganda may be summarized as follows:

The basic rule is that the state is not responsible under international law for acts of propaganda by private individuals and corporations. To this general rule, however, there are the following identifiable exceptions:

When nations have made actual treaties between themselves assuming the greater responsibility for acts of individuals, this greater responsibility applies to the parties to the treaty.

Subversive propaganda by individuals which goes to the extreme of terroristic activity, and most clearly incitement to assassination, engages the responsibility of the state under international law.

Every state is under a duty to act in order to suppress a hostile expedition being prepared on its soil against a foreign government, therefore also to suppress propaganda directly connected with such a hostile expedition as an overt act.

Because of a long history of international diplomatic custom, a state is responsible for defamation by individuals directed against foreign diplomats.

Finally, because of the universal relatively great degree of control of governments over radio, the better view, in spite of some disagreement, is that states are bound by international law to assure that their territory is not used for the emission of radio signals which would be in the category of war-mongering, subversive, or defamatory propaganda.

Chapter VIII

Individual Responsibility
for Propaganda

INDIVIDUAL RESPONSIBILITY FOR STATE PROPAGANDA

States, like corporations, can only act through human beings. Although up to this point we have talked entirely of responsibility of states, obviously behind each state action was an individual person or a number of persons who made the decision to act, wrote the offensive words, spoke the damaging radio message, or directed the war-mongering or subversive propaganda campaign.

Since the purpose of this book is to examine the extent to which the law can be pressed into service to reduce the propaganda threat to peace, the relevant question for present purposes is this: Can international law act upon individual persons in such a way as to strengthen the deterrent to harmful propaganda?

The law on this subject is dominated by the Nuremberg Judgments. These judgments held that waging aggressive war was a crime, that preparing for and inciting aggressive war through propaganda was also a crime, and that individuals who were responsible for the commission of these acts could be convicted of crime and punished. As mentioned earlier in connection with the general subject of illegality of war-mongering propaganda, its criminality as such was indicated by its inclusion in the indictments, the evidence and the judgments themselves.[1]

The conviction of Rudolph Hess identified propaganda as one part of the crime for which he was convicted. The same was true of the conviction of Rosenberg, the ideologist of the Nazi Party. Streicher was sentenced to death for crimes which were almost entirely in the category of propaganda.

Since there has been so much controversy about the Nuremberg

[1] Supra, pp. 76 ff.

167

Trials, it is essential for our purposes to sort out the non-controversial from the controversial doctrines established by the trials and see whether the element of controversy invades any of the doctrines that are to be relied on here.

The first controversial feature of the Nuremberg Trials was the holding that aggressive war was a crime in 1939. As already noted, this controversy did not affect our present legal analysis, since the United Nations Charter has now removed doubt on this point.

The second controversial aspect of the case was the constituting of a special Tribunal manned in part by representatives of the victorious countries. Some critics asked where such a Tribunal got its authority and whether the impression was not inevitably created that winners were punishing losers because they were losers. It would undoubtedly have been much better if the judges had been taken entirely from countries not involved in the war. On the other hand, no effort was spared to provide the most elaborate safeguards of the rights of defendants to prepare their cases, have the best available legal counsel, and enjoy the full range of protections which the Anglo-American tradition throws around an accused criminal. In any event, whatever the merits of the controversy surrounding the Tribunal, for our purposes we can indulge the assumption that any future tribunal that might apply the rules here discussed would not be subject to similar legal questionings.

As to the propriety of holding individual persons responsible for offenses under international law, this raises no special difficulties, once it is clear that the offense is indeed an offense.[2]

Criticism of the Nüremberg Trials has not so much been directed at the principle of individual liability as such. Rather it has been directed at making the basis of conviction "crimes against peace" instead of war crimes and crimes against humanity, for which the Nazi leaders could have been convicted ten times over without the slightest difficulty.

But even as to this controversy, the element of dispute has now been largely removed by the outlawing of war in the United Nations Charter and by the affirmation of the Nuremberg principles in a unanimous resolution of the General Assembly passed on December 11, 1946.

The question may be raised: How much good does it do to add individual responsibility to official state responsibility, so far as deterrence of harmful propaganda is concerned? This sort of thing is impossible to measure. No one could prove whether, at the moment

---

[2] Oppenheim, *International Law* (8th ed., H. Lauterpacht, 1955), Vol. 1, p. 20. See also: W. W. Gould, *An Introduction to International Law*, New York, 1957, pp. 205-12, esp. pp. 206-07; M. S. Korowicz, *Introduction to International Law*, The Hague, 1959, pp. 325-89, esp. pp. 385-89.

of making a decision to utter some illegal morsel of propaganda, the official finds creeping into the back of his mind the thought, "Perhaps someday I shall be convicted and punished under international law for this." All one can say is that, if he does ever experience such a thought, it may help to add a little to whatever other deterrence exists.

More important might be helping get rid of the kind of official attitude which assumes that no individual culpability attaches to official governmental actions. The Nuremberg Trials revealed that this attitude was almost universal in the Nazi hierarchy. The third echelon official hid behind orders from the second echelon; the second echelon pleaded that it acted under instructions from the first echelon; and so on. Ultimately, according to the defendants at Nuremberg, no individual had any responsibility for the appalling crimes of the regime except Hitler himself—and Hitler died in a bunker under Berlin. This familiar refrain was heard again in the defense of Eichmann. It is true that, as noted in the discussion of war-mongering as an international offense, the Nuremberg Court went very far in excusing a person like Fritsche on the plea that he uttered his vicious propaganda only as a "conduit" for Goebbels.

Any legal support for the proposition that policy-making governmental officials must be conscious of personal legal responsibility for their decisions will be a healthy thing. If it gradually penetrates the attitudes of officials around the world and displaces the prevalent attitude of official irresponsibility, it may have some useful impact on improving the standards of official conduct.

INDIVIDUAL RESPONSIBILITY FOR PRIVATE PROPAGANDA

We now come to the last of the four possible combinations of conduct and responsibility: the liability of the private individual for private acts of propaganda.

When the act for which the individual is being charged is not an official act on behalf of the government, as in the last section, but a private act in the form of articles in a privately owned newspaper, or broadcasts over a private radio or television station, or pamphlets printed and distributed by agitators, refugees, or irredentist groups, some of the difficulties of the last section disappear and new ones arise to take their place.

There is here no difficulty about the principle of individual responsibility for the act, since obviously an individual is fully responsible for his own individual act. The new difficulty is this: while a wrongful act by a state, or by an individual acting for the state, can readily be found to be an offense under international law, the act of an individual in a private capacity raises the fundamental question whether any law has been broken at all. To answer this question we will look first at international law and then at domestic law. As to international law, the problem will be the controversial question whether there can be pieced together out of the various sources of international law enough evidence of the rule to make the conduct unlawful. As to domestic law, the problem is simpler. It is merely one of taking brief note of the existence within certain countries of domestic laws forbidding certain kinds of private propaganda.

International Law of Individual Responsibility for Private Propaganda

International law on individual responsibility for private propaganda has to be extracted largely from the writings of publicists or from corollaries and analogies in other fields of international law. The reason has to do with the practical question: How would this kind of responsibility find its way into an actual tribunal? If the individual were brought before a tribunal in the country where the propaganda was originated by him, the court would be concerned with its own domestic laws governing the alleged offense— a subject which will be considered in the last part of this chapter. If by some chance he fell into the hands of the "victim" country, that country would probably not be at a loss for local laws under which to prosecute him, if the acts were in the nature of subversion, defamation and the like. The possibility of the point arising in some third country is remote. And as to international tribunals, there is no regular court before which such an individual offense could be heard. The International Court of Justice deals only with cases between states.

Nevertheless, it is useful to round out the overall pattern by filling in this area of law as far as possible, even if the result be largely theoretical, and consists more of *lex ferenda* than *lex lata*.

The most interesting possibility is one which has already been discussed in another connection: the possibility of labeling individual war-mongering a crime at international law, a *délit du droit des gens*. This question was discussed under the heading of state responsibility for the practical reason that, if there were such an international crime, the point would be more apt to arise in the form of state responsibility for failure to suppress such crimes by individuals under its control. The jurisdictional problem noted above would be, at least theoretically, less troublesome here, since if the act is a *délit du droit des gens* any state having possession of the person accused of such an international law crime would have the legal right to try him. This would place war-mongering by individuals in the same category as piracy, counterfeiting, and the white-slave traffic. As noted earlier, some writers believe that war-mongering propaganda is rightfully included in this category.[3] Others have questioned this view. The conclusion formulated has been that matters have not yet reached the point where the present existence of such a *délit du droit des gens* can be established.

As to subversive propaganda, we have observed also the existence of a broad view which, under a statement like the following by Rivier, would apply to individuals as well as to states:[4]

> Agitations fomented, undertaken, even simply tolerated in one country against the integrity of the territory of another . . . are directly contrary to the right of conservation and constitute, as such, positive violations of international law.

Here again, we noted that, partly because of the strong insistence by the British and Americans on a narrower rule, this concept of general, broad responsibility cannot be considered to represent existing customary international law. On the other hand, several specific kinds of subversive activity were identified as being of sufficiently special character to engage state responsibility. These included incitement to assassination, overt act preparing for hostile armed action against another country, the defaming of foreign diplomats and probably the use of international radio for harmful propaganda. Applying the principle of corollary reasoning, we could suggest this conclusion: If a given act of propaganda committed by an individual is of such character that it arouses the concern of international law, and if it is of such seriousness and relevance to international order that international law imposes a derivative liability upon the state for the act performed by an individual, then there must be a primary liability of the individual himself for the wrongful act.

Except where an actor is legally incapable of assuming responsibility, as in the case of an insane person or a very young child, it is difficult to conceive how there can properly be a derivative liability upon entity B for the acts of entity A, when there is no primary liability on the part of entity A from which the liability of B can be derived. In all the cases in question, the nature of the liability of the state is purely secondary. That is to say, the state itself has not committed an act of propaganda; its fault lies exclusively in the fact that it has somehow failed to prevent the individual from committing the substantive act constituting the wrong. It seems a permissible conclusion, then, that at least in the four particular situations where state

---

[3] Supra, p. 158. A recent writer, discussing the draft Statute for an International Criminal Jurisdiction, deplores its failure to include an article establishing individual criminal responsibility for false propaganda which places in danger the peace and security of mankind. García-Mora, *op. cit.*, p. 44.

[4] Rivier, *op. cit.*, Vol. I, p. 266.

liability exists for failure to prevent individual subversive propaganda, individual liability should also exist under international law.

This still leaves open the question of how, as a practical matter, an individual is apt to be called to account for this violation of international law. If a regular international court capable of trying individuals for crimes under international law were established, as has been proposed, the answer would be much easier. In addition, one can imagine at least hypothetical combinations of circumstances under which the courts of a third country or the originating country might adduce the rule of international law if they had occasion to try the offender.

The technique of corollary may be applied also to the liability discussed in the last section: the liability of an individual for official acts of war-mongering propaganda. The argument would run as follows: The promulgation of propaganda to foment initiation of aggressive war is an international crime under the United Nations Charter and the Nuremberg Judgments when conducted by a state; any difficulty of holding an individual liable for his crime merely because he is an individual has been overcome by the Nuremberg Trials; propaganda inciting war is no less a violation of international law when carried on unofficially rather than officially; therefore there is no reason why an individual should not be held guilty of an offense under international law because he is guilty of private acts of war-mongering propaganda.

Suppose, for example, that there could have been brought before the Nuremberg Tribunal a defendant whose acts were admittedly exclusively non-governmental and unofficial, but the substance of whose conduct was the same as that of the convicted defendants. There seems to be nothing in the judgments to indicate that the defendant would have been considered any less guilty of the international crime. As a matter of fact, in the case of Streicher, since he had almost no administrative or military role in the crimes for which he was convicted, we may actually have precedent for individual liability for individual propaganda. The conduct for which he was convicted consisted mostly of the incitement to murder and extermination contained in the anti-Jewish publication Der Sturmer, of which he was publisher and editor.

Similarly, in the conviction of Rosenberg, a very large part of the crime for which he was found guilty took the form of essentially private expressions, such as his book, *A Myth of the Twentieth Century,* and other books and periodicals.

As has already been stressed, war-mongering and propaganda in favor of war are comparatively recent offenses because the outlawing of war is itself a comparatively recent development. There has therefore not been much time for a body of customary international law to grow up supporting the thesis of illegality of war propaganda by individuals. However, in view of the above strong arguments from analogy and corollary, and in view of the extent to which the Nuremberg Judgments were based on unofficial as well as official propaganda, it is at least a permissible conclusion that war-mongering propaganda by individuals should be considered an offense under international law for which they are individually responsible.

Domestic Law of Individual Responsibility for Private Propaganda

There has already been occasion in various connections to bring forward domestic statutes and decisions bearing on the illegality of certain kinds of propaganda, but up to this point the operative function of domestic law in which we have been most interested has been its function as evidence of customary international law or a general principle of law recognized by civilized nations.

We are now ready to look briefly at this source of law in its more straightforward function of acting directly upon the conduct of individuals within the particular domestic jurisdiction.

Under the heading of State Responsibility for Individual War-Mongering Propaganda, there were cited at least 25 states which provide in their domestic laws for the prosecution of individuals urging the state to go to war against a foreign state.[5] Thus, a Polish law forbids communications inciting the Polish state to an act of aggression and outlaws propaganda tending to incite any state to such an act. The Constitution of Brazil in Article 141 states that "Propaganda for war . . . shall not be tolerated," and Article 6 of the Constitution of the Democratic Republic of Germany also outlaws war propaganda. The Peace Defense Law of 1951 of the USSR states that war propaganda is "The gravest crime against humanity" and punishes it as a "most grave criminal offense," no matter who the person may be and no matter what state is the object of the incitement to war.[6]

As to subversive propaganda by individuals, it has been noted that Belgium since 1858 has made it a criminal offense to attempt the destruction or modification of the form of government of a foreign state or incite its inhabitants to arm against their leaders.[7] Similar laws forbidding attempts against the security of a foreign country, or instigating rebellion in foreign states, exist in Spain, Czechoslovakia, Greece, Switzerland, Finland, Yugoslavia, Liechtenstein, Bel-

---

[5] *Supra,* p. 156.
[6] For the above, see p. 157,, *supra.*
[7] *Supra,* p. 136, 142.

gium and Israel.[8] The United States statute imposing criminal penalties for assisting organization of an armed invasion of another country has also been noted.[9]

We have also described earlier the various domestic laws aimed specifically at the problem of agitation by refugees. The expulsion of King Carol ordered in 1928 has been noted[10] and the expulsion of General Boulenger by the Belgians in 1889 as well as similar expulsions by the Swiss.[11]

As to defamatory communications, we have noted that attacks on foreign diplomats are made illegal in most countries. All or practically all of 51 states studied showed legal protection under domestic law for foreign diplomats against defamatory attack.[12] We have also seen that as early as 1794 it was considered criminal libel in the United States to insult a foreign minister, and that again in 1898 the Secretary of State of the United States expressed the opinion that it would be criminal libel to charge a foreign diplomatic representative with the operation of a spy system.[13] As to libelous attacks on foreign heads of state, the prevalence of protection under municipal law is less widespread. Twenty-eight were found to give protection to foreign sovereigns or heads of state, three to sovereigns only, and 20 of those studied do not.[14] The history of the law in Britain has also been reviewed in the chapter on Defamatory Propaganda showing a number of convictions, particularly in earlier times, for libels against heads of foreign states. Perhaps the most famous case is that of Jean Peltier, who was convicted for a libel on Napoleon because of the theory that such libels increase the danger of a clash between the two countries,[15] and also because the offensive material contained incitements to assassination.

It has been noted that both the United States and Great Britain have tended to reduce rather than increase the protection afforded by domestic law so far as heads of foreign states are concerned.[16]

In France, under Articles 36, 37, 84 and 85 of the French Penal Code it appears to be possible to prosecute persons committing libels against the heads of foreign states, and one such prosecution was noted in 1896.[17] However, very few cases of this kind have been reported.

The Swiss law was noted, which goes even further and punishes

---

[8] *Supra* p. 136.
[9] *Supra* p. 138-140.
[10] *Supra* p. 145.
[11] *Supra* p. 145.
[12] *Supra* p. 149.
[13] *Supra* p. 151.
[14] *Supra* pp. 149 ff.
[15] *Supra* p. 151.
[16] *Supra* p. 151.
[17] *Supra* p. 152.

outrages against a foreign nation as well as foreign heads of state. Some of the expulsions under this statute have been mentioned above.[18]

In the aggravated case of terroristic activities such as incitement to assassination, we noted that even in Britain a strong line has been taken under domestic law, and that a conviction was upheld in 1881 of a person who had published a pamphlet in Britain urging the assassination of the Czar of Russia. This was found to be both a scandalous libel at common law and a violation of a statute on conspiring to murder, a statute which applies also when the intended victim is outside the realm.[19]

We have also noticed the existence of special domestic laws in the field of radio, such as the laws in Mexico, Peru and Uruguay.[20]

FALSE NEWS

If the offensive propaganda takes the form of false news, another category of domestic controls may come into play.

Many states have attempted through their local legislation to deal with the problem of false news. Such laws fall roughly into three categories. First, some countries merely leave false news unpunished, so long as the particular communication does not come within some established category of prohibited messages, for example, libel, offenses against public morals, messages dangerous to public health and safety, or words tending to a breach of the peace.[21] These coun-

---

[18] *Supra* p. 152.

[19] *supra* p. 139, 153.

[20] *Supra* p. 155.

[21] In 1275 there was enacted a statute, *De Scandalis Magnatum,* which declared:

"Whereasmuch as there have been afore times found in the country devisers of tales . . . whereby discord or occasion of discord hath arisen between the king and his people or great men of this realm . . . it is commanded that none be so hardy as to tell or publish any false news or tales whereby discord or occasion of discord or slander may grow between the king and his people or the great men of the realm; he that doth so shall be taken and kept in prison until he hath brought him into the court which was the first author of this tale." (Quoted in Veeder, "The History of the Law of Defamation," 3 *Select Essays on Anglo-American Legal History,* 453 (1909).

In some form this statute remained in force until 1887, although the last action under it occurred in 1710. *Id* at 454. Its purpose, of course, was to prevent breaches of the peace that otherwise might arise from false rumors. See Plucknett, *Concise History of the Common Law,* pp. 456 et seq.; Scott, "Publishing False News," 30 *Canadian Bar Review* 37, 38 (1952). Stephen's *Digest of the Criminal Law* stated in 1878 that:

"Everyone commits a misdemeanour who cities or publishes any false news or tales whereby discord or slander may grow between the Queen and

tries rely on the organ publishing the news in question or other media, or perhaps on the passage of time to correct the error and attenuate its evil consequences.[22]

Among the countries which believe that the best antidote for false or distorted reports is to provide for wider sources of information, we find the United Kingdom, which reported, in response to a United Nations inquiry, that "False reports published by one organ are, provided there is free access to the appropriate news source, generally offset by correct reports in other." The dangers inherent in attempts by governmental action to clamp down on newspapers in this matter were emphasized as follows: "Great abuses are likely to arise from any attempt by administrative action to prevent the publication of 'false,' 'distorted' or 'tendentious' news, more especially if arbitrary power is conferred on executive authorities to determine what constitutes falsehood, distortion and tendentiousness."[23] Apparently the difficulties of proving error and motive are held to be so great that any prohibition would be ineffective. States holding this view include Belgium, Denmark, Italy, Great Britain and the United States. In a second group of states, the publication of false news is declared to be unlawful provided that the publication is malicious and results in actual harm, or at least is likely to produce harm. Such laws are found in Canada, France, Egypt,[24] the Sudan, Luxembourg, Sweden, Brazil, Chile, Colombia and Lebanon. Uruguay punishes "the malicious diffusion of false news liable to prejudice the order, the public peace, the economic interest or the external security of the State."[25] A third group of laws includes those which seek to ensure the conviction of the offender by omitting the requirement of proof of bad faith. All that is demanded is a demonstration that the news in question may gravely disturb the peace; if so, the bad faith of the author is presumed. Yugoslavia, Spain, Mexico and Nicaragua have this type of law.[26]

---

her people, or the great men of the realm (or which may produce other mischiefs)." P. 62 (1st ed. 1878).
The English case reports and textwriters reveal considerable authority for the proposition that it was punishable to spread false news that would produce public mischief or injury. See citations in Scott, *supra*.

[22] Terrou and Solal, *op. cit.*, Vol. 1, pp. 288 ff.

[23] From reply of United Kingdom to U.N. request for information on this problem; *Freedom of Information, A Compilation,* New York (United Nations), 1950, 2 vols., Vol. I, p. 217.

[24] *The Egyptian Penal Code. Article 188.* Whoever publishes, by any of the same means (indicated in Article 171), false news, fabricated or falsified documents or lies attributed to others, when these documents are related to the public peace or to the public interest, will be punished with imprisonment not exceeding one year and with fine from LE20 to LE100 or with either of the punishments, if the accused does not present a proof of his good faith.

[25] Terrou and Solal, *op. cit.*, p. 289.

[26] Ibid., pp. 289-290.

176

In most countries, notably those where the law against false news requires proof of bad faith, convictions have been very rare. Nevertheless, in theory at least, many of these laws would apply to the case of false news found injurious to foreign nations. Some legislation specifically covers the publication of false reports injurious to other countries if of a nature to disturb the peace. The law of Sweden punishes "the dissemination of rumors or other false statements liable to endanger the safety of the kingdom, the food supply of the population, public order and internal security."[27] And the Rumanian code proposed in 1933 read: "He who outrages a foreign nation by attributing to it untrue acts and thus exposes it to hatred and public shame will be punished."[28]

Fernand Terrou and Lucien Solal, who prepared for UNESCO in 1951 a survey of local legislation dealing with the publication of false news, follow their pessimistic appraisal of the value of laws designed to attenuate the purely domestic evils of such practice, with an even more bearish view of laws aimed at international repercussions of false news when harm is done another nation or to the interests of world peace. This appraisal follows:[29]

> A *fortiori*, the law will be quite unable to penalize false news about foreign countries. This is the most dangerous kind of false news, because it may destroy good international relations and lead to war. But it is hardly possible to prove in court that such news is false. Witnesses would have to be brought from abroad and examined through an interpreter. Further, at times of crisis, such prosecutions would do more harm than good; the declarations of a foreign government might be treated as false by the national judges, and these latter, ill-informed and influenced by public opinion, might decide for the truth of news that was in fact false. . . Useful results could, however, be achieved by means of diplomatic agreements.

The French government, equally pessimistic, has pointed out the difficulties inherent in any attempt on the international level to verify the "truth" of information; such difficulties, it maintains, are "practically insuperable."[30]

The treatment of various kinds of illegal propaganda under domestic law has, up to this point, generally presupposed a situation in which the particular state is acting upon citizens or others within its borders. The basis for the illegality has been somewhat indirect. That is, war-mongering, subversion, and defamation by people within the jurisdiction but aimed at foreign countries has been considered illegal because of the assumed unfavorable effects on a country of

---

[28] Cited by Pella, "La Protection de la Paix par le Droit Interne," *Rev. Gén. de Dr. Int. Pub.*, Vol. 40 (1933), pp. 479-480.

[29] *Op. cit.*, p. 290.

[30] *Freedom of Information, op. cit.*, Vol. I, p. 209.

origin, whether in the form of increased risk of war, retaliation by other countries, or other disturbance of peaceful international relations. In addition, nations will sometimes pass domestic laws or conduct domestic prosecutions on the theory that there is a rule of international law obliging them to do so.

But now suppose that the prosecuting country is itself the victim of foreign propaganda. Suppose, for example, that the circumstances are such that it finds within its jurisdiction a foreign propagandist who has been broadcasting or sending into the country subversive, war-mongering or defamatory propaganda.

In the case of subversion and defamation, or in the case of outright treason, for which Lord HawHaw was tried and convicted by the British, domestic law raises no particular problems beyond, of course, the necessity of obtaining possession of the offender or at least his property. The same might be true of war-mongering propaganda if the particular country had a statute making this a domestic offense.

One question of law which might be raised is the question whether, if a broadcast is sent from a foreign country, the offense sufficiently takes place within the receiving country to give it jurisdiction. The law on this is quite clear. The target state may assume jurisdiction over such cases on the ground that the crime took place where the force impinged, in other words, where its effect took place. Broadcasting to a state is not very different from shooting a bullet from across a frontier line. This principle was reaffirmed by the Permanent Court of International Justice in the famous *Lotus* Case, which upheld the right of Turkey to try the captain of the French steamer which on the high seas had run down and sunk a Turkish ship; the crime was held to have taken place where the force impinged, namely, on the Turkish ship which in the view of the court was assimilated to Turkish territory.[31] Many cases from domestic courts could be cited in support of this doctrine. Thus the German Reichsgericht decided in 1889 that the crime of sedition had been committed on German soil by a person who, from French territory and within hearing distance of the German frontier, had shouted "Viva la France!"[32] And in the *Savarkar* case, where the defendant, from England, had directed a revolt in India, sending to that country tracts and arms for this purpose, the British court held that the crime took place in India, which thus could properly assume territorial

---

[31] *The S. S. Lotus*, P.C.I.J., Series A, No. 10.

[32] *Entscheidungen des Reichsgerichts*, Vol. 20, p. 146; cited by Preuss, *op. cit.* ('International Responsibility for Hostile Propaganda. . .'), p. 665. Sténuit, *op. cit.*, pp. 37 ff. See discussions in Harvard Research Study of Jurisdiction with Respect to Crime, *Am. J. Int. Law*, Vol. 29 (1935), Supp., July 1935, pp. 480 ff.

jurisdiction over the crime.[33] A similar rule has been laid down by a high American tribunal with respect to radio propaganda itself. In *Horwitz et al v. United States,* the operation of a radio broadcasting station in Mexico soliciting participation in a lottery among American listeners was held to constitute an overt act within the United States, as a wrongful solicitation to misuse the United States mails. Circuit Judge Sibley, in his concurring decision, said as follows:

> The radio communications in English were also clearly solicitations to misuse the United States mail intended to reach the people of the United States. And, although more like poison gas than bullets, I think their intended effect when accomplished in the United States constitutes an overt act there. Jurisdiction exists from the standpoint of international law.[34]

The injured (target) state in these circumstances could assume jurisdiction over the broadcaster and prosecute him on another ground based on excellent authority. This is the doctrine laid down by the Institute of International Law, namely, that "Every state has the right to punish acts committed outside its territory, even by foreigners, when the act constitutes: a) an attempt against its security. . ." Many countries already claim such jurisdiction.[35]

In summary: the extent to which domestic law acts upon the kind of propaganda by individuals which is the subject of this discussion is somewhat spotty and irregular. In certain areas, such as those of restraining irredentist or refugee campaigns, domestic legislation may be quite important. It does have the one great advantage of directness and unquestionable enforceability where it is operative. On the other hand, as has been stressed throughout the discussion, by far the greatest part of the modern propaganda problem consists of propagandistic activity by states themselves. Deficiencies in remedies against individuals, then, while they should be the subject of efforts at improvement, should not be allowed to create an impression of general weakness in the law of propaganda out of proportion to the importance of the individual and domestic aspects of the subject.

The substantive law of propaganda, as it establishes the illegality of war-mongering, subversive, and defamatory propaganda by states, and with some gaps and omissions also by individuals, has now been set forth. Even with the deficiencies that have been noted, it is fair

---

[33] Affaire Savakar, *Journal du Dr. Int. Privé,* 38th year(1911), pp. 626-634, citing *Law Times Report,* Vol. 104, p. 473.

[34] 63 Fed. 2d, 706 (1933) at p. 709.

[35] *Annuaire, I. D. I.,* 1879-1880, Vol. I, p. 281, discussed by Bourquin, *op. cit.,* (*Hague Recueil,* Vol. 16 [1927], pp. 164 ff.). See discussion in Research in International Law, Harvard Law School, "Jurisdiction with Respect to Crime," *Am. J. Int. Law,* Vol. 29 (1935), Supp., pp. 543 ff.

to conclude this portion of the book by stating that the principal difficulty of bringing international propaganda within a rule of law does not lie in the lack of substantive law creating and defining the offenses and the liabilities. Rather, the principal difficulties lie in the area to be discussed in the next part of the book: the matter of remedies, and how to make them more effective.

PART III

REMEDIES
AND IMPROVEMENTS

Chapter IX

Monitoring and the Right of Reply

The best hope for improved compliance with the standards established by the international law of propaganda lies first in wider knowledge of the law, and second in much more complete exposure of the facts to which that law applies.

No nation wants to stand before the world branded as a law breaker. Up to the present time, there has been no particular danger that a state will be branded as a law breaker on account of propagandistic activities for two reasons. First, the existence of a body of international law on the subject has not been demonstrated and called to the attention of nations and individuals; and second, the actual facts of broadcasts and other propaganda that might be questionable have not been authoritatively placed before world opinion.

As to the first problem: it is hoped that the present exposition of the law will be followed, not only by further studies expounding the law and enriching its sources, but also by widespread efforts to bring the law's existence to the attention of every country in the world. As to the second problem: methods should be devised for bringing the facts wherever possible out into the open in an authoritative way. One proposal to this end is entitled to immediate attention, both because it has real potentialities for rounding out the process described above, and because it is an action of such relative simplicity that it ought to be capable of achievement even under the strained conditions of today's world.

MONITORING

The proposal is to have the United Nations undertake systematic monitoring of international radio broadcasts.

A brief resume of the history of this proposal in the United Nations will indicate that there is nothing unrealistic about pressing this proposal as a concrete step well within the realm of possibility. President Eisenhower, in his historic speech on August 13, 1958, before the General Assembly of the United Nations, included in his comprehensive proposal for peace in the Near East a suggestion for a system of monitoring inflammatory broadcasts. He said,[1]

> I believe that this Assembly should reaffirm its enunciated policy and should consider means for monitoring the radio broadcasts directed across national frontiers in the troubled Near East area. It should then examine complaints from these nations which consider their national security jeopardized by external propaganda.

An interesting precedent for President Eisenhower's proposal was that put forward in 1953 by Salvador P. Lopez, Rapporteur on Freedom of Information for the Economic and Social Council:[2]

> It would be useful, if with the cooperation of the profession, an annual survey were made of the general situation with regard to the dissemination of false or distorted information on international affairs. In cases where there is damage or harm to international understanding, an investigation might be made with a view to recommending corrective or disciplinary action. Cases requiring governmental action should, of course, be brought promptly to the attention of the Economic and Social Council. Where, moreover, the Council considers a report likely to provoke or encourage a breach of the peace or an act of aggression, it could "furnish information to the Security Council" under Article 65 of the Charter. This is a possibility which obviously needs further study; such study could be entrusted to a rapporteur on freedom of information . . .

A somewhat similar suggestion was offered by Chester Bowles in an article on the African situation. As part of a comprehensive agreement to aid the new states of that continent, he proposes:[3]

> A pledge by all nations to refrain from agitating propaganda within Africa and to end all efforts at direct or indirect subversion. The United Nations could be authorized to investigate all charges of violation and to report to the General Assembly.

Unfortunately no action followed President Eisenhower's proposal, although the speech inspired several of the delegates who followed him to comment favorably on his proposal. Thus Mr. Lloyd, for the United Kingdom, remarked:[4]

> I do not believe that it is consistent with our ideas of a world

---

[1] *Dept of State Bulletin,* Vol 39, No. 1001, September 1, 1958, pp. 337-342, at p. 339; *Gen. Ass. Off. Rec.,* Plenary Meetings and Annexes, 3d Emergency Special Session, August 13, 1958, pp. 7-10.

[2] Salvador P. Lopez, "Freedom of Information, 1953," ECOSOC, *Official Records,* 16th Session, Supp. No. 12. UN, E/2426, May 6, 1953, p. 19.

[3] Chester Bowles, "Great Challenge to the U.N.—Africa," *New York Times Magazine,* August 21, 1960, pp. 15, 108.

[4] *United Nations Review,* September, 1958, p. 47.

order that the official radio of one country should seek to promote bloody revolutions in other countries, and, incidentally to congratulate itself upon its success in so doing. . . I believe that we should all of us submit to a certain discipline in this matter. I think there could be no quicker way of easing tension than for countries to give up this conception that the radio should be used to impose views upon other countries or to subvert their peoples or to incite them to violence and to bloodshed.

Believing that a different standard of behavior should be accepted among nations, he suggested that as a first step the United Nations give serious consideration to the possibility of reports being submitted to member states at periodic intervals on the kind of material being broadcast throughout the world.

Mr. Rifai, speaking for Jordan, complained that

> The persistent attempts of the United Arab Republic to overthrow Jordan's constitutional regime continue in the form of propaganda, shameful press attacks, radio incitement, conspiracies and plots prepared in Cairo and Damascus or on the borders of the Arab Republic with Jordan.[5]

Referring to President Eisenhower's suggestion, he said:

> However, it is imperative that a stop should be put to hostile and inciting propoganda, both in broadcasting and in the press. On this point my Government will not object to the establishment of a United Nations committee or a special international organ to monitor broadcasts and press used for incitement and interference in other countries' international affairs.[6]

Mr. Zorlu (Turkey) praised the proposal, but felt the monitoring should not be confined to the Near East, since a number of other regions, notably parts of Asia and Africa, had been targets of inflammatory and subversive broadcasts. His own state, he said, had been one of the victims.[7] The proposal was also welcomed warmly by Mr. Ahdoh of Iran, but he also thought monitoring should be extended to cover broadcasts throughout the world in general.[8] Mr. Gromyko was not impressed by President Eisenhower's proposal. He complained of the emissions by Radio Free Europe and the Voice of America, and said if the United States and the United Kingdom were indeed worried about the influence of broadcasting, they should accept the proposals of the Soviet Union for the condemnation of war propaganda.[9]

President Eisenhower's proposal would appear to offer a feasible

---

[5] *Ibid.*, pp. 49-50.
[6] *Ibid.*
[7] *United Nations Review,* September, 1958, p. 51.
[8] *Ibid.*, p. 52.
[9] *Ibid.*, p. 62.

remedial procedure, not only for the Near East, but for the entire world.[10] In fact, the proposal is proof that there still is an opportunity for fruitful innovation in this field. True, the monitoring of broadcasts is not new. It was an invention of the inter-war period, widely used by dictatorships and then adopted by all the belligerents on a broad scale in World War II. Today the monitoring of foreign broadcasts is an accepted adjunct of the intelligence services of all the leading powers. But monitoring by a great world organziation is something new.

Investigation and publicity, leading to deliberation and recommendation, constitute highly valuable procedures for peaceful settlement, even in a world of cold war. These procedures proved their worth once more during the war scares over Suez, in Jordan and Lebanon, and in the Cuba crisis.

Where charges and counter-charges of the misuse of radio and other media of propaganda are made, especially international subversion and war-mongering, broadcasts could be monitored and transcribed by an official agency of the United Nations, located perhaps at Geneva. As a result, the participants could be called on to explain the source and nature of an offensive communication before a committee of the United Nations, or perhaps before the Security Council or General Assembly. In any event, there would be worldwide subjection of the text of the broadcast to the white light of publicity. This in itself would be something that has never been done before. A nation now accused of improper propaganda can always quibble about authenticity of the charge, deny that the broadcast was ever made, blame it on some unofficial source, question the translation, or in other ways sufficiently muddy the waters to prevent a clear exposure of the case to world public opinion. Moreover, the world is full of little-known propaganda battles of unusual virulence which seldom come to the attention of even the best informed persons. The systematic monitoring and publicizing by the United Nations of some of these minor league verbal brawls would strip from them the screen of virtual secrecy in which they have been operating because of the failure of the rest of the world to pay much attention to them. To haul all of these broadcasts out into the open and let the fresh air of public attentioin blow through them might well, over a sustained period of time, go a long way toward curbing the worst excesses.

In any case, getting the facts out in the open is an indispensible first step toward curbing the evils of harmful propaganda. Once this has been done, other remedies and devices may be considered as ways of following up the start thus made. One such device, to be considered in the next section, is the right of reply and correction.

---

[10] Whitton, "Radio Propaganda—A Modest Proposal," *Am. J. Int. Law,* Vol. 52 (1958), pp. 739-745.

THE RIGHT OF REPLY

Many countries provide by law for a right of reply, or even a right of compulsory retraction, for use by any individual considering himself injured by a published statement.[11] This remedial procedure is founded on fundamental considerations of common sense and justice. It stands as a legitimate means of self-defense. It assumes that the most practical and the most efficacious remedy available to anyone injured by a communication is a regular legal institution for the establishment of the truth, so as to undo promptly, so far as this is possible, the harm caused by the original publication. The provision for a right of reply, although not common in the United States, is strongly in accord with the familiar American view that the best antidote for propaganda is the assurance of wider sources of news. The person attacked puts into operation certain machinery whereby a new source of information is provided, enabling him to set forth his own version in opposition to the version originally published.

If the complainant in a case of a defamation is given the opportunity to have a reply to the offensive statement published, he may thus be assured in certain circumstances of relief much more substantial than he could procure through any civil action. As every lawyer knows, the requirements governing proof of a charge of libel are extremely technical. Also, moral damage may result from subtle insinuations which cannot be brought within the precise technical definition of libel or slander. Many communications, for example statements in court or in legislatures, are privileged, and cannot be made the basis for civil or criminal action. Trials in actions for defamation are usually costly and may take months or even years to complete. Even if the plaintiff wins the case his reputation may never fully recover from the effects of the original defamatory communication. And, after an extended trial, despite convincing proof of the guilt of the defendant, the plaintiff may have to be satisfied with a symbolic judgment of a few dollars or even cents. Hence the utility of the right of reply, particularly since the complainant is not required to prove material or moral prejudice.

---

[11] For a review of the laws of certain members of the United Nations in this matter, see *Freedom of Information, op. cit.*, Vol. I, pp. 245-253. See also Albert Exhenry, *De Droit de Réponse en Matière de Presse dans les Législations d'Europe*, Lausanne, 1929; Zechariah Chafee, Jr., *Government and Mass Communications*, 2 vols., Chicago, 1947, Vol. I, pp. 145-195, and David Riesman, *Columbia Law Review*, Vol. 42 (1942): "Democracy and Defamation: Control of Group Libel," pp. 727-780, "Democracy and Defamation: Fair Game and Fair Comment I," pp. 1085-1123; "Democracy and Defamation: Fair Game and Fair Comment II," pp. 1282-1318; UN Doc. E/2698, March 14, 1955: "Legal Aspects of the Rights and Responsibilities of Media of Information," (Study prepared by Secretary-General); Martin, *op. cit.*, p. 242, n. 82.

Chafee says of the libel action:[12]

> The crude Anglo-Saxon notion of vindicating honor by getting cash has become unsatisfactory to many decent people. They want a less sordid and more convenient procedure, which will focus its attention on what most concerns them, the mistakes in the defendant's statement. It would be desirable for a court to be able to do something tangible to reduce the injurious effect of those mistakes, without having to bother about any of the hard-fought questions of damages which now take up so much time in a libel suit.

Donnelly writes in the same vein: "A successful libel suit is, at best, almost as unusual as a successful action to break a will. It is the rare exception."[13] The laws of various countries on the rights and responsibilities of information media are dealt with in a study prepared by the United Nations Secretariat and transmitted in 1955 to appropriate information enterprises and professional associations.[14]

Numerous domestic precedents from other countries for the institution of an international right of reply can be cited, although it is not widely used in Anglo-American jurisprudence.

In 1950 the United States government informed the United Nations that Nevada was the only state which expressly provided in its laws for a right of reply.[15] But twenty states offer to the plaintiff, as an optional remedy, the right to demand a retraction, and if the defendant publishes this retraction (or if the plaintiff fails to ask for it), the recoverable damages are reduced, some states cutting off punitive damages, others general damages as well.[16]

A score of nations now provide for mandatory publication and right of reply.[17] An interesting example is the Cuban Presidential Decree of August 3, 1950, which reads:[18]

> (1) Any individual or corporate body referred to directly or indirectly in any radio broadcast in offensive terms, whether explicit or veiled, touching his reputation, or to whom acts have been attributed falsely or in a distorted form shall have the right to request the Ministry of Communications, through the Directorate of Radio, that the correction of such remarks shall be published by the broadcasting undertaking used for the transmission of the said version, the appro-

---

[12] Zechariah Chafee, "Possible New Remedies for Errors in the Press," *Harvard Law Review,* Vol. 6 (1946), pp. 1-43, at p. 7.

[13] Richard C. Donnelly, "The Right of Reply: An Alternative to an Action for Libel," *Virginia Law Review,* Vol. 34 (1948), pp. 867-900 at p. 874.

[14] E/2698 and Add. 1; *U. N. Yearbook 1955,* pp. 166-167.

[15] *Nevada, Compiled Laws, Hillyer,* 1929, Sec. 10506. *Freedom of Information,* U. N. 1950, Vol. I, p. 253. Mississippi also gives the injured party a right of reply. If the newspaper fails to print the reply it is liable for actual damages or $500 punitive damages, whichever is larger. Mississippi Code Annoted, §3175.

[16] *Freedom of Information,* U. N. 1950, Vol. I, p. 245.

[17] Martin, *op. cit.,* p. 242, n. 82. See also Riesman, *op. cit.,* p. 1114

[18] Martin, *op. cit.,* p. 148.

priate announcement being read either by the station's announcer or by the person concerned himself.

In 1819 the first such law was passed in France. Originally its purpose was to enable the government to reply effectively to injurious press statements. Later this right was made available to civil servants, and eventually it was offered to anyone considering himself injured by published materials. The basic law in France is the Act of July 29, 1881 as modified by the law of September 29, 1919, Art. 13.[19] The French example was followed by many other countries.[19a]

When, after the First World War, international propaganda was first recognized as a serious international problem, it was only natural —given the tendency of international lawyers to invoke analogies to local law as a means of solving international problems—that an attempt should be made to institute an international right of reply.[20] One of the earliest of such proposals was made in 1929, when the International Juridical Congress on Radio, at its fourth congress, adopted a *voeu* (opposed by the American delegation), favoring the extension to broadcasting of the right of reply then in use in some countries for defamatory articles appearing in the press.[21] At about the same time, a French court decided that the right of reply, designed for articles in the press, was not applicable to broadcast messages.[22] (It was reported to the United Nations in 1950 that a new draft broadcasting act would establish in France as regards radio, *mutatis mutandis*, a right of reply similar to that already existing for the press.)[23] In 1931, the International Federation of League of

[19] Exhenry, *op. cit.*, pp. 11 ff.

[19a] The Third Committee of the 16th General Assembly discussed a proposal for an individual right of reply as part of the Draft Convention on Freedom of Information, at its 1125th through 1132rd meetings. The discussions were extremely enlightening, since they not only reflected the individual views of many nations, but demonstrated the many problems which the operation of such a right would entail. The Article 4 of the proposed Draft Convention on Freedom of Information, whose consideration was postponed by the General Assembly until the 17th session (G. A. Res. 1681 [XVI], 18 Dec. 1961) reads as follows:

"The Contracting States recognize that the right of reply is a corollary of freedom of information and may establish appropriate means for safeguarding that right."

(See Report of Third Committee: A/5041).

[20] Whitton, "An International Right of Reply?" *Am. J. Int. Law*, Vol. 44 (1950), pp. 141-145; Maxime Tardu, "Les Aspects Internationaux du Droit de l'Information," unpublished thesis, Faculty of Law, Paris, 1951.

[21] Compte Rendu, 4e Congrès, pp. 115-140; Lapie, "Droit de Réponse et Radiophonie," *Rev. Jr. Int. Radioélectr.*, 5th year (1929), p. 16; Saudemont, "Le Droit de Réponse en Radiophonie," *ibid.*, p. 166.

[22] *Ibid.*, 5th year (1929), p. 57, 6th year (1930), p. 36.

[23] *Freedom of Information, op. cit.*, Vol. I, p. 248. On December 9, 1959, a bill was filed the effect of which would have been to extend the right of reply to radio and television. The bill was revived on May 16, 1961, and sent to a committee for discussion. *Sénat*, No. 212, Annèxe au procès-verbal de la 2e séance du 16 mai 1961.

Nations Societies favored the establishment of a right of reply on behalf of any state objecting to a press or radio report which was inexact or calculated to disturb international relations.[24] A similar view was voiced by the International Federation of Journalists at its conference held at Brussels in 1934.[25] Other similar proposals could be cited.[26] On the other hand, the 1936 Geneva convention on radio propaganda made no reference to an international right of reply, apparently because of the negative recommendation of the Committee of Experts who prepared material for the conference. These experts believed that the right, being designed for the printed word, was inapplicable to cases of defamation by radio. While the insertion of a reply or rectification in a newspaper is lasting, it was said, a similar reply sent out over the air waves would be quite ephemeral. Futhermore, it was felt that the obligation to allot time for replies over the air would be unduly burdensome to the broadcasting company. Other practical difficulties were mentioned.[27] The most plausible suggestion—the insertion in a newspaper of a concise article correcting the error appearing in a broadcast, followed by a brief explanation—was not adopted.[28]

Such a right, however, actually does exist under the laws of Indiana. A 1937 law requires that in case of the broadcasting of defamatory remarks, the aggrieved party, three days before commencing a defamation suit, must serve on the company a notice in writing specifying the words or acts alleged to be false or defamatory; the company then has ten days within which to make a "full and fair retraction." In such case, if it is proved at the trial that the emission was made in good faith, and was due to mistake or a misapprehension of the facts, then the plaintiff may recover only actual damages.[29]

Some authorities, however, have argued that in many cases the wiser course would be to ignore entirely the objectionable statements, whether printed or broadcast, for fear that insistence on a right of reply might only serve to aggravate the injury by giving it even greater publicity, thus playing into the hands of the propagandist. Thus Alphonse XII, who suffered an insult while on a state visit in

---

[24] Meeting at Budapest, May 1931. L. O. N. Doc. C. 602, M. 240. 1931 IX-IX. Disarmament 1931 IX. 19, p. 4.

[25] L.O.N. *Bulletin of Information on the Work of International Organizations,* Vol. VII (1935), pp. 50-51.

[26] For example, see *Sixième Congrès Juridique Internationale de la Radio-électricité,* (held at Brussels), Paris, 1936. The delegates voted in favor of a right of rectification in case of inexact or injurious allegations.

[27] *Broadcasting and Peace* (Studies and Projects in the Matter of International Agreements), Paris, 1933, p. 26.

[28] *Ibid.,* p. 190.

[29] Acts 1937, Ch. 37, Sec. 2, p. 231, cited by Stuart Sprague, "More Freedom of the Air," *Contemporary Law Pamphlets* (New York Univ., School of Law), Series 1, No. 26 (1940), pp. 9-10.

Paris, could have insisted that the offender be punished under existing French law, but wisely chose to make no complaint.[30]

At the United Nations Conference on Freedom of Information, held at Geneva in March and April, 1948, a draft convention concerning the establishment of an international right of correction, the so-called "French Convention," was adopted. According to this text, if a contracting state alleges that news reports likely to injure its relations with other states transmitted from one country to another country by foreign correspondents or by news agencies and disseminated abroad are false or distorted, it may submit its own version of the facts. This draft, in substantially the same form, was approved by the General Assembly of the United Nations on May 14, 1949, as part of the first world Convention on the International Transmission of News and the Right of Correction.[31] Later the General Assembly separated the right of reply, and in substantially the same form opened it formally for signature on December 16, 1952 as the Convention on the International Right of Correction.

Under this convention the "right of correction" becomes operative when a state party to the convention contends that: 1) a news dispatch is capable of damaging either its relations with other states or its national prestige or dignity; (a Mexican proposal for the compulsory correction of *any* report was voted down after much debate); 2) it is transmitted from one country to another country by correspondents or information agencies; 3) it is published or disseminated abroad; and 4) it is false or distorted. In such case the injured party may submit its version of the facts—the *communiqué*—to the contracting state or states within whose territory the report was published or disseminated. A copy of the *communiqué* goes to the news agency or correspondent concerned to enable it to correct the objectionable dispatch. This *communiqué* can only refer to the news dispatch and must contain no comment or expression of opinion and must be "not longer than is necessary." The text of the objectionable dispatch must accompany it, plus evidence that the dispatch was transmitted to the agency whose correspondent was responsible, if its agency.[32] With the least possible delay—and within at least five days —the *communiqué* must be released to the correspondents and information agencies operating in the territory in question and also be transmitted to the agency whose correspondent was responsible, if its headquarters are located within the national territory. In case the receiving state fails so to publicize the *communiqué* within the time

---

[30] Whitton, *op. cit.* ("The United Nations Conference on Freedom of Information . . . ."), p. 80; Edouard Clunet, "Offenses et Actes Hostiles Commis par des Particuliers contre un État Étranger," *J. de Dr. Int. Pub.*, Vol. 14 (1887), pp. 5, 19.

[31] Res. 630 (VII), *U. N. Yearbook,* 1952, pp. 463-465.

[32] Letter from United Nations Secretariat.

limit, it may be submitted by the complainant government, together with the original dispatch, to the Secretary-General of the United Nations, so informing the state complained against. The latter within five days may submit its comments to the Secretary-General, who, within ten days, must give appropriate publicity through the information channels at his disposal of both *communiqué,* dispatch and comments.

This convention is now in force for the ratifying parties, as of August 25, 1962, thirty days after Sierra Leone deposited its instrument of ratification. The terms of the text require ratification by at least six states. Other ratifying states are Cuba, El Salvador, Guatemala, United Arab Republic, and Yugoslavia. Now that as a result of the adoption of this convention by the necessary minimum number of countries, there is in effect for the first time an actual right of reply on the international scene, the discussion of the merits and difficulties of this remedy have passed from the realm of theory to the realm of actuality.

The theoretical advantages of the right of reply have been generally supported by analogy from right of reply in domestic legislation, and indeed it is possible to make out a persuasive case for the appropriateness of this remedy as between nations. It is argued that the remedy is found, not in the attempt to punish the offender, but in the nature of the assistance rendered the victim, and that therefore the general interest—concern for peaceful international relations —is brought into harmony with the individual right of free expression. Thus, given general application, the right of correction could offer within the offending nation, including a dictatorship if it would accept such a remedy, an opportunity to an injured power to answer officially inspired campaigns against it or its leaders. And, on the other hand, it could give considerable satisfaction even to a dictatorship considering itself unjustly attacked by the free press in the democracies. This is particularly significant, since the governments of such free countries, because of constitutional guarantees of freedom of the press, have often found themselves unable to do more than express regrets—hardly a satisfactory remedy for the aggrieved government.

Moreover, the beneficial effect of the existence of a right of reply may extend beyond the mere correction of a particular item. It may have a salutary long-range effect. If everyone knew that his utterances might be subjected to this official procedure, he might be more careful about the accuracy and propriety of his statements.

When we turn to the difficulties of applying the right of reply in practice, we begin to encounter administrative problems of considerable complexity. The heart of the problem lies in the question whether some degree of discretion must not be allowed to the body administering the remedy.

If a demand for right of reply is made upon the offending country and complied with, no difficulty arises. But if the alleged offender declines to afford a right of correction through its own channels, and if the complainant exercises his right of appeal to the United Nations under the convention just discussed, the question would arise whether some room for judgment on appropriate action should be allowed. This room for judgment might be necessary on two principal questions: First, whether there was in fact any ground for making a correction at all; and second, whether the proposed statement put forward by the complainant is itself correct.

It might be argued that this discretion is not necessary to make the right of reply workable, but the Secretary-General should be compelled to give publicity to a countervailing statement whenever asked to do so. The theory would be that if both statements were inaccurate and offensive, at least both sides would have had an opportunity to say what they have to say and the inaccuracies could cancel each other out. Against this it could be argued that two blacks do not make a white, and two wrongs do not make a right, and two false and offensive statements, far from solving the problem, might make it twice as bad as it was before.

Even under the terms of the convention now in effect between six nations, there appears to be an area in which the Secretary-General must exercise some judgment. The *communiqué* must contain no comment or expression of opinion and must be no longer than is necessary. Suppose, then, that in an exchange between Cuba and Guatemala, a *communiqué* under the right of reply is submitted to the Secretary-General which contains a great deal of abusive, inflammatory and opinionated material. Someone would obviously have to decide whether this violated the limitations contained in the convention, and that someone would presumably have to be the Secretary-General. T   does
not itself place   decide
whether the o   t does
place upon l   istinc-
tion betwee   d, and
factual c   re, the
right of rep   r pressing the communications facilities of the United Nations into service in disseminating the worst kinds of national propaganda.

There seems to be no insuperable reason why the Secretary-General could not set up procedures within his office to undertake the function of making this type of decision. As a last resort, there is

193

always the possibility of the referral of a question to the International Court of Justice for an advisory opinion. Such referrals would probably be very rare, but the residual availability of this ultimate resort to the highest authority within the United Nations on international law would purge the procedure of any taint of purely administrative arbitrariness.

Perhaps this is about as far as any discretion could realistically go, quite apart from the desirability of broader discretion. As to the question of the truth of the original statement, and the truth of the reply, a satisfactory determination would in some cases necessitate the most elaborate kind of investigation and trial, going far beyond anything that the Secretary-General could reasonably be expected to undertake. Suppose, for example, that the United States demanded a right of reply to reports that it had engaged in germ warfare in Korea. One shudders to think of the magnitude of the resulting litigation, if both sides were to be satisfied that they had a chance to present their cases in full. Or suppose that the United States demanded the right to reply to charges that it was involved in the assassination of the Syrian Deputy Chief of Staff in April, 1957. A full airing of the truth of the charges and countercharges involved would presumably require nothing short of the equivalent of a full scale murder trial.

On balance, therefore, the tentative conclusion at this point should probably be that the Secretary-General must rightly exercise sufficient discretion to confine all of the statements in the right of reply procedure to statements of fact as distinguished from opinion and comment, but that it would be administratively unworkable to expect him to pass upon the inherent truth or falsity of either the original statement or the proffered correction. Whether the right of reply, within these limitations and subject to these imperfections, can be made into an effective instrument of propaganda control can probably only be learned by further research, and particularly by further experience with the remedy in actual operation.

Chapter X

Freedom of Information

The two specific remedies so far considered, monitoring and right of reply, both rely for their efficacy on the salutary effect of the widespread exposure of the truth as an antidote to the false and sinister. The present chapter considers a more general application of this therapy: the overall movement for greater freedom of information.

Although this book is mostly concerned with the task of curbing harmful propaganda, it goes without saying that there are two parallel duties to be performed by any effort in the field of international communication. The one function is to minimize damaging propaganda. The other function is to maximize freedom of communication. The two functions are closely interrelated, and the one cannot be considered apart from the other. For example, inevitably when controls on harmful propaganda are being considered, a point is reached at which it must be asked whether the gains to be achieved through suppression of damaging propaganda are overbalanced by the losses that ensue in the form of undue restraints on free communication between peoples. So also in the present chapter the relationship between the two is close. The more freedom of information can be achieved, the more difficult it will be for distorted propaganda to survive the competition of truth.

FREEDOM OF INFORMATION ACTIVITY IN THE UNITED NATIONS

Since 1945 collective efforts of remarkably wide scope and intensity in the field of freedom of information have been made continuously by a number of United Nations agencies. The post-war movement was given considerable impetus by President Roosevelt's Four Freedoms Speech during the war, and at San Francisco, largely due to pressure from the United States, the cause of freedom of information was consecrated in the United Nations Charter as one of the human rights and fundamental freedoms. The matter has been before the General Assembly, the Third Committee of that body,

195

ECOSOC, and the Commission of Human Rights. It has been delegated to a Sub-Commission, a single Rapporteur (who prepared the admirable Lopez Report of 1953), an *ad hoc* committee, and a Committe on Freedom of Information, which since 1957 has been the agency mainly responsible for effort in this field. The high point for an effort which since then has been adversely affected by the Cold War was the Geneva Conference of 1948 on freedom of information and of the press. From this meeting, as we show later, came three conventions, of which the most notable was the convention on international correction or right to reply discussed in the previous chapter.

Nor should we fail to note significant gains of a technical nature accomplished through the Specialized Agencies, notably UNESCO, International Telecommunications Union, Universal Postal Union, Food and Agricultural Organization, and International Labor Organization, usually in cooperation with the appropriate agencies of the General Assembly and Secretariat.[1] UNESCO, through technical missions, has sought to expand communications facilities in the underdeveloped nations, train news personnel, and supplement facilities for the provision of newsprint. Other specialized agencies have aided in overcoming legal and administrative obstacles to the flow of information, especially with respect to telegraph rates, assignment of frequencies, postal facilities, tariffs, copyrights, etc. Also, these agencies have produced a long series of studies and reports, and have collected and published statistics and other data, especially legislation (domestic laws of libel, provisions for a right of reply, barriers to communication), which have proved to be of great value to workers in this field.

It would be an impossible task to cover this immense activity in a volume of this kind. Much of the work of the United Nations bearing directly or indirectly on freedom of information is covered in other chapters, notably in our treatment of monitoring, a right of reply, the movement against jamming, and a code for newsmen. In the present section we propose to deal with the collective efforts of the United Nations, through international legal obligations, to promote and even guarantee freedom of information throughout the world. But even here, we must, within the general scheme of this inquiry, concentrate on those efforts which have to do with the problem of hostile international propaganda.

The first specific reference to freedom of information in United Nations meetings occurred at the second session of the Preparatory Commission, in November and December 1945, which decided that the Commission on Human Rights should formulate recommendations, among other matters, dealing with freedom of information.[2]

[1] See Lopez Report, E/2426, 6 May 1953, pp. 6-10
[2] Doc. PC/20

The first General Assembly, in 1946, debated and approved a resolution introduced by the Philippine delegation calling for an international conference on freedom of information.[3] In this resolution it was stated that "freedom of information requires as an indispensable element the willingness and capacity to employ its privileges without abuse," and that it "requires as a basic discipline the moral obligation to seek the facts without prejudice and to spread knowledge without malicious intent."[4]

The Economic and Social Council was directed to make preparations for this conference, which was held in 1948 as described below.

At its meeting in May and June 1946, the Economic and Social Council authorized the establishment of a Sub-Committee on Freedom of Information and of the Press. It also discussed the problem of human rights. During this discussion the representative of the United Kingdom stated[5]

> . . . if we are to have the fullest guarantees for the freedom of the press, we must also, in cooperation with the press, and let me add, with the authorities who control the radio systems of the world, we must in cooperation with them, find some way in which we can restrain irresponsible perversion or suppressions of the truth. Everybody knows that in the period before the war, large parts of the press in various important countries, and in smaller countries too, belonged to vested interests, and I know . . . how powerful that influence was—the vested interests' influence in destroying the work of the Disarmament Conference.

At this same meeting the representative from Belgium proposed an international convention requiring the insertion in the world's press of information supplied by the United Nations, with the object of insuring that information be supplied to the public objectively and fully "and not as in the past, deformed by the press organs."[6]

The Commission on Human Rights began its extended deliberations on the matter of freedom of information in January and February of 1947, when it discussed the constitution and terms of reference of the proposed Sub-Commission on Freedom of Information and of the Press.[7] Particularly interesting was this statement from the representative of Lebanon:

> We believe there can be no real peace anywhere in the world so long as the truth in any of its forms is withheld or artificially controlled. There may indeed be peace, but only for a time.[7a]

---

[3] U. N. Yearbook 1946-1947, p. 77
[4] Ibid., p. 176
[5] E/P/V/5, p. 71
[6] Ibid., p. 61 ff.
[7] U. N. Yearbook 1946-1947, pp. 471, 526
[7a] E/CN.4 Sub 1/38, p. 9

The representative of Yugoslavia urged the Commission to examine the "measures to be taken against those who abuse the freedom of information or influence the public opinion in a way that could put in danger the friendly relations between nations by publishing false information."[8] And the French delegate emphasized that freedom of the press had often been used by enemies of freedom against freedom itself by utilizing the press, for example, to prepare a nation to accept Nazism. He believed that some responsibility should accompany liberty of the press and that both governments and private individuals should be held responsible for abuses, and that some type of international organization of the press was needed which could serve to counteract false information.[9]

Further preparations for the United Nations Conference on Freedom of Information and of the Press were made by the Sub-Commission in May and June 1947[10] and by the drafting committee of the Commission on Human Rights, also in June 1947.[11] When the Economic and Social Council met in July and August, 1947, to consider the report of the Sub-Commission, the debate that then took place was particularly significant because several typical points of view clearly emerged. While all parties admitted that there had been abuses in the press, there was sharp disagreement as to the best method to overcome them. For example, the delegate of Norway felt that the main reliance must be placed on professional organizations of journalists and newspapermen. The representatives of the Communist bloc again urged the acceptance by all states of firm obligations to impose severe legal controls to suppress abuses, and wanted the press to take a positive stand in the fight against Fascism. The Soviet representative insisted that "if the press is to perform its highest task, it can only do so if it fights for the principles of democracy . . . if it helps the development of friendly relations between nations based on mutual respect and democracy." This last viewpoint was attacked by the representative of France who stated: "It is impossible to order the press, to orchestrate it, with a view to synchronized campaigns, even if we earnestly believe in the aims in view." Along the same line, a statement by the representative from Canada reads: "We do believe that to say that the object of the press is not to tell the truth but to promote democracy or to promote any other set of values, however good, is mistaken in philosophy and profoundly dangerous in practice." The Soviet delegate again insisted on the necessity for repressive measures, saying in the course of his speech:[12]

---

[8] *Ibid.*, p. 4
[9] *Ibid.*, pp. 4-5
[10] *Ibid.*, p. 9
[11] *Ibid.*, p. 11
[12] For this exchange of views, see *ibid.*, pp. 15 ff.

If we must forbid the use of opium and sign a convention against the harm that the use of opium and other narcotic drugs can bring to mankind, if we have a convention against obscene publications, then it is also our sacred duty to forbid any fostering of war or any activities which are contrary to the main principles of the United Nations, against peace and security in the world. Is it more important to fight the harm done by opium and obscene publications than to fight propaganda against peace, against friendly relations among nations, against the main objectives of the United Nations?

These preliminary steps finally culminated in the calling of the United Nations Conference on Freedom of Information, held at Geneva in March and April, 1948, and the drafting and signing of three major conventions and a large number of resolutions.[13] The major objective of the Conference was the improvement in the means of sending information across frontiers in accordance with the view, solemnly affirmed by the Conference, that freedom of information is "a fundamental human right and . . . the touchstone of all the freedoms to which the United Nations is dedicated." But the negative aspects of the problem were not neglected. Considerable attention was given to measures proposed to curb the use by nations in their mutual relations of various types of harmful propaganda. In fact, the two resolutions passed at the 1947 General Assembly, already mentioned—the one condemning war propaganda, the other directed against false and distorted information—were specifically referred to this conference for attention.

Three draft conventions were adopted, namely, the United States Convention on the Gathering and International Transmission of News, the French Convention for an International Right of Correction and the British Convention on General Principles of Freedom of Information. The Conference also approved a draft article for inclusion in the proposed United Nations Declaration and Covenant of Human Rights, and passed 43 resolutions of varying importance, some of which it was hoped might eventually become international conventions.

We cannot do justice here to the enormous output of the Conference, and so will confine ourselves to those matters having a direct bearing on the problem of international propaganda. Such matters may be divided arbitrarily into three classes: 1) Measures of a gen-

---

[13] For an account of the work of this conference, see "United Nations Conference on Freedom of Information, Geneva, Switzerland, March 23-April 21, 1948, Report of the United States Delegates with Related Documents," *Dept. of State, Publ. 3150, International Organizations and Conferences*, p. 5; Whitton, "The United Nations Conference on Freedom of Information and the Movement Against International Propaganda," *Am. J. Int. Law*, Vol. 43 (1949), pp. 73 ff.

eral nature. 2) Measures condemning propaganda. 3) Proposals for remedies or for further efforts.

1) Since many of the evils of international propaganda would tend to disappear with a sufficient increase in the dissemination of ideas and information across frontiers, it is worth noting that the Conference declared that freedom of information is a fundamental right; that each individual has the right to freedom of thought and expression; and that he may hold opinions without interference, and seek, receive and impart information and ideas by any means and regardless of frontiers. The right to listen was specifically confirmed and a number of measures to this end were proposed; for instance, the distribution of inexpensive radio sets to make this "right" more effective. Since censorship and the propaganda bureaus go hand in hand, it is significant that the Conference condemned peacetime cen- ·sorship and that Convention One contained the obligation to confine censorship in peace to measures required by the needs of national military security. ("Military security" was changed later to "national defense"). Even such censorship was surrounded with meticulous conditions designed to make it as innocuous as possible.

2) Several of the resolutions adopted condemn the use by states of harmful propaganda. Resolution 2, endorsing the two anti-propaganda resolutions passed at the 1947 General Assembly already referred to, declares that war propaganda and the spreading of false and distorted reports are contrary to the purpose of the United Nations and "condemns solemnly all propaganda either designed or likely to provoke or encourage any threat to the peace, breach of the peace, or act of aggression and all distortion and falsification of news through whatever channels, private or governmental." Among other provisions this resolution asserts that only a free press—one "free to seek and to disseminate the truth"—can hope to counteract Nazi, Fascist, or other propaganda of aggression or of racial, national and religious discrimination. Resolution 3 makes a number of suggestions for the implementation of Resolution 2, while Resolution 4 is aimed at the dissemination of racial and national hatred and prejudice, suggesting as the best remedy for such evils the widest possible dissemination of free information through a diversity of sources, and provision for suitable non-legislative measures in addition to appropriate legislative measures by states "within their constitutional limits."

3) Among other remedies, Resolution 26 calls for the appointment of a committee of jurists to formulate a body of fundamental rules and principles with respect to the law of libel, a matter closely connected with certain types of international propaganda, but in the opinion of the delegates not yet ready for action without further research. Resolution 36 recommends additional study of the project for

an international code of honor for journalists and an international court of honor. Finally, Resolution 39 includes a paragraph suggested by the Russians directing the Sub-Commission to study the problems caused by the dissemination of false or distorted information, and to recommend means to spread "true information to counteract Nazi, Fascist, or other propaganda of aggression or of racial, national, and religious discrimination."

The three conventions and the 43 resolutions were all adopted by overwhelming majorities, such as votes of 32-5 or thereabouts. The Communist bloc, led by the U.S.S.R., maintained a stubborn opposition throughout, refusing even to sign the Final Act, and its obstructionist tactics in the Economic and Social Council, when that body considered the results of the Conference in August 1948, effectively blocked any action other than the discussion of Convention One. As a result, the Economic and Social Council was forced to submit the entire matter without action or recommendation to the General Assembly.

On May 13, 1949, the General Assembly, after extended debates there and in the Third Committee, adopted by a vote of 33-6, (all affirmative but the Soviet bloc) and with 13 abstentions, the "Convention on the International Transmission of News and the Right of Correction."[14] This convention was an amalgamation of two of the three draft conventions adopted at Geneva, namely, the so-called American and French Conventions.

This convention contains much of interest concerning the problems here under discussion. In the preamble we find full recognition of the danger of friction and war caused by false or distorted reports and of the necessity of combatting war-mongering propaganda. But the enormous difficulties in the way of effective international action are underlined by the statement that "it is not at present practicable to institute, on the international level, a procedure for verifying the accuracy of a report which might lead to the imposition of penalties for the publication of false or distorted reports." Remedies for these evils must be sought primarily in a wider circulation of news, heightening the sense of responsibility of those engaged in news dissemination, and the institution of an international right of correction.[15]

Numerous provisions are contained in the body-proper of the convention to improve the gathering and international transmission of news. A few of these are of concern for the present study. The contracting states are required to expedite, in a manner consistent with their immigration laws, the administrative procedures for the entry, residence, travel and egress of correspondents. Correspondents are protected against expulsion due to what they may have lawfully re-

---

[14] *U. N. Yearbook 1948-1949,* p. 564, Preamble to the Convention.
[15] *Ibid.*

ported, and their access to sources of news is facilitated in many ways. Censorship in peacetime is confined to regulations "relating directly to national defense," and these rules are strictly defined and circumscribed.[16] The right of contracting states to make and enforce laws and public regulations for the protection of national security and public order is reserved, and their right to prohibit news material which is blasphemous or contrary to public morals or decency. This convention's international right of correction, limited however to reports that are false or distorted, has already been mentioned.

An attempt by the Soviet bloc to qualify the definition of "news material" as that *not* of a nature to provoke or encourage threats or breaches of peace or acts of aggression, and *not* intended as a dissemination of false or distorted reports, was voted down as a subterfuge; it would merely have permitted a state to exclude almost anything from the purview of the treaty, on the mere pretext that it was false, distorted, or of a war-mongering nature, or otherwise prejudicial to its relations with other states.[17] Similarly, a Mexican proposal to impose on correspondents a legal duty to report the facts properly was defeated. The Mexican representative, supported by many Latin American delegations, and those of the Middle East, India and the Soviet bloc, proposed the following text:

> It is the duty of information agencies and foreign correspondents to report the facts without discrimination, to promote respect for human rights and fundamental freedoms, to further international understanding and cooperation and to contribute to the maintenance of international peace and security.[18]

While the United States delegate approved of the objectives of this proposal, he stated that his country could never accept such legal obligations, for fear of approving the totalitarian thesis that government should dictate the functions of the press. By merely accusing correspondents of failing to comply with this definition of their functions, any government could deprive the individual of all benefits of the convention.[19]

The approval of the other treaty drafted at Geneva in 1948—the Convention on Freedom of Information—as well as the question of opening up for signature the news-gathering convention, came before the General Assembly at its Fourth Session, in September, 1949. Here further action on the convention was postponed until the next session

---

[16] Art. VII, Art. XII.
[17] Doc. A/C.3/416, April 7, 1949.
[18] Doc. A/C.3/SR202, April 26, p. 12.
[19] Extensive debates on the Mexican proposal are summarized by Samuel De Palma in "Freedom of the Press, An International Issue," *Dept. of State Bulletin,* November 14, 1949, reprinted as Dept. of State Publication 3687, January, 1950, pp. 10 ff.

of the General Assembly, pending receipt of the Covenant on Human Rights from the UN Commission on Human Rights. It was pointed out that the Assembly would not be in a position to determine intelligently what action to take on a specific convention before it had first reached agreement on a statement of the general concept of this freedom, to appear in the Covenant on Human Rights.[20]

The Commission on Human Rights, at its meeting March to May, 1950, while completing three years of work on the drafting of the proposed International Convention on Human Rights, adopted its article on freedom of expression. This article (Article 14) was drafted in general terms to provide that

> Everyone shall have the right to freedom of expression; this right shall include freedom to seek, receive and impart information and ideas of all kinds, regardless of frontiers, either orally, in writing or in print, in the form of art, or through any other media of his choice.[21]

But this freedom is not absolute; it has special duties and responsibilities, and is subject to penalties, liabilities and restrictions "necessary for the protection of national security, public order, safety, health or morals, or the rights, freedoms, or reputations of others." Although some members of the Commission sought to restrict freedom of information further by other specific limitations, the Commission rejected these proposals and decided to limit freedom of expression only in general terms along the same lines as the limitations (Articles 13, 15 and 16) concerning the freedoms of religion, assembly and association.

Another conference of interest in this connection was the meeting of the United Nations Sub-Commission on Freedom of Information and of the Press, at its fourth session, in Montevideo in May of 1950. One of the session's concluding acts was to adopt a draft proposal submitted by Mr. Azkoul concerning the implementation of the resolutions Two and Three of the UN Conference on Freedom of Information, condemning war propaganda and the dissemination of false information. By a vote of 6-0 (5 abstentions) it requested the Secretary General to submit a report on measures taken by governments pursuant to these resolutions. Also, a code of ethics for news personnel was adopted after lengthy debate. This draft was adopted by a vote of 8-1 with the representatives of the United States and the United Kingdom abstaining because of serious doubts as to the desirability of such a code.[22] Their representatives argued that any such code should be drafted and adopted by the news profession itself on a purely voluntary basis. It was feared that any code sug-

---

[20] *U. N. Yearbook 1948-1949*, pp. 572-576; U. N. Doc. A-1010.

[21] U. N. Economic and Social Council, *Official Records*, 5th year, 11th Session, Supp. 5 (E/1681), 1950, p. 17.

[22] *U. N. Weekly Bulletin*, June 15, 1950, pp. 521 ff.

gested by the United Nations might be used by certain governments as a means of controlling their press. The debates were as significant for the proposals voted down as for the articles actually adopted. For instance, the member from Yugoslavia insisted that all news was basically propaganda and that for this reason every journalist should be guided by the causes he was promoting. Along this same line, two paragraphs in the original text stated that news personnel should promote friendly international relations, human rights and solutions for economic and social problems. These articles were attacked on the ground that they attempted to make of the journalist a sort of evangelist or, even worse, a propagandist rather than a reporter presenting facts as he sees them. This proposal was also criticized as totalitarian in concept and was rejected. Another unsuccessful amendment introduced by the Yugoslav delegate would have forbidden a correspondent to "advocate the infringement of the rights set forth in the universal Declaration of Human Rights, or the purposes of the United Nations to strengthen universal peace and to develop friendly relations between nations, based on respect for the principles of equal rights and self-determination of peoples."[23]

An important resolution was adopted (8-3) condemning the jamming of radio broadcasts as a violation of the accepted principles of freedom of information. This resolution, introduced by the United States delegate, Carol Binder, also recommended that the General Assembly be asked to request all member governments not to interfere with the rights of their peoples in this regard. This was undoubtedly a reference to Article 14 of the draft covenant on Human Rights already referred to which affirms the "freedom to seek, receive and impart information . . . regardless of frontiers."[24]

At this conference a "grim and depressing" report on the general state of the world in the matter of freedom of information was presented by UNESCO. It stated that as of December, 1949, censorship in 44 countries or territories was in force; since December, 1948, 13 countries had adopted measures restricting the flow of information. Ten had prohibited certain newspapers, periodicals, and films; 7 had instituted new restrictions on the import of the latter; 12 had curtailed freedom of foreign correspondents or news agencies; and 9 had refused entry visas to correspondents or had expelled them.[25]

That this situation has not improved is shown by a recent report. *Time* Magazine on January 26, 1962, published this account of current restrictions on its distribution:

> *Time* of course is not on the newsstands in Communist countries, though a number of copies go to top officials, curious, we suppose,

[23] *Ibid.*, p. 524.
[24] *Ibid.*
[25] *Ibid.*, p. 525; *New York Times*, May 25, 1950.

about what's going on in the world, or at least what a Western journal says is going on in the world. Though there is no official ban on us in Cuba, distributors are afraid to handle *Time* there for fear of trouble. In the past year, nine issues of *Time* have been confiscated in the Dominican Republic (about as many under Ramfis Trujillo as under his assassinated father). We are currently banned in Spain and Portugal and their colonies, and in Indonesia too. We have run into trouble in the past year in Laos, Iran, and Jordan for stories that displeased the censors. In Ghana, a local distributor, on his own initiative, prudently burned all copies of one issue that reprinted a cartoon from the Manchester *Guardian* showing Nkrumah gagging the press. In Arab countries, censors sometimes wield their scissors as if they were scimitars. Saudi Arabia, Egypt, Syria and Libya have confiscated or cut pages out of issues in recent months, and in Iraq the censor has objected to stories about Middle Eastern politics, to cartoons, to a classically painted nude, and to stories, and even an ad, about Israel.

We think this is an instructive list. During this same period we have on occasion said things as harsh or harsher about political figures or government policies in Britain, France, West Germany, Italy, Canada, Brazil, Japan, Belgium, Australia, Mexico (among many others) without being censored.

As to restrictive activities by the United States, there may be mentioned the provision in the postal bill, H.R. 7927, passed October 5, 1962, which requires interception of all mail originating in a foreign country, except sealed letters and mail to schools, public libraries, professional institutions and government agencies and mail covered by reciprocal international agreements, if determined by the Secretary of the Treasury to be Communist political propaganda. The Act requires notification of the addressee and permits delivery of such matter only upon declaration by the addressee that he wants the material. The definition of Communist political propaganda used is that stated in the Foreign Agents Registration Act of 1938, and includes any propaganda, used by or on behalf of a Communist country, which attempts to influence a recipient with reference to political or public interests, policies, or relations of a foreign government or political party or with reference to the foreign policies of the U. S., or which promotes U. S. racial, religious or social dissensions.[26]

Since the meeting of the Sub-Commission on Freedom of Information at Montevideo, freedom of information has been thoroughly discussed in numerous United Nations bodies, notably in the General

---

[26] According to the Congressional Quarterly for September 28, 1962 (39 C. Q. 1692), "The provision was opposed by the Administration as lacking clear guidance on what constituted propaganda, as being administratively unfeasible, and as likely to provoke retaliation against U.S. mail to Communist countries." For a detailed discussion of the background and issues, see "Distribution of Communist Propaganda through the Mails," by Mollie Z. Margolen, The Library of Congress Legislative Reference Service, 172/272, April 16, 1962.

Assembly itself, its Third Committee, ECOSOC and the Commission on Human Rights. We cannot cover all this activity, and will only refer briefly to certain portions directly pertinent to the present study.

In recent years the main discussion has centered on the Draft Convention on Freedom of Information, first drawn up in 1948 on the great Geneva convention and revised in 1951 by an *ad hoc* committee of the General Assembly. Extensive debates on this draft were held in the Third Committee in 1959 and 1960, but actual progress was confined to the approval of a Preamble and Articles 1 and 2. Further debate took place before the Third Committee of the 1961 (17th) General Assembly.[27] The tenor of this latter debate is given below.

The significant matters in these discussions, for our purposes, are found first, in certain basic differences of opinion among the delegates, and second, in the reactions to the exceptions to absolute freedom of information set forth in Article 2. These two matters will now be discussed.

The clash of opinions which marked these debates was very similar to that at the 1948 Geneva conference on freedom of information, except that some delegations now showed even less enthusiasm for a convention than they did earlier. Most of the democratic countries of the West, notably the United States, the United Kingdom, Sweden and Australia, felt that a convention at this time would be premature, especially as there were such wide divergencies between the nations. A number of these delegations actually feared that a convention would be a step backward, in that it seemed to emphasize the restrictions on freedom of information more than the freedoms themselves. Also, the insistence on "fair, honest and reliable information" raised the specter of state controls, with preventative censorship a prime bugaboo. Some, for instance Sweden and Australia, favored self-discipline in place of binding obligations, and expressed confidence that with a democratic press the truth would ultimately prevail. Some felt, on the other hand, that freedom uncontrolled was itself a real danger, in that it left the press and other media free to disseminate false news and hatred propaganda. In this connection the Communist bloc continued its compaign to include in the convention a direct obligation on the parties to suppress propaganda for war, for Fascism, or for racial discrimination. The French, as usual, pressed for a right of correction as a remedy for abuses, and the Australians favored a code of ethics for newsmen.

Article 2, accepted by the Third Committee only with the greatest difficulty, constitutes the crux of the draft convention, for it sets

---

[27] *U. N. Yearbook,* 1959 pp. 212 ff.; A/4636, Dec. 9, 1960; *International Organization,* Winter, 1959, pp. 107-108; Winter, 1960, pp. 151 ff.; Winter, 1961, pp. 121-126; Winter, 1962, pp. 134-136. See also, "Issues Before the Seventeenth General Assembly," *International Conciliation,* No. 539 (September, 1962), pp. 142-145.

forth the permitted exceptions to the principle of freedom of information. This principle, found in Article 1, establishes the "freedom to gather, receive and impart without government interference, save as provided in Article 2—information and opinions orally, in writing, or in print, in the form of art or by duly licensed visual or auditory devices." The important section of Article 2 is as follows:

> The exercise of the freedoms referred to in Article 1 carries with it duties and responsibilities. It may, however, be subject only to such necessary restrictions as are clearly defined by law and applied in accordance with the law in respect of: national security and public order (*ordre public*); *systematic dissemination of false reports harmful to friendly relations among nations and of expressions inciting to war or to national, racial or religious hatred;* attacks on founders of religions; incitement to violence and crime; public health and morals; the rights, honour and reputation of others; and the fair administration of justice. (Italics added)

Prior censorship is prohibited. The italicized words in this paragraph are significant for our purposes. They *authorize* the parties to the draft convention to suppress propaganda dangerous to good international relations. But they do not *oblige* the parties to do so. Thus the draft represents a compromise between what may be called the Soviet and the Western theses. But the leading Western powers are not happy over this provision, for fear it will be used by dictatorial regimes as an added device to control their own press even more severely than ever, and also as a weapon against any criticisms of their policies which they find objectionable in the media of other states.

At the 16th General Assembly, the Third Committee continued the discussion and adopted as Article 3, without amendment, a text proposed ten years earlier. It read as follows:

> Nothing in the present Convention may be interpreted as limiting or derogating from any of the rights and freedoms to which the present Convention refers which may be guaranteed under the laws of any Contracting State or any conventions to which it is a party.

But the most interesting debate for our purposes occured in connection with a proposed Article 4, providing for a right of reply, which after considerable argument and amendment was adopted in the following form:

> The Contracting States recognize that the Right of Reply is a corollary of freedom of information and may establish appropriate means for safeguarding that right.

That this debate was pertinent to problems dealt with in the present study is clear from a mere statement of issues prominent in the discussion: Was the right available to governments, or only to individuals? If to governments, was the matter not already covered in the Convention on the International Right of Correction? How would the exercise of the right apply to media other than the press— radio and television? Did the right of reply and its remedies differ fundamentally from those associated with defamation, already covered in Article 2?[28]

Another United Nations effort in this same field is the movement to draft a Declaration (as distinguished from a Covenant) of freedom of information. Many feel that this is a more practical approach to the problem, and invoke the example of the Universal Declaration of Human Rights, which undoubtedly has had great influence, and real moral authority. A revised draft of such a declaration, approved by the Social Committee, meeting April 7-20, 1960, was postponed for consideration to the 16th General Assembly, and by the latter to the Seventeenth.[29] In this text, instead of the more specific exceptions to

the principle of freedom of information contained in Article 2 of the Covenant, just discussed, we find a general exception (Article V) which would confine the permissible restrictions "only to such limitations as are determined by law solely for the purpose of securing due recognition and respect for the rights and freedoms of others and of meeting the just requirements of morality, public order and the general welfare in a democratic society."[30]

In the Social Committee the Soviet delegate continued the fight for a specific article condemning war propaganda. It offered this amendment:

> All Governments have the responsibility to combat all forms of war propaganda and to oppose the dissemination of false or distorted reports which are offensive to the national dignity of the peoples and engender hatred or prejudice against other States or individual persons or groups of different race, language, religion or outlook.[31]

From this summary it can be seen that the freedom of information movement within the United Nations has not in itself as yet produced any binding law, except the Convention on Internationl Right of Correction adopted by six countries. It has undoubtedly had considerable moral value in keeping constantly alive the emphasis on the value of freedom of information. It has also laid the groundwork for possible concrete action on such specific measures as right of reply, restrictions on jamming, which will be discussed next, and

---

[28] Report of Third Committee, A/5041. Further debate was postponed to the 17th General Assembly, A/RES/1681 (XVI).

[29] A/RES/1683 (XVI).

[30] E/AC./7/L.355, *U. N. Yearbook,* 1959, p. 217.

[31] *United Nations Review,* May, 1960, p. 48.

a code of ethics which will be treated in a later chapter. In addition, it has clearly highlighted some fundamentally different points of view on the relation between the values of free speech and the values of controlling propaganda, a subject which will also be examined in more detail in a separate chapter.

Chapter XI

Restraints on Jamming

Jamming is the deliberate use of interfering radio signals sent from one or more transmitters to garble emissions from other transmitters in order to make them unintelligible at reception. An objective discussion of jamming in the present setting must consider it from two points of view. Under present conditions, it is tempting to think of jamming only in terms of interference with free communication. At the same time it must be analyzed as a possible kind of "self-help" remedy which may be claimed by the target state.

May the target state, victim of propaganda, defend itself from radio attacks coming from abroad which, being defamatory, subversive or war-mongering, threaten to cause it serious harm? When Goebbels, for instance, was directing his poisoned darts of hatred and subversion across frontiers to the Sudeten Germans, would Benes have been within his rights had he taken measures to jam the offensive and dangerous messages? In that particular case, the answer is definitely yes. Benes would have had the law on his side. This difficult problem will be discussed later in this chapter.

Jamming has become today a matter of keen current interest, and a subject of continued controversy. Its origins go back some twenty-eight years. In 1934 the Dollfuss Government attempted in this way to prevent the Austrians from hearing the Nazi attacks on his regime.[1] During the Second World War jamming was practiced by several belligerents in an attempt to exclude enemy and even neutral broadcasts considered deleterious to the national morale. The BBC, sticking as it did closely to the truth and thus gaining a well-deserved reputation for veracity, was particularly resented by Mr. Goebbels. After the war, in 1946, Soviet Russia resumed the practice of jamming. This campaign, mild at first, did not become acute until 1948, when Soviet Russia began to jam on a large scale the Russian-

---

[1] Earlier, in 1932, Roumania attempted, but without much success, to jam hostile radio broadcasts from Soviet Russia. Sidney S. Biro, "The International Aspects of Radio Control," *Journal of Radio Law*, Vol. II (1932), pp. 60-61.

language programs of the United States concomitantly with the inauguration of a vast program of abuse against the United States and the non-Communist world. By 1949 the Soviet Union was using over 1000 stations to jam Russian-language programs originating in the West, many of them beamed to Soviet bloc countries. In June, 1949, Assistant Secretary of State Allen admitted that this jamming was 70-75 per cent effective.[2] The American government protested both to the United Nations and to the International Telecommunications Union but in vain.[3]

Since then, as a characteristic feature of the Cold War, the Soviets have extended and improved their complicated paraphernalia of radio jamming, despite the disapproval of the practice of jamming by three agencies of the United Nations in 1950.[3a] Commencing about the middle of 1961, the Cuban radio has been jamming radio transmissions from the United States. The United States has responded by stepping up the power of its stations, four of which now use a million watts of power—twenty times the power of the strongest commercial station in the United States. On February 21, 1962, it was reported by the Director of the Voice of America that the Government was engaged in a 50 million dollar program, with three new powerful overseas transmitters which will give an additional 8½ million watts of transmitting power, to double present strength.[3b]

The General Assembly on December 14, 1950, by a vote of 49-5, adopted a resolution condemning jamming as a violation of the accepted principles of freedom of information, and as a denial of the right of all persons to be fully informed. It also "invites all governments to refrain from radio broadcasts that would mean unfair attacks or slanders against other peoples anywhere and in so doing to conform strictly to an ethical conduct in the interests of world peace by reporting facts truly and objectively."[4]

Two subsidiary agencies of the United Nations likewise frowned on jamming. In fact one of these, the United Nations Sub-Commission on Freedom of Information and the Press, in May, 1950, specifically condemned Soviet Russia for "deliberately interfering with the

---

[2] Martin, op. cit. p. 87, and p. 223, n. 94.

[3] Ibid., p. 85.

[3a] Moscow's jamming is occasionally an assistance to the United States. Selective jamming indicates to the Voice of America what matters to stress. It throws light on delicate matters of Soviet domestic and international policy. Thus in January 1962, Soviet and Communist bloc broadcasts of President Kennedy's State of the Union message carefully jammed the President's optimistic reference to American agricultural progress in contrast with Soviet failures. New York Herald-Tribune, January 18, 1962.

[3b] New York Times, February 22, 1962.

[4] General Assembly, Official Records: Fifth Session, Supp. No. 3 (A/1345), 1950, p. 67, and Supp. No. 20 (A/1775), Resolutions, p. 44. For vote, see, G. A. Official Records, Plenary Meetings, 5th Session, 1950, p. 666.

reception by the people of the U.S.S.R. of certain radio signals originating beyond the territory of the U.S.S.R."[5] And in August of that same year, jamming was condemned by a vote of the Economic and Social Council, despite the vigorous opposition of the Communist bloc, especially Soviet Russia. Moscow claimed it was merely acting in self-defense, complaining of the "slander and lies" sent out to its detriment by Britain, the United States, France, and even Spain.[6]

In 1959, during the pre-summit *détente* in the Cold War, the Soviets temporarily ceased their jamming, but then resumed it on a selective basis. This was particularly evident during Mr. Khrushchev's first visit to the United States. For instance, on September 17, after a brief cessation of the practice, the speech of Secretary of State Herter to the General Assembly of the United Nations was jammed. Mr. Khrushchev attempted to rationalize this action by explaining that the Soviet Union resorted to jamming only because the Voice of America did not really represent the voice of the Americans and "to avoid our people getting the wrong view of the American people."[7] In 1949, at the U. N., Mr. Vishinsky made a similar statement to defend jamming, saying that the Russian action was designed to protect the West from the Russian people, who would rise up in "indignation, anger, ire and wrath" at such "nonsense and trash" if they could hear it.[8] Officials estimated, according to the *New York Times,* that the Soviet jamming network consisted of more than 1500 transmitters at 300 sites in the Soviet Union plus some 750 transmitters at approximately ninety locations in Czechoslovakia, Hungary, Rumania and Bulgaria. It was estimated that the installation of this network cost about $250 millions, and that the annual operating expenditure amounted to about $185 millions. In contrast, the United States Information Agency was spending at the time $100 millions a year for all of its activities, of which broadcasting constituted only a portion.[9] The lack of fair play which characterizes Soviet jamming was demonstrated on May 24, 1960, when the Soviet radio carried Foreign Minister Gromyko's charges of United States espionage, but when Ambassador Lodge sought to answer him, jamming ensued midway in the speech.[10]

[5] ECOSOC, *Off. Rec.,* 11th Session, Supp. No. 5A, Ch. II, p. 2, May 26, 1950. "Considering that the duly authorized radio operating agencies of the USSR are deliberately interfering with the reception by the people of the USSR of certain radio signals operating beyond the territory of the USSR . . . . Declares these types of interference to be a violation of the accepted principles of freedom of information . . . Condemns all measures of this nature. . . ."
[6] *New York Times,* December 5, 1950.
[7] *Ibid.,* September 16, 19, 1959.
[8] Lowell M. Clucas, Jr., "Piercing the Iron Curtain," *Yale Review,* Vol. 39 (1950), pp. 603-619 at p. 614; *New York Times,* November 17, 1949.
[9] *New York Times,* September 19, 1959.
[10] *Ibid.,* May 25, 1960.

In this situation, what are the rights of the target state? Are the Russians correct in their contention that their jamming, designed to exclude hostile propaganda, is justified as a measure of self-defense, a recognized right in all domestic and international law? Is this exclusion of communications from abroad analogous to similar measures motivated by the need to keep out pornographic literature, or to stop the importation of opium or other noxious drugs constituting a danger to the public? This is a difficult problem: the nature and the extent of the right of a sovereign government to prevent the broadcasting into its territory of information which, for reasons of its own, that government deems to be harmful to its national interests.

A RIGHT TO JAM IN THE ABSENCE OF TREATY?

In their analyses of the legal problem of the right to jam, many authors have been led into learned discussions of the doctrine of sovereignty over the so-called "ether."[11]

It is not possible to discuss here in detail the various theories dealing with the status of the ether, but a great deal of ink has flowed since the beginning of the century, particularly in France and Germany, in an effort to reach some agreement in this matter. Three theories have predominated:

1. *The view that each state may exclude from its territory Hertzian waves coming from abroad.* There is excellent doctrinal authority for this view, notably Lauterpacht-Oppenheim.[11a] This contention is based on a claim of sovereignty, by analogy to the now admitted right of exclusive sovereignty over the airspace. Support for this view can be found in certain early treaties, and in discussions of learned associations, such as the Institute of International Law at its 1906 meeting.[12] A moral ground in support of this concept is the fact that there is no practical way, other than by jamming, to exclude hostile radio

---

[11] One of the most complete treatments is: Johann Joeden, "Die Funksende-freiheit der Staaten," *Jahrbuch für Internationales Recht*, Vol. III (1954), pp. 85-128, Vol. IV (1954), pp. 71-119.

[11a] *Op. cit.*, 8th ed., Sec. 197 f.

[12] *Annuaire*, I. D. I., Vol. 21 (1907), especially pp. 77 ff., 299 ff.; Paul Fauchille, "La Télégraphie sans fil et le droit international," *Rev. de droit Int. et de Lég. Comparée*, 3d series, Vol. I (1920), pp. 7 ff.; H. Thurn, *Die Funken-telegraphie im Recht*, Munich/Berlin/Leipzig, 1913; Alphonse Rivier, *Principes du Droit des Gens*, Paris, 1896, Vol. I, pp. 140-141; Alexandre Mérignhac, *Les Lois et Coutumes de la Guerre sur Terre*, Paris, 1903, p. 198, n. Review of early theories in Harold D. Hazeltine, *The Law of the Air*, London, 1911, pp. 9 ff., and J. Hostie, "Quelques Réflexions sur le Droit International Commun en Matiére de Radiocommunications," *Rev. de Droit Int. et de Lég. Comparée*, 3rd series, Vol. 18 (1937), pp. 10 ff. Review of all theories, old and new, in Joeden, *op. cit.*, Vol. III, pp. 86 ff.

messages, in contrast with written propaganda, whose dissemination can be prevented by the customs officials and the censor.

2. *The view that the ether is free,* and that therefore no state may object to the passage of Hertzian waves over its territory. This concept also relates to the doctrine of sovereignty: sovereignty is based on a physical right to control, which is absent.[13] Even jamming cannot control or exclude foreign waves; it can only make their messages incomprehensible and cannot always do that. Consequently, there can be no valid claim to sovereignty over the ether. The ether and the air being totally different, it is immaterial that a right of exclusive sovereignty over the airspace is everywhere recognized.[14] Again, it is pointed out that jamming has been condemned by the United Nations and many private international bodies.[15] It is also shown that in practice few states have made claims to possess sovereignty over the ether.[16] Moral grounds are also invoked; the fact that jamming violates one of the basic human rights—freedom of information—and if not curbed is bound to end broadcasting entirely and thus do great damage to the essential welfare of the international community.[17]

3. *The view that while the ether is free, and jamming in principle condemned, it is permitted if required to exclude hostile propaganda by radio.*[18] Assuming that the ether is free, this freedom, like every other domestic or international freedom, is subject in this view to reasonable limitation in the general interest. This limitation on the freedom of the ether, from which the right to jam is deduced, is based on the fundamental right of self-defense. A typical statement of this legal right of self-defense is that of Bowett:

> For example, where the delict involves the broadcasting of propaganda the state may have recourse to "jamming," which may be illegal *prima facie* but justifiable as self-defense. Thus the decision of

[13] See discussion by Institut de Droit International, 1902, *Annuaire*, Vol. 19 (1902), pp. 32 ff.; Hazeltine, *op. cit.*, p. 27; Sténuit, "Projet de Convention Internationale de la Radioélectricité," *Rev. Int. de la Radioélectricité*, 1935, pp. 137 ff.; Hostie, *op. cit.*, p. 18.

[14] E. de Gaspar, "Le Principe de la Liberté de l'Air dans ses Rapports avec la Navigation Aérienne et la Circulation des Ondes," *Rev. Int. de la Radioélectricité*, 1938, pp. 99 ff.

[15] *Supra*, p. 211.

[16] Joeden, *op. cit.*, Vol. III, p. 96.

[17] *Ibid.*

[18] Most authors maintain today that while the air may be "free," this cannot be said of the "ether," through which the Hertzian waves flow; in other words, radio is *sui generis*. Arrigo Cavaglieri, "Principes de Droit International Régissant la T. S. F.," *Rev. Dr. Int.*, Vol. II (1928), pp. 860 ff. The older view was to consider the "air" and the "ether" to be governed by the same principles of state sovereignty. *Supra* p. 285, n. 3. But since 1930 the ether has been generally considered to constitute a special domain. Hostie, *op. cit.*, pp. 16 ff.; Joeden, *op. cit.*, Vol. III (1954), pp. 98 ff.; de Gaspar, *op. cit.*, pp. 103 ff.

the British government to "jam" the broadcasts from Athens Radio in January, 1956, was justifiable as a measure of self-defense against delictual conduct by Greece. . .[19]

In some cases jamming may likewise be justified as a reprisal.[19a] Support is found in disputed articles of various treaties (notably Atlantic City, Buenos Aires, Geneva), the same, by the way, which are invoked by proponents of conflicting theories.[20] Also, stress is placed on reservations made by several parties to the 1936 Convention for the Use of Radio in the Cause of Peace, and by reservations to the United Nations resolutions condemning jamming.[21] Again, the deliberations of certain learned societies are in point, especially the resolutions of the Institute of International Law at its 1927 meeting.[22] Here certain moral arguments are advanced: that this compromise between Views 1 and 2 is the only one which can respond to the basic needs of the international community; both the unlimited freedom concept, and the doctrine of exclusive sovereignty, if carried to the extreme, would result in chaos and would undermine the intercommunications potentialities made possible by the miracle of radio, which is so essential for the development of mutual understanding among the nations.[23]

The uncertainty of the legal rights and duties in relation to jamming was strikingly demonstrated in a statement made by the late Secretary of State Dulles on February 20, 1956, in reply to a question from 40 Congressmen concerning radio broadcasting to the Soviet world. He said as follows:

> That is another question, I think, where international law is quite obscure: whether you have a right to send ether waves carrying messages into another country or whether you have the right to try to jam those waves. We have tried, as you know, at the last Geneva conference to get an agreement that what you might call straight news broadcasts would be recognized and not sought to be jammed, but we could not get very far with the Soviets on that score. What the law is, I don't know, but it is a case where I suppose it would be extremely difficult to make any rule that you couldn't send radio mes-

---

[19] D. W. Bowett, *Self-Defense in International Law*, New York, 1958, p. 54.
[19a] Joeden, *op. cit.*, Vol. IV, pp. 109 ff.
[20] *Post*, pp. 216 ff.
[21] Joeden, *supra* n. 19a. *Am. J. Int. Law*, Vol. 32 (1938), Supp., pp. 119-120.
[22] *Annuaire*, IDI, Vol. III (1927), pp. 286, 342. See especially Art. 5, IDI text: "If the emissions by radio of one State cause grave troubles to the emissions of another State, this fact will cause it to incur an international responsibility exposing it to the usual sanctions. . . ." Also: "It is the same if a State does not take the measures at its disposal in order to prevent radio emissions which by their content are of a nature to trouble the public order of another State, when such emissions have been brought to the latter's attention."
[23] Hyde, *op. cit.*, Vol. I, Sec. 192.

sages into another country because they automatically go there.[24]

However, there is no great need to discuss in detail the problem of the status of the ether, for this reason: since those states addicted to jamming and their victims are members of the International Telecommunication Conventions and Regulations annexed thereto, the legality of jamming is essentially a problem of treaty interpretation, not of customary international law.

JAMMING IN THE LIGHT OF THE TELECOMMUNICATIONS CONVENTIONS

On first sight, under the telecommunications conventions binding on most states, including the United States and the Soviet Union, it would appear that the jamming of radio broadcasts when such broadcasts originate abroad and are sent out over assigned wave lengths constitutes a violation of duties burdening the receiving state in international law. As maintained by the General Assembly in its resolution condemning jamming, the practice is undoubtedly a violation of the "freedom to listen," one of the rights embodied in the Universal Declaration of Human Rights.[25] (Article 19). The U. N. Resolution condemns "measures of this nature as a denial of the right of all persons to be fully informed concerning news, opinions, and ideas *regardless of frontiers.*"[26] (Italics added.) However, this alleged prerogative is still a simple moral right, for the famous Declaration, while of great historic importance, with undoubted prestige, has never been transformed into universal convention, nor does anyone contend that it has ripened by custom into a rule of positive law. The right to listen, however, is set forth in the European Convention for the Protection of Human Rights and Fundamental Freedoms, signed at Rome on November 4, 1950. This Convention has the force of law between the ratifying states. Article 10 states: "Everyone has the right to freedom of expression. This right shall include freedom to hold opinions and to receive and impart information and ideas without interference by public authorities and regardless of frontiers." The convention makes provision for a European Commission of Human Rights, and a European Court of Human Rights.[27]

The most important point, for our purposes, is the fact that in principle jamming appears to violate a treaty obligation binding on Soviet Russia, the United States, and most other nations. Article 44

---

[24] *Dept. of State Bulletin,* Vol. 34, No. 869, February 20, 1956, pp. 284-285.
[25] *Supra* p. 211.
[26] *Supra* p. 211.
[27] *Am. J. Int. Law,* Vol. 45 (1951), Supp., pp. 24 ff.; *U. N. Yearbook of Human Rights for 1950,* pp. 418-422.

of the International Telecommunications Convention (Atlantic City, 1947, now revised as Article 47 at the ITU Conference at Geneva in 1959) provides that

> All stations, whatever their purpose, must be established and op-
> perated in such a manner as not to result in harmful interference to the
> radio services or communications of other Members or Associate
> Members or of recognized private operating agencies, or of other duly
> authorized operating agencies which carry on radio service, and which
> operate in accordance with the provisions of the Radio Regulations.[28]

As an adjunct to Article 47, Article 14 of the Radio Regulations annexed to the Convention provides that:

> All stations are forbidden to carry out
> —unnecessary transmissions;
> —the transmission of superfluous signals and correspondence;
> —the transmission of signals without identification.[29]

This position has been upheld by the United States representative during discussions of jamming in the United Nations.[30] From the provisions just cited one might conclude that the jamming of a radio emission, when the latter is sent on an authorized frequency and conforms to agreed technical standards, would be unlawful in the countries which are parties to the Telecommunications Convention and its Regulations. But before reaching such a conclusion, we must consider two articles of the Buenos Aires Telecommunications Convention of 1952. These are Articles 29 and 30, currently still effective (as Articles 31-32) between, among many others, the United States and Soviet Russia. Article 29 refers to private telegrams only, and states that any of them may be stopped if "dangerous to the security of the state or contrary to their laws, to public order or to decency." Article 30 goes further; it permits the suspension of the "international *telecommunication* service," which, of course, includes radio trans-missions, "for an indefinite time, either generally or only certain rela-tions and/or for certain kinds of correspondence, outgoing, incoming or in transit." The only condition here is that all members and as-sociate members of the ITC must be notified.[31] While this article would seem to refer merely to the right of a state to halt *its own*

---

[28] *International Telecommunication Convention* (Final Protocol to the Con-vention, Additional Protocols to the Convention, Resolutions, Recommendations and Opinion), Geneva (ITU), 1959, p. 36.

[29] "International Telec. Conferences: Atlantic City," *Dept. of State Pub-lication 3177, Int. Org. and Conference Series,* Vol. I, No. 4. Radio Regulations, with appendices and additional protocol (Message from the President of the United States), 86th Congress, 2d Sesssion, Senate Executive I, Washington, June 9, 1960, p. 165.

[30] Reviewed by Joeden, *op. cit.,* Vol. IV, pp. 111 ff.

[31] *Supra* p. 215.

services, the Soviet delegate at this same Buenos Aires conference voiced his approval of Article 29 and 30 on the ground that they be understood to authorize the censorship of news containing anything that would constitute "incitement to aggression, to war, to the use of force."[32] In the absence of any provision for obligatory arbitration it is thus open to Soviet Russia, without fear of effective sanction, to claim the right to consider foreign broadcasts some kind of "incitement" and to proceed to jam them. Unfortunately, efforts to overcome by official action the alleged discrepancy between Articles 29 and 30 of the Buenos Aires Convention, and the provisions accepted at Atlantic City and revised at Geneva, referred to above, have thus far proved unsuccessful.[33]

At all events, it is reasonable to assume that none of the regulations quoted above would rule out the right of the target state to defend itself from messages constituting a real danger to its security and public order. Such communications would include those which could be properly considered to be defamatory, subversive or warmongering. Thus, with proper impartial interpretation, there would be no discrepancy between the Buenos Aires and Atlantic City rules, in the light of the limited exceptions voiced by the Soviet delegate at Buenos Aires. Furthermore, the target state would seem to be within its rights if it sought to exclude emissions which are obscene, unfit for children (for instance even many of the crime stories which appear today on American radio and television), or those likely to cause panic, thus constitutiong a clear and present danger.

An interesting example of the prevention of panic by jamming was presented when one of the authors in the course of his United States Information Agency duties was visiting the late Premier of Iraq, Nuri as-Said. Nuri launched the conversation with an immediate and brusque demand that the United States furnish him with jamming equipment. In support of his demand, he cited a broadcast alleged to have been made by Radio Cairo charging Nuri with the personal murder of several of the holiest men of Islam within one of the holiest mosques of Islam. According to Nuri, this broadcast had set off severe rioting, bloodshed and civil disorder. (Under American policy, the request for jamming equipment could not be complied with.)

The target state in the various circumstances would be justified in using all reasonable means to exclude such harmful emissions from its territory. And as jamming is the most practicable if not the only method of obliterating the offensive radio signal, the resort to this practice would appear in such circumstances to be legitimate exercise

---

[32] George A. Codding, Jr., "Jamming and the Protection of Frequency Assignments," *Am. J. Int. Law,* Vol. 49 (1955), pp. 384 ff.

[33] DePalma, *op. cit.,* pp. 13-14.

218

of the right of self-defense provided, of course, that after proper protest has been lodged with the offending state, no remedial action results. We might note that at the meeting of the Juridical Committee on Radioelectricity, meeting in Rome in 1928, it was declared that all powers had the right to oppose the passage of sound waves if required to protect their "essential interests," the national defense and finally for "the accomplishment of its international obligations."[34] And, in signing the 1936 convention on broadcasting, Belgium declared that the right "to jam by its own means improper transmissions emanating from another country" was not affected by the convention, in so far as such a right existed in law or by treaty. Spain made similar declarations. Soviet Russia and Egypt took this same position in United Nations debates over this issue.[35]

The broad outlines, then, of the substantive law applicable to jamming can be summed up as follows: under the telecommunications conventions jamming is *prima facie* a violation of an international treaty obligation. This obligation has two identifiable sources of exception: the reservation by the Soviet delegate at the Buenos Aires conference of the right to censor news constituting an incitement to aggression, to war and to the use of force, and the inherent right of a state to defend itself from messages constituting a genuine danger to its security and public order.

If the international community were equipped with courts of obligatory jurisdiction, there would probably be no insuperable difficulty to applying these principles to actual cases. The unilateral claim of necessity ascribed to self-defense is not in itself conclusive either under domestic law or under international law, as was established at the Nuremberg Trials. In an orderly adjudication therefore, an impartial tribunal would have the task of deciding whether particular broadcasts of the Voice of America, for example, were really a threat to legitimate Soviet interests. The American government in its administration of the Voice of America has adopted as a fixed policy the broadcasting of nothing but truth.[36] But what Washington considers the simple truth may become in the eyes of Moscow harmful propaganda. Nevertheless, an impartial body, applying legal and judicial techniques, and free from the possible bias that might be present on either side, could form an independent and objective judgment on the reasonableness of the claim of self-defense. This is admittedly saddling the court with a very difficult task. But the task is similar in principle to that thrust upon any domestic court when required to judge the reasonableness of the apprehensions of an in-

---

[34] "Congrès de Rome du Comité Juridique de la Radioélectricité," *Rev. Int. de la Radioélectricité*, 5th year (1928), No. 16, p. 305.

[35] *Supra* p.

[36] See U.S.I.A. Basic Guidance Paper, Appendix A.

dividual who asserts that he committed assault or murder because he thought the other fellow was about to attack him.

What all this adds up to, so far as jamming is concerned, is that, while further amplification of the legal rules on jamming can be of value as adding moral force to the general condemnation of unjustified jamming, a satisfactory solution cannot be expected unless either the political atmosphere sufficiently improves to produce voluntary cessation of jamming, or unless the obligatory jurisdiction of the International Court of Justice or some other tribunal is accepted by the state involved.

Chapter XII

Other International Measures

United Nations actions, already traced out and discussed at many points in this book, have been addressed both to substantive law and to remedial procedures.

It has been shown that the many resolutions of the United Nations and its subsidiary bodies, as well as of the League of Nations, have helped to strengthen the body of international propaganda law by supplying evidence of accepted practice and standards among nations. The cumulative effect of such actions, even when the individual actions fall short of treaty status, has gone a long way toward clarifying customary international law in this field. Reliance on this type of source is by no means a one-sided matter. In a complaint to the Netherlands filed in 1948 against an article appearing in a Dutch newspaper discussing possible Soviet tactics in the event of war, the Soviet government itself invoked a United Nations resolution banning propaganda for war.[1] Moscow also based a protest on this resolution when it objected to an article in a leading American weekly describing the defensive measures the United States Air Force would be likely to take in case of war with Russia.[2]

As to remedies, the proposals for various lines of action by the United Nations have also been noted, but here the tangible results are less visible than in the substantive law field.[3] Among the remedies that have been discussed as figuring in United Nations deliberations are: monitoring, the freedom of information movement, Communist-

---

[1] Reported by Martin, *op. cit.*, p. 177.

[2] June 11 and 30, 1948. Also, on November 13, 1948, Vishinsky decried an article in the *Saturday Evening Post* allegedly urging a preventive war. *New York Times*, November 14, 1948.

[3] It must be admitted that much of the collective effort in this field has ended in failure. There is one more which has had little publicity. It was reported from London, May 10, 1960, that the United States, the United Kingdom and France had planned to ask the USSR to support a declaration of principle at the planned summit conference (which never took place), calling on statesmen to refrain from making aggressive speeches on Africa, Asia and the Middle East, and not to interfere in the politics of such countries. *New York Times*, May 10, 1960.

backed resolutions requiring domestic legislation to control war-mongering propaganda and other improper utterances by private sources, restraints on jamming, and the right of reply and correction in the case of false news.

Are there any other measures the United Nations might consider to help translate the substantive law on propaganda into effective compliance?

A UNITED NATIONS BROADCASTING SERVICE

There is one practical action which, although it has a precedent in the League of Nations,[4] has had little current attention. This action would be the creation of a United Nations broadcasting service.[5] The idea would be to put into the hands of the United Nations the facilities for world-wide radio broadcasting of materials in aid of its own programs for peace and also in aid of specific enforcement of remedies against illegal propaganda. Both purposes would be relevant to the propaganda problem. The regular broadcasting of the facts on current affairs by an almost universally representative organization would in itself go a long way toward meeting the problem of counteracting deceptive propaganda. Many other benefits could be foreseen, including the opportunity to keep the world much better informed on the many particular programs of the United Nations.

The most directly pertinent reason for creating such an operation would be to afford a vehicle for specific remedies against illegal propaganda. It would be most useful in connection with the right of reply. If the right of reply and correction were established under the procedures discussed in Chapter 12, there might remain the problem of conveying the correction effectively to a large enough audience. If the offending source refused or neglected to comply with

---

[4] Codding, *op. cit.*, p. 66; Arno Huth, "Radio Today: The Present State of Broadcasting," *Geneva Studies*, Vol. 12 (July, 1942), pp. 136-137, referring also to *Radio-Vaticana*. Also, Childs-Whitton, *op. cit.*, pp. 10-11. "But the most vital function of radio was neglected, namely, the active propagation of the League idea during those crises when everything depended on mobilizing public opinion for the maintenance of world peace and order." *Ibid.*, p. 10.

[5] The United Nations Radio does not own its transmitting facilities. But it beams programs to all parts of the world over rented short-wave transmitters. According to Codding, its programs "are regularly rebroadcast by stations in 73 Member States and in 44 non-Member States. In addition, certain stations in the United States and Canada receive programmes by direct wire from United Nations Headquarters in New York." United Nations, Department of Public Information, *Broadcasts from the United Nations*, New York, November I, 1957. See also, Leon Gordenker, "Policy Making and Secretariat Influence in the U. N. General Assembly: The Case of Public Information," *Am. Pol. Sci. Rev.*, Vol. 54 (1960), pp. 359-373.

its obligation to publish the correction, the United Nations broadcasting service itself could proceed to publish this correction with as much thoroughness as necessary to undo the damage.

Similarly, the function of monitoring would be strengthened by the availability of this device. Since the salutary effect of monitoring rests on the assumption that exposure to public opinion is a corrective against illegal propaganda, availability of a mechanism for accomplishing effective exposure would be a valuable adjunct here also.

It has already been mentioned that the League of Nations for a time, operated out of Geneva, a broadcasting service called Radio Nations. This effort did not survive, but so many things have changed since the days of the League that any present venture should be judged primarily on today's needs and conditions. Plenty of difficulties can be foreseen in the path of any such undertaking, but at least it would be useful to bring the proposal under active study and consideration. As to the technical problem of creating the necessary facilities, it is quite possible that, for a time at least, the United Nations could utilize the resources of existing systems under some kind of lease arrangement.

United Nations Enforcement Sanctions

There remains to be considered the question whether outright sanctions for violations of the law of propaganda can be devised and imposed by the United Nations.

Most of the remedies so far discussed have been somewhat indirect in character, relying upon such things as public opinion and the effectiveness of correction and freedom of information. But now let us suppose the following set of facts: Country A makes broadcasts which are a clear violation of the law of propaganda; it is authoritatively and impartially determined that the law has been violated; Country A is called upon to desist but continues to break the law. What sanctions can be imposed to enforce the law?

In answering this question, we must avoid the two extremes that appear in much of the discussion of enforcement of international law.

The one extreme is to adopt the cynical view that there is really no effective way of enforcing international law at all. There are in fact a number of weapons in the armory of international law enforcement, including diplomatic sanctions, economic measures, attachment of property belonging to the debtor's estate, enforcement through municipal courts, various kinds of enforcement through international organizations, and enforcement measures under international arrangements apart from the United Nations. In addition, in light of the expanded role of the United Nations Force in the Congo, it is plain that the use of force to back up United Nations decisions is a real factor and will probably increase in importance.

However, we should not go to the other extreme and assume that raw force is the best and only way to enforce international law. Some people who hold this view are apt to conclude that there can be no effective international law short of world government backed by an overwhelmingly powerful police force. This is not so. Indeed, even if such a police force were available, its use in many enforcement situations would be inappropriate and probably ineffective. Specifically, if the violation of law in question were the broadcasting of illegal propaganda, would it be appropriate to invade the country with United Nations troops and seize the radio station by force? It is difficult to believe that a remedy so disproportionate to the offense would be adopted even if it were available.

The key to devising sanctions which are both effective and practical in today's world is this: the sanction should as far as possible operate upon the category of activity in which the violation falls. The idea is "to make the punishment fit the crime." A specific example will make this much clearer than the generalization. Under the International Civil Aviation Convention, if the Council of the organization finds that a member nation has refused to comply with a final decision of the International Court of Justice or of an arbitral body, the contracting states undertake not to allow the air line of the offending state to operate in their territory.[6] This is a sanction of obvious potency. Indeed, so far as the international traffic of the delinquent country is concerned it amounts to a death sentence. The significant feature for our purpose is that for a violation in the field of aviation activities there is imposed a penalty in the field of aviation.

Can we find a counterpart to this principle in the area of propaganda? The field involved here is communications. The penalty therefore ought to act upon communications. Our search should therefore lead us to ask what privileges the United Nations has within its power that it can withhold to punish the offender, or what other penalties are within its present power to apply.

The greatest privilege that the United Nations has to give or withhold is membership. Practically every country in the world places a tremendous value on this privilege. Membership in the United Nations is the one thing that, more than any other factor, gives real meaning to independent nationhood so far as the smaller countries

---

[6] Articles 85-88, Chicago Convention, 1944. *Final Act and Related Documents,* Dept. of State Publication 2282, Conference Series 64, Washington, D. C., 1945. For bibliography, see Oppenheim, *op. cit.,* 8th ed., Vol. I, p. 516, and John C. Cooper, *The Right to Fly,* New York, 1947, basic documents in Appendix.

are concerned. If it were not for the United Nations, it would mean far less to be Prime Minister of some small country in the interior of Africa. But, because of United Nations membership, the Prime Minister can go to New York, can hobnob with the world's leaders from all countries, can be entertained in Washington at Blair House, can cast the same vote in the General Assembly as Great Britain or France, can speak on the floor of the General Assembly and expound his own country's views on every subject that comes up, can see his remarks faithfully reproduced in the *United Nations Review* and in the press of the entire world, and can make his voice heard in various other organs and agencies of the United Nations. The value placed on United Nations membership is also attested to by the persistence of such countries as Mainland China in seeking membership, and in the reluctance of such countries as the Soviet Union to withdraw from membership even when repeatedly thwarted in efforts to change the organization more to their liking.

However, although expulsion from the United Nations is a theoretically possible sanction under the United Nations Charter, it is undesirable, inappropriate, and extremely unlikely. It is undesirable because the effectiveness of the United Nations is diminished when its membership is cut down. It is inappropriate because it is much too severe and irrevocable for the kind of offense that would probably be involved. It is unlikely because it would be subject to the veto. We should therefore look for something short of expulsion, and something if possible bearing upon communications.

Perhaps the greatest propaganda platform in the world is the floor of the General Assembly.[7] It is here submitted, therefore, that an appropriate and feasible sanction would be to bar the representatives of the defaulting nation from speaking on the floor of the General Assembly until the nation has come into compliance with the law.

This sanction has the advantage of being readily within the power of the General Assembly by a simple vote of its own membership. The action would not be dependent upon anything the Security Council might or might not do, and the availability in the Security Council of veto would therefore be immaterial.

One could go from here to suggest additional actions within the power of the General Assembly, requiring neither Security Council assent nor United Nations Charter revision, to increase the weight of the communications sanctions imposed upon the recalcitrant state

---

[7] Unfortunately, many cases of hostile propaganda heard in this forum could be cited. None, however, could be much more violent than the speech by the representative of Saudi Arabia in October 1961, and which was called "without doubt the most vicious and obscene ever heard from a UN platform." He referred to Israel as "barbarism seated in gangsterism rooted in Nazism" and declared "Israel is another Eichmann" *New York Herald Tribune,* October 18, 1961.

if necessary. For example, all United Nations publications could place an embargo on the utterances of the violator. The General Assembly could recommend to member nations that they take various individual actions against the violating country which might otherwise be questionable. Under Article 11, paragraph 2, which authorizes it to "make recommendations" to states on "any questions relating to the maintenance of international peace and security" it could probably recommend that countries jam the offending broadcasts, and this authorization would relieve the jamming of any taint of violating the principles of freedom of information. It might even further recommend that all members place an embargo on all communications to and from the guilty country. This would be an action of extreme gravity, not to be undertaken unless everything else should fail.

These are some of the communication actions that are within the control of the United Nations, and it is difficult to believe that any country would place so much importance on the continuation of offensive broadcasts that it would risk bringing down on its head this succession of penalties.

A related type of sanction involving the International Telecommunications Convention would be to initiate action depriving the country of its right to use certain radio frequencies. If this were done by appropriate procedures, the effect would be not only to cut down the country's international audibility, but even to interfere seriously with its domestic broadcasting, particularly when neighboring countries began to use the frequencies thus released.

Although the resort to sanctions particularly relevant to communications has been stressed here, it remains true that all the other sanctions mentioned above would also be available, as they are in any problem of international law enforcement.

All this presupposes, of course, the political willingness of United Nations members to adopt the particular disciplinary action. The effort here is merely to find appropriate devices which could be pressed into service if the community of nations wished to do so.

Discussion of enforcement action also presupposes the existence of a decision-making and dispute-settling mechanism adapted to the nature of the problem.

The appropriate mechanism could be patterned after the type of administrative-judicial pattern that now exists in many countries including the United States. There could be a special office under the Secretary General handling the entire array of activities connected with propaganda and communications, including the operation of the broadcasting service, the monitoring, the administration of the right of reply, and the application of sanctions. This special office could make an administrative decision in the first instance on any controverted question, observing the usual administrative law standards of fair play and fair hearing. The decision, however, should be essentially a judicial one, not a political one. That is, it should be an application of the existing law of propaganda to the facts as found by the administrator. There could perhaps be various provisions for rehearing and review at the administrative level. There should also be an ultimate appeal to the International Court of Justice, in the form of a referral for an advisory opinion on the law.

Realistically, one should not count on Communist backing of these proposals for remedies, particularly in view of the Soviet mistrust of the principle of impartial adjudication within the United Nations framework or anywhere else. But since many of the remedies suggested can be taken by the General Assembly, the dissent of the Communist countries would not be fatal. Some other countries interested in keeping a free hand for their propaganda activities might also object. But, on the whole, the general trend in the Assembly now is a surge of active responsibility, caused partly by the Security Council veto. In such actions as the Uniting for Peace Resolution, the extension of the Korean action to China, the Korean embargo, the setting up of the United Nations Expeditionary Force in the Middle East, the approval of the Secretary-General's actions in the Congo, and the creation of an armed force and temporary regime in West Irian, the General Assembly is showing that it is determined to shoulder more and more operating responsibility. The general justification is that the United Nations as a whole was created to keep the peace by dealing effectively with threats to international security and order. If the Security Council is unable to play the major part it was intended to play, this does not mean that the purposes of the United Nations stated in Article 1 have been abandoned. It follows that somebody has to carry out those purposes, and if the Security Council fails to act, this puts the job squarely in the hands of the General Assembly and the Secretary-General. Accordingly, we may expect to see more examples of functions assumed by the General Assembly which fifteen years ago would have been thought to belong solely to the Security Council.

The question might be raised whether the United States and the democracies would go along with the proposals for remedies here discussed. In a later chapter, there is presented a more detailed discussion of the reasons why the United States, the United Kingdom and others have sometimes been found on the side of opposition to United Nations actions on propaganda. There is a difference, however, between that problem and the one discussed here. What the democracies object to is the attempt to enlarge the substantive content of the international law of propaganda by creating an obligation on the state to control the utterances of private persons. However, for purposes of the present issue of remedies, that problem does not arise. We are here taking the substance of international law as we find it. As shown earlier, under present international law, except where nations have specifically adopted some such obligation by treaty, there is no general obligation on governments to control the utterances of private persons except in several specific and extreme cases. For all practical purposes, then, the responsibilities with which the United Nations would be concerned in applying these remedies would be responsibilities of states for their own acts. They would be applying a body of law which is acceptable to the democracies, and which indeed the democracies have had a large share in building up. The one point at which United Nations actions might impinge upon private expression would be in the device of right of reply and correction. However, this in no way circumscribes freedom of speech, nor does it require any government to adopt a more restrictive attitude toward freedom of speech within its own borders. It merely supplies an antidote when freedom of speech has allegedly gone too far.

All in all, there appears to be no reason why the democracies and most of the other countries of the world should not support this array of remedies. In the past, the drive to take united action against harmful propaganda has unfortunately consumed most of its force in reaffirmations of the substantive law of propaganda, that is, the illegality of war-mongering, subversive and defamatory international communications. Perhaps this was done partly under the impression that it was somehow necessary to create substantive law on these points. However, as the analysis in the first part of the book has shown, the substantive law, while it is strengthened by these declarations, is not dependent upon them and can at the crucial points be demonstrated independently of them. It is to be hoped, therefore, that future United Nations efforts will be concentrated on a systematic adoption of the kind of practical remedies here discussed.

Additional Treaty Action

Of the remedies so far discussed, all but one are by nature designed for United Nations administration, and the remaining one would be greatly strengthened by United Nations participation. The device of monitoring requires United Nations administration. It could not be effectively achieved by treaty, since the performance of this function by anything less than an overall world organization would not command the necessary respect. Similarly, the proposed operation of the United Nations broadcasting service is by definition a United Nations function. The general enforcement of existing law against illegal propaganda through administrative and judicial decision-making and application of the various sanctions suggested is also clearly a United Nations activity. Conceivably regional arrangements of a similar sort could be worked out by treaty, but they would have neither the advantage of existing administrative and judicial machinery nor the sanctions inherent in the nature of the present relation of states to the United Nations.

What then are the functions that can best be performed by treaties, or that treaties can help carry out? By a process of elimination, it is possible to narrow these functions down to two or three. These are: the creation of the right of reply and correction; imposition of a duty to pass domestic legislation curbing excessive propaganda by individuals; and possibly the establishment of dispute-settling procedures between the parties in matters of propaganda.

It will be noted that the function of substantively outlawing certain kinds of propaganda is conspicuously missing from this list. The reason the omission is conspicuous is that this function has usually been the primary and sometimes almost exclusive concern of past treaty attempts, as well as of various proposals by scholars. Examples of attempted or fragmentary treaties have been cited in previous chapters.[8] The most complete treaty on propaganda was the 1936 Geneva Convention on Broadcasting and Peace,[9] while the three draft conventions and the numerous resolutions adopted at Geneva in 1948 at the Conference on Freedom of Information and of the Press contained many significant provisions.[10] In addition, numerous bilateral treaties exist, notably those designed to curb subversive propaganda spread by refugees. Some of these treaties are of ancient date, and others in considerable numbers were signed during the years following the First World War. Professor Pella as early as 1933 prepared a draft treaty designed to outlaw untrue accusations, false news, and communications calculated to stir up hatred between peoples.[11] The committee of experts appointed to prepare the 1936 Conference on Broadcasting and Peace, after long deliberations, drafted a model treaty against propaganda by radio.[12] *The International Law of the Future*, a formulation of the fundamental principles of international law prepared by American International Lawyers during the Second World War, contains an article whose purpose was to oblige a state to "prevent the organization within its territories of activities calculated to foment strife in the territory of any other state" (Prin-

---

[8] For an excellent treatment, with numerous citations, of past and existing treaties in this field, see Martin, *op. cit.*, Ch. 5: "Control by International Agreement."

[9] *Supra* pp. 70, 125 ff.

[10] *Supra* pp. 70, 199 ff.

[11] *Supra* p. 177, n. 28.

[12] *Broadcasting and Peace*, Paris, 1933.

ciple 4). [13] The comment on this principle makes it apply clearly to subversive radio broadcasting. In preparation for the Madrid Radio Conference a draft convention was drawn up, unfortunately never considered by the meeting itself, according to which the signitories were to agree to take necessary measures against the emission of false news.[14] Moreover, in his *Unwritten Treaty*, James P. Warburg has included a comprehensive model convention dealing with the evils of international propaganda.[16]

Despite all of these efforts, there is a prevalent feeling that in today's embittered international situation there is little hope of achieving a general convention for outlawing the publication of false reports and the proscribing of defamatory, subversive and war-mongering communications. In his remarkable report as United Nations Rapporteur on Freedom of Information, Mr. Salvador P. Lopez concluded in 1953: "It is not feasible, for the present at least, to seek the outright prohibition and suppression of hostile propaganda and of false or distorted information by means of international legislation."[16] He added that "it would be unrealistic at the present time to attempt to draw up a convention which would bind individual states to introduce legislation aimed at the suppression of objectionable reports."

It is submitted that the effort to apply treaties to the propaganda problem would be more effective if it consumed less of its energies on the substantive law and concentrated more on remedies. Of course, any treaty which specifically outlaws a particular kind of propaganda adds just that much more to the strength of the substantive law. But, as the first part of this book has demonstrated, it would be a mistake to approach a propaganda treaty on the assumption that a substantive legal vacuum exists which must first be filled. On the whole, there already exists substantive law outlawing the most dangerous kinds of international propaganda. Therefore if treaty makers limit themselves to declarations on substantive law, they may conceivably do more harm than good. For one thing, they run the risk of bogging down in quibbling about definitions, phrasings, and shadings of meaning defining the various offenses. Moreover, in the very process of negotiating such substantive points they may appear to cast doubt on the present existence of law on the subject. Worst of all, particularly

---

[13] The comment states: "The advent of the radio has brought in new possibilities of disturbances in the political life of peoples, and as recent experience has shown propaganda broadcast from the territory of one State to people living in the territory of another State may be as effective in fomenting political strife as the despatch of armed ships and armed forces." *International Concilation*, No. 399 (1944), pp. 250, 297-298.

[14] Robert Homburg, "The Next World Conference at Madrid and the International Regulation of Electric and Radioelectric Transmissions," *Journal of Radio Law*, Vol. I (1931), pp. 220 ff.

[15] James P. Warburg, *Unwritten Treaty*, New York, 1946, Ch. 17.

[16] *Op. cit.*, p. 18.

if the number of nations involved is large, substantive declarations may be adopted which are actually weaker than existing law on the same subject.

It is a familiar observation about treaties that the larger the number of nations participating, the more diluted the content of the treaty is apt to be. Since the object of a multilateral treaty is to attain the signatures of all the participants, the attempt to satisfy everyone tends to drive the content of the treaty to the lowest common denominator.

The treaties, conventions and proposals mentioned above also contain some treatment of remedies, but the point here is that an intensive concentration on remedies, taking the existence of a working body of substantive law for granted, would probably be more fruitful under present world conditions.

The remedy which could benefit most from the treaty process is the right of reply and correction. The reason is that the creation of this system involves the calling into existence of a new kind of obligation between the nations affected.

In an oblique way, the right of reply could perhaps be partially enforced by United Nations action. If the United Nations adopted the function suggested above of determining the existence of illegal propaganda and then applying various sanctions to the offender, it could also offer the offender the opportunity to escape or diminish the sanctions by agreeing to publish appropriate replies and corrections. This would be closely parallel to certain state defamation statutes cited in the chapter on right of reply. At best, however, this would be an indirect and incomplete way of using the right of reply as a remedy. The forthright method would be to achieve the adoption by as many countries as possible of an agreement on mutual right of reply and correction.

Such an agreement would not be self-executing. The chapter on right of reply describes the necessity for at least a minimum amount of impartial decision-making. It would be quite possible for the parties to a treaty to create a special body to handle this function. However, if the United Nations were prepared to do this job, it would be much better to use its facilities, as the present Convention or International Right of Reply does, than to go to the trouble of setting up a new organization with less universality and prestige.

This leads to an observation about the treaty approach to international problems generally. One of the lessons that is being taught with increasing cogency by experience in international law is this: a treaty is apt to be no better than the administrative arrangements that are set up to see that it is carried out. The idea that nations can sign an agreement binding them to certain standards of conduct, and then simply go away and leave it in the expectation that the objectives of the treaty will automatically flow from the agreement, is increasingly coming into question. By contrast, the more successful treaties appear to be those which are accompanied by the creation of some kind of commission which has the full time responsibility of overseeing their execution, settling the disputes they engender and making recommendations on keeping the treaties up to date. An example of this kind of treaty is the agreement between Canada and the United States governing problems arising between the two countries along their common boundary—an agreement which was wisely accompanied by the creation of a mixed U.S.-Canadian Commission which continues to give the treaty everyday meaning.[17]

One may also note the contrast between two agreements between Pakistan and India. Reference has already been made to the April 1948 agreement between these countries in which they promised to "insure that their respective organizations handling publicity, including publicity through radio and the film, refrain from and control" propaganda against the other dominion, or news "likely to inflame or cause fear or alarm to, the population or section of the population in either dominion."[18] In the absence of an accompanying administrative procedure for insuring day to day compliance with these promises, the inflammatory propaganda has continued. By contrast, the more recent treaty dealing with the explosive problem of the sharing of the Indus waters carries with it an elaborate organizational plan which promises to dispose of this almost impossibly difficult dispute in a way which never could have been achieved merely through some agreement which did no more than enunciate a principle of sharing.[19]

As a general matter, then, the mere signing of additional treaties agreeing to refrain from harmful communication would not be of first line importance in the solution of the problem, although such accords would, if strong enough in their terms, serve to bolster the law on the subject. The more productive course is to strive for agreed remedies accompanied by agreed administrative structures to put them into effect. Herein lies the particular virtue of the United Nations, since it supplies a ready-made administrative structure which could carry on various kinds of operations to translate agreements into tangible results.

There is one other possible remedy that figures in actual or proposed treaties. This is a device of agreeing by treaty to impose certain restraints on propaganda by private persons, presumably through domestic legislation. This will be treated in the next chapter.

---

[17] C. J. Chacko, *The International Joint Commission Between the United States of America and the Dominion of Canada,* New York, 1932.

[18] *Supra,* pp. 88, 147.

[19] India-Pakistan, Indus Waters Treaty, September 19, 1960. *Am. J. Int. Law,* Vol. 55 (1961), pp. 797-821.

Chapter XIII

Strengthened Domestic Legislation

The question of strengthening domestic legislation may come about in two ways. As mentioned in the last chapter, it may arise as part of the obligation of a treaty binding the parties to restrain certain kinds of actions by private individuals. But it may also arise as the purely unilateral and voluntary act of a particular state.

In either event, the heart of the issue is the same. It is the question whether democracies like the United States can do more than they are already doing to restrain harmful propaganda by individuals without unduly endangering the values of free speech and free press. The broad question of freedom of speech in relation to control of all kinds of propaganda is examined in the next chapter. At this point, we are principally concerned with the specific question whether it is possible to devise domestic legislation which acts upon the more serious kinds of propaganda without at the same time endangering traditional freedom of speech.

One gets the impression that, in most of the United Nations debates and in various conferences concerned with propaganda conventions, the American and British delegates have assumed as a matter of course that even the slightest additional restraint on private individuals is absolutely unthinkable, as if they thought the free speech tradition were not only sacred but fragile. Certainly it is understandable that the spokesmen for western democracies would reject sweeping Communist proposals under which governments could suppress all communications that tend to injure relations between nations or that are identified by some flexible language which could become the excuse for almost unlimited censorship in a totalitarian society. On the other hand, it is salutary to remind ourselves that we have found it perfectly possible to impose limitations on freedom of speech on our own initiative when the evil to be dealt with was sufficiently grave. Such restrictions already exist as to expressions that are defamatory, obscene, dangerous to national security, or in other ways harmful to the common welfare. Even Blackstone wrote long ago: "that is true, and it is well recognized, that to punish abuses of the press, or license, is to maintain its liberty."[1]

In May, 1962, the long story of the Soviet-American dialogue on this question took a turning which would have been amusing but for the serious nature of the issue at stake. For many years the Soviet Union had been monotonously demanding an agreement binding nations to suppress war propaganda, and the United States had been monotonously reaffirming its position that this would jeopardize its traditions of freedom of speech. When the eighteen nation disarmament conference convened in the Spring of 1962, the Soviet delegate, Valerian A. Zorin, insisted that the first thing that must be agreed upon was a ban on war propaganda. Mr. Arthur H. Dean, the United States negotiator, at first adopted the traditional American position and countered with a statement supporting free flow of information as an antidote to propaganda. He enlivened the discussion by suggesting on April 10, 1962, that Moscow outlaw books by Marx, Lenin and Stalin containing assertions that war was inevitable.

Several weeks later a remarkable thing happened. A six-point declaration was worked out in private sessions as a result of modifications of the positions of both sides, and on May 25, 1962, the declaration was adopted unanimously by the eighteen nation conference sitting as a committee of the whole.[2] The key provision called upon

---

[1] William Blackstone, *Commentaries on the Laws of England,* Oxford, 1759, Bk IV, Ch. 11.

[2] The complete text, as carried in the *New York Times,* May 26, 1962, with a Reuters May 25, 1962, Geneva dateline is as follows:

The Government of the states participating in the eighteen-nation Disarmament Committee in Geneva:

Considering that in the preamble of the Charter of the United Nations the peoples express their determination "to practice tolerance and live together in peace with one another as good neighbors:"

Considering that Article 2, Paragraph 4, of the Charter lays down the obligation that all members shall refrain in their international relations from the threat or use of force against the territorial integrity or political independence of any state:

Recalling that the joint statement of agreed principles of disarmament negotiations affirms that it is important for the achievement of disarmament that all states refrain from any action which might aggravate international tensions:

Convinced that the younger generation of today should be brought up in the spirit of peace, mutual respect and understanding among peoples:

Determined to promote by every means at their disposal friendly relations among states in accordance with the purposes and principles of the United Nations:

Recognizing that war propaganda, meaning propaganda in whatsoever form or country conducted which can provoke or encourage a threat to, or breach of, the peace, is incompatible with the United Nations Charter and can lead to acts of aggression and war:

Recognizing that an end to such propaganda could facilitate the conclusion of an agreement on general and complete disarmament:

234

all states "to adopt, within the limits of their constitutional systems, appropriate practical measures, including measures in a legislative form in the case of states which consider such form appropriate, with a view to giving effect to this declaration against war propaganda . . ."

The agreement was immediately hailed as a good omen by participants who had been thirsting for some kind of agreement on something for ten long weeks, and stories about the newly buoyant atmosphere radiated from Geneva throughout the week-end that ensued.

When work resumed the following week, however, Mr. Zorin had received instructions from Moscow which obliged him to retract his acceptance. He then put forth some different proposals which were unacceptable to the United States.

The buoyant mood collapsed as abruptly as it had arisen.

Of course, one could merely write off the episode as a classical exercise in what the Russians themselves call "demonstrative diplomacy"—this time an exercise which failed—with whatever general lessons are to be learned for other similar Soviet-American negotiations in which the Soviet Union appears in the role of proposer of grandiose reforms while the United States conscientiously takes on the unpopular role of saying, "Let's be practical and realistic and take one step at a time." But for purposes of the specific problem of dealing with war propaganda, we cannot leave the matter there. Quite apart from Russian proposals, of whatever degree of sincerity, the United States and other democracies should give more serious

---

1. Solemnly affirm their support for the United Nations General Assembly Resolution 110 (11) which condemned "all forms of propaganda, in whatsoever country conducted, which is either designed or likely to provoke or encourage any threat to the peace, breach of the peace, or act of aggression":
2. Condemn appeals for war and for the settlement of disputes between states by the use of force, and also statements to the effect that war is necessary or inevitable:
3. Affirm their conviction that in our day, war can no longer serve as a method of settling international disputes and their desire to educate the younger generation in this conviction and to promote the ideas of peace, mutual respect and understanding among peoples:
4. Undertake to promote by every means at their disposal the widest possible circulation of news, ideas and opinions conducive to the strengthening of peace and friendship among peoples, and to extend cultural, scientific and educational relations with a view to better dissemination of the ideas of peaceful and friendly cooperation among states, and general and complete disarmament;
5. Call upon all states to adopt, within the limits of their constitutional systems, appropriate practical measures, including measures in a legislative form in the case of states which consider such form appropriate, with a view to giving effect to this declaration against war propaganda:
6. Call upon all other states to support this declaration.

235

study to the extent to which they can indeed adopt effective measures within the limits of their constitutional systems.

It is submitted that there is a hard-core minimal offense in the propaganda field that could and should be prohibited by domestic legislation and that would involve no increase in the threat to the principle of freedom of speech. This minimal provision would follow the pattern already established in American legislation of distinguishing between words as words, and words as acts. Thus, when words are used to incite to arson, pillage or murder, it is the act (provocation) that is punishable, rather than the expression of an opinion or a doctrine. The expression "has moved out of the half-world between thought and action; it has become a deed."[3] In the words of Montesquieu: "Les paroles qui sont jointes à une action prennent la nature de cette action . . . Ce ne sont point les paroles que l'on punit, mais une action commise, dans laquelle on emploie les paroles."

Thus, in *Lazar v. Commonwealth of Pennsylvania*,[4] a state statute was upheld which forbade any utterance which advocates or teaches the duty, necessity, or propriety of engaging in crime, violence, or any form of terrorism as a means of accomplishing political reform or change in government. See also *Gitlow v. New York*:[5] "That a State in the exercise of its police power may punish those who abuse this freedom by utterances inimical to the public welfare, tending to corrupt public morals, incite to crime, or disturb the public peace, is not open to question . . . Thus it was held by this Court in the *Fox Case*[6] that a State may punish publications advocating and encouraging a breach of its criminal laws . . ."

As Judge Medina said in his charge to the jury in the trial of the eleven Communists:[7] "But no one could suppose nor is it the law that any person has an absolute and unbridled right to say or to write and to publish whatever he chooses under any and all circumstances. If he did have such a right and if such were the law the words

> We the people of the United States, in order to form a more perfect Union, establish Justice, *insure domestic Tranquility,* provide for the common defense, *promote the general Welfare,* and secure the Blessings of Liberty to ourselves and our Posterity, do ordain and establish this Constitution for the United States of America.

---

[3] *De l'Esprit des Lois,* new ed., Paris, 1871, Bk. 12, Ch. 12, p. 181: "Elles ne deviennent des crimes que lorsqu'elles préparent, qu'elles accompagnent ou qu'elles suivent une action criminelle."

[4] 157 Atl. 701, appeal dismissed, 268 U. S. 532 (1932).

[5] 268 U. S. 652 (1925), at p. 667.

[6] 236 U.S. 273 (1915).

[7] *New York Times,* October 14, 1949; Hawthorne Daniel, *Judge Medina,* A *Biography,* New York, 1952, pp. 319 ff.

as contained in the Preamble to the Constitution would be no more than empty phrases. Doubtless you observed that I placed emphasis on the 'insure domestic Tranquility' and 'promote the general Welfare' clauses of the Preamble. Words may be the instruments by which crimes are committed, as in many familiar situations; and it has always been recognized that the protection of other interests of society may justify reasonable restrictions upon speech in furtherance of the general welfare."

Statutes have been upheld by American courts which impose liability for the publication or utterance of statements injurious to public order, provided that in the special circumstances of the case they constitute a "clear and present danger." This is the famous rule first formulated by Justice Holmes in the *Schenck Case.* Affirming the conviction of defendants for mailing circulars in pursuance of a conspiracy to obstruct the recruiting and enlisting service, in violation of the Espionage Act of 1917, the court said: "The question in every case is whether the words used are used in such circumstances and are of such a nature as to create a clear and present danger that they will bring about the substantive evils that Congress has a right to prevent."[8] The rule was refined by Brandeis and Holmes in *Whitney v. California,*[9] upholding the constitutionality of a California criminal syndicalism statute. "To justify suppression of free speech there must be reasonable ground to fear that serious evil will result if free speech is practiced . . . The wide difference between advocacy and incitement, between preparation and attempt, between assembling and conspiracy, must be borne in mind. In order to support a finding of clear and present danger it must be shown either that immediate serious violence was to be expected or was advocated, or that the past conduct furnished reason to believe that such advocacy was then contemplated." The joint opinion of Holmes and Brandeis adds:[10]

> But, although the rights of free speech and assembly are fundamental, they are not in their nature absolute. Their exercise is subject to restriction, if the particular restriction proposed is required in order to protect the state from destruction or from serious injury, political, economic or moral. That the necessity which is essential to a valid restriction does not exist unless speech would produce, or is intended to produce, a clear and imminent danger of some substantive evil which the state constitutionally may seek to prevent has been settled.

In the case of *Dennis* v. *The United States,* the majority decision somewhat softens the rule as to the degree of proof of clear and present danger. The court adopted the formula authored by Judge

---

[8] 249 U.S. 47 (1919), at p. 52.
[9] 274 U.S. 385 (1927), at p. 376.
[10] *Ibid.,* p. 373.

Learned Hand in the lower court: "In each case [courts] must ask whether the gravity of the 'evil,' discounted by its improbability, justifies such invasion of free speech as is necessary to avoid the danger." Also it was said: "And this analysis disposes of the contention that a conspiracy to advocate, as distinguished from the advocacy itself, cannot be constitutionally restrained, because it comprises only the preparation. It is the conspiracy which created the danger."[11]

Perhaps the most significant American law for present purposes is a statute which was first enacted in 1794 and has been re-enacted several times since, most recently on June 25, 1948:

> Whoever, within the United States, knowingly begins or sets on foot or provides or prepares a means for or furnishes the money for, or takes part in, any military or naval expedition or enterprise to be carried on from thence against the territory or dominion of any foreign prince or state, or of any colony, district, or people with whom the United States is at peace, shall be fined not more than $3,000 or imprisoned for not more than three years, or both.[12]

This is one of the first statutes in history on the books of any nation which was designed to crystalize into national law a principle of customary international law.

This statute has been interpreted and applied in a large number of cases. It is fair to say that the following excerpt is representative of the breadth of interpretation that has been applied to this statute.

> This language is very comprehensive and peremptory. It brands as a national offense the first effort or *proposal* by individuals to get up a military enterprise within this country against a friendly one. It does not wait for the project to be consummated by any formal array or organization of forces, or declaration of war; but strikes at the *inception of the purpose*, in the first incipient step taken, with a view to the enterprise, by either engaging men, munitions of war, or means of transportation, or funds for its maintenance; and even further, it is not necessary that the means shall be actually provided and procured. The statute makes it a crime to procure these means. This would clearly comprehend the making ready, and the tender or offer of such means to encourage or induce the expedition; and may probably include also any plan or arrangements, having in view the aid and furtherance of the enterprise.[13] (Italics added)

It has been stated in *U. S. v. Lumsden*,[14] that mere words showing a purpose to do the forbidden act are not enough to constitute the crime. There must be an overt or definite act. However, the overt act may be an "incipient step." For example, in the O'Sullivan case it was definitely said that the use of words to contract for recruits would be within the statute. Starting from this point, one could easily go on

---

11 341 U.S. 494 (1951), at pp. 510-511.
12 *U.S. Statutes at Large*, Vol. 62 (1948), Part I, pp. 745-746.
13 *U.S. v. O'Sullivan*, 27 Fed. Cas. No. 15,975 (1851) 380, at 383.

to conclude that the statute would be violated by such actions as publishing recruiting notices in the papers, using words for active recruiting, using words for raising money or assembling supplies and so on. In other words, the use of words merely to express opinions or intentions about a possible expedition would not be a crime; but the use of words to plan, organize, equip, finance, transport or in other tangible ways forward the forbidden venture would be prohibited.

The purpose of this statute was expressly stated in the O'Sullivan case to be prevention of disturbances to international peace. When the statute was first passed, and throughout much of its history, the kind of conduct prohibited by this statute was probably the major illegal form of disturbing international peace. At that time there was nothing illegal about declaring and waging war openly. Now, however, war has been made illegal by the United Nations Charter, except in two principal exceptional situations, and we are entitled to ask whether it would not be appropriate to have a counterpart of the 1794 statute addressed to the kind of conduct that might threaten the peace under modern conditions. True, violations of the 1794 statute still occasionally take place and have a damaging effect on international harmony. The most notable example was the invasion of of Cuba in the Spring of 1961, which was a clear violation of this statute.[15] But the world's most serious problem is the threat of outbreak of open war between the major powers. Certainly it is logical to say that any conduct, although in the form of words, sufficiently overt to come with in the statute of 1794 when the objective is to organize an armed expedition to attack a friendly country should also be a criminal offense if its object is to bring about actual war.

It has been shown in the discussion of the Nuremberg Judgments that the use of propaganda in a sustained and deliberate effort to bring about aggressive war is a punishable crime.[16] The western democracies themselves were principally responsible for establishing, or at least recognizing and applying, that rule of law. If this is so, what excuse would these democracies have for refusing to write this international crime into their domestic statute books? If the democracies refuse to do so, they will indeed be vulnerable to the charge that they imposed a rule of law as victors upon a defeated enemy which they would not be willing to have applied to themselves.

Any such statute forbidding overt conduct, whether words or deeds, in aid of bringing on war would have to be carefully drawn

---

[14] 26 Fed. Cas. No. 15,641 (1856) 1013.

[15] See Larson, "The Cuba Incident and the Rule of Law," *Saturday Review*, May 13, 1961, pp. 23, 53; Richard A. Falk, "American Intervention in Cuba and the Rule of Law," *Ohio State Law Journal*, Vol. 22 (1961), p. 546.

[16] *Supra* p. 76.

to deal only with real war-mongering and not with peripheral or figurative uses of the expression. The Soviet Union, for example, has a habit of accusing people of war-mongering when they do no more than talk frankly about the possibility of war and the way it would be waged and the horrors that would ensue. There was mentioned at the beginning of Chapter XII a pair of protests to the Netherlands and to the United States in which the Soviet Union complained of alleged war-mongering articles, both of which were essentially descriptive analyses of how war would be waged if it came. The Russians constantly complain of the writings of such people as Herman Kahn and Kissinger, whom they regard as war-mongers because they write openly and candidly about what they consider the realities of hydrogen war if it should happen.

However, this need not deter the United States from dealing in its own way with the most extreme forms of overt war-mongering conduct. It may seem to some people that the number of cases of this kind would be virtually non-existent. However, as time goes on there may be developments that we cannot predict. There are extremist and fringe organizations, small but highly vocal, that in the past have shown themselves capable of campaigns just as irrational as a deliberate campaign to launch a preventive war. At the time of the invasion of Cuba in the Spring of 1961, there were some people who were openly demanding that the United States wage all-out war on Cuba, and demands of this kind have continued to be heard. If these utterances were to go beyond mere casual expressions of opinion and were to take the form of concrete and organized activity to bring about an illegal aggressive war and to aid in specific actions and steps toward this end, surely they should be just as punishable as supporting, by active propaganda amounting to incitement, the organization of armed bands to invade another country under the 1794 statute.

This limited proposal, then, is not a new and unprecedented inroad into free speech. It is logical application to modern threats to peace of a principle which has been in force almost since the United States was founded.

Why, in the view of the probable rarity of such offenses, would it be worth the trouble to pass such a statute? One good reason is to anticipate and block the development of any such kind of activity in case anyone is tempted to try this sort of thing in the future. Another useful result would be to show that the democracies are willing within the framework of their own constitutional traditions to do everything they can with their domestic law to help solve the propaganda problem. This would help clear the way to get on with more essential moves, such as the adoption of genuine remedies through the United Nations and through treaties.

Chapter XIV

Freedom of Speech and the
Restraint of Propaganda

In the course of the debates that were held in the United Nations commissions and in international conferences since 1945 on the question of propaganda, an unfortunate pattern developed which, perhaps more than any other factor, blocked progress toward effective action. The appearance was created that the Soviet Union was on the side of strong repressive measures to eliminate propaganda that tends to stir up war, while the United States resisted practically all measures designed to curb propaganda on the ground that the dangers to free speech outweighed the gains and that, in any event, the best cure for propaganda was more freedom of information.

Other countries, while rarely siding with the Soviet bloc, did not always see eye to eye with the American position. It has been stated that

> Current national concepts of freedom of the press or freedom of information, far from being characterized simply by the gap between the Soviet thesis of the state indoctrinated society and the democratic thesis of the society free to reach its own consensus on the basis of competing sources of news, are more accurately described as being ranged in a continuous ideological spectrum. This spectrum is bounded by the U.S.S.R. at one extreme and the United States at the other, with every country ranged between.[1]

Certain smaller powers, their press services hampered by the lack of such facilities as are enjoyed by the American press and press agencies, have manifested a genuine fear of possible American domination, and this preoccupation is one reason why they have favored certain types of governmental aid and intervention which the United States has opposed as inconsistent with the doctrine of freedom of information. Some small states have complained that, through either

---

[1] De Palma, *op. cit.*, p. 17.

ignorance or sensationalism, their policies have been misrepresented by powerful agencies of information and their national cultures ignored or distorted. Others, like the French and Belgians, have been more ready than the Americans to accept, on general principles, legal obligations and machinery to curb propaganda. In this matter, the British, too, while approving the American view that the best antidote for propaganda is greater dissemination of news and more diversified sources, have looked with greater favor than the Americans on proposals for the international control of propaganda.

The trouble with this whole picture of a spectrum with the United States at one end and the Soviet Union at the other is that it misses the essence of the international propaganda problem. As has been demonstrated throughout this book, the greatest propaganda problem is that of the utterances of governments themselves. One has merely to skim through the examples given throughout the various chapters to see that the really dangerous items are in modern times almost entirely governmental in origin. The problem of freedom of speech in the constitutional sense simply does not arise when the government itself is doing the speaking.

The area in which the danger to traditions of free speech and free press is involved, therefore, is a relatively subsidiary one in the total problem. It is confined largely to printed material originating in the western democracies at the hands of private individuals and corporations. But the problem is not even this broad. It is narrowed further by the fact that any country can stop printed materials at its borders and thereby obliterate almost completely any effect these printed materials might have on its own people. This leaves the effect on the people of the originating country and third countries to be considered. The third countries can also ban the publications on demand of the offended country, but if they do not, it is probably an indication that the third country does not agree with the complaining country's appraisal of the situation. The problem, then, proves to be mainly that of printed material read within the originating country. Of course this is a problem, and may conceivably take forms that would have a serious impact on world peace. But in any accurate appraisal of its relative importance to the total problem, it must be admitted that it is a secondary factor compared with the everyday penetration by international radio of target countries and third countries all over the world by communications carrying the full authority of the very governments which hold the ultimate decision of peace and war.

All of the United Nations remedies already discussed could be adopted without any perceptible impact on domestic constitutional rights of free speech and press. If discussion could be concentrated on these essentials, therefore, the lineup would look quite different.

There is no reason why the United States and the other democracies should not throw their full weight behind these proposals. The right of reply, even if applied to private utterances, would not cut down on freedom of the press. Anyone could continue to print anything he could print before. The only difference would be that offending statements might be offset by the publication of a correction or a reply. No censorship would be involved. Moreover, as to the possibility of strengthened domestic legislation discussed in the previous chapter bearing upon private publications, the recommendations here made are carefully restricted to actions which involve no more invasion of traditional free speech of principles than do existing neutrality and sedition laws.

As long as the international dialogue on propaganda continued to follow the rut it had been in since 1945, it was certain to result in deadlock. The chasm between the Soviet and American attitudes and values appeared too deep to be crossed. Such basic terms as "freedom" and "democracy" receive irreconcilable interpretations. This is no academic debate over niceties of definition, but a reflection of profound divergencies in philosophy of law and principles of government. To the Russions the only "free" press is one controlled by the government. Censorship, they say, is necessary to assure the rights of the people, and to prevent by severe controls the use of information to promote war, fascism, and racial discrimination. To the liberal democracies, a free press is one unfettered by peacetime censorship. Freedom of the press can be restrictd only for carefully designed purposes, for example to prohibit communication which is defamatory, obscene, or dangerous to national security. And such restrictions must be interpreted and enforced by an impartial tribunal—in short, be subjected to the careful control of the rule of law. In the United Nations resolution on the freedom of information there is a condemnation of peacetime censorship except when it can be justified by the exigencies of national defense. The lengthy debates on this subject are full of interest. The Soviet delegation, while forced to admit that censorship did exist in Russia, maintained that its only purpose was to protect the "real freedom of information" existing in Russia and to prevent serious abuses. According to the Russians the Soviet press was the freest and most democractic in the world. It was in this connection that the Eastern bloc made one of the most violent attacks on the American press, alleging that it was the victim of "hidden censorship" and the slave of advertisers and monopolists of wealth. The Communist conception of "freedom" was revealed by the Hungarian delegate when he said that, while freedom of the press existed in his country, this did not mean freedom for fascists, defenders of dispossessed landowners or instigators of racial and national hatred. As to remedies, the Communist bloc's point of view is illustrated by the declaration of the Yugoslav delegate that "every country should take appropriate steps to prevent its press from spreading false rumors which were a provocation to war."[3] In a similar vein, a Soviet memorandum deplored the absence of any article in the conventions prohibiting fascist or aggressive propaganda, or the dissemination of false or deformed news. These viewpoints were pressed by members of the Communist bloc on every possible occasion.[4]

The American delegation, in its official report on the 1948 Geneva Conference, stated that "stripped of propaganda phraseology designed to confuse, the Soviet offensive amounted to a drive for the institution in other countries of a state-controlled press system, with governments deciding what is true and what is false and what is friendly and what in unfriendly."[5] Similarly, Mr. Forsythe, the Australian representative, made the following statement before the General Assembly on December 11, 1954:

> It is perfectly clear that the aim of the Soviet group in presenting and supporting this Czechoslovak draft resolution is a one-sided verbal disarmament. What they want is to gag us while leaving themselves free to pour forth propaganda in favor of Communist domination. They want the United Nations to adopt a resolution which would leave Soviet propaganda machinery completely free to operate, but which could be appealed to by the Soviets as authority for the suppression of any voice raised in any democratic country to criticize the Soviet Union and to awaken the people of the world to the Soviet Union's policies of aggression and subversion.[6]

The British point of view was less absolute, however, as shown by the British Draft Convention on Freedom of Information, approved at Geneva by a majority without the American vote. It expressly stipulates in Article 2 that freedom of information is subject to restrictions clearly defined by law, a list of which is given. The last specifically refers to international propaganda, as follows: "The systematic diffusion of deliberately false or distorted reports which undermine friendly relations between peoples or states."[7]

American delegates have often invoked the safeguards of American constitutional law in explanation of their opposition to plans for

---

[3] Whitton, op. cit., (infra, p. 250, n. 8), p. 82.

[4] Ibid.

[5] "Report of the United States Delegates with Related Documents," Dept. of State Publication 3150, International Organization and Conference Series III, 5, pp. 4-5. See also, Carroll Binder, "Freedom of Information and the United Nations," International Organization, Vol. VI (1952), pp. 210-226.

[6] U. N. Gen. Ass., Off Rec., Plenary Meetings, 9th Session, 1954, p. 472. Answering the Soviet delegates claim that revolutions were not fomented by it because it violated their principle of non-intervention, Mr. Forsythe added: "Perhaps revolutions cannot be exported, but we are quite certain that subversive activities can be."

[7] "Report of the U.S. Delegates," op. cit., p. 22.

legal controls to repress harmful international propaganda. As to the constitutional guarantees of free speech and press, this position could be modified by agreeing to adopt such measures as are clearly within the limits permitted by our constitutional framework. No country can be asked to do more. In addition, it is sometimes argued that under the 10th Amendment the obligations in question would require the passing of new laws by each of the 50 states and it is therefore not possible for the Federal Government to accept over-all obligations to restrain propaganda. This objection is by no means new. It had been raised for many years by American delegations at international conferences in connection with proposals for international labor legislation. The opposition is based more on political than an legal grounds in the present instance. The case of *Missouri v. Holland*[8] makes it clear that the United States may through treaty accomplish ends of this kind under the 10th Amendment. But the storm over the Bricker Amendment shows how strong the feeling is against too broad a use of the treaty power.[9] In any event, the subject matter here is the conduct of the external relations of the United States, the broad question of peace and war, and the impact of domestic events on international relations. The sort of legislation here discussed would constitutionally be as proper a subject for federal action as the neutrality statutes of 1794, which have the same object of preventing repercussions that might endanger the peace.

The picture of the debate, which since 1945 has seemed to cast Russia in the role of active condemner of war propaganda and the United States in the role of cautious opponent of anti-propaganda action (because of freedom-of-speech fears) has finally been made obsolete by the 1962 Geneva episode described in a previous chapter. The roles of the parties were not only altered by this incident, but almost reversed. The United States, having modified its 17-year-old position of shying away from any agreement on repression of war propaganda emerged from that episode as the nation which was and still is willing to go through with arrangements aimed at control of war propaganda—an agreement accepted unanimously by all participants in the conference including the Russian delegate, while the group sat as a committee of the whole. The Soviet Union, in turn,

---

[8] 252 U. S. 416 (1920). Here J. Holmes said: "We do not mean to imply that there are no qualifications to the treaty-making power; but they must be ascertained in a different way. It is obvious that there may be matters of the sharpest exigency for the national well being that an act of Congress could not deal with but that a treaty followed by such an act could, and it is not lightly to be assumed that, in matters requiring national action, 'a power which must belong to and somewhere reside in every civilized government' is not to be found." (P. 433).

[9] John B. Whitton and J. Edward Fowler, "The Bricker Amendment—Fallacies and Dangers," *Am. J. Int. Law,* Vol. 48 (1954), pp. 23-56.

having reneged on its agreement, emerged from the same episode looking like the man who has thrown his shoulder mightily against a door which he thought was securely locked, only to find that someone has suddenly opened the door. Or, to put the matter more bluntly, the Soviet refusal to go through with an agreement that was actually in hand could not help but lead to speculation that the Soviet Union's demands for a war propaganda agreement all these years had been something less than perfectly sincere.

Perhaps this revealing incident will help to clear the air by creating a more accurate impression of the true attitudes of the parties, and by demonstrating the advantages of studying fresh approaches and avoiding stereotyped positions.

The issue of freedom of speech appears in another form in the propaganda debate. On a number of occasions the democracies have taken the position that the way to overcome the evils caused by harmful propaganda is to provide wider sources of information. This thesis has venerable and respectable support. As Professor Hocking has pointed out, both Milton and Mill contended that in a free public contest of opinion the truth was bound to prevail, and that men who set out to suppress what they considered to be error will end by suppressing the truth.[10] As early as 1875 the Belgian government, replying to Prussian charges against subversive propaganda sent out by certain Belgian bishops, invoked the principle of freedom of the press and said that the best way to overcome harmful propaganda was to give free rein to such freedom.[11] Experience had shown, it was said, that the best way to counter the preachings of the Internationale was to bring them into the light of day where they succumbed before the good sense of the population. In a similar vein, Dr. Evatt (Australia), in the First Committee of the U.N. General Assembly in October 1947, stated that the remedy for propaganda should be sought in providing such a large number of newspapers, with full access to news and opinion in its own or in other countries, that every responsible view could get a fair hearing.[12] The Swiss with some eloquence have expressed the same thought.[13] The *New York Times*,

---

[10] William Ernest Hocking, *Freedom of the Press, A Framework of Principle*, Chicago, 1947, pp. 91, 106 and *passim;* Jacques Bourquin, *La Liberté de la Presse*, Paris, 1950.

[11] *Archives Diplomatiques*, Vol. II, (1876), p. 298.

[12] *U. N. Weekly Bulletin*, November 4, 1947, pp. 583-584.

[13] *Freedom of Information, op. cit.*, Vol. I, p 214: "The existence, in Switzerland, of newspapers of various shades of political opinion and propensities is in itself a guarantee that any attempt to institute or to spread false ideas by the systematic dissemination of false reports would be uncovered and condemned by the press itself. To the Swiss way of thinking this constitutes the best safeguard against 'demonstrably false or tendentious reports which confuse the peoples of the world. . . .'"

in an editorial of December 20, 1952, questioning the validity of an international right of reply then under consideration by the United Nations, expressed a similar view in the following passage.[14]

> This is not the way of getting at truth. The real way—and in fact the only way—is to abolish the censors, to throw open the channels of information and communication; and then—even though irresponsible journals and irresponsible governments will continue to produce some lying, distorted and propagandistic stories, falsehood will not be able to master truth in the ultimate competition of the public forum.

The United States Supreme Court, through Vinson, has itself said that "propaganda will answer propaganda" but in the same paragraph has cautioned that free speech "is not an unlimited, unqualified right, but that the societal value of speech must, on occasion, be subordinated to other values and considerations."[15] Also, Justice Douglas, in his dissent in the same case, italicized Justice Brandeis' dictum in the *Whitney* case: *"If there be time to expose through discussion the falsehood and fallacies, to avert the evil by the processes of education, the remedy to be applied is more speech, not enforced silence."*[16]

There are several difficulties in relying too heavily on this admittedly salutary principle when the problem at stake is prevention of propaganda tending to cause war.

One difficulty has to do with insuring that the real truth does in fact have free flow, and therefore an opportunity to compete with falsehood and drive it out. As White and Leigh have said, "The surest antidote for ignorance and deceit is the widest possible exchange of objectively realistic information—true information, not merely *more* information."[17] The existence of sheer quantity and variety of sources cannot necessarily guarantee that the true story will be told with completeness and freedom from bias.

Another question is whether this principle can work at all outside the free democratic states. In the dictatorships, where there is in effect only a single news outlet, it seems unrealistic to rely on proposals for more avenues of information. Mr. McNeil, speaking for the United Kingdom in 1947 before the First Committee of the General Assembly, said that "nobody could say that the British press was perfect, but at least if a newspaper published incorrect news there would be another paper to put it right, whereas if *Pravda* were mis-

---

14 *New York Times,* December 20, 1952.

15 *Dennis* v. *U. S.,* 341 U. S. 494 (1951), at p. 503.

16 *Ibid.,* at p. 586, citing *Whitney* v. *California,* 274 U. S. 357 (1927), at pp. 376-377.

17 Llewellyn White and Robert D. Leigh, *Peoples Speaking to Peoples,* Chicago, 1946, p. 2.

taken there would be no other paper to correct the error."[18]

Still another problem is that of timing. This question was suggested by Mr. Lopez, reporting on freedom of information to the United Nations, when he declared that "while it is undoubtedly true that the free flow of information will ultimately drive out the false, history shows that this process of purgation does not always come quickly enough to avert the catastrophe of war."[19]

Finally, the most dangerous propaganda is not amenable to this antidote. A sustained propaganda campaign aimed at subversion, for example, is not corrected by mere freedom of information. This is recognized in Judge Hand's decision affirming the conviction of eleven Communists in 1950, when he said:

> The only justification which can be suggested is that in spite of their efforts to mask their purposes . . . discussion and publicity may so weaken their power that it will have ceased to be dangerous when the moment may come. That may be a proper enough antidote in ordinary times and for less redoubtable combinations; but certainly it does not apply to this one. *Corruptio optimi pessima.*[20]

Similarly, violent and unremitting defamation designed to stir up hostility between countries, or outright war-mongering campaigns, or any other types of propaganda in which the essence is not the truth or falsity of statements but the deliberate use of words to incite violence and war are outside the reach of this remedy; and it must be stressed again that these are the most important part of the problem.

In conclusion then, it is strongly urged that, while undoubtedly the democracies should continue to stress the values of greater freedom of information as an antidote to propaganda and should continue to insist that the values of free speech and free press must not be sacrificed in the effort to control propaganda, they should in the future concentrate their efforts on obtaining the kind of United Nations and treaty actions that will supply effective remedies bearing on the central problem of international communications by governments. At the same time they should temper the absoluteness of opposition to restraints on private propaganda by devising appropriate controls for the most extreme and overt offenses, since this can be done readily without going beyond existing traditions and precedents on freedom of speech and press.

---

18 U. N. Gen. Ass. 1947, *Off. Rec.., 1st Committee,* p. 230. On October 13, 1961, the United States formally protested to Russia that while the American public could freely read Russian publications and hear its speakers, the Russian people were denied similar freedom. *New York Times,* October 14, 1961.

19 Lopez, *op. cit.,* p. 18.

20 *U. S. v. Dennis,* 183 Fed. 2nd, 201 (1950), at p. 213.

Chapter XV

Private Action

We have so far considered three main categories of remedial actions: United Nations actions, treaty actions and domestic legislation. There remains the question: What contribution to alleviating the propaganda problem can be made by non-governmental organizations?

A Newsman's Code?

In past discussions of the problem at hand, considerable reliance has been placed in international press conferences on the role of press associations or similar private agencies in keeping news free from justified criticism. Such proposals were particularly popular before the rise of Hitler, when the press, and associations of the press, were more free from governmental restraints than later. As early as 1893 the responsibility of the press for the avoidance of international friction was discussed.[1] Excellent resolutions were adopted by a meeting of press experts in 1927, called by the League of Nations Assembly stating that "newspapers and news agencies of the world should deem it their duty to take stringent measures to avoid the publication or distribution" of news that was "obviously inaccurate, highly exaggerated, or deliberately distorted"; also to avoid that which was "calculated to cause undesirable misunderstanding among nations and suspicions detrimental to international peace." Despite these sentiments, as usual no machinery was provided for their implementation or enforcement.[2] A few years later, in 1930, the International Federation of Journalists, representing 25,000 members from twenty-two nations, decided at its meeting in Berlin to create a tribunal of professional honor, with power to declare unworthy of exercising the profession of journalist anyone publishing mendacious information capable of arousing the public against a foreign nation.[3]

[1] At the first World Press Conference, held in Chicago. Martin, *op. cit.*, p. 67.

[2] L. O. N., Conference of Press Experts, Geneva, August 24, 1927. Publications of the League of Nations, General 1927.5, p. 15.

[3] Julien Luchaire, *Le Désarmement Moral*, Paris, 1932, pp. 119 ff.

In 1931 this same body, at The Hague, actually set up such a tribunal of honor.[4] Similarly, in 1932, the International Radiophony Union outlawed all political or nationalistic propaganda, and decided to exclude from membership any nation permitting such propaganda.[5] In 1946 White and Leigh attempted to revive this proposal, suggesting "The organization in all principal news centers of the world of foreign correspondents' corps with strict, self-administered codes of ethics; the requirement that all newspaper, magazine and radio reporters and all authors and photographers (including newsreel cameramen) who join these corps be bound by their codes; specific authority for the corps to handle all disputes among members or with host-governments, with right of appeal to a unit of the United Nations Economic and Social Council . . ." This body would receive complaints of violations, investigate and report on alleged cases of distortion of facts or the fomenting of international discord.[6] This idea was reconsidered at the Geneva Conference on Freedom of Information and of the Press, urged on by a resolution of the International Organization of Journalists at their 1948 meeting at Brussels.[7] But no action was taken, other than a request to the Economic and Social Council to study the proposal, submitted by UNESCO, to establish an International Institute of Press and Information (Resolution No. 34). The proposal for an international press card was withdrawn after objections had been voiced by Soviet Russia, Britain, and the United States. Furthermore, it was not found practicable to establish an international court of honor as proposed by Peru and Colombia, with the support of the Netherlands and India. This project, together with a proposal for an international honor code for journalists, was referred back to the Sub-Commission.[8] As already remarked, the code of ethics approved two years later at the Montevideo Conference (1950) was opposed by the American and British delegates on the ground that such a code was a task for private organizations, but hardly for governments.[9]

The code of ethics, proposed by the United Nations Sub-Commission on Freedom of Information and of the Press in 1950, and revised in 1952, if adopted and respected, would make the task of the propagandist or the purveyor of false news extremely difficult. Thus, under Article I, communicators "should do all in their power to ensure that the information the public receives is factually accurate.

---

[4] Yves de la Brière, "Aspect Juridique du Désarmement Moral," *Rev. Gén. de Dr. Int. Pub.*, Vol. 41 (1933), pp. 129-139, at p. 132.

[5] White and Leigh, *op. cit.*, p. 108.

[6] *Ibid.*

[7] Martin, *op. cit.*, p. 68.

[8] For the above, see Whitton, *op. cit.* ("United Nations Conference on Freedom of Information. . . ."), pp. 79-80.

[9] *U. N. Weekly Bulletin*, June 15, 1950.

They should check all items of information to the best of their ability. No fact should be wilfully distorted and no essential fact should be deliberately suppressed." The code condemns wilful calumny, slander, libel and unfounded accusations. It requires information harmfully inaccurate to be spontaneously and immediately rectified. Rumor and unconfirmed news should be identified and treated as such. (Article II.) When charges against the reputation or moral character are made, the code requires that an opportunity be afforded for a reply. (Article III.) Communicators dealing with events in foreign lands should acquire the knowledge of such country necessary if accurate reports and comments are to be made. (Article IV.)[10] The General Assembly in December 1952, and again in November, 1953, directed the Secretary General to take steps to prepare for a professional conference to consider the code. It was made clear, as the United States representative particularly insisted, that the job was one for professional members of information enterprises, without interference from governments. No action, however, has been taken as yet, nor do the chances seem good, to judge by the scepticism of American, French and United Kingdom representatives. Typical of their views was that expressed by the U.K. delegate before the Sub-Commission, which reviewed the text of the draft and passed it on to the Economic and Social Council.[11]

> Mr. Waithman (United Kingdom) was inclined to share the doubts expressed by the Canadian Association of Broadcasters that there was any real justification for the promulgation of the International Code of Ethics. In the first place, a good, honest and experienced journalist hardly required to be told what correct professional conduct was. In the second place, the existing dangers to freedom of information, as the body he had cited had observed, came not from journalists but rather from governments themselves and from organized minority groups within certain communities.

In 1954 the General Assembly decided to take no further action toward the organization of a conference of professionals, and merely voted to send relevant data pertaining to the draft code, for their information, to the enterprises and associations with which they had been communicating.[12]

A survey of the codes of ethics as they existed among members of the United Nations in 1948 did not yield very encouraging results. Of thirty-three members who replied to the U.N. questionnaire, less than half stated they possessed a code of honor or similar instrument. Among the responses, there was very little sign of any sense of direct

---

[10] An International Code of Ethics for Information Personnel, United Nations, 1952, ST/SOA/12. See also A/C.3/L.381.

[11] E/2190.

[12] *U.N. Yearbook,* 1954, p. 242.

responsibility on the part of the press for news stories of a nature to disturb international harmony and peace. On the other hand, some of the codes included general principles of conduct apparently limited to the domestic scene which, if applied strictly, could make a signal contribution also in the field of international relations.[13] The Australian code, for example, called on newsmen to "report and interpret the news with scrupulous honesty."[14] Several, i.e., the Canadian, United Kingdom and American codes, enjoined strict objectivity.[15] Almost all insisted on accuracy. The American code called for a disposition to rectify errors. But only three emphasized the direct international responsibility of the journalist. India proscribed scurrilous attacks against leaders or communities, and all incitements to violence. This precept could be considered to apply to news and radio emissions of international importance. It was also stated: "Items of news calculated to make for peace and harmony and to help in the restoration and maintenance of law and order shall be given prominence and precedence over other news."[16] The Union of South Africa had this provision in its code: "In discussing editorially internal or foreign affairs, members should abstain from abusive or vituperative language."[67]

The Standards of Practice for American Broadcasters (1948) had some admirable provisions which, if followed honestly by communicators around the world, could accomplish wonders for better relations among the nations. Broadcasters were enjoined to "Respect the rights and sensitivities of all people;" "protect and uphold the dignity and brotherhood of all mankind;" "provide for the fair discussion of matters of general public concern; engage in works directed toward the common good; and volunteer our aid and comfort in times of stress and emergency." Also, "news reporting should be factual, fair and without bias."[18]

Unfortunately the American Television Code of the National Association of Broadcasters (1959) is much less precise in formulating standards having application to international propaganda. There seems to be little comprehension here of how much damage to good international relations can be done by television, especially by creating a false image of other countries, for example by presenting disparaging stereotypes of foreign peoples. Nor is there here any sign that the broadcasters realize how much good might be accomplished for mutual understanding among the peoples of the world by the right kind of programs. One is glad to discover, however, a condemnation of "words (especially slang) derisive of any race, color, creed, na-

---

13 *Freedom of Information,* Vol. I, pp. 254 ff., and Vol II, pp. 208 ff.
14 *Ibid.,* Vol. II, p. 208.
15 *Ibid.,* pp. 208, 212, 213.
16 *Ibid.,* p. 209.
17 *Ibid.,* p. 211.
18 *Ibid.,* p. 210.

tionality or national derivation," although one suspects that this provision is meant to apply exclusively to the home front. As to news, the code fortunately calls for reporting which is factual, fair and without bias, and enjoins that news should be telecast in such a manner as to "avoid panic and unnecessary alarm."[19]

It also seems unfortunate that in the "Code of Ethics or Canons of Journalism of the American Society of Newspaper Editors," one looks in vain for any indication that the American newsmen accept any responsibility relating to news which may be good or bad from the point of view of international peace.[20] Of course, this Code does lay great stress on sincerity, truthfulness and accuracy, and frowns on printed material which would supply incentives to base conduct. But the absence of a precise treatment of the type of news and editorial writing bearing on international tensions, particularly when defamation, subversion and war-mongering dangerous to international peace are involved, is greatly to be regretted.

The new (1960) Standards of Good Practice for the Radio Broadcasters of the United States of America exhibit a keener comprehension of responsibilities in the international field.[21] The code calls on broadcasters to respect the rights and sensitivities of all people, and to protect and uphold the dignity and brotherhood of all mankind. Particularly in the field of newscasting one discovers a number of excellent precepts. Newscasters must exercise constant professional care in their selection of sources "for the integrity of the news and the consequent good reputation of radio." News reporting must be factual and objective. Morbid, sensational or alarming details not essential to factual reporting should be avoided. This latter is an excellent standard for communications in time of international crisis. As to editorials, "the reputation of a station for honesty and accuracy in editorializing depends upon willingness to expose its convictions to fair rebuttal." Equality of opportunity for the discussion of public issues is also enjoined.

[19] *The Television Code* (The National Asociation of Broadcasters), 5th ed., March, 1959, Washington, D.C. It also states: "Televised drama shall not simulate news or special events in such a way as to mislead or alarm."

[20] Off-print received from the A. S. N. E.

[21] Issued by the National Association of Broadcasters, Washington, D. C., first promulgated in 1937, latest edition 1960. The film industry in America, in an effort at self-regulation, has a "Production Code," an important section of which states: "The history, institutions, prominent people and citizenry of all nations shall be represented fairly." Toward this aim of objectivity, all major film studios engage international specialists to review scripts, the locale of which is set abroad, in order to determine whether any element of the story might be construed as offensive. Also, "No picture shall be produced that tends to incite bigotry or hatred among peoples of differing races, religions or national origins." *The Motion Picture Production Code*, Motion Picture Association of America, Inc., Washington/New York/Los Angeles, December, 1956,

There is little doubt that private associations of journalists, broadcasters, cameramen, etc., could become under appropriate circumstances an excellent influence in preventing the dissemination of materials dangerous to good international relations. Their usefulness, however, in some totalitarian countries is doubtful, to say the least; in Germany under the Nazis for example. Nevertheless, it must be apparent that the effort to curb pernicious international communication would be greatly facilitated by the development throughout the world of a corps of newsmen inspired by high ideals of professional conduct, provided that they are free to put these ideals into practice without interference from advertisers, owners, or state directors of "information and enlightenment." Such ideals for the guidance of all those engaged in the dissemination of information to the public were admirably phrased at the 1948 Geneva Conference:[22]

> (a) to report facts without prejudice and in their proper content and to make comments without malicious intent;
> (b) to facilitate the solution of the economic, social and humanitarian problems of the world as a whole and the free interchange of information bearing on such problems;
> (c) to help promote respect for human rights and fundamental freedoms without discrimination;
> (d) to help maintain international peace and security;
> (e) to counteract the persistent spreading of false or distorted reports which promote hatred or prejudice against states, persons or groups of different race, language, religion or philosophical conviction.

A recent formulation along these lines is the declaration on freedom of the press, approved by the Social Committee of ECOSOC (U.N.) on April 20, 1960, by a vote of 15-0 and three abstentions. Particularly significant is Article IV—"Those who disseminate information must strive in good faith to ensure the accuracy of the facts reported and respect the rights and dignity of nations . . ."[23]

In our search for an appropriate code of conduct, let us recall here once again the almost-forgotten but excellent 1936 treaty on radio broadcasting, entitled the International Convention Concerning the Use of Broadcasting in the Cause of Peace, which called on the signatories to do certain things which, if carried out in good faith, would have made great inroads on the evils of propaganda. Besides requiring the parties to rectify any incorrect statements at the earliest possible moment, the convention obliges them to:[24]

1) Prohibit emissions of such a character as to incite the popula-

---

[22] *Supra* p. 199. This is from Article 3 of the Draft Convention on Freedom of Information, known as The British Convention.
[23] E/3359.
[24] *Supra* p. 125.

tion of any territory to acts incompatible with internal order and security (i.e., subversive propaganda);

2) Ensure that domestic emissions "shall not constitute an incitement either to war against another High Contracting Party or to acts likely to lead thereto;" (war mongering)

3) Prohibit "any transmission likely to harm good international understanding by statements the incorrectness of which is or ought to be known to the persons responsible for the broadcast;" (false news; defamation; war mongering)

4) Ensure, "especially in time of crisis, that stations . . . shall broadcast information concerning international relations the accuracy of which shall have been verified . . . by the persons responsible for broadcasting the information." (To promote peace, perhaps curb war-mongering).

It is notable that in 1954, when the General Assembly took note of the existence of this treaty, it considered steps to improve it, suggesting the addition of new articles calling on the contracting states to "refrain from radio broadcasts that would mean unfair attacks or slanders against other peoples anywhere and in so doing to conform strictly to an ethical conduct in the interest of world peace by reporting facts truly and objectively, and to provide that each High Contracting Party shall not interfere with the reception, within its territory, of foreign radio broadcasts."[25]

It is to be hoped that the efforts to evolve and perfect codes of ethics and to create appropriate tribunals of honor to administer them will be further pursued by responsible associations. To help toward this end, a suggested draft of a code of ethics is attempted in the next chapter.

_____

25 *U. N. Yearbook* 1954, p. 235. Also, see Codding, *op. cit.*, p. 73.

Chapter XVI

A Code of Ethics for
International Communicators

In the following pages a system of ethical rules is proposed for newspapers, periodicals, books, radio, television, films and other media of information. We submit that if these rules were respected by those in management or control of mass media throughout the world, both governmental and non-governmental, the greater part of the hostile propaganda which today poisons the international atmosphere would be eliminated.

These precepts are intended as guides or standards of good professional conduct. They are not presented as legal norms, although some of them are already rules of international law, and others, for instance the rules against defamation, exist as part of domestic law in virtually all countries. Many of these principles can already be found in the professional codes of ethics formulated by national and international organizations for the several media of mass communication.

No attempt is made here to suggest one code for countries in which the mass media are controlled by the state, and another for those in which the media are independent. Subversive communications originating on the soil of State A and directed against the established government of State B are dangerous to the peace whether the radio in State A is a government monopoly or is privately owned and controlled. Theoretically the duty to refrain from hostile propaganda can be more easily enforced when the government has complete control over the mass media. In the "free" state, responsibility is so dispersed that a government desirous of curbing communications objectionable to foreign countries must, except in extreme cases, rely almost wholly on persuasion, in which case success depends on the voluntary cooperation of the medium, or it must perhaps fall back on such uncertain remedies as an apology presented to the offended nation *après coup.* Such a government, attempting to influence its own press in the interest of international harmony, might find the present code of ethics quite useful as persuasive authority, especially if the code received the badge of approval of international organizations, both public and private. In the same way, the Universal Declaration of Human Rights, although without legal force, is often cited with persuasive effect, and its provisions have been written into a number of national constitutions and legal codes.

When the draft "International Code of Ethics for Information Personnel" was prepared by the United Nations Sub-Commission on Freedom of Information and of the Press in 1950 and revised in 1952, various objections were raised, and similar objections might be made to the draft here submitted. It was first objected that the code contained nothing new.[1] This may have been true of that particular draft code, but the present text is much more comprehensive, and at any rate many codes have proved of great value although not "new." It was also remarked that any such code would merely provide totalitarian regimes with further pretexts for the suppression of freedom of information.[2] But so little freedom exists in such countries, and so many grounds are already available there for the suppression of the news, that a code of ethics would make little difference in this matter. Nevertheless, such a code would not be without effect even in totalitarian countries. Code proscriptions against hate propaganda could be invoked both by the West against Moscow's hostile broadcasts, and by the Soviets against objectionable communications concerning Russia appearing in free newspapers of the West.

Some also doubted whether any effective code could ever achieve universal acceptance. The same objection, however, was made when the United Nations embarked on its task of drawing up a Declaration of Human Rights.[3] Even if such an attempt to achieve a Code of Ethics should fail, the effort alone, particularly the publicity thereby engendered, should have a beneficial effect, persuasive and educational, on international relations.

A final objection, urged by a Canadian delegate, was that the good newsman did not need to be told what was honest and correct reporting.[4] But while this may be true of the press, or at least much of it, in that particular country, the vast amount of harmful communication generally characteristic of international relations today hardly substantiates this argument. Also, it must be remembered that many of the abuses in question are not the fault of the individual newsman, but rather of his masters—in totalitarian regimes, his government, and,

---

[1] Lopez, *op. cit.* pp. 11 ff; ST/SOA/12, August 12, 1952; *U. N. Weekly Bulletin,* June 15, 1950, pp. 521 ff.

[2] *Ibid.*

[3] H. Lauterpacht, *International Law and Human Rights,* New York, 1950, Ch. 13, "The Substance and the Enforcement of the Bill of Rights."

[4] E/2190, Annex A.

in free countries, the owners or managers of the medium. The present code is addressed to all of these.

The essential duty of every communicator, whether governmental or non-governmental, and whether his message is addressed to the home population or to some foreign country, is to be truthful—to search for and stick to the truth in reporting, explaining and interpreting facts. He should be prepared to furnish accurate information, whatever the consequences. But it is also his duty, so far at it is reasonably possible, to "protect and uphold the dignity and brotherhood of all mankind," by avoiding messages of a nature to cause ill-will and hatred, especially by the systematic diffusion of false or distorted news which undermine friendly relations between nations. For while freedom to communicate, as asserted by the United Nations General Assembly, is a sacred human right, it is a right burdened with important duties. In the words of the General Assembly, "Freedom of information requires as an indispensable element the willingness and capacity to employ its privileges without abuse. It requires as a basic discipline the moral obligation to seek the facts without prejudice and to spread knowledge without malicious intent."[5] Thus the communicator must refrain from sending forth messages which constitute a clear and present danger to peaceful international relations. Defamation, subversion and war-mongering, hate propaganda and false reports, are to be condemned. He should do his best to respect the rights and sensitivities of all peoples. In the following pages, these general propositions will be presented in more detail.

SUGGESTED DRAFT CODE

I. Special Precriptions for the Communicator

1) INTEGRITY

Every one engaged in the processes of mass communication is endowed with a high public trust. Hence he is under a duty not to seek any personal advantage through the promotion of a selfish private interest, or any other unworthy purpose contrary to the general welfare of the international community. While naturally sensitive to the demands of a legitimate patriotism, he should not forget his responsibility toward the cause of international good will and world comradeship.

2) KNOWLEDGE AND TRAINING

It is the duty of the communicator (and of him who prepares his material), if he undertakes to comment on or present facts relating to a foreign country, to acquire a degree of knowledge and under-

---

[5] Resolution 59 (1),*U. N. Yearbook 1946-1947*, p. 176.

standing of such country reasonably adequate to enable his reports thereon to be unbiased, accurate and fair.

II. Rights of the Communicator

As affirmed in Article 19 of the Universal Declaration of Human Rights, "Everyone has the right to freedom of opinion and expression; this right includes freedom to hold opinions without interference and to seek, receive and impart information and ideas through any media and regardless of frontiers."[6] Thus all communicators should be free from peacetime censorship which restricts or controls freedom of information. And freedom to communicate to consumers, either at home or in foreign lands, may be limited only by a recognition of and respect for the rights of others, and in order to protect, but only as provided by law, the freedom, welfare and security of all. The exercise of these freedoms carries with it duties and responsibilities.

"It may, however, be subject only to such necessary restrictions as are clearly defined by law and applied in accordance with the law in respect of: national security and public order (*ordre public*); systematic dissemination of false reports harmful to friendly relations among nations and of expressions inciting to war or to national, racial or religious hatred; attacks on founders of religions; incitement to violence and crime; public health and morals; the rights, honor and reputation of others; and the fair administration of justice.

"The restrictions specified in the preceding paragraph shall not be deemed to justify the imposition by any state of prior censorship on news, comments and political opinions and may not be used as grounds for restricting the right to criticize the government."[7]

III. Rights of the Public, or "Target"

All peoples have a right to be fully and truthfully informed, not only as a prerequisite to the effective operation of democratic processes of government, but as a necessary precondition to the maintenance of international understanding and peace. This basic right—the right to know—includes the right to listen and the right to read. The right to listen must be protected by the avoidance of the jamming of non-hostile broadcasts originating abroad, and the right to read must be protected by the avoidance of prior peacetime censorship, and may be limited only by certain restrictions clearly defined by law, as explained in the last article.

---

[6] As adopted by the General Assembly on December 10, 1948. *These Rights and Freedoms,* United Nations, 1950, p. 173.

[7] Gen. Ass., *Off. Rec.,* 15th Sess., *Annexes,* Agenda Item 35 (A/4636), December 9, 1960. *United Nations Review,* May, 1960, p. 43.

IV. *Prescriptions as to Content*

1) FAIRNESS

In his references to a foreign country, notably concerning its history, culture, institutions, prominent personalities, people, and foreign and domestic problems and policies, the communicator should endeavor to limit himself to verified facts, presenting them fairly and free from bias. When commentary, opinion or news analysis are offered, they should be clearly identified as such. If a given report is based on rumor, it should be so stated. When an issue is controversial, and materially affects the welfare of nations and the cause of world peace, the communicator should endeavor to present or discuss the issue without bias, prejudice or distortion.

2) ACCURACY

It is the duty of the communicator to do all in his power to ensure that the information he is disseminating to the public, either at home or abroad, is factually accurate, in short as near an approximation to the truth as is humanly possible. As Professor Walter Williams stated in his well-known Journalists' Creed: "I believe that clear thinking and clear statement, accuracy, and fairness are fundamental to good journalism. . . I believe that suppression of the news, for any consideration other than the welfare of society, is indefensible."[8]

The communicator is not to be excused for lack of thoroughness or accuracy which are within his control, nor for failure to obtain command of these qualities when this is possible. Those in charge of mass media should endeavor to stop without delay the diffusion of any material, the inaccuracy of which is known, especially if it is of a nature to harm the cause of good international understanding. If such material has already been published or broadcast, the communicator should be prepared to offer appropriate reparation, as indicated below.

In countries in which peacetime censorship is permitted and operative in accordance with the law of the land, the censor should take all reasonable means to prevent the dissemination of news, opinion or commentary which is inaccurate or false. In other countries, this duty must be shouldered by the owners or managers of the medium in question, as well as by the editors and individual communicators.

3) DEFAMATION

It is the duty of every communicator to refrain from wilfully libellous or slanderous attacks and unfounded accusations against prominent foreign personalities, especially heads of states, governmental leaders, and diplomatic agents. This precept is based, first, on

---

[8] School of Journalism, Univ. of Missouri, 1958.

the respect which nations mutually owe to each other and to their representatives, and, secondly, on the fact that such attacks cause resentment and constitute a danger to peaceful international relations. Also, and mainly for the second reason just mentioned, the communicator should avoid the diffusion of material tending to hold up to derision or obloquy any foreign people, or any group or minority thereof, because of race, color, creed or national origin, thus causing bigotry or hatred, with the consequent danger of violence. Particularly important in this connection is the avoidance of the use of epithets, in the form of slang or other expressions which tend to create or perpetuate stereotype images of a disparaging, insulting or degrading nature, thus causing misunderstanding, resentment, and international tension. The truth of such attacks is no defense if the object of the communication is to weaken the loyalty of a given people vis-a-vis its government or to urge one nation to engage in aggression against another, or is otherwise malicious.

Criticism of the policies and aims of a foreign government is permissible if based on the truth, is non-malicious, and is in the best interests of the international community. Fair, unbiased criticism of aggressive policies of a foreign government, if founded on accurate information and not inspired by malice, can be a service to the cause of security and peace.

4) SUBVERSIVE PROPAGANDA

It is the duty of the communicator to refrain from disseminating material, whether true or false, which is designed or is of a nature to disrupt peaceful relations existing between a friendly foreign government and its citizenry, or to foment a rebellion against the government by the use of force. With respect to radio broadcasting, the agency in control of the station in question must prohibit, and, if occasion arises, stop without delay the broadcasting to a foreign country of any transmission which to the detriment of good international understanding is of such a character as to incite the population to acts incompatible with the internal order or the security of such foreign state.

This article does not purport to prohibit popular manifestations of mere moral support on the soil of one state favoring an insurrectionary movement in another state, provided that the communicator is not disseminating propaganda in direct connection with the commission of an overt act of support to such insurrection, notably the preparation of armed bands which are planning to cross the frontier to give active armed aid to the movement. Radio broadcasts beamed or directed to persons in a foreign country urging them to rebel against their government are particularly harmful to good international relations and a real danger to peace.

5) WAR-MONGERING

It is the duty of communicators to avoid the dissemination of any material which is of a nature, whether so designed or not, to incite or provoke the decision-makers of a given state, or the people therein, to threats or acts of aggression against another state with whom it is at peace. This includes the use of words, signs, symbols or any visible or audible representations which are likely to promote feelings of enmity or hatred, or promote a war-spirit, between different peoples. Incitement to threats or acts of aggression is not the less reprehensible if it fails of its object. It is immaterial that such war-mongering propaganda employs argument based on fact, if the motive be malicious.

It is particularly dangerous to international peace for a commentator to make false charges of aggression alleged to have been prepared or committed by a foreign government or its people.

6) COMMUNICATION IN TIME OF CRISIS

In time of grave international tension, particularly when an international crisis occurs during which peace is seriously endangered, communicators should be especially careful not to diffuse unsubstantiated reports or inflammatory comment of a nature to cause alarm or panic either among governmental leaders or their citizenry. At such times particular care should be taken to verify the sources of all news stories and reports, and also to avoid publicizing matter based on unfounded rumor. At the very least, rumor should be clearly identified as such.

V. Remedies

In the event of a violation by a communicator of any of the principles set forth in this code, an aggrieved party, or a government acting on his behalf, may, through resort to one or more of the following remedies, seek reparation for the injury suffered. It is the duty of the state in which the offending communication originates to give satisfaction to the complaining party through cooperation in the operation of such remedies.

1) Rectification by the offending medium itself of a communication which is false or erroneous, defamatory, subversive or warmongering, or otherwise harmful to good international relations.

2) Operation of a right of reply in accordance with domestic or international law, where such a right is in effect for the interested parties.

3) Apology by the government of the state in which the offense occurs, offered to the offended government after request by the latter.

4) Punishment of the offending communicator in accordance with constitutional law and procedures. If the communication com-

plained of is a libellous or defamatory attack on an individual of the complaining state, the proper remedy may be an action for damages pursued in the court of the state in which the offense took place.

5) Award and payment of damages where appropriate.

6) Submission of the matter to the United Nations after complaint and failure to obtain adequate satisfaction, for investigation, report, and such other action as may be appropriate in the circumstances, and in accordance with the provisions of the Charter and existing precedents.

7) In case of dispute involving a question of international law, submission of the matter to the International Court of Justice, unless the parties agree upon some other mode of settlement.

Chapter XVII

Summary of Proposals and Prospects

Whenever a major public issue like propaganda is discussed, the final question is always: "What can we do about it?" Answers to this question have been suggested at appropriate points throughout the book, but it might be useful to bring the principal suggestions together here in the form of a brief summary. They may be grouped under the headings of substantive law and remedies.

As to substantive law: it has been stressed that the need for action is less acute here than in respect to remedies. Nevertheless, there is much that could be done to strengthen and sharpen the body of law of international propaganda.

As to treaty law, continued efforts to make existing law more specific are all to the good. Bilateral treaties, or regional arrangements, under which the parties assume clearly defined duties on freedom of information and avoidance of harmful propaganda are probably more promising than attempted universal conventions. As to customary international law and particularly the "general principles of law recognized by civilized nations" there is an opportunity for a contribution by scholars and research workers. International law still suffers not merely from the deficiency of relevant law on particular points, but even more from the failure to find and make the most effective use of law that already exists. This has been conspicuously true in the case of the law of international propaganda. Much more can be done to bring out and apply to the problem the evidences of customary international law on the subject. An even more challenging task is that of exploiting the "general principles"—a task which obviously is one of great difficulty and magnitude. It should involve investigations of all the great legal systems of the world on the particular points relevant to propaganda, the comparison of the principles found to identify common elements, a careful appraisal to eliminate semantic errors, and a creative transposition of these principles to the international law counterpart of the domestic principles found.

Another large task is that of bringing the existence of the law of illegal propaganda to the consciousness of the people all over the world. It is quite possible that, if average people and even public leaders in various countries were asked about the law governing propaganda, nine out of ten would stare blankly and declare that they were not aware that there was any such law. Certainly a large part of official conduct around the world seems to be carried on as if the area were a legal vacuum. Here then is a task of public education for everyone concerned with education and communications.

As to remedies: a number of specific actions have been suggested.

The institution of a universal monitoring system operated by the United Nations is a first step. It would have a strong deterrent effect in its own right, and would lay the basis for the other remedies.

The provision of an international right of reply and correction is another moderate step which can be achieved either directly through treaty action, or indirectly through use as an alternative to more severe sanctions by the United Nations.

The operation of a United Nations Broadcasting Service is also suggested. It could make a large contribution by providing an unimpeachable source of everyday truth about international affairs. It could also be the vehicle for giving effect to the right of reply and correction, and would have many incidental educational benefits.

The direct enforcement of the law of propaganda by the United Nations is also here proposed. This would include an administrative decision-making process to pass on the merits of controverted cases, and a judicial review which could be accomplished within existing mechanisms. General Assembly action would be sufficient to impose the most obvious sanction, which is deprivation of use of United Nations facilities of communication including access to the floor of the Assembly for speech-making purposes. A number of other follow-up sanctions have also been sketched out.

Since the decision-making process is fundamental to the success of any such enforcement, any action which will strengthen the International Court of Justice and enlarge its acceptance by the members of the United Nations would be of value here. Therefore, the world-wide movement to increase the number of declarations accepting the jurisdiction of the International Court over future disputes involving international law and treaties deserves to be listed here as a tangible action important to the solution to the propaganda problem.

Some room for action in the field of improved domestic legislation has also been indicated. At the minimum, this would take the form of legislation prohibiting propaganda which amounts to an overt act in aid of bringing about aggressive war. International treaties agreeing to take such actions domestically, within the constitutional and traditional framework of the particular country, are a step in this direction and, as so limited, should not be resisted.

At the same time, efforts should be continued to break down barriers to freedom of communication, including restrictions on printed matter, jamming of radio broadcasts, censorship of dispatches, and the like. Treaties to this end should be pursued.

Private associations should redouble their efforts to formulate a code of ethics for communicators, and to accompany it with a tribunal of honor and other appropriate administrative mechanisms to apply its standards to everyday conduct.

These, then, are some of the specific actions that could make contributions to solving the problem of illegal propaganda. They do not presuppose sweeping United Nations Charter revisions, or any Charter revisions at all. Nor do they presuppose some miraculous change in the cold war attitudes or in national policies and characters. However, they do presuppose that the large majority of nations of the world are thoroughly disgusted with excessive propaganda, are sincere in their desire for peace, and are aware of the fact that unrestrained propaganda is a formidable and growing threat to the peace. In the last analysis, self-interest is the most reliable motivation in international affairs. Every nation has a vital interest in avoiding the outbreak of another world war, and the task is to build upon this fact in order to convince the world that each nation has a vital interest in eliminating the threat to peace represented by hostile propaganda.

In conclusion, there is one way in which self-interest may be working in support of the effort to curb illegal propaganda. There is some reason to believe that a new phase in the history of propaganda is in its early beginnings—a phase in which emphasis on facts begins to displace frenzy and invective. Undoubtedly the British Broadcasting Corporation deserves primary credit for this turn of events. Over a period of years, the BBC, by calmly reciting factual news including the rough with the smooth, succeeded in building up a reputation for credibility that was almost legendary. The United States Information Agency for a number of years has done everything in its power to achieve a similar degree of acceptance and believability.[1] Indeed, the shortest way of describing to USIA employees the kind of tone and content to be observed under this policy was simply to tell them to emulate the BBC. It was one of the brighter moments in the history of the USIA when a poll showed that, among Hungarian refugees, the Voice of America had actually attained a higher degree of believability than the BBC.

It is too early to say whether this new phase shows any visible traces in parts of the world which have produced the most aggressive propaganda.[2]

---

[1] See Appendix: *U.S.I.A. Basic Guidance Paper*

[2] The following may be noted as signs of concern in the Middle East, about illegal propaganda:

266

But if there is any truth in the hypothesis that propagandists may gradually become convinced that factual reporting is more effective propaganda than violent and distorted invective, the prospects of strengthened observance of the law will be increased. As listeners become more sophisticated or more calloused, propagandists may find that their more extreme efforts not only misfire but backfire. On the broad issue of peace and disarmament the world's best hope lies in the universal realization that the crime of war does not pay. So too, in achieving disarmament in the war of words, it is to be hoped that nations will realize that this specific crime—the use of war-mongering, subversive and defamatory propaganda—also does not pay.

---

1) A resolution passed at the Shturah conference of Arab Foreign Ministers in August 1960, and re-endorsed at Baghdad conference in February 1961, calling on Arab States to discontinue radio and press attacks on each other.

2. An item of news which appeared in *Al-Ahram*, the leading Egyptian daily newspaper on June 7, 1961, which reads:

"The People Move to Face Communist Aggression
The Popular Arabic Organization Move to Face the Battle of Psychological War which the Soviet Propaganda Directs Against Us"

"In Cairo the Press Association held a special meeting after which it issued a statement declaring that the Soviet Press and all other organs of propaganda emanating from Moscow, overstepped all the established rules of etiquette in the press profession and its international treaties.

"The statement also said:
'There is still time for the press of the Soviet organs of propaganda to amend the erroneous attitude which it took without reason. Otherwise it will be the direct cause of destroying all the values which our press cherishes in its international relations with our friends the Soviet people.'

"The committee of the Press Association in its statement denounced the behaviour of one of the papers that is published in Arabic in Lebanon, which is a friendly country. This paper takes the liberty of being amenable in the hands of the Soviet propaganda. It fabricates lies and spreads them, thus giving the Soviet propaganda organs the opportunity to copy these lies and later to use them as a means to interfere in our internal affairs. The Lebanese Government prohibited the publication of this newspaper because it intended to hurt relations between the United Arab Republic and Lebanon.

"At the end the statement said:
'The Press Association denounces vehemently all these attacks which the press and other means of information use as a means of pressure against nations and independent governments and to dictate certain policies and doctrines which contradict customs, principles and the desire of nations to be independent and free.'"

APPENDIX

Excerpts from

U.S.I.A.

BASIC GUIDANCE PAPER

1957

Arthur Larson, Director

"The purpose of the United States Information Agency shall be to submit evidence to peoples of other nations by means of communications techniques that the objectives and policies of the United States are in harmony with and will advance their legitimate aspirations for freedom, progress, and peace."

—President Dwight D. Eisenhower

I.

TONE AND METHOD: ". . . TO SUBMIT EVIDENCE. . ."

A.   *What is "evidence"?*
  1. *Facts* about current events.
  2. *Facts* about the background of events and about history.
  3. *Facts* about what our foreign policy is, as expressed in official utterances by policy-makers.
  4. *Facts* about the reasons for and the significance of our foreign policy.
  5. *Facts* about the policies and attitudes of other countries, as expressed by their spokesmen.
  6. *Facts* about American and world opinion and attitudes, as seen in editorial comment or expressions of public figures.
  7. *Facts* about American life, culture, thought, and history which aid in understanding us and our policies.
  8. *Facts* refuting communist lies and discrediting the false pretensions of communist ideology.

B.   *What is not "evidence"?*

  1. Any material whose appeal is based not on facts but on emotion or rhetoric is outside our statement of purpose.
     This ban extends to all kinds of polemics and denunciation, to any tone which is sarcastic or boastful or self-righteous, and to any style

which employs loaded phrases and purple adjectives. E.g., "bloody hands."

2. Drawing obvious morals should be avoided.

Implicit in the idea of "submitting evidence" is the further idea that you let the audience draw its own conclusions. You provide the facts and explanation—but you then give your audience credit for enough intelligence to form its own judgment. E. g., having described a series of revolutionary Supreme Court decisions, you do not conclude by saying, "And thus once more has been demonstrated the dynamic and flexible nature of the American system."

This applies particularly to material addressed to the people in countries with governments which we do not entirely approve. We may display before them the facts of their own government's shortcomings. But if we then, speaking on behalf of the United States Government, proceed to pass judgment and use uncomplimentary phrases, innate local pride may cause a revulsion against us.

Our material should always be purposeful. We are not in the business of news or art or literature or entertainment or education for their own sake. Our output should in fact form the basis of conclusions that support our foreign policy and objectives. The point of this subsection is merely to emphasize that these conclusions will be more readily reached as a result of a skillful and imaginative exposition of facts stopping short of announcing a moral, than by a presentation which assumes to tell the audience what they ought to believe.

C   *Analysis and explanation*

Under this factual approach, analysis, background, explanation and interpretation of facts and policies are not only permissible but highly desirable, since they help to make the facts and policies meaningful.

Every effort should be made, through imaginative use of facts, through highest-quality standards of editing and presenting material, and through skilful use of art, humor, local interests, and fresh, creative techniques, to make our unfolding of the facts attractive as well as understandable.

It is within our mission to present the issues between the communist and the democratic ideologies in a calm and reasoned manner.

As to policy utterances, these should ordinarily not be undertaken on the authority of the U.S. Information Agency or any of its spokesmen or media, but should be accomplished in one of two ways:

> —official, by direct or indirect quotations from those who have authority to express policy, such as the President, the Secretary of State, the Under Secretary of State, and the Ambassador to the United Nations.

—unofficial, by quotations from Congressional opinion, editorial opinion, statements of public figures, and statements, whether official or unofficial, by leaders in other countries.

D. *Why the factual approach?*

1. *Dignity of the United States*

Since we speak as a part of the United States Government, every item of our output must be consistent with the dignity and traditions of the United States. If any other country wishes to adopt a posture of being loud-mouthed, hysterical, frantic, bad-tempered and bad-mannered, that is its business.

Our posture must remain one of calmness and confidence.

The communists can never reveal themselves for what they really are. Instead they must constantly obscure the truth and create illusions. Our strength lies in precisely the opposite direction—to reveal what we actually are and stand for, and to dispel misleading illusions.

2. *Effectiveness*

The factual approach is designed, not to weaken or soften our impact, but rather to strengthen it.

Except in a few places, most of the people in our intended audience are now "wise to" old-fashioned propaganda, with its exaggerations, half-truths and big lies. Moreover, they are resentful of it, and react against it.

On the other hand, they are eager to have straight information that they can believe and use. The factual approach, therefore, makes the information service both believed and welcome. If an information service is not believed, it is nothing. In fact, it is worse than nothing. Therefore, believability is the beginning of effectiveness.

All our output must be invariably checked against the one sovereign test: Will this bring us nearer the day when people all over the world will say, "If you hear it from the U.S. Information Service, it's true."

This may occasionally mean foregoing a short-term "propaganda coup." But such a coup, if achieved by violating these standards, may undermine a long-term reputation which has taken years of patient effort to build.

This does not mean the Agency has the obligation, as might a commercial news service, to carry news merely because it is news.

However, our standards may on occasion require us to relate facts which are unfavorable to us, when failure to do so would damage our believability. In doing this, the two purposes of handling unfavorable material should be kept constantly in mind as determining the extent and nature of the treatment: (a) the necessity of main-

270

taining credibility and integrity, and (b) the desirability of placing unpalatable facts in their proper proportion and setting. Since news of the unpleasant fact, such as the Little Rock episode, will probably be widespread anyway in various degrees of accuracy, we can do more good by giving a straight account and restoring a sense of perspective as to how the unfavorable fact relates to the over-all picture of favorable progress than by ignoring the story . . . .

II

CONTENT: THE "MUTUALITY" THEME

A.   *Their aspirations and our policies.*

The aspirations of the other country for freedom, progress and peace are the beginning-point of our content.

Starting with these aspirations, we then go on to submit evidence that what we stand for will advance their hopes and plans.

Here again, we can be completely factual, since the facts indeed support this conclusion.

As to *freedom*: the United States, through its history, constitution, literature, and traditions, has always been the inspiration of peoples working toward national independence and personal freedom.

As to *progress*: nations struggling toward a better standard of life can identify the United States and its policies not only with a high degree of productive vigor inherent in its system but also with a willingness to help others technically and financially.

As to *peace*: the facts of our history and our current conduct prove repeatedly our active devotion to the maintenance of peace. Cogent examples include our willingness to stand by small nations when attacked, and our willingness to go much more than halfway to get a workable first-step disarmament agreement.

There are several reasons why we stress the mutuality theme.

One is that our over-all objective is a harmonious family of nations which recognize a common interest in vital issues, and support each other on these issues—while denying support to elements inimical to this mutual interest.

Another reason has to do with effectiveness. It is human nature to be much more interested and receptive when someone is talking about you rather than just about himself.

Indeed, the more local the item of self-interest is, the more effective the tie-in will usually be. It is highly desirable to find ways of associating our policies and objectives with easily-understood vital local issues.

Not only will our output be more effective when put in these terms —it will also be more welcome. The mutuality approach automatically avoids the pitfalls of seeming to talk too much about ourselves and perhaps even bragging about our achievements.

The mutuality theme may sometimes mean omitting perfectly true items, since, if the audience cannot relate them to anything in their experience, they may actually sound false and offensive. Thus, while accounts of the wages and living standards of American workers may be useful

271

in areas where the stage of industrialization makes the comparison intelligible, these same accounts in the ears of remote agrarian populations may sound like the wildest fantasy and only serve to damage our credibility.

Similarly, the mutuality theme may in many countries suggest "deglamorizing" our output, in the sense of cutting through some of the cliches that have grown up about America, particularly on the materialistic side. We should attempt to obtain understanding of the real fabric and pattern of American life and thought in depth, rather than in terms of superficial manifestations.

The mutuality concept will also be served by recognizing that we, like everyone else, are far from perfect, and have our share of unsolved problems. A posture of perfection is the surest way to disassociate ourselves from others.

Moreover, we can add to the feeling of mutuality by being quick to express appreciation for what we have learned from other countries and continue to learn from our association with them.

B. *What we are FOR.*

1. *Accentuate the positive.*

The Agency's statement of purpose is cast in affirmative, not negative, terms. It is what we are *for* that will advance the aspirations of other countries.

Of course, to do the positive job we must also work tirelessly to clear away the underbrush of communist lies, distortions, and exaggerations. But it is wrong to conceive of the Agency's mission as being primarily negative, defensive, and reparative—i.e., going about mopping up after the communists to undo the mischief they have earlier done.

It is easy to succumb to the temptation of letting the communists choose the arena. They put forward a positive program for revolutionizing the world and solving all its ills, including poverty, inequality and oppression. Their program is fallacious, unworkable and fraudulent in the extreme, but it has the advantage that any over-simplified panacea has in the eyes of restless, dissatisfied and disfavored people. But if we consume our energies doing no more than answering communist lies, we place ourselves at a severe disadvantage. The positive is always much the most appealing; the negative is unpopular, unrewarding, and unsatisfying.

We must ourselves be in the position of holding up a positive ideal and vision for the future that the world can rally round. Every American should be able to express in simple terms what we are for. He can then go on to show others how this identifies us with their aspirations.

2. *The broad common bond.*

How can we be sure that our mutuality-of-interest theme is in fact valid? Why are we so confident that what we stand for is in line with the aspirations of other peoples? It is because we know that, whatever their society or form of government, all people share something called "human nature." And human nature everywhere, with few exceptions, has at its core certain common drives and characteristics.

It is in showing forth this identification that the portion of our program dealing with life and culture in the United States becomes crucial.

There is no better way of reminding everyone of this common bond than through learning about each other's everyday life, sports, music, graphic arts, theatre, and literature.

3. *Our ideal for the future.*

In holding forth a positive ideal, we must above all avoid the mistake of seeming to say to the world: "Look at us—our bustling economy, our standard of living, our political institutions, our personal freedoms; now all the rest of you have to do is try to scramble along the road we have travelled and try to reach where we are."

Instead, we should say something like this: "We are all groping toward an ideal of a better world and better life—an ideal that we all fall far short of attaining now. But we are generally agreed on our direction, and, although we know that we shall never ever come to rest at a final destination, we do know that our common goal is a world of self-fulfillment and self-realization, in which the common impulses toward freedom, justice, individuality and human dignity, property and religion can have maximum expression."

BIBLIOGRAPHY

Bibliography

A

Almond, Gabriel, *The American People and Foreign Policy*, New York, 1950.

——, *The Appeals of Communism*, Princeton, 1954.

Andrews, T. Cutler, *The North Reports the Civil War*, Pittsburgh, 1955.

Anonymous, "Developments in the Law of Defamation," *Harvard Law Review*, Vol. 69, Part 2 (1955-1956), pp. 876-960.

Anonymous, "Mob Violence, Group Defamation and Civil Rights," *Northwestern University Law Review*, Vol. 54 (1959), pp. 616-628.

Auxier, G. W., "The Propaganda Activities of the Cuban Junta in Precipitating the Spanish-American War, 1895-1898," *Hispanic American Historical Review*, Vol. 19 (1939), pp. 286-305.

B

Barghoorn, Frederick C., *The Soviet Cultural Offensive: The Role of Cultural Diplomacy in Soviet Foreign Policy*, Princeton, 1960.

Barrett, Edward W., *Truth Is Our Weapon*, New York, 1953.

Bartlett, F. C. *Political Propaganda*, New York, 1940.

Basdevant, Jules, *La Révolution Française et le Droit de la Guerre Continentale*, Paris, 1901.

Batsell, Walter B., *Soviet Rule in Russia*, New York, 1929.

Beller, Elmer A., *Propaganda in Germany During the Thirty Years War*, Princeton, 1940.

Bent, Silas, "International Broadcasting," *Public Opinion Quarterly*, Vol. 1 (1937), pp. 117-121.

Binder, Carroll, "Freedom of Information and the United Nations," *International Organization*, Vol. 6 (1952), pp. 210-226.

Biro, Sidney S., "The International Aspects of Radio Control," *Journal of Radio Law*, Vol. 2 (1932), pp. 45-65.

Boeck, Charles de, "L'Expulsion et les Difficultés Internationales qu'en Soulève la Pratique," *Recueil de l'Académie de Droit International de la Haye*, Vol. 18 (1927), pp. 447-647.

Bogart, Leo, "A Study of the Operating Assumptions of the United States Information Agency," *Public Opinion Quarterly*, Vol. 19 (1955-1956), pp. 369-377.

Bolsover, George H., "Soviet Ideology and Propaganda," *International Affairs*, Vol. 24 (1948), pp. 170-180.

Bourquin, Jacques, *La Liberté de la Presse*, Paris, 1950.

Bowett, D. W., *Self-Defense in International Law*, New York, 1958.

Briggs, Asa, *The Birth of Broadcasting*, New York, 1961.

Brinton, Crane, *A Decade of Revolution 1789-1799*, New York/London, 1934.

Broadcasting and Peace (Studies and Projects in the Matter of International Agreements), Paris, 1933.

Bruntz, George G., *Allied Propaganda and the Collapse of the German Empire in 1918*, Stanford/London, 1938.

Butter, Oscar, "La Presse et les Relations Politiques Internationales," *Recueil de l'Académie de Droit International de la Haye*, Vol. 45 (1933), pp. 223-245.

C

Caldwell, Louis G., "Legal Restrictions on the Contents of Broadcast Programs," *Air Law Review*, Vol. 9 (1938), pp. 229-249.

Cantril, Hadley, and Allport, Gordon W., *The Psychology of Radio*, New York, 1935.

Cantril, Hadley, *The Invasion from Mars: A Study in the Psychology of Panic*, Princeton, 1940.

——, *Tensions That Cause Wars*, Urbana, 1950.

——, *The Politics of Despair*, New York, 1958.

——, *Soviet Leaders and Mastery Over Man*, New Brunswick, 1960.

Carr, E. H., *Propaganda in International Politics*, (Oxford Pamphlets on World Affairs), Oxford, 1939.

Carroll, Wallace, *Persuade or Perish*, Boston, 1948.

Castberg, Frede, *Freedom of Speech in the West* (A Comparative Study of Public Law in France, the United States and Germany), Copenhagen, 1960.

Cavaglieri, Arrigo, "Principes de Droit International Régissant la T.S.F.," *Revue de Droit International*, Vol. II (1928), pp. 860-872.

Chafee, Zechariah, Jr., *Free Speech in the United States*, Cambridge, 1941.

——, "Possible New Remedies for Errors in the Press," *Harvard Law Review*, Vol. 60 (1946), pp. 1-43.

——, *Government and Mass Communication*, Chicago, 1947. 2 vols.

Chakhotin, Sergei, *The Rape of the Masses: The Psychology of Totalitarian Political Propaganda*, London, 1940.

Childs, Harwood L., ed., *Propaganda and Dictatorship*, Princeton, 1936.

Childs, Harwood L. and Whitton, John B., *Propaganda by Short Wave*, Princeton, 1942.

Clucas, Lowell M., Jr., "Piercing the Iron Curtain," *Yale Review*, Vol. 39 (1950), pp. 603-619.

Clunet, Edouard, "Offenses et Actes Hostiles Commis par des Particuliers Contre un Etat Etranger," *Journal de Droit International Public*, Vol. 14 (1887), pp. 5-21.

Codding, George A., Jr., "Jamming and the Protection of Frequency Assignments," *American Journal of International Law*, Vol. 49 (1955), pp. 384-388.

——, *Broadcasting Without Barriers*, The Hague (UNESCO), 1959.

Committee on Public Information, *Complete Report of the Chairman of the Committee on Public Information*, Washington, 1920.

Cooper, John C., *The Right to Fly*, New York, 1947.

Costikyan, Simon, *Twelve Years of Communist Broadcasting, 1948-1959*, (Office of Research and Analysis, U.S. Information Agency), Washington, 1960.

Creel, George, *How We Advertised America*, New York/London, 1920.

Crowley, Thomas H., and others, *Modern Communications*, New York, 1962.

"Cuba," *Department of State Publication 7171*, April, 1961.

D

Dambmann, Gerhard, *Propaganda im Friedensvolkerecht*, Frankfort, 1953.

Daugherty, William E., and Janowitz, Morris, *A Psychological Warfare Casebook*, Baltimore, 1958.

Davidson, Philip, *Propaganda and the American Revolution, 1763-1783*, Chapel Hill, 1941.

Davis, Elmer, and Price, Byron, *War Information and Censorship*, Washington, D.C., 1943.

Davison, W. P., and George, A. L., "An Outline for the Study of International Political Communications," *Public Opinion Quarterly*, Vol. 16 (Winter 1952-1953), pp. 501-511.

Davison, W. P., "Pragmatic Approaches to Political Communication," *World Politics*, Vol. XII (1959), pp. 120-131.

Delbez, Louis, "La Responsabilité Internationale pour Crimes Commis sur le Territoire d'un Etat et Dirigés Contre la Sûreté d'un Etat Etranger," *Revue Générale de Droit International Public*, Vol. 37 (1930), pp. 461-475.

Dickinson, Edwin D., "The Defamation of Foreign Governments," *American Journal of International Law,* Vol. 22 (1928), pp. 840-844.

Dizard, Wilson P., *The Strategy of Truth: the Story of the U.S. Information Service,* New York, 1961.

Domenach, Jean-Marie, "Leninist Propaganda," *Public Opinion Quarterly,* Vol. 15 (1951), pp. 265-273.

Donnelly, Richard C., "The Right of Reply: An Alternative to an Action for Libel," *Virginia Law Review,* Vol. 34 (1948) pp. 867-900.

Doob, Leonard W., *Propaganda, Its Psychology and Technique,* New York, 1935.

——, *Public Opinion and Propaganda,* New York, 1948.

——, "Goebbels' Principles of Propaganda," *Public Opinion Quarterly,* Vol. 14 (Fall 1950), pp. 419-442.

Dovring, Karin, *Road of Propaganda: the Semantics of Biased Communication,* New York, 1959.

Driencourt, Jacques, *La Propagande, Nouvelle Force Politique,* Paris, 1950.

Dryer, Sherman H., *Radio in Wartime,* New York, 1942.

Dunn, Frederick S., *War and the Minds of Men,* New York, 1950.

Dyer, Murray, *The Weapon on the Wall,* Baltimore, 1959.

E

Eek, Hilding, *Freedom of Information as a Project of International Legislation: A Study of International Law in Making,* Upsala and Wiesbaden, 1953.

Ettinger, Karl E., "Foreign Propaganda in America," *Public Opinion Quarterly,* Vol. 10 (Fall 1946), pp. 329-342.

Ettlinger, Harold, *The Axis on the Air,* New York, 1943.

Evans, Frank Bowen, ed., *Worldwide Communist Propaganda Activities,* New York, 1955.

Exhenry, Albert, *Du Droit de Réponse en Matière de Presse dans les Législations d'Europe,* Lausanne, 1929.

F

Falk, Richard A., "American Intervention in Cuba and the Rule of Law," *Ohio State Law Journal,* Vol. 22 (1961), pp. 546-585.

Farago, Ladislas, "British Propaganda," *United Nations World,* Vol. 2 (1948), pp. 22-26.

Fauchille, Paul, "La Télégraphie Sans Fil et le Droit International," *Revue de Droit International et de Législation Comparée,* 3d series, Vol. I (1920), pp. 7-18.

Fay, Sidney B., *The Origins of the (First) World War,* 2d ed., New York, 1931. 2 vols.

Fenwick, Charles G., "The Use of the Radio as an Instrument of Foreign Propaganda," *American Journal of International Law,* Vol. 32 (1938), pp. 339-343.

——, "Intervention by Way of Propaganda," *ibid.,* Vol. 35 (1941), pp. 626-631.

——, "Proposed Control Over the Radio as an Inter-American Duty in Cases of Civil Strife," *ibid.,* Vol. 48 (1954), pp. 289-292.

Foster, H. Schuyler, "The Official Propaganda of Great Britain," *Public Opinion Quarterly,* Vol. III (1939), pp. 263-271.

Fraser, Lindley M., *Germany Between the Wars: A Study of Propaganda and War-Guilt,* New York, 1945.

——, *Propaganda,* London/New York/Toronto, 1957.

Freedom of Information, A Compilation, New York (United Nations), 1950. 2 vols.

Friedmann, W., "Some Impacts of Social Organization in International Law," *American Journal of International Law,* Vol. 50 (1956), pp. 475-513.

G

Garcia-Mora, Manuel R., *International Responsibility for Hostile Acts of Private Persons Against Foreign States*, The Hague, 1962.

George, Alexander L., *Propaganda Analysis: A Study of Inferences Made from Nazi Propaganda in World War II*, White Plains, 1959.

Godechot, Jacques, *La Grande Nation: l'Expansion Révolutionnaire de la France dans le Monde 1789-1799*, Paris, 1956. 2 vols.

Gordenker, Leon, "Policy Making and Secretariat Influence in the U.N. General Assembly: The Case of Public Information," *American Political Science Review*, Vol. 54 (1960), pp. 359-373.

Grandin, Thomas, "The Political Use of the Radio," *Geneva Studies*, Vol. 10 (August 1939), pp. 7-116.

Graven, J., "Les Crimes Contre l'Humanité," *Recueil de l'Académie de Droit International de la Haye*, Vol. 76 (1950), pp. 433-607.

Graves, Harold W., Jr., *War on the Short Wave*, (Foreign Policy Association Pamphlet), New York, 1941.

H

Hartmann, Frederick H., "The Swiss Press and Foreign Affairs in World War II," *University of Florida Monographs*, Social Sciences, No. 5 (Winter 1960).

Hatin, Louis Eugène, *Histoire Politique et Littéraire de la Presse en France*, Paris, 1859-1861. 8 vols.

Hazeltine, Harold D., *The Law of the Air*, London, 1911.

Hocking, William E., *Freedom of the Press: A Framework of Principle*, Chicago, 1947.

Holt, Robert T., *Radio Free Europe*, Minneapolis, 1958.

Holt, Robert T., and van de Velde, Robert W., *Strategic Psychological Operations and American Foreign Policy*, Chicago, 1960.

Holtman, Robert B., *Napoleonic Propaganda*, Baton Rouge, 1950.

Honig, G., "The Cold War as an Instrument of Policy," *Yearbook of World Affairs*, Vol. 7 (1953), pp. 45-70.

Hostie, J., "Quelques Réflexions sur le Droit International Commun en Matière de Radiocommunications," *Revue de Droit International et de Législation Comparée*, 3d series, Vol. 18 (1937), pp. 10-33.

Huth, Arno, *La Radiodiffusion, Puissance Mondiale*, Paris, 1937.

——, "Radio Today: The Present State of Broadcasting," *Geneva Studies*, Vol. 12 (July 1942), pp. 1-160.

Hyde, Charles Cheney, *International Law, Chiefly as Interpreted and Applied by the United States*, 2d rev. ed., Boston, 1945. 3 vols.

Hyman, Sidney, "State Responsibility for the Hostile Utterances of its Officers," (unpublished M. A. dissertation, University of Chicago), Chicago, 1938.

I

Inkeles, Alex, *Public Opinion in Soviet Russia: A Study in Mass Persausion*, Cambridge, 1950.

——, "The Soviet Characterization of the Voice of America," *Columbia Journal of International Affairs*, Vol. 5 (1951), pp. 44-55.

——, "The Soviet Attack on the Voice of America: A Case Study in Propaganda Warfare," *American Slavic and East European Review*, Vol. 12 (1953), pp. 319-342.

"International Law of the Future: Postulates, Principles, Proposals," *International Conciliation*, April, 1944 (No. 399).

Irwin, Will, *Propaganda and the News*, New York, 1936.

J

Joeden, Von Johann, "Die Funksendefreiheit der Staaten" *Jahrbuch für Internationales Recht*, Vol. III (1954), pp. 85-128; Vol. IV (1954), pp. 71-119.

K

Klineberg, Otto, *Tensions Affecting International Understanding: A Survey of Research* (Social Science Research Council, Bulletin No. 62), New York, 1950.

Kohler, Foy D., "Effectiveness of the Voice of America," *Department of State Bulletin*, May 14, 1951, pp. 780-783.

Krause, Günter B., *Beiträge zum Rundfunkrecht*, Hamburg, 1960.

——, "Der Runfunkfriedenspakt von 1936," *Jahrbuch für Internationales Recht*, Vol. IX (1960), pp. 33-57.

Kris, Ernst, and Speier, Hans, *German Radio Propaganda: Report on Home Broadcasts During the War*, London/New York/Toronto, 1944.

L

Labin, Suzanne, *Il Est Moins Cinq*, Paris, 1960.

Larson, Arthur, "The Cuba Incident and the Rule of Law," *Saturday Review*, May 13, 1961, pp. 23, 53.

——, *When Nations Disagree*, Baton Rouge, 1961.

Lasswell, Harold D., *Propaganda Technique in the World War*, New York, 1927.

——, *Propaganda and Promotional Activities: An Annotated Bibliography*, Minneapolis, 1935.

——, (With Blumenstock, Dorothy) *World Revolutionary Propaganda*, New York/London, 1939.

——, "The Strategy of Soviet Propaganda," *Proceedings of the Academy of Political Science*, Vol. 24 (1951), pp. 66-78.

——, "Psychological Policy Research and Total Strategy," *Public Opinion Quarterly*, Vol. 16 (Winter, 1952-1953), pp. 491-500.

Laurent, François, *Histoire du Droit des Gens et des Relations Internationales*, Paris, 1851-1870, 18 vols.

Lauterpacht, H., *Private Law Sources and Analogies of International Law,* London, 1927.

——, "Revolutionary Propaganda by Governments," *Transactions of the Grotius Society,* Vol. 13 (1928), pp. 143-164.

——, "Revolutionary Activities by Private Persons Against Foreign States," *American Journal of International Law,* Vol. 22 (1928), pp. 105-130.

——, *International Law and Human Rights,* New York, 1950.

Lavine, Harold, and Wechsler, James, *War Propaganda and the United States,* New Haven, 1940.

League of Nations: "Final Act, Intergovernmental Conference for the Conclusion of an International Convention Concerning the Use of Broadcasting in the Cause of Peace," C.399 (a), M. 252 (a) 1936. XII.

Lenin, Nikolai, and Trotsky, Leon, *The Proletarian Revolution in Russia,* (Louis C. Fraina, ed.), New York, 1918.

Lerner, Daniel, *Sykewar: Psychological Warfare Against Germany, D-Day to VE Day,* New York, 1951.

——, *Propaganda in War and Crisis,* New York, 1951.

LeRoy, Howard S., "Treaty Regulation of International Radio and Short-wave Broadcasting," *American Journal of International Law,* Vol. 32 (1938), pp. 719-737.

Linebarger, Paul M. A., *Psychological Warfare,* Washington, 1954.

Lippmann, Walter, *Public Opinion,* New York, 1922.

Loewenstein, Karl, "Legislative Control of Political Extremism in European Democracies," Part I, *Columbia Law Review,* Vol. 38 (1938), pp. 591-622; Part II, pp. 725-774.

Lopez, Salvador P., "Freedom of Information, 1953," *Economic and Social Council, Official Records,* 16th Session, Supplement No. 12, E/2426, May 6, 1953.

Lowenthal, Leo, (guest editor), "International Communications Research," *Public Opinion Quarterly* (special issue), Vol. 16 (Winter 1952-1953), pp. 481-701.

Lumley, Frederick E., *The Propaganda Menace*, New York, 1933.

M

McDonald, Joseph A., and Grimshaw, Ira L., "Radio Defamation," *Air Law Review*, Vol. 9 (1938), pp. 328-351.

Margolen, Mollie Z., "Distribution of Communist Propaganda Through the Mails," *The Library of Congress Legislative Reference Service*, 172/272, April 16, 1962.

Markel, Lester J., and others, *Public Opinion and Foreign Policy*, New York, 1949.

Martin, L. John, *International Propaganda; Its Legal and Diplomatic Control*, Minneapolis, 1958.

Marx, Karl, and Engels, Frederick, *Communist Manifesto*, (authorized English translation annotated by Frederick Engels), Chicago, c. 1888.

Matter, Paul, *Cavour et l'Unité Italienne*, Paris, 1925-1927. 3 vols.

Mock, James R., and Larson, Cedric, *Words that Won the War: the Story of the Committee on Public Information*, Princeton, 1939.

Mott, Frank, (ed.), *Journalism in Wartime*, Washington, 1943.

Munson, Gorham B., *Twelve Decisive Battles of the Mind: the Story of Propaganda During the Christian Era, with Abridged Versions of Texts That Have Shaped History*, New York, 1942.

Myrdal, Gunnar, "Psychological Impediments to Effective International Cooperation," *Journal of Social Issues* (Supplement Series, No. 6), New York, 1952.

N

Naurois, Abbé Louis de, "Diffamation et Injures Envers les Collectivités," *Revue de Science Criminelle et de Droit Pénal Comparé*, 1948, pp. 1-23.

O

Odgers, W. Blake, *A Digest of the Law of Libel and Slander,* London, 1896.

Oppenheim, L., *International Law, A Treatise,* Edited by H. Lauterpacht, Vol. I (Peace), 8th ed., London, 1955; Vol. II (Disputes, War and Neutrality), 7th ed., London, 1960.

P

Padover, Saul K., "Psychological Warfare in an Age of World Revolution," *Columbia Journal of International Affairs,* Vol. 5 (1951), pp. 3-12.

Palma, Samuel de, "Freedom of the Press, an International Issue," *Department of State Publication 3687,* January, 1950.

Pella, V., "Un Nouveau Délit: la Propagande pour la Guerre d'Agression," *Revue de Droit International* (1929), pp. 174-179.

———, "La Protection de la Paix par le Droit Interne," *Revue Générale de Droit International Public,* Vol. 40 (1933), pp. 401-505.

Périvier, A., *Napoléon Journaliste,* Paris, 1918.

Peterson, H. C., *Propaganda for War: the Campaign Against American Neutrality 1914-1917,* Norman, Oklahoma, 1939.

Pompe, C. A., *Aggressive War an International Crime,* The Hague, 1953.

Potter, Pitman B., "League (of Nations) Publicity: Cause or Effect of League Failure?", *Public Opinion Quarterly,* Vol. II (1938), pp. 399-412.

Preuss, Lawrence, "La Répression des Crimes et Délits Contre le Sûreté des Etats Etrangers," *Revue Générale de Droit International Public,* Vol. 40 (1933), pp. 606-645.

———, "International Responsibility for Hostile Propaganda Against Foreign States," *American Journal of International Law,* Vol. 28 (1934), pp. 649-668.

"Propaganda in World Affairs," *Columbia Journal of International Affairs,* Vol. 5 (Spring, 1951), pp. 1-64.

R

Raestad, Arnold, "Les Ondes Hertziennes et le Droit International," *Journal des Télécommunications* (1935), pp. 213 ff.

——, "Le Projet de Convention sur la Radiodiffusion et la Paix," *Revue de Droit International et de Législation Comparée*, Vol. 62 (1935), pp. 289-298.

Raffaele, J. A., "United States Propaganda Abroad: Notes on the U.S.I.S. in Italy," *Social Research*, Vol. 27 (1960), pp. 277-294.

Rappaport, E. S., "Propagande de la Guerre d'Agression comme Délit du Droit des Gens," *Revue Pénitentiaire de Pologne*, Annex 13, Warsaw, 1939.

Riegel, O. W., *Mobilizing for Chaos*, New Haven, 1934.

——, "Press, Radio and the Spanish Civil War," *Public Opinion Quarterly*, Vol. I (1937), pp. 131-141.

Riesman, David, "Democracy and Defamation: Control of Group Libel," *Columbia Law Review*, Vol. 42 (1942), pp. 727-780; "Democracy and Defamation: Fair Game and Fair Comment I," pp. 1085-1123; "Democracy and Defamation: Fair Game and Fair Comment II," pp. 1282-1318.

Rogers, Cornwell B., *The Spirit of Revolution in 1789*, Princeton, 1949.

Rolo, Charles J., *Radio Goes to War*, New York, 1942.

Roosevelt, Kermit, Jr., "Propaganda Techniques of the English Civil Wars— and the Propaganda Psychosis of Today," *Pacific Historical Review*, Vol. 12 (1943), pp. 369-379.

Rudolph, Walter, "Informationsfreiheit und Rundfunk im Völkerrecht," *Jahrbuch für Internationales Recht*, Vol. V (1955), pp. 256-288.

S

Sarnoff, David, *Radio Communication and its Import in International Relations*, Princeton, 1946.

Schramm, Wilbur, (ed.), *Mass Communications,* Urbana, 1949.

Saudemont, A., Le Droit de Réponse en Radiophonie," *Revue Juridique Internationale de la Radioélectricité,* 5th year (1929), pp. 166 ff.

Schwartz, William, "The Reign of the Verbal Tyrant in the Domain of International Law," *Boston University Law Review,* Vol. 40 (1960), pp. 196-209.

Schwarzkopf, Dietrich G., "Responsibility of National States for Hostile Propaganda Campaigns," *Journalism Quarterly,* Vol. 29 (1952), pp. 194-206.

Scott, Jonathan F., *Five Weeks: the Surge of Public Opinion on the Eve of the Great War,* New York, 1927.

Selznick, Philip, *The Organizational Weapon: a Study of Bolshevik Strategy and Tactics,* New York, 1952.

Seton-Watson, Robert W., *From Munich to Danzig,* London, 1939.

Siegal, Seymour N., "Radio and Propaganda," *Air Law Review,* Vol. 10 (1939), pp. 127-145.

Siepmann, Charles A., *Radio in Wartime,* Boston, 1942.

——, "Propaganda and Information in International Affairs," *Yale Law Journal,* Vol. 55 (1946), pp. 1258-1280.

——, *Radio's Second Chance,* Boston, 1946.

——, *Radio, Television and Society,* New York, 1950.

Sington, Derrick, and Weidenfeld, Arthur, *The Goebbels Experiment: A Study of the Nazi Propaganda Machine,* New Haven, 1943.

Smith, Bruce L., Lasswell, Harold D., and Casey, Ralph D., *Propaganda, Communication, and Public Opinion; A Comprehensive Reference Guide,* Princeton, 1946.

Smith, Bruce L., and Smith, Chitra M., *International Communication and Political Opinion; A Guide to the Literature,* Princeton, 1956.

Smith, J. W. Brabner, "Subversive Propaganda, the Past and the Present," *Georgetown Law Journal,* Vol. 29 (1941), pp. 809-828.

Sorel, Albert, *L'Europe et la Révolution Française,* Paris, 1889-1904. 8 vols.

Speier, H., "The Future of Psychological Warfare," *Public Opinion Quarterly*, Vol. 11 (Spring, 1948), pp. 5-18.

——, "International Political Communication: Elite Versus Mass," *World Politics*, Vol. 4 (1952), pp. 305-317.

——, *Social Order and the Risks of War*, New York, 1952.

Squires, James D., *British Propaganda at Home and in the United States from 1914 to 1917*, Cambridge, 1935.

Standards of Good Practice for Radio Broadcasters of the United States of America (National Association of Broadcasters), Washington, 1960.

Steinberg, Charles S., *The Mass Communicators. Public Relations, Public Opinion and Mass Media*, New York, 1958.

Sténuit, René, *La Radiophonie et le Droit International*, Brussels/Paris, 1932.

Stephens, Oren, *Facts to a Candid World; America's Overseas Information Program*, Stanford, 1955.

Stone, Julius, *Legal Controls of International Conflict*, New York, 1954.

——, *Aggression and World Order*, Berkeley/Los Angeles, 1958.

Stowe, Leland, *Conquest by Terror*, New York, 1952.

Stowell, Ellery C., "Respect Due to Foreign Sovereigns," *American Journal of International Law*, Vol. 31 (1937), pp. 301-304.

T

Tanenhaus, Joseph, "Group Libel," *Cornell Law Quarterly*, Vol. 35 (1950), pp. 261-302.

Tardu, Maxime, "La Protection Juridique des Groupes Sociaux Contre la Propagande d'Hostilité," *Revue Internationale de Droit Pénal*, 1956, pp. 59-91.

——, "Les Aspects Internationaux du Droit de l'Information," (unpublished doctoral dissertation), Faculty of Law, Paris, 1951.

Taylor, Edmond, *The Strategy of Terror, Europe's Inner Front*, Boston, 1940.

Television Code (National Association of Broadcasters), 5th edition, Washington, 1959.

Terrou, Fernand, and Solal, Lucien, "Legislation for Press, Film and Radio," United Nations, *Economic and Social Council, Publication No. 607*, Paris, 1951.

Thimme, Hans, *Weltkrieg ohne Waffen: Die Propaganda der Westmächte gegen Deutschland, ihre Wirkung and ihre Absehr*, Stuttgart/Berlin, 1932.

Thomas, Ann van Wynen, and Thomas, A. J. Jr., *Non-Intervention, the Law and its Import in the Americas*, Dallas, 1956.

Thomson, Charles A. H., *Overseas Information Service of the United States Government*, Washington, 1948.

Tomlinson, John D., *The International Control of Radiocommunications*, Geneva, 1938.

Trial of the Major War Criminals Before the International Military Tribunal, Nuremberg, 1947. 42 vols.

U

United Nations, "United Nations Conference on Freedom of Information, Final Act." E/Conf. 6/79. April 22, 1948.

"United Nations Conference on Freedom of Information, Radio Broadcasting and Freedom of Information" (Memorandum Prepared by the Secretary General). E/Conf. 6/30, March 19, 1948.

United Nations: "An International Code of Ethics for Information Personnel," St/SOA/12, 1952. Also, A/C.3/L.381.

United Nations. "Legal Aspects of the Rights and Responsibilities of Media of Information" (Study Prepared by the Secretary General), E/2698, March 14, 1955.

United Nations. "Broadcasts from the United Nations," (Department of Public Information), New York, November 1, 1957.

"United Nations Conference on Freedom of Information, Geneva, Switzerland, March 23-April 21, 1948. Report of the United States Delegates with Related Documents," *Department of State, International Organizations and Conferences, Publication 3150*, Washington, 1948.

United States Congress. "An Act to Promote the Better Understanding of the United States Among the Peoples of the World and to Strengthen Cooperative International Relations," (the "Smith-Mundt Act"). Public Law 402, 80th Congress, 1948.

United States Senate. "The Soviet Propaganda Program," (Subcommittee on Overseas Information Programs of the United States), *Staff Study No. 3*, Senate, 82nd Congress, 2d Session, 1952.

United States Senate. "Report of the Committee on Foreign Relations: Foreign Information Programs," *Senate Report No. 1984*, 82nd Congress, 2nd Session, 1952.

United States Senate. "Report of the Committee on Foreign Relations: Overseas Information Programs of the United States." 83rd Congress, 1st Session, *Senate Report No. 406*, June 15, 1953 (generally known as "The Hickenlooper Report"). Final Report, same committee, 83rd Congress, 2nd Session, *Senate Report No. 936*, February 10, 1954.

United States Senate. "Overseas Information Programs of the United States," (Committee on Foreign Relations). Other *Hearings* and *Reports*, at intervals since 1941.

V

Vagts, Alfred, *A History of Militarism*, New York, 1937.

Van Dissel, G. F., "League of Nations Wireless Station," *Proceedings of the Institute of Radio Engineers*, Vol. 22 (1934), pp. 430-448.

Van Dyke, Vernon, "The Responsibility of States in Connection with International Propaganda," (unpublished doctoral dissertation, University of Chicago, 1937).

——, "The Responsibility of States for International Propaganda," *American Journal of International Law*, Vol. 34 (1940), pp. 58-73.

W

Warburg, James P., *Unwritten Treaty*, New York, 1946.

Whitaker, Urban G., Jr., (ed.), *Propaganda and International Relations*, San Francisco, 1960.

White, Llewellyn, and Leigh, Robert D., *Peoples Speaking to Peoples*, Chicago, 1946.

Whitton, John B., "Propaganda and International Law," *Recueil de l'Académie de Droit International de la Haye,* Vol. 72 (1949), pp. 545-659.

——, "The United Nations Conference on Freedom of Information and the Movement Against International Propaganda," *American Journal of International Law,* Vol. 43 (1949), pp. 73-87.

——, "An International Right of Reply?", *ibid.,* Vol. 44 (1950), pp. 141-145.

——, "Cold War Propaganda," *ibid.,* Vol. 45 (1951), pp. 151-153.

——, "Radio Propaganda—A Modest Proposal," *ibid.,* Vol. 52 (1958), pp. 739-745.

——, " 'Subversive Propaganda' Reconsidered," *ibid.,* Vol. 55 (1961), pp. 120-122.

—— and others, *Propaganda and the Cold War,* Washington, 1963.

Whitton, John B., and Fowler, J. Edward, "The Bricker Amendment—Fallacies and Dangers," *American Journal of International Law,* Vol. 48 (1954), pp. 23-56.

Wilcox, Francis O., "The Use of Atrocity Stories in War," *American Political Science Review,* Vol. 34 (1940), pp. 1166-1177.

Wilkerson, Marcus M., *Public Opinion and the Spanish American War: A Study in War Propaganda,* Baton Rouge, 1932.

Willert, Arthur, "Publicity and Propaganda in International Affairs," *International Affairs,* Vol. 17 (1938), pp. 809-826.

Wilson, Robert R., "International Law and Proposed Freedom of Information," *American Journal of International Law,* Vol. 39 (1945), pp. 790-793.

Wisan, Joseph E., *The Cuban Crisis as Reflected in the New York Press, 1895-1898,* New York, 1934.

Wright, Quincy, *A Study of War,* Chicago, 1942. (2 vols.).

——, "The Crime of 'War-Mongering,' " *American Journal of International Law,* Vol. 42 (1948), pp. 128-136.

——, "Subversive Intervention," *ibid.,* Vol. 54 (1960), pp. 521-535.

——, *The Study of International Relations,* New York, 1955.

Table of Cases

INDEX

Cavaglieri, A., 161, 214
Cavell, Edith, 32
Cavour, C. B. di, as propagandist, 93
Cereti, C., 162
Chacko, C. J., 232
Chafee, Z., Jr., 187, 188
Chalandon, F., 15
Chauvelin, F.-B., 19
Cheng, B., 57
Childs, H. L., 25, 35, 36, 38, 39, 99, 222
Churchill, Winston, and propaganda, 39, 42
Civil Law, and fair comment, 116; group libel, 121; libel and slander, 113; solicitation, 72
Clark and Marshall, 71
Clucas, L. M., 212
Clunet, E., 191
Codding, G. A., Jr., 6, 35, 44, 218, 222
Code of ethics for newsmen, appraisal of, 254; critique of, 257; examples of, 251, ff.; at Geneva 1948 radio conference, 201; history of proposals for, 249-255; text of proposed code, 259-263.
Comintern, 26
Common law, and fair comment, 116; group libel, 120-121; libel and slander, 112 ff.; solicitation, 71 ff.
Communist China, propaganda from, 44, 46
Communist Manifesto, 26
Condorcet, M. J. de, 17
Conference on Freedom of Information (1948), 197 ff., 229, 254; code of ethics at, 250-251, 254; condemnation of war propaganda by, 70; Great Britain and, 245; right of reply at, 191 ff.; U.S. and, 159, 244; USSR and, 244
Consensus of San Jose, 100
Cooper, J. C., 224
Costikyan, S., 46
Craies, W. F., 139
Creel, G., 32
Cromwell, Oliver, 16
Crowley, T. H., 7
Cuba, dispute with U.S. over propaganda, 106-107, 111, 211; jamming by, 211; invasion of, 239; propaganda from, 94-95; war propaganda, Spanish-American War, 30, 63; Voice of America and, 51
Curran, J. W., 72

Curzon, Lord, 28
Customary law, as source of international law, 57, 134; and war-mongering propaganda, 69 ff.; and subversive propaganda, 97; and defamatory propaganda, 111.
Czecho-Slovakia, laws against propaganda, 6.
Dambmann, G., 55, 83
Daniel, H., 236
Davidson, P., 29
Déak, F., 156
Defamatory propaganda, definition of, 10-11, 104; domestic laws on, 111, 174; international law on, by state: writings of publicists, 110; customary law, 111, "general principles," 111 ff.; treaties, 124-131; judicial decisions, 131-132; international law on propaganda by individuals, 147 ff.: treaty law, 147; attacks on diplomats, 148; attacks on heads of state, 149; attacks on a state, 154-156.
DeGaulle, General, 42
Délit du Droit des Gens, 75, 158-159, 170-171
DeLouter, J., 136
DePalma, S., 202, 218, 241
Despagnet, F., 135
Dickinson, E. D., 55, 105, 155
Dickinson, G. L., 30
Diplomatic agents, defamation of, 148-149
Disarmament, and propaganda, 8; see also Remedies
Dizard, W. P., 49-50
Domenach, J., 44
Dominican Republic, and dispute with Haiti over propaganda, 130; domestic laws, 150; subversive propaganda by, 4, 84-85.
Donnelly, R. C., 188
Doob, L. W., 9
Driencourt, J., 9
Dulles, J. F., 215-216
Dumouriez, C., 21-22, 24, 154
Egypt, domestic laws on false news, 176; subversive propaganda, 89 ff. See also, Arabs, Nassar, Radio Cairo.
Eisenhower, President, proposal for monitoring, 183-184
Ems Telegram, as propaganda, 30
Engels, F., 26
Evans, F. B., 44
Exhenry, A., 187, 189

Fair comment, and laws of libel and slander, 115 ff.
Falk, R. A., 239
False news, 175 ff.; domestic laws on, 175-179; as war-mongering, 65
Fauchille, P., 96, 135, 141, 145, 213
Fay, S. B., 98
Fenwick, C. G., 55, 102, 128, 129, 130
Ferdinand, Archduke, assassination of, 3
Foster, H. S., 37
Fowler, J. E., 245
France, disputes, with Britain over propaganda, 18, 139, 153; with U.S., 165; domestic laws and propaganda, 122, 141-142, 151-152, 155, 174, 176, 177; and false news, 176, 177; and refugee propaganda, 141, 146; and right of reply, 189; use of propaganda by: in French Revolution, 16 ff.; 19th Century, 98; World War I, 30; early use of radio, 35; between the wars, 38, 87; in World War II, 39 ff.; restraints on propaganda, attitude toward, 242. See also, French Revolutionary Propaganda.
Fraser, L. M., 35
Freedom of information, Belgium and, 153-154; draft convention on, 205-208; draft declaration on, 208; France and, 20; Geneva Convention on (1948), 70, 159, 191, 197, ff., 229, 244; Great Britain and, 20-21, 227, 233, 251; radio and, 163; restraints on, 21, 160, 205-206, 210 ff., 233-234, 235 ff.; right of reply and, 207-208; sub-commission on, 213-214; U.S. and, 233, 236-239; USSR and, 208, 243 ff.
French Revolutionary Propaganda, 16 ff.; army and, 23; comparison with Soviet Revolution, 25-26; Decree of 1792 as propaganda, 18, 97; dispute with Britain over, 18 ff., 139; reactions to, 18 ff.; Russia and, 21, Switzerland, 21, 154, Germany, 21, Belgium, 21, Italy, 22, Spain, 22.
Fritzsche, H., 80, 169

Galantière, L., 52
Garcia-Mora, M. R., 55, 96, 135, 138, 158
Garraud, R., 142, 143, 152
Gaspar, E. de, 214
"General principles of law", and propaganda: for war, 71 ff., for subversion, 103, for defamation, 111 ff.; as source of law, 57 ff., 60
Geneva Radio Convention (1936), see "Broadcasting in the Cause of Peace."
Germany, anti-Jewish propaganda by, 78, 80, 122; disputes over propaganda: with Austria, 125-141, Belgium, 153, in French Revolution, 21, with Switzerland, 120, U.S., 105, 165, USSR, 28; domestic laws on propaganda, 156; propaganda from: in World War I, 30, 32, 41; inter-war period, 35 ff., Second World War, 36 ff., 76-82; propaganda treaties, 101, 125. See also, Civil Law, Nuremberg Trials.
Godechot, J., 17, 21, 22
Goebbels, P. J., 35, 37, 40, 81, 169, 210
Goering, H., 120
Goodrich, L. M., 69
Gordenker, L., 222
Gorky, Maxim, 28
Gould, W., 168
Grandin, T., 36, 37, 39
Great Britain, disputes over propaganda with France, 18 ff., 139, U.S., 153, Russia, 28; expulsion of King Carol, 145, 174; and false news, 176; freedom of press, 20; narrow responsibility doctrine favored, 137, 174; overt act doctrine, 140; propaganda by refugees, 144-145; propaganda in World War I, 31, 41, early use of radio, 35, in inter-war period, 36, 87, in World War II, 39 ff., 41; remedies, attitude of toward, 227, 233, 251. See BBC.
Greece, propaganda in Ancient Greece, 13; and subversive propaganda, 10, 86, 93, 98
Grenville, 19
Group libel, domestic laws of, 120-123
Guggenheim, P., 57
Guichen, Vicomte de, 23
Guizot, F. P., 16, 23
Gustave III, 21

Hackworth, G. H., 137, 138, 154
Haiti, dispute with Santo Domingo, 130
Hall, W. E., 82
Harriman, W. A., 119
Hartmann, F. H., 120
Hatin, E., 15
"Haw-Haw, Lord", 42, 178
Hawkesbury, Lord, 20, 21

Hazeltine, H. D., 213, 215
Hearst, W. R., 30, 63, 133
Hess, R., 79, 103, 167
Hétairie, Le, 85
Hitler, Adolph, as propagandist, 35, concept of propaganda, 32, 36; in inter-war period, 36 ff., 99, 125; Mein Kampf as propaganda, 79; responsibility of, 169.
Hocking, W. E., 124, 246
Holland, pioneer in use of radio, 35; propaganda dispute with USSR, 221, 240
Holmes, Justice, 160, 237, 245
Holt, R. T., 40, 52
Holtman, R. B., 23
Holtzendorff, F. von, 118
Homburg, R., 230
Hostie, J., 213, 214
Huber, G., 31
Hudson, M. O., 57, 128, 163
Human Rights, Commission on, 203; Convention on (1950), 144; freedom of information, and, 196 ff., 202; European Convention on, 216; jamming and, 216; Universal Declaration on, 257, 259.
Hurwicz, E., 123
Hussein, and radio broadcasts, 5; propaganda victim, 91.
Huth, A., 35, 36, 222
Hyde, C. C., 29, 99, 105, 110, 111, 131, 149, 155, 161, 215
Hyman, S., 55, 119
India, propaganda dispute with Pakistan, 88, 232; subversive propaganda by, 96-97; treaty with Pakistan, 88-89, 147, 232

Institute of International Law, on jurisdiction over crime, 179, sovereignty, 214, 215, radio, 161, 215, refugee propaganda, 146
International law of propaganda, bibliography, 55, pattern of, 55 ff., sources, 57 ff., weaknesses, 59-60; state responsibility for propaganda by state: war-mongering, 65 ff., subversive, 83 ff., defamatory, 104 ff; state responsibility for propaganda by individuals, 134 ff.; summary of law, 166
International Law Commission, and Nuremberg rules, 77

International Telecommunications Conventions, 216 ff., 226
Intervention, propaganda as, 96
Iran, and Soviet propaganda, 107 ff.
Islamic law, on incitement, 73, on fair comment, 116-117, on group libel, 123, on libel and slander, 113 ff.
Italy, domestic laws, 122; propaganda by radio, inter-war period, 35-36, World War II, 43

Jamming of radio broadcasting, by Austria, 210, Britain, 213-214, Cuba, 211, Rumania, 28, 210, USSR, 6, 210-211, 212; condemned by U.N., 204, 211, 216; definition of, 210, Iraq and, 218, protests against, by U.S., 211; international law and, 213 ff.; bibliography on, 213; the law in absence of treaty, 213-216, as reprisal, 214, in self-defense, 214, under Telecommunications Conventions, 216-210; summary of law, 219-220; Voice of America and, 211, 218; in World War II, 210, in Cold War, 211-212
Japan, propaganda between the two world wars, 36, by radio, 36; propaganda dispute with U.S., 105
Jenks, C. W., 57
Jessup, P. C., 156
Joeden, J., 10, 55, 75, 83, 162, 213, 214, 215, 217
Judicial decisions, and defamation, 105, 150-151, 174; and freedom of information, 237, 245-248; group libel, 120; solicitation, 72; and international law of: war-mongering propaganda, 76 ff., subversive propaganda, 103, defamatory propaganda, 131 ff.; as source of law, 59.

Kaas, A., 27
Kaulek, J. B., 21
Kertesz, S. D., 48
Khrushchev, N. S., propaganda dispute with Greece, 88; and jamming, 212
Kohler, F. D., 7
Kopelmanas, L., 57
Korowicz, M. S., 168
Krause, G. B., 55, 70, 162
Kris, Ernst, 35, 37, 38, 40
Lamartine, A. M., 18
Lapie, P., 189
Laprade, W. T., 19

Larson, Arthur, and Basic Guidance Paper, USIA, 269; cited, 140, 239; Director, USIA, 50; and "General Principles," 57; and Iraq, 218
Larson, Cedric, 31, 32
Lasswell, H. D., 13, 16, 31, 33, 34, 44
Latin-America, Soviet propaganda to, 45-46. See also, PAU and OAS
Laurent, F., 17
Lauterpacht, H., 18, 55, 57, 83, 106, 137, 138, 142, 145, 161, 164, 168, 213, 257
Lavisse, E., 18
Lazarovics, F. de, 27
League of Nations, and aggressive war, 66; Convention on Broadcasting in the Cause of Peace (1936), 70, 125 ff., 147, 190, 215, 229, 254-256; and fair comment, 118; and press code, 249; "Radio Nations," 35, 36, 223; and terrorism, 141-142; and war propaganda, 69.
Leigh, R. D., 247, 250
Leites, N., 26, 27
Lenin, N., 26-27
Léonoff, R., 86
Lerner, D., 40
LeRoy, H. S., 125
Libel and Slander, civil law and, 113; in common law, 112, 148-154; domestic laws of, 104, 111 ff., 200; "fair comment" and, 115 ff.; and group libel, 120 ff.; Islamic law of, 113 ff.
Liszt, F., von., 135, 155
Lockwood, H. C., 19
Loewenstein, K., 6
Loomis, H., 7
Lopez, S. P., report to U.N. on freedom of information, 184, 196, 230, 257
Louis-Philippe, 23
Luchaire, J., 249
Ludden, R., 48, 49
Lumley, F. E., 13, 14, 16, 34

McConaughy, J. B., 46
McDougal, M. S., 57
McNeal, E. H., 14
Magie, D., 13
Margolen, M. Z., 205
"Marseillaise", as propaganda, 17
Martens, F. F., 83, 101, 144
Martin, L. John, 35, 38, 55, 101, 125, 136, 143, 144, 146, 148, 149, 155, 156, 187, 188, 211, 221, 229, 250
Marx, K., 26

Mason, E. S., 24, 25
Matter, P., 93
Maurach, R., 72, 73, 122
May, T. E., 20
Medina, Judge, 236
Mein Kampf, as propaganda, 79
Mérignhac, A., 213
Mexico, propaganda disputes with U.S., 99, 105, 137, 140
Mock, J. R., 31, 32
Moniteur Universal, 14
Monitoring, Eisenhower proposal in U.N., 183-184; as remedy for dangers of propaganda, 183 ff.; summary and appraisal, 186
Montesquieu, C. L. de, 236
Moore, J. B. (Digest), 84, 105, 137, 148, 151, 153, 154
Morozov, G. I., 157
Murrow, E. R., 50
Mussolini, B., and radio propaganda, 36

Napoleon Bonaparte, dispute with Britain over propaganda, 20, 150; and freedom of press, 20; as propagandist, 23
"Narrow responsibility school", 137-139
Nassar, broadcasts by, 5; propaganda by: war-mongering, 63-64, subversive, 89 ff., dafamatory, 109.
Naurois, Louis de, 123
Northcliffe, Lord, 32, 33
Nuremberg Trials, criticisms of, 168; evidence of Nazi propaganda at, 36, 40, 65; and international law rule against war-mongering, 67, 68, 76-82, 239; and subversive propaganda, 103; and individual responsibility for propaganda, 167 ff.; United Nations and, 77, 168

OAS, (Organization of American States) anti-propaganda treaties, 101 ff., 127 ff.; handling of dispute, Santo Domingo v. Haiti, 130; and outlawry of war, 66.
Odgers, W. B., 104, 119
Oppenheim, L., 57, 76, 95, 106, 110, 132, 168, 213, 224
OSS, (Office of Strategic Services), 46
OWI (Office of War Information), 40, 47
Paine, T., 29
Pakistan, agreement with India, 88-89, 147; and subversive propaganda, 88

301

302

Remington, F., 30
Renvoi doctrine, 142-143
Responsibility, definition and categories of, 56 ff.; responsibility of individual, 170 ff.
Riegel, O. W., 36
Riesman, D., 121, 187, 188
Right of reply, appraisal of, 192-194, 231, bibliography, 187; French proposal for, 191, 199, 206; history of, 189 ff., 207-208; as remedy for propaganda, 187-194, 207, 231, 243, 265; U.N. action on, 193, 207-208.
Rivier, A., 136, 213
Robespierre, M. F. de, 17
Roederer, P. L., 23
Rolo, C. J., 39
Rome, ancient, propaganda in, 13
Roosevelt, F. D., 34, 39, 195
Root, E., 119
Rosenberg, A., 79, 167, 172
Rothenberg, I, 148
Rudolph, W., 55
Rumania, and jamming, 28

Saar, Nazi propaganda in, 38, 99
Sackville, Lord, 84
Santo Domingo, dispute with Haiti, 130
Sarnoff, D., 7
Saud, King, propaganda by, 5
Saudemont, A., 189
Scharfeld, A. W., 155
Schmitt, B. E., 30, 32
Schwartz, W., 55
Scott, F. R., 175
Scott, J. F., 98
Self-defense, and aggressive war, 67, 68; and jamming, 214
Serbia, and war-mongering propaganda, 2, 10
Shapiro, L., 101
Siegal, S. N., 55
Smith-Mundt Act, 48
Smith, Senator H. A., 48
Smith, B. L. and C. M., 42
Smith, J. S. B., 55
Solal, L., 55, 136, 176, 177
Sorel, A., 14, 18, 20, 21, 22, 145
Sorensen, T. C., 50
Sovereignty, over airspace, 213-216
Spain, and propaganda during Commune, 25, French Revolution, 22, war with U.S., 29-30, Spanish Civil War, 36; disputes over propaganda, 110, 138, 165; domestic laws on, 136, 176

Speier, H., 35, 37, 38, 40
Sprague, S., 190
Squires, J. D., 31
Stalin, J. V., 24, 27
Sténuit, R., 55, 158, 162, 178, 214
Stephen's Digest, 175
Stone, J., 55, 67, 76
Stowell, E. C., 83, 96, 136
Strategy of terror, 43
Strausz-Hupé, R., 15
Streibert, T. C., 50
Streicher, J., 79 ff., 167, 172
Subversive propaganda, categories of, 85; definitions, 10, 83 ff.; examples of, 10, 38, 84 ff.; irridentist propaganda, 92 ff.; ordinary subversive propaganda, 85 ff.; revolutionary, 94 ff.; prohibited in code of ethics, 261; relation to war-mongering, 63, 83
Subversive propaganda, international law and, by state, 95 ff.; under customary law, 86, 97 ff.; general principles of law, 103; as intervention, 96; judicial decisions, 103; treaties, 101 ff.; writings of publicists, 97-98; U.N. and 99-100
By individuals, 134 ff.; broad responsibility school, 134-137, 171; code of ethics and, 261; moral support not prohibited, 136-137; narrow responsibility school, 137-139; refugee propaganda, 143-147; renvoi doctrine, 142-143; rule of overt act, 140; terroristic propaganda, 141.
Switzerland, domestic laws against propaganda, 6, 152, 155, 174-175; propaganda disputes, with France 21, 154, with Nazi Germany, 120; refugee propaganda, 145-146; and state responsibility for radio, 162
Tardu, M., 122, 123, 189
Taylor, E., 43
Television, and propaganda potentialities, 8
Telstar, 7
Terroristic propaganda, 141, 142, 152
Terrou, F., 55, 136, 176, 177
Thatcher, O. J., 13
Thimme, H., 31, 32
Thirty Years War, and propaganda, 15
Thomas, A. V. and A. J., 96, 97
Thompson, J. W., 16
Thomson, C. A. H., 38, 40
Thurn, H., 213
Tomlinson, J. D., 35
Toynbee, A., 28, 125

Treaties, defamatory propaganda and, 124-131, 147; proposals for new treaties, 229; on refugees, 144; as source of law, 57, 163; and subversive propaganda, 101, 129 ff.; and war-mongering, 76 ff.

Trotsky, L., 26

Truman, H. S., 47, 48

Tsar of Russia, dafamatory attack against, from Britain, 153, 175; and subversive propaganda, 85, 98.

Turkey, propaganda dispute with Russia, 86, 106; and subversive propaganda, 85, 86, 93, 98

United Nations, broadcasting by proposed, 222-223; and Code of Ethics, 250-257; and Convention on Use of Broadcasting in Cause of Peace, 127, 131; and Diplomatic Immunities Conference, 149; and freedom of information, 195 ff., 259; and monitoring proposal, 183-186; and Nuremberg Rules, 168; propaganda in, 106, 225; and right of reply, 189 ff.; sanctions against propaganda, 223-228; subversive propaganda and, 99-100; and terrorism, 142; and war (Charter provisions), 66, 168, 239; and war propaganda, 67, 69-70, 75; USSR and propaganda in, 234-236, 241, 245-246; U.S. and propaganda in, 106, 241, 183-184, 227, 245-246.

United States, and code of ethics, 251; disputes over propaganda: with Austria, 165; Britain, 153, Cuba, 106-107, 111; Czecho-Slovakia, 106, Egypt, 109, France, 165, Japan, 105, Mexico, 99, 105, 137, 140; Nazi Germany, 105, 165; Spain, 110, 138, 165; Russia, 27-28, 99, 106, 107 ff., 119, 159, 164, 221, 240, 245. Domestic laws: on foreign mail, 6, 205, on libel and slander, 113, 151, on false news, 176, on right of reply, 188, 190; propaganda by: 29 ff., 154, 97; in World War I, 32, 34, World War II, 39 ff., since World War II, 47 ff., (see USIA and Voice of America); and narrow responsibility doctrine, 137, 138, 174, 233, 241; and neutrality statute, 138, 140, 238-240; and treaties against propaganda, 126, 159, 227; and refugee propaganda, 146; and restraints on freedom of information, 206, 236-239, 241; U.N., activities in, 106, 183-184, 227, 241, 245-246.

United States Information Agency, 46 ff.; 266. And see Voice of America.

USSR
army and propaganda, 25; comparison with French Revolutionary propaganda, 25-26; disputes over propaganda: with Britain, 28, France, 29, Germany, 28, Greece, 87 ff., Holland, 221, 240, Iran, 81 ff., 107 ff., 111, Rumania, 28, Turkey, 87, USA, 28-29, 99, 107 ff., 119, 159, 164, 221, 240; domestic laws and propaganda, 74-75, 115, 117-118, 123, 150, 156, 157, 243-244; history of use of propaganda: early efforts, 27-28, inter-war period, 36, World War II, 39, since World War II, 44 ff.; and freedom of information, 198-199, 243; and jamming, 6, 210-212; monitoring proposal and, 185, 243; and radio propaganda, 27-28, 164; and remedies for propaganda, 227, 243; and subversive propaganda, 91, 92, 94; treaties prohibiting propaganda, 101, and war propaganda, 65, 241; activities concerning propaganda within U.N., 106, 185, 208, 227, 234-236, 241, 245

Vabres, D. de, 159

Vagts, A., 31

Van de Velde, R. W., 40

Van Dissel, G. F., 36

Van Dyke, V., 18, 55, 83, 86, 98, 99, 144, 149, 155

Vattel, E., 96, 105

Veeder, V. V., 175

Venezuela, and subversive propaganda, 4, 84-85

Verdross, A. von, 57

Vidal, C., 146

Voice of America, basic guidance paper, 268-273; criticisms of, 49-50; and Cuban Crisis, 51, 211; history of: origins, 40, since World War II, 47 ff., 109; and jamming, 211, 219; Korean War, effect on, 48; policies of, 219, 268; reorganization of, 49. Smith-Mundt Act and, 48.

Von Papen, F., 81-82

Von Shirach, B., 80

Vyshinsky, A. Y., 118, 212, 221